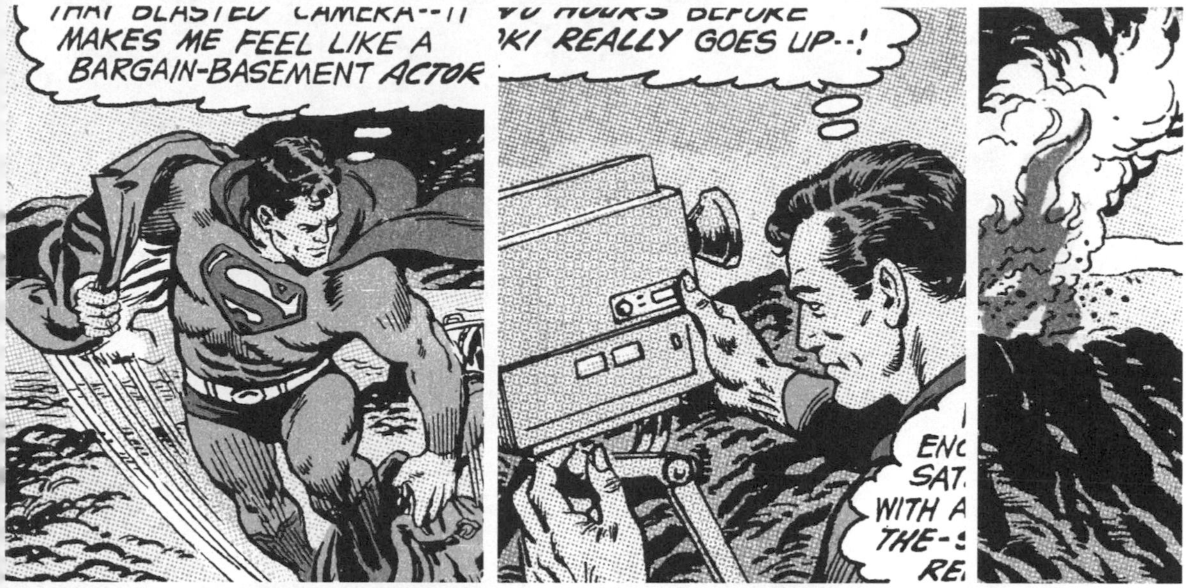

MAKES ME FEEL LIKE A
BARGAIN-BASEMENT ACTOR
REALLY GOES UP--!

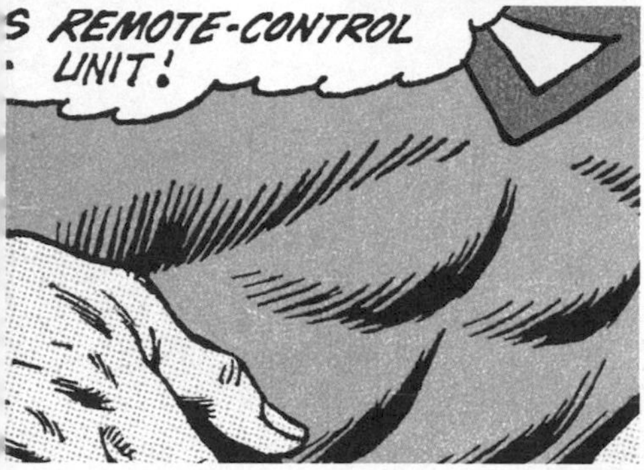

REMOTE-CONTROL
UNIT!

DC COMICS CLASSICS LIBRARY

SUPERMAN

KRYPTONITE NEVERMORE

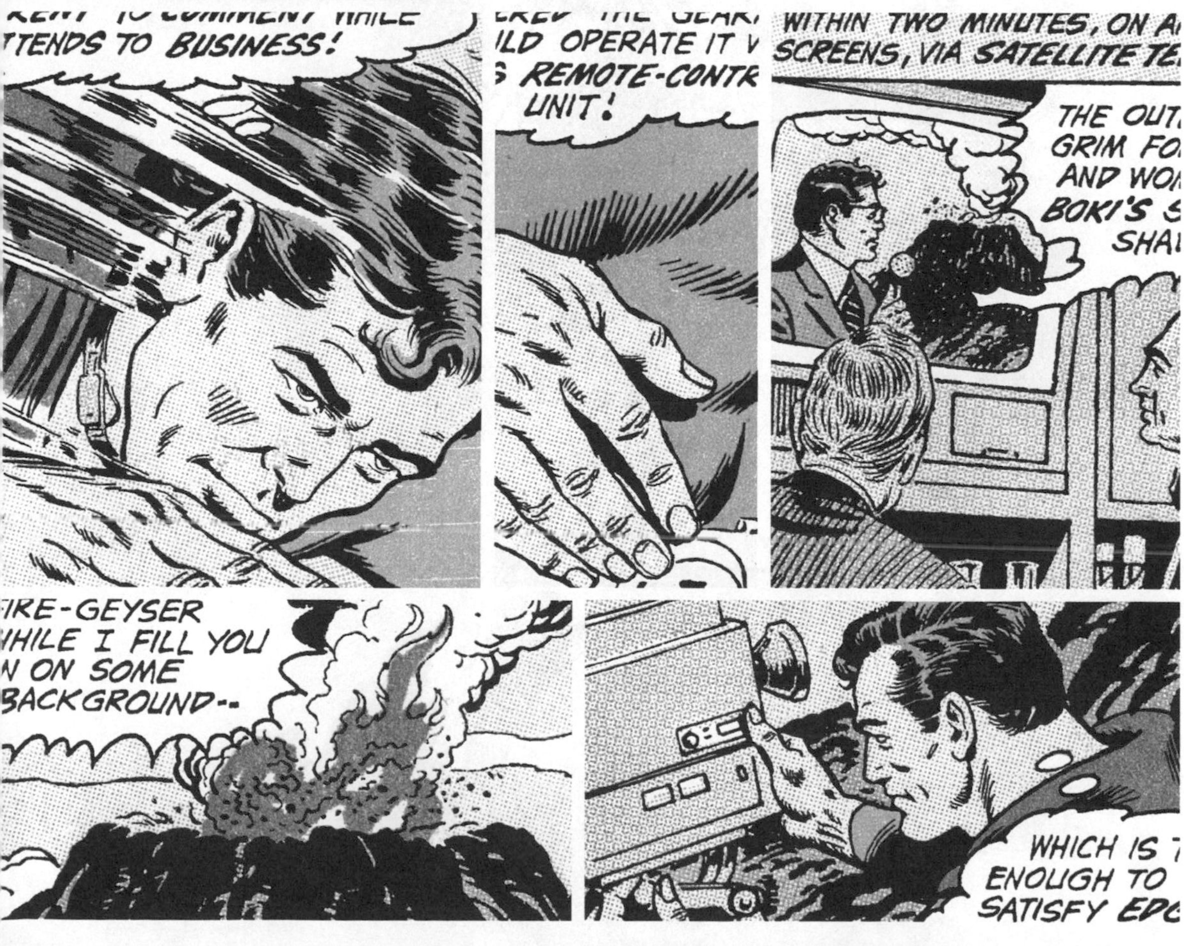

TO BUSINESS!
OPERATE IT
REMOTE-
UNIT!
WITHIN TWO MINUTES, ON
SCREENS, VIA SATELLITE
THE
GRIM
AND
FIRE-GEYSER
WHILE I FILL YOU
ON SOME
BACKGROUND--
WHICH IS
ENOUGH TO
SATISFY

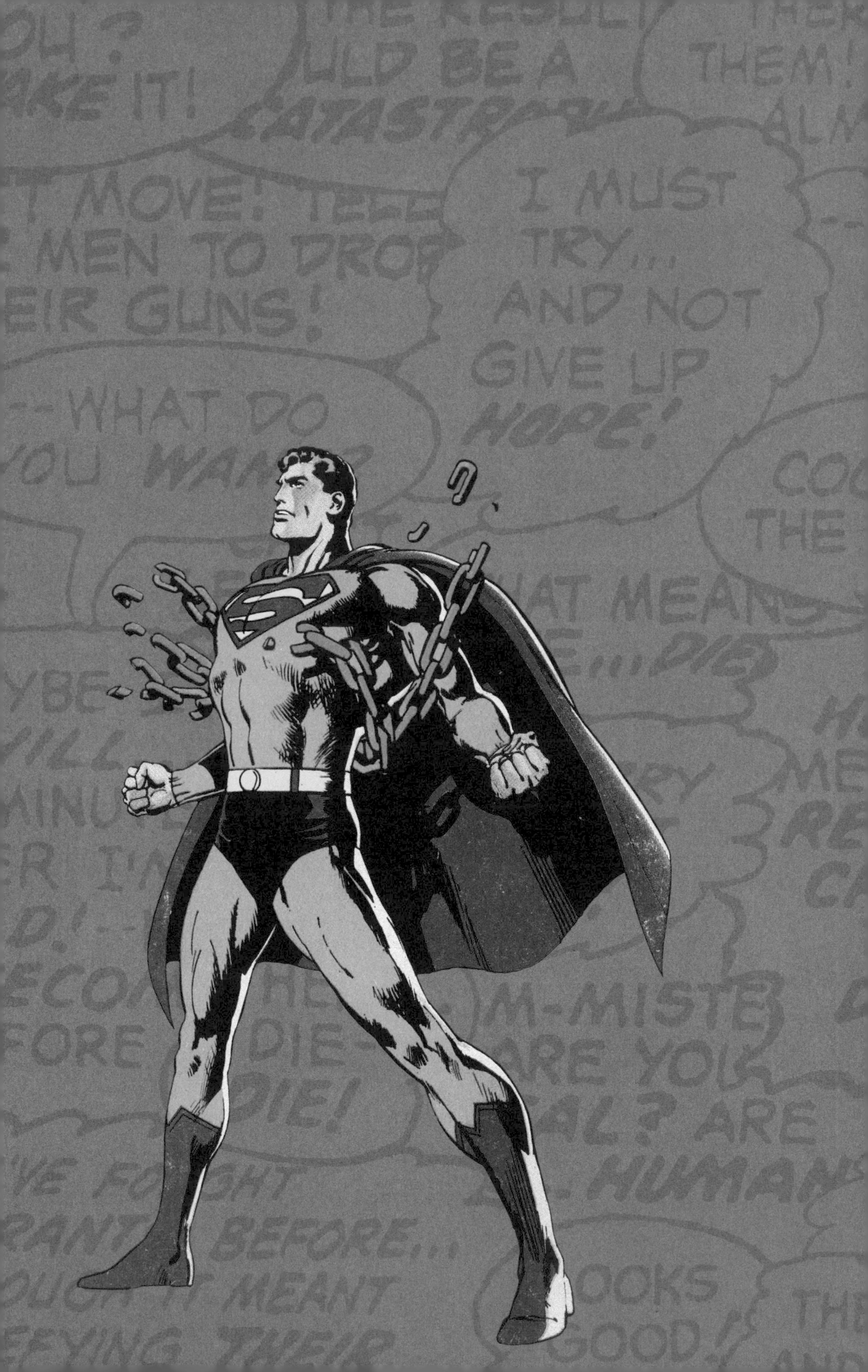

I MUST TRY... AND NOT GIVE UP HOPE!
MEN TO DROP
EIR GUNS!
--WHAT DO YOU
M-MISTE ARE YOU
AL? ARE
ANT BEFORE...
LOOKS GOOD!

DC COMICS CLASSICS LIBRARY

SUPERMAN

KRYPTONITE NEVERMORE

writer **Dennis O'Neil**
penciller **Curt Swan**
inker **Murphy Anderson**

Superman created by Jerry Siegel and Joe Shuster

Dan DiDio Senior VP-Executive Editor **Julius Schwartz** Editor-original series **Bob Joy** Editor-collected edition
Robbin Brosterman Senior Art Director **Paul Levitz** President & Publisher **Georg Brewer** VP-Design & DC Direct Creative
Richard Bruning Senior VP-Creative Director **Patrick Caldon** Executive VP-Finance & Operations
Chris Caramalis VP-Finance **John Cunningham** VP-Marketing **Terri Cunningham** VP-Managing Editor
Amy Genkins Senior VP-Business & Legal Affairs **Alison Gill** VP-Manufacturing **David Hyde** VP-Publicity
Hank Kanalz VP-General Manager, WildStorm **Jim Lee** Editorial Director-WildStorm
Gregory Noveck Senior VP-Creative Affairs **Sue Pohja** VP-Book Trade Sales **Steve Rotterdam** Senior VP-Sales & Marketing
Cheryl Rubin Senior VP-Brand Management **Alysse Soll** VP-Advertising & Custom Publishing
Jeff Trojan VP-Business Development, DC Direct **Bob Wayne** VP-Sales

Cover art by Neal Adams with Curt Swan and Murphy Anderson. Recolored by Allen Passalaqua.

DC COMICS CLASSICS LIBRARY
SUPERMAN: KRYPTONITE NEVERMORE

Published by DC Comics. Cover, text and compilation Copyright © 2009 DC Comics. All Rights Reserved.

Originally published in single magazine form in SUPERMAN 233-238, 240-242. Copyright © 1971 DC Comics.
All Rights Reserved. All characters, their distinctive likenesses and related elements featured in this publication
are trademarks of DC Comics. The stories, characters and incidents featured in this publication are entirely fictional.
DC Comics does not read or accept unsolicited submissions of ideas, stories or artwork.

DC Comics, 1700 Broadway, New York, NY 10019
A Warner Bros. Entertainment Company
Printed in the USA. First Printing.
ISBN: 978-1-4012-2085-3

Contents

THE DC COMICS CLASSICS LIBRARY
continues DC's tradition of making our best and most
historically significant publications available in lovingly restored,
carefully produced volumes. When we launched the DC ARCHIVES
SERIES, two decades ago, it was our goal to republish for the first time in
sequential form key DC series from the Golden Age and Silver Age of comics.
Over time, that was expanded to include some titles from other publishers as well, and
with over 150 volumes released, entire runs of such seminal titles as THE SPIRIT and ALL-STAR
COMICS have been "archived" and made easily accessible to fans, collectors, scholars and
libraries. Over those years, it's become common for comics to be published as hardcover graphic
novels, and DC has rereleased many wonderful comics in collected, permanent formats.

Looking over our now-groaning bookshelves, however, we realized that certain stories had been
overlooked in this process: stories that had been published before the hardcover graphic novel format
was common, and which had either not been part of an extended run that had been archived, or
which had been "lost" in such a run without a chance for readers to easily discover them. With the
help of our readers, we identified a list of stories that were at least ten years old, had not been sepa-
rately collected as a hardcover edition, and were identifiably "classic" as peak moments in our
characters' history or important in the creative evolution of comics.

We invite you to share in the pleasure of reading and owning these classics.

—**Paul Levitz**
President & Publisher DC Comics

A Word from the Publisher

SEE--THE EXPLOSION CHANGED IT... TO ORDINARY IRON!
IMPOSSIBLE!
'TE!
GET IT AWAY FROM HERE, YOU FOOL! IT CAN KILL SUPERMAN!

Introduction

November 5, 1971: More than three decades after Superman became the first American comic book character to receive his own regularly published title, SUPERMAN #233 was published, beginning the classic tale of "Kryptonite Nevermore!"

Longtime editor Mort Weisinger had retired, after guiding Superman's adventures from his return from World War II through the height of the Vietnam War, and overseeing an explosion in the depths of mythology built around the hero. Replacing him as the Man of Steel's steward was Julie Schwartz, a friend since the earliest days of science fiction fandom, who had also gone on to a stellar career in SF and comics (launching Solar Sales Service, the first SF literary agency, with Mort, and then playing a pivotal role in launching the Silver Age of comics). Julie was the field's expert on updating concepts and styles of super hero comics from his work on launching new versions of The Flash and Green Lantern, and his run of the "New Look" Batman, which restored him to his pulp and detective fiction roots. He sharpened his editor's pencil and went to work.

Gone were the armies of other survivors of Krypton who had accreted over the years — the denizens of the bottle city of Kandor (with its tiny Superman Emergency Squad), the wispy criminals of the Phantom Zone, even the animals from Krypto the Super-Dog to Beppo the Super-Monkey. They weren't destroyed, or written out of canonical history (as comics are wont to do in more recent reboots), just studiously ignored and banished from the pages. Along with them went the powerful Superman robots and other handy story devices. And Kryptonite (which by then had blossomed under Mort to appearing in green, red, white, blue and even jeweled colors) was going to disappear as well.

The life of Clark Kent would change too. The glamour of newspaper reporting having faded, the Daily Planet newsroom, which had been the centerpiece of so many Superman stories, was set aside and Clark moved to become a television newsman.

And behind the scenes, Julie made many other shifts as well. Mort's regular writers were sent off, replaced by Denny O'Neil, then simultaneously handling his now-legendary GREEN LANTERN/GREEN ARROW run and some of the best-remembered BATMAN tales of what would become a four-decade association with the character. Denny would never have the same comfort with the Man of Steel, rhetorically asking once how he could write stories about a hero who "could destroy a galaxy by listening hard." But his tension in the assignment permeated the work, making the changes in the story's tone echo more loudly. The art would change, too: even though Curt Swan remained on the team while the rest of Mort's pencillers exited, he was joined by Murphy Anderson, Julie's favorite inker, in a style-setting collaboration that fans would laud as a high point in both men's extraordinary careers.

Even the very structure shifted. For the first time in its run, SUPERMAN became a monthly comic, still a rarity at DC for a single character title. And it was all announced by a cover that became one of the most famous, iconic images of the Man of Steel, as Neal Adams unleashed him from the symbolic chains of Kryptonite.

Welcome to this classic moment...

Paul Levitz
President & Publisher
DC Comics

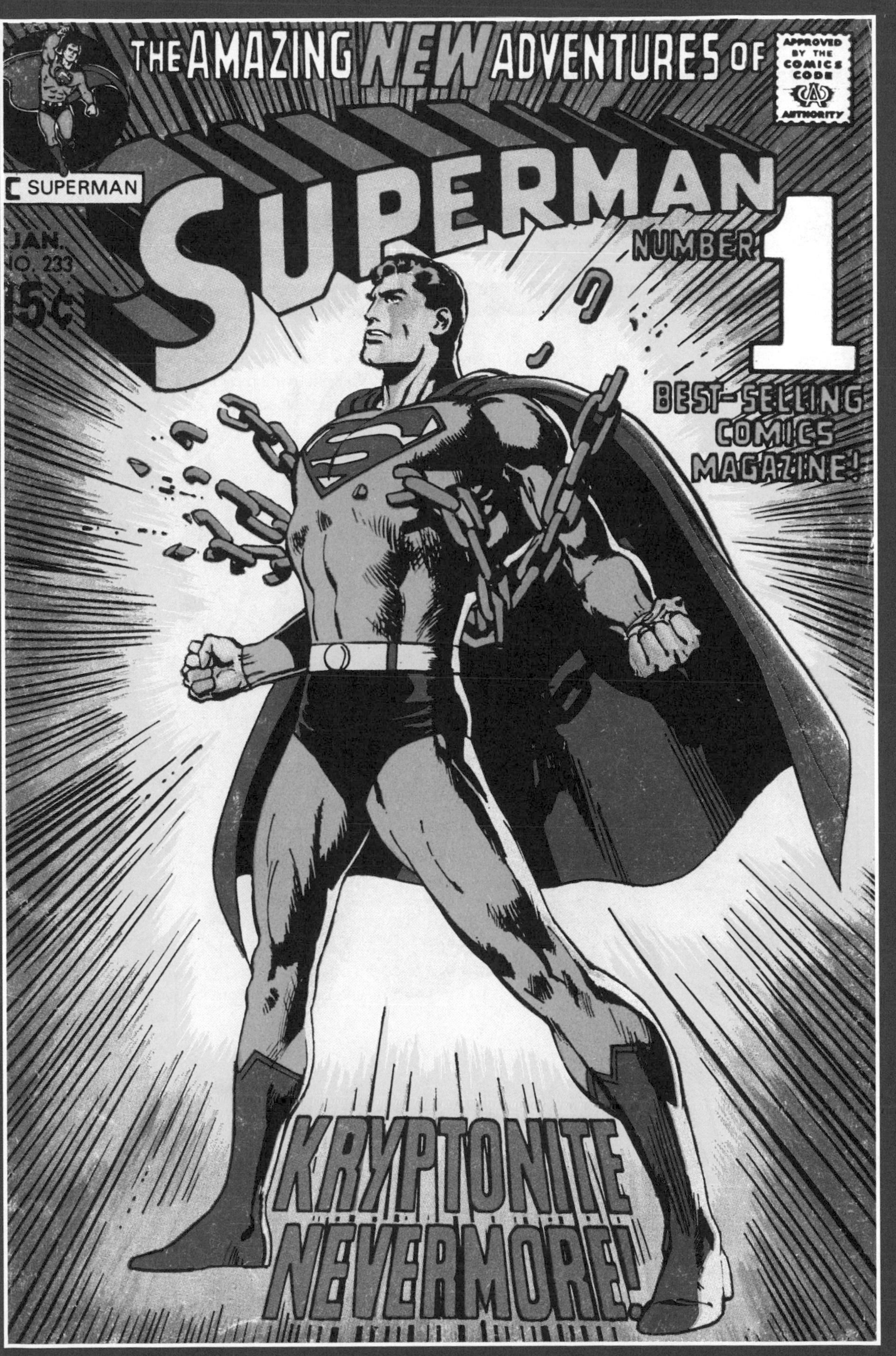
THE AMAZING NEW ADVENTURES OF
APPROVED BY THE COMICS CODE AUTHORITY
SUPERMAN
SUPERMAN
JAN. NO. 233
15¢
NUMBER 1
BEST-SELLING COMICS MAGAZINE!
KRYPTONITE NEVERMORE!

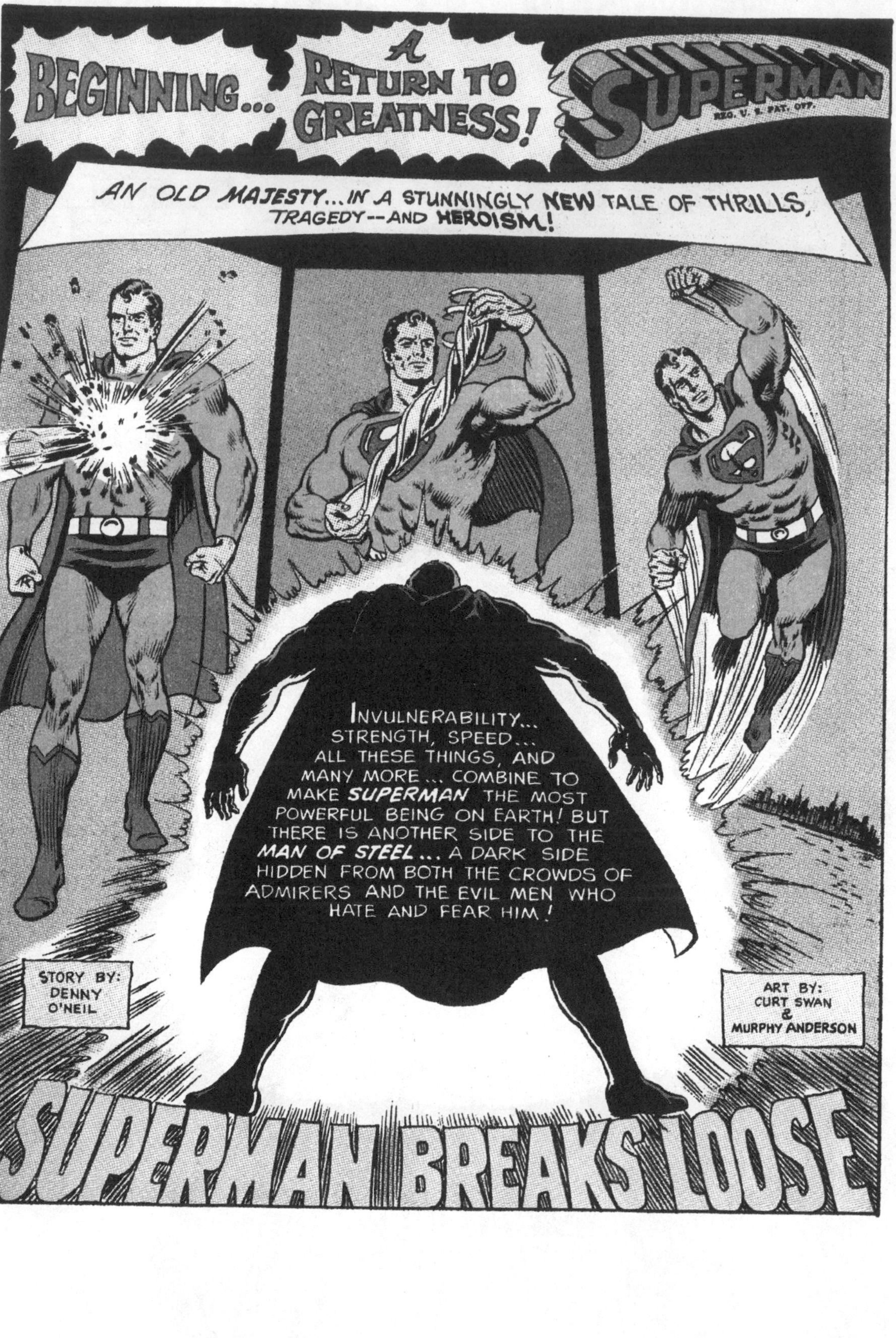

BEGINNING... A RETURN TO GREATNESS!
SUPERMAN
REG. U. S. PAT. OFF.
AN OLD MAJESTY... IN A STUNNINGLY NEW TALE OF THRILLS, TRAGEDY--AND HEROISM!
INVULNERABILITY... STRENGTH, SPEED... ALL THESE THINGS, AND MANY MORE... COMBINE TO MAKE SUPERMAN THE MOST POWERFUL BEING ON EARTH! BUT THERE IS ANOTHER SIDE TO THE MAN OF STEEL... A DARK SIDE HIDDEN FROM BOTH THE CROWDS OF ADMIRERS AND THE EVIL MEN WHO HATE AND FEAR HIM!
STORY BY: DENNY O'NEIL
ART BY: CURT SWAN & MURPHY ANDERSON
SUPERMAN BREAKS LOOSE

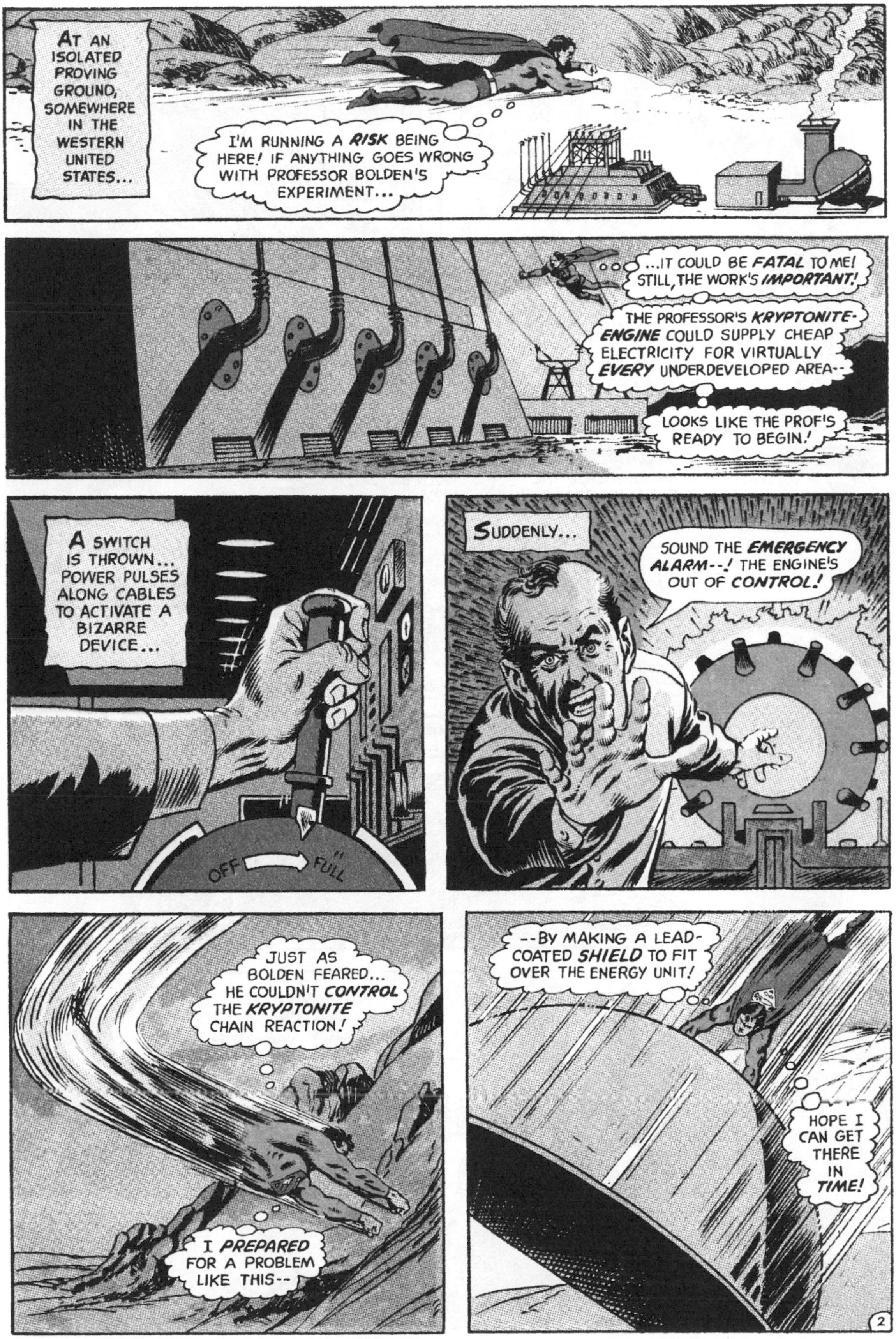
AT AN ISOLATED PROVING GROUND, SOMEWHERE IN THE WESTERN UNITED STATES...
I'M RUNNING A RISK BEING HERE! IF ANYTHING GOES WRONG WITH PROFESSOR BOLDEN'S EXPERIMENT...
...IT COULD BE FATAL TO ME! STILL, THE WORK'S IMPORTANT!
THE PROFESSOR'S KRYPTONITE-ENGINE COULD SUPPLY CHEAP ELECTRICITY FOR VIRTUALLY EVERY UNDERDEVELOPED AREA--
LOOKS LIKE THE PROF'S READY TO BEGIN!
A SWITCH IS THROWN... POWER PULSES ALONG CABLES TO ACTIVATE A BIZARRE DEVICE...
OFF
FULL
SUDDENLY...
SOUND THE EMERGENCY ALARM--! THE ENGINE'S OUT OF CONTROL!
JUST AS BOLDEN FEARED... HE COULDN'T CONTROL THE KRYPTONITE CHAIN REACTION!
I PREPARED FOR A PROBLEM LIKE THIS--
--BY MAKING A LEAD-COATED SHIELD TO FIT OVER THE ENERGY UNIT!
HOPE I CAN GET THERE IN TIME!
2

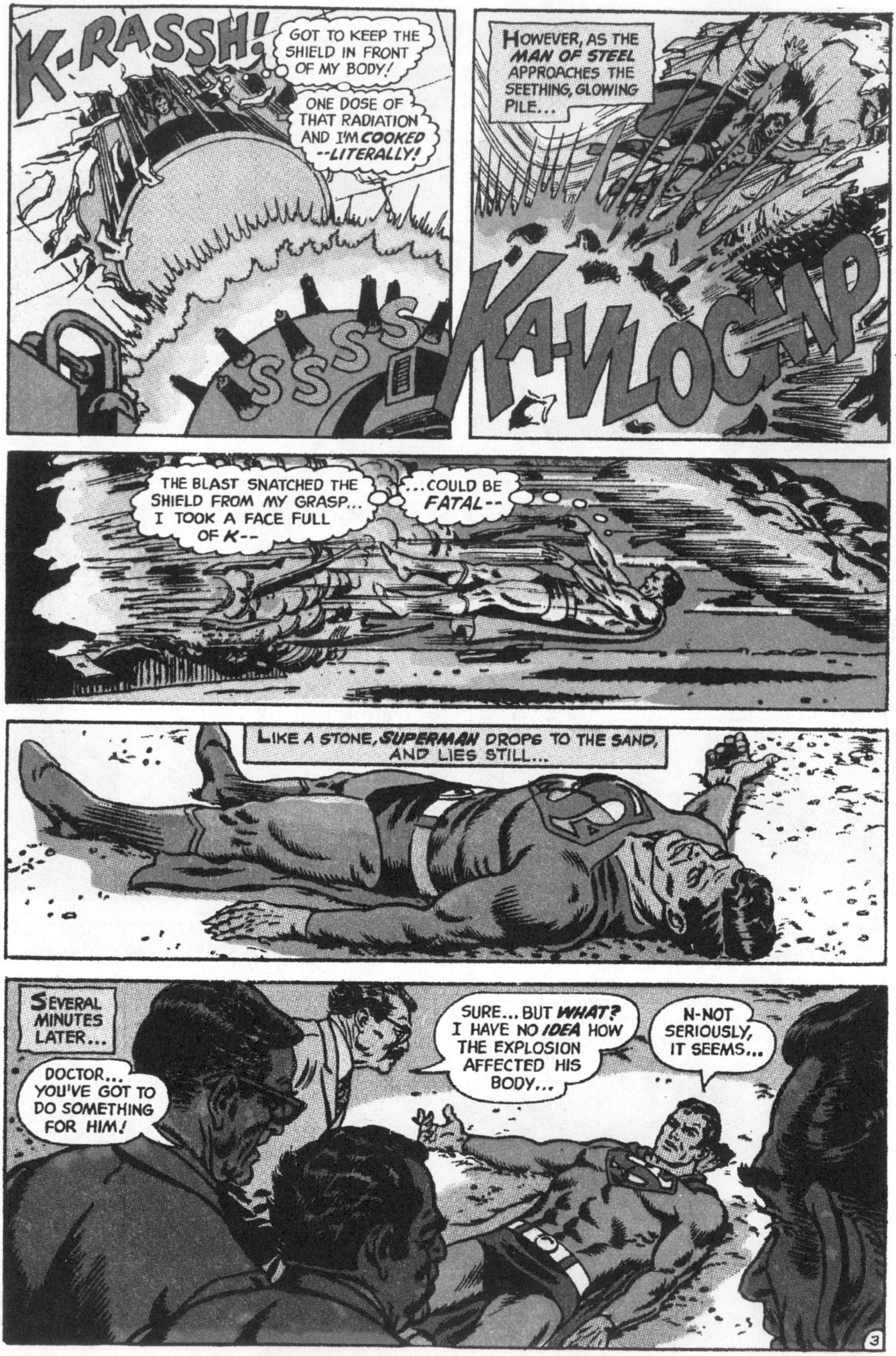
K-RASSH!
GOT TO KEEP THE SHIELD IN FRONT OF MY BODY!
ONE DOSE OF THAT RADIATION AND I'M COOKED --LITERALLY!
SSSSSS
HOWEVER, AS THE MAN OF STEEL APPROACHES THE SEETHING, GLOWING PILE...
KA-VLOOMP
THE BLAST SNATCHED THE SHIELD FROM MY GRASP... I TOOK A FACE FULL OF K--
...COULD BE FATAL--
LIKE A STONE, SUPERMAN DROPS TO THE SAND, AND LIES STILL...
SEVERAL MINUTES LATER...
DOCTOR... YOU'VE GOT TO DO SOMETHING FOR HIM!
SURE... BUT WHAT? I HAVE NO IDEA HOW THE EXPLOSION AFFECTED HIS BODY...
N-NOT SERIOUSLY, IT SEEMS...
3

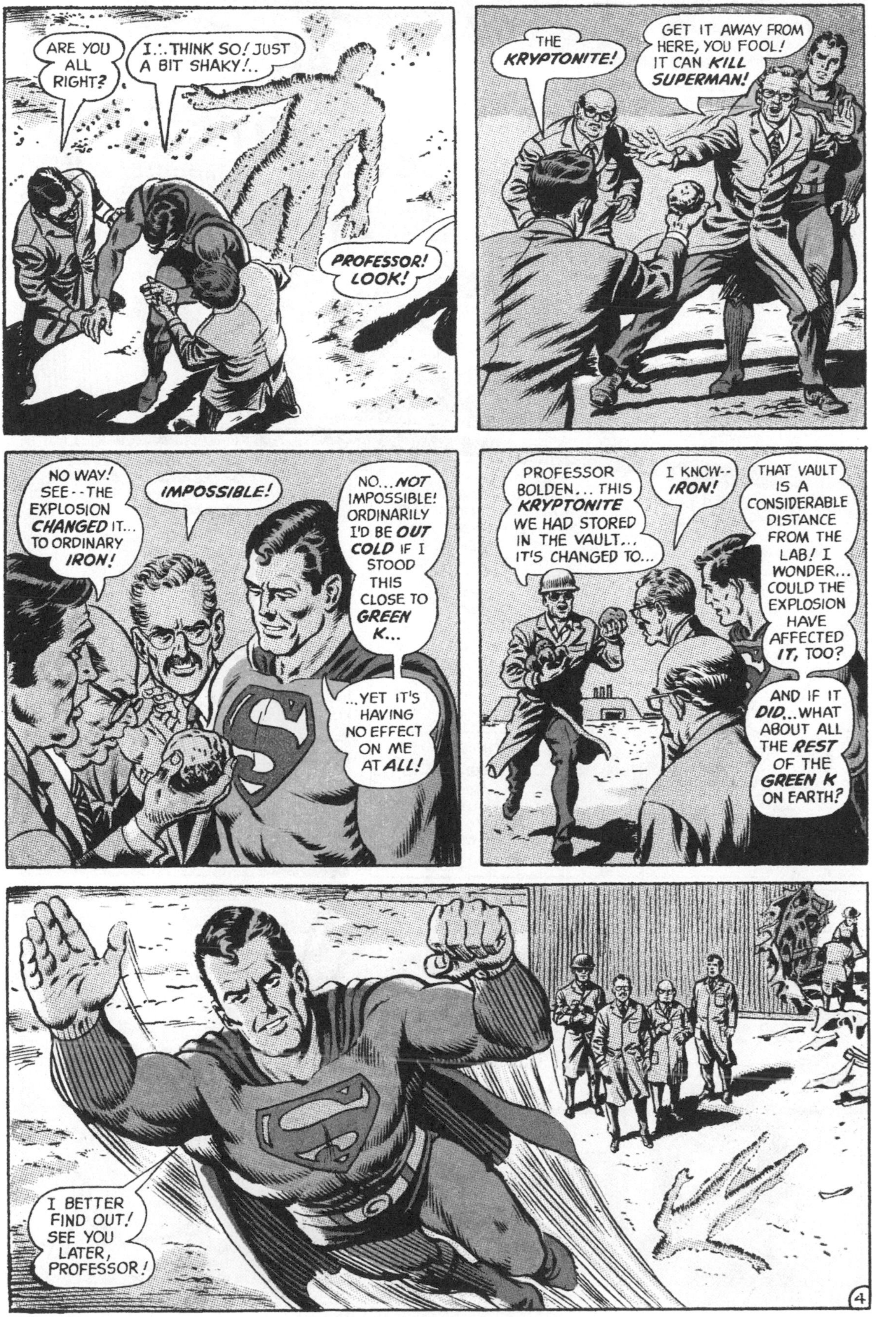

ARE YOU ALL RIGHT?
I...THINK SO! JUST A BIT SHAKY!..
PROFESSOR! LOOK!
THE KRYPTONITE!
GET IT AWAY FROM HERE, YOU FOOL! IT CAN KILL SUPERMAN!
NO WAY! SEE--THE EXPLOSION CHANGED IT... TO ORDINARY IRON!
IMPOSSIBLE!
NO...NOT IMPOSSIBLE! ORDINARILY I'D BE OUT COLD IF I STOOD THIS CLOSE TO GREEN K...
...YET IT'S HAVING NO EFFECT ON ME AT ALL!
PROFESSOR BOLDEN... THIS KRYPTONITE WE HAD STORED IN THE VAULT... IT'S CHANGED TO...
I KNOW-- IRON!
THAT VAULT IS A CONSIDERABLE DISTANCE FROM THE LAB! I WONDER... COULD THE EXPLOSION HAVE AFFECTED IT, TOO?
AND IF IT DID...WHAT ABOUT ALL THE REST OF THE GREEN K ON EARTH?
I BETTER FIND OUT! SEE YOU LATER, PROFESSOR!
4

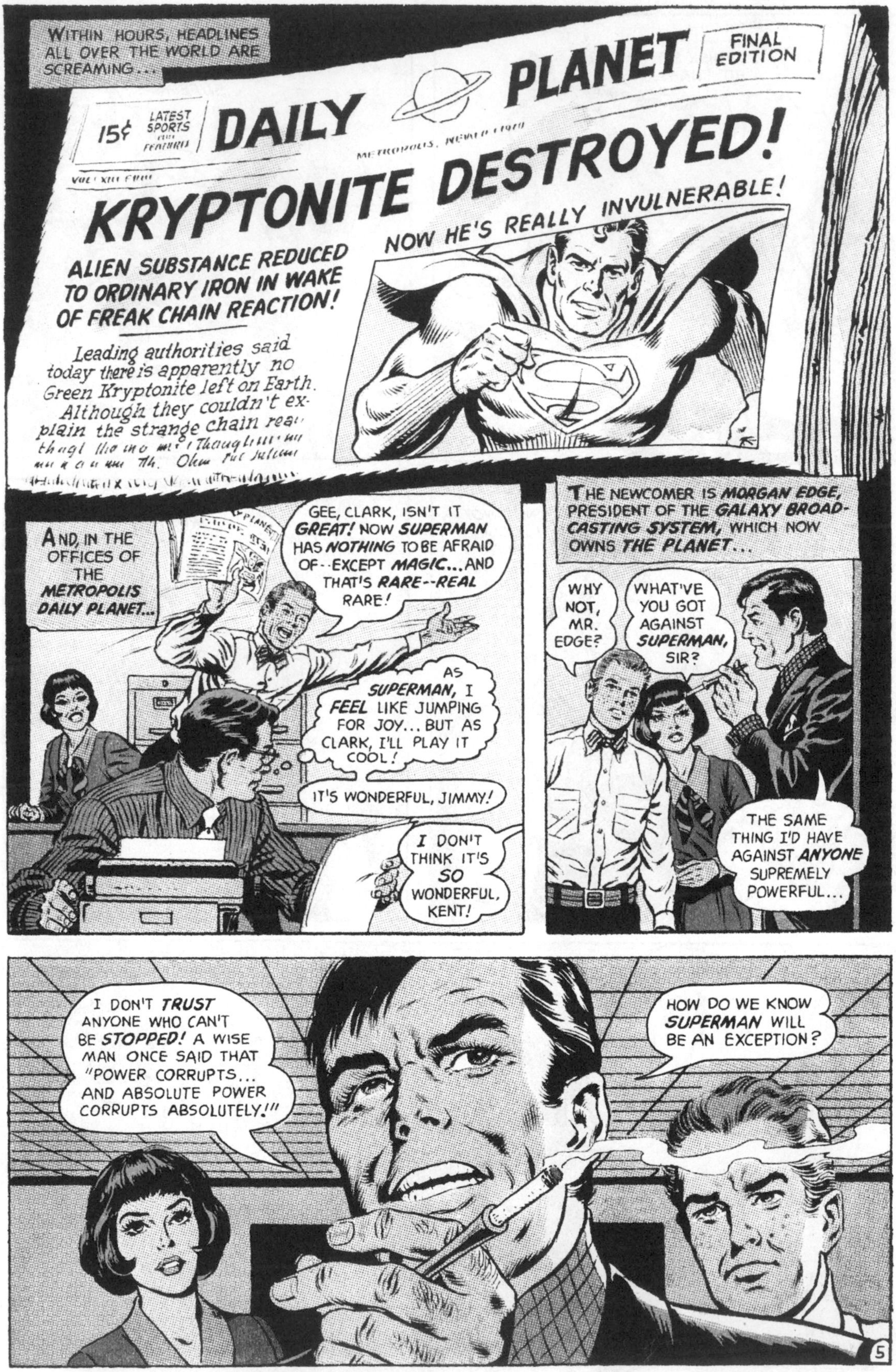

WITHIN HOURS, HEADLINES ALL OVER THE WORLD ARE SCREAMING...
DAILY PLANET
FINAL EDITION
15¢
LATEST SPORTS
KRYPTONITE DESTROYED!
ALIEN SUBSTANCE REDUCED TO ORDINARY IRON IN WAKE OF FREAK CHAIN REACTION!
Leading authorities said today there is apparently no Green Kryptonite left on Earth. Although they couldn't explain the strange chain rea-
NOW HE'S REALLY INVULNERABLE!
AND, IN THE OFFICES OF THE METROPOLIS DAILY PLANET...
GEE, CLARK, ISN'T IT GREAT! NOW SUPERMAN HAS NOTHING TO BE AFRAID OF--EXCEPT MAGIC...AND THAT'S RARE--REAL RARE!
AS SUPERMAN, I FEEL LIKE JUMPING FOR JOY... BUT AS CLARK, I'LL PLAY IT COOL!
IT'S WONDERFUL, JIMMY!
I DON'T THINK IT'S SO WONDERFUL, KENT!
THE NEWCOMER IS MORGAN EDGE, PRESIDENT OF THE GALAXY BROADCASTING SYSTEM, WHICH NOW OWNS THE PLANET...
WHY NOT, MR. EDGE?
WHAT'VE YOU GOT AGAINST SUPERMAN, SIR?
THE SAME THING I'D HAVE AGAINST ANYONE SUPREMELY POWERFUL...
I DON'T TRUST ANYONE WHO CAN'T BE STOPPED! A WISE MAN ONCE SAID THAT "POWER CORRUPTS... AND ABSOLUTE POWER CORRUPTS ABSOLUTELY!"
HOW DO WE KNOW SUPERMAN WILL BE AN EXCEPTION?
5

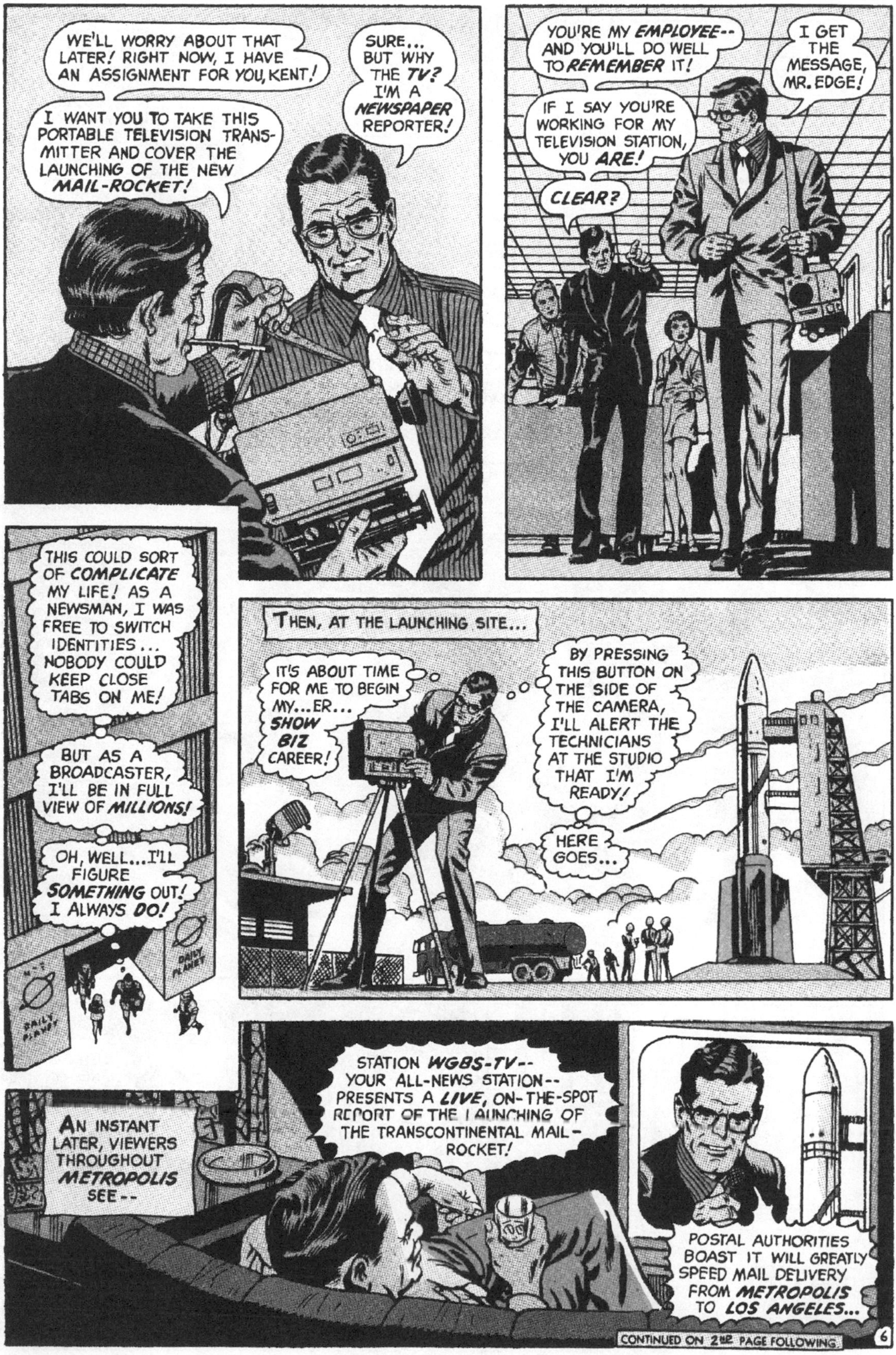

WE'LL WORRY ABOUT THAT LATER! RIGHT NOW, I HAVE AN ASSIGNMENT FOR YOU, KENT!
I WANT YOU TO TAKE THIS PORTABLE TELEVISION TRANSMITTER AND COVER THE LAUNCHING OF THE NEW MAIL-ROCKET!
SURE... BUT WHY THE TV? I'M A NEWSPAPER REPORTER!
YOU'RE MY EMPLOYEE-- AND YOU'LL DO WELL TO REMEMBER IT!
IF I SAY YOU'RE WORKING FOR MY TELEVISION STATION, YOU ARE!
CLEAR?
I GET THE MESSAGE, MR. EDGE!
THIS COULD SORT OF COMPLICATE MY LIFE! AS A NEWSMAN, I WAS FREE TO SWITCH IDENTITIES... NOBODY COULD KEEP CLOSE TABS ON ME!
BUT AS A BROADCASTER, I'LL BE IN FULL VIEW OF MILLIONS!
OH, WELL...I'LL FIGURE SOMETHING OUT! I ALWAYS DO!
DAILY PLANET
DAILY PLANET
THEN, AT THE LAUNCHING SITE...
IT'S ABOUT TIME FOR ME TO BEGIN MY...ER... SHOW BIZ CAREER!
BY PRESSING THIS BUTTON ON THE SIDE OF THE CAMERA, I'LL ALERT THE TECHNICIANS AT THE STUDIO THAT I'M READY!
HERE GOES...
AN INSTANT LATER, VIEWERS THROUGHOUT METROPOLIS SEE--
STATION WGBS-TV-- YOUR ALL-NEWS STATION-- PRESENTS A LIVE, ON-THE-SPOT REPORT OF THE LAUNCHING OF THE TRANSCONTINENTAL MAIL-ROCKET!
POSTAL AUTHORITIES BOAST IT WILL GREATLY SPEED MAIL DELIVERY FROM METROPOLIS TO LOS ANGELES...
CONTINUED ON 2ND PAGE FOLLOWING.
6

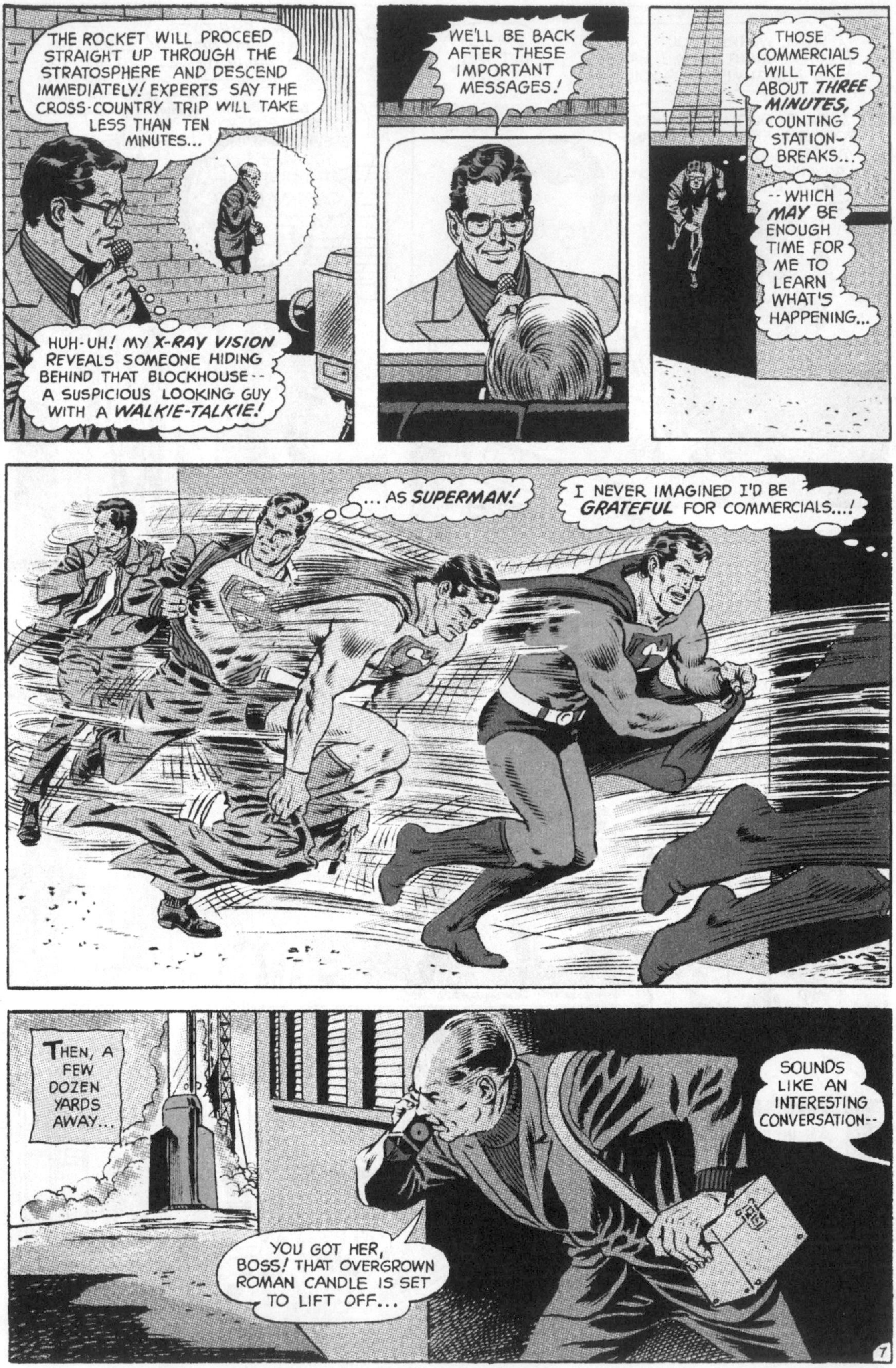

THE ROCKET WILL PROCEED STRAIGHT UP THROUGH THE STRATOSPHERE AND DESCEND IMMEDIATELY! EXPERTS SAY THE CROSS-COUNTRY TRIP WILL TAKE LESS THAN TEN MINUTES...
HUH-UH! MY X-RAY VISION REVEALS SOMEONE HIDING BEHIND THAT BLOCKHOUSE-- A SUSPICIOUS LOOKING GUY WITH A WALKIE-TALKIE!
WE'LL BE BACK AFTER THESE IMPORTANT MESSAGES!
THOSE COMMERCIALS WILL TAKE ABOUT THREE MINUTES, COUNTING STATION-BREAKS...
--WHICH MAY BE ENOUGH TIME FOR ME TO LEARN WHAT'S HAPPENING...
... AS SUPERMAN!
I NEVER IMAGINED I'D BE GRATEFUL FOR COMMERCIALS...!
THEN, A FEW DOZEN YARDS AWAY...
YOU GOT HER, BOSS! THAT OVERGROWN ROMAN CANDLE IS SET TO LIFT OFF...
SOUNDS LIKE AN INTERESTING CONVERSATION--
7

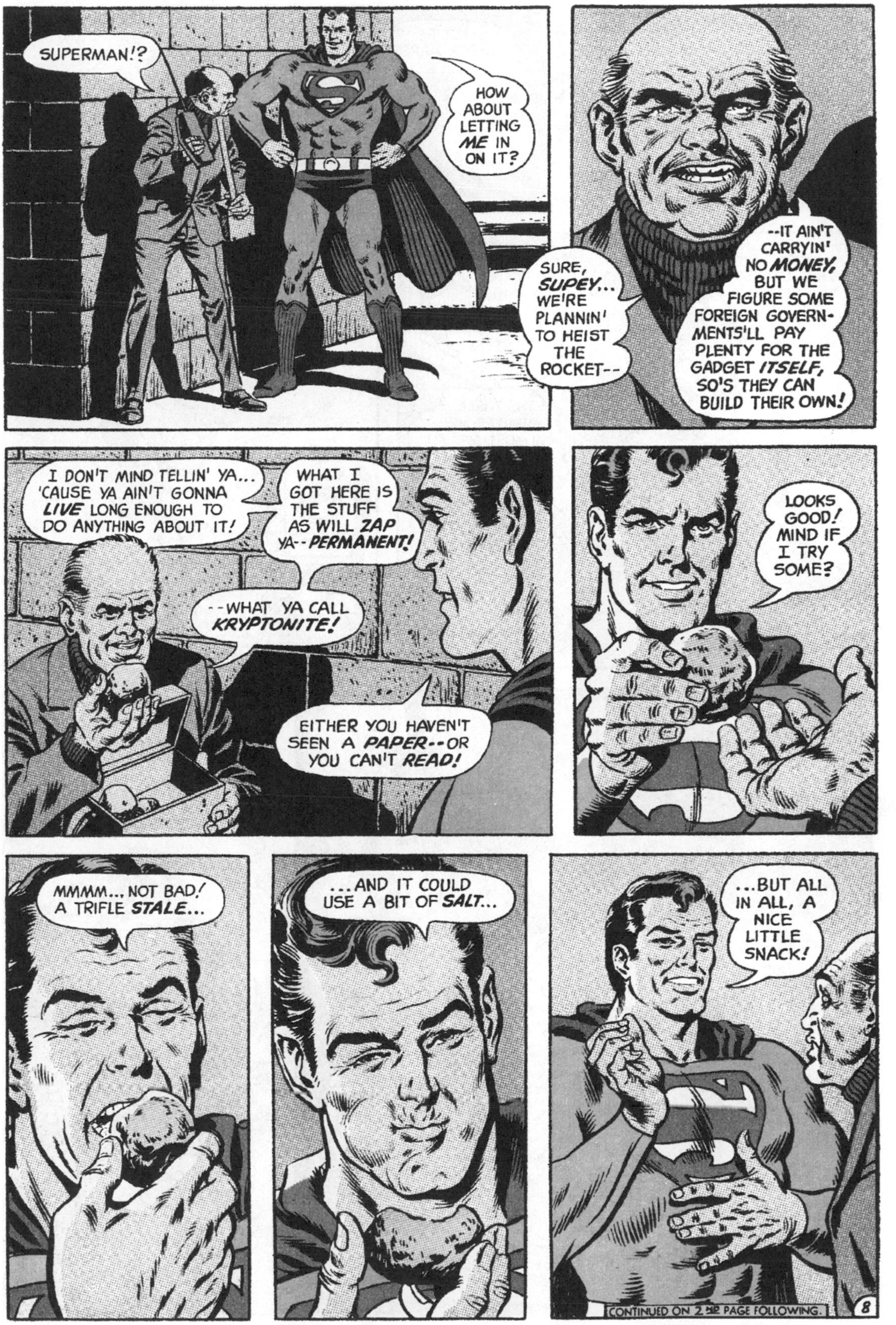
SUPERMAN!?
HOW ABOUT LETTING *ME* IN ON IT?
SURE, *SUPEY*... WE'RE PLANNIN' TO HEIST THE ROCKET--
--IT AIN'T CARRYIN' NO *MONEY*, BUT WE FIGURE SOME FOREIGN GOVERNMENTS'LL PAY PLENTY FOR THE GADGET *ITSELF*, SO'S THEY CAN BUILD THEIR OWN!
I DON'T MIND TELLIN' YA... 'CAUSE YA AIN'T GONNA *LIVE* LONG ENOUGH TO DO ANYTHING ABOUT IT!
WHAT I GOT HERE IS THE STUFF AS WILL *ZAP* YA--*PERMANENT!*
--WHAT YA CALL *KRYPTONITE!*
EITHER YOU HAVEN'T SEEN A *PAPER*--OR YOU CAN'T *READ!*
LOOKS GOOD! MIND IF I TRY SOME?
MMMM..., NOT BAD! A TRIFLE *STALE*...
...AND IT COULD USE A BIT OF *SALT*...
...BUT ALL IN ALL, A NICE LITTLE SNACK!
CONTINUED ON 2ND PAGE FOLLOWING.
8

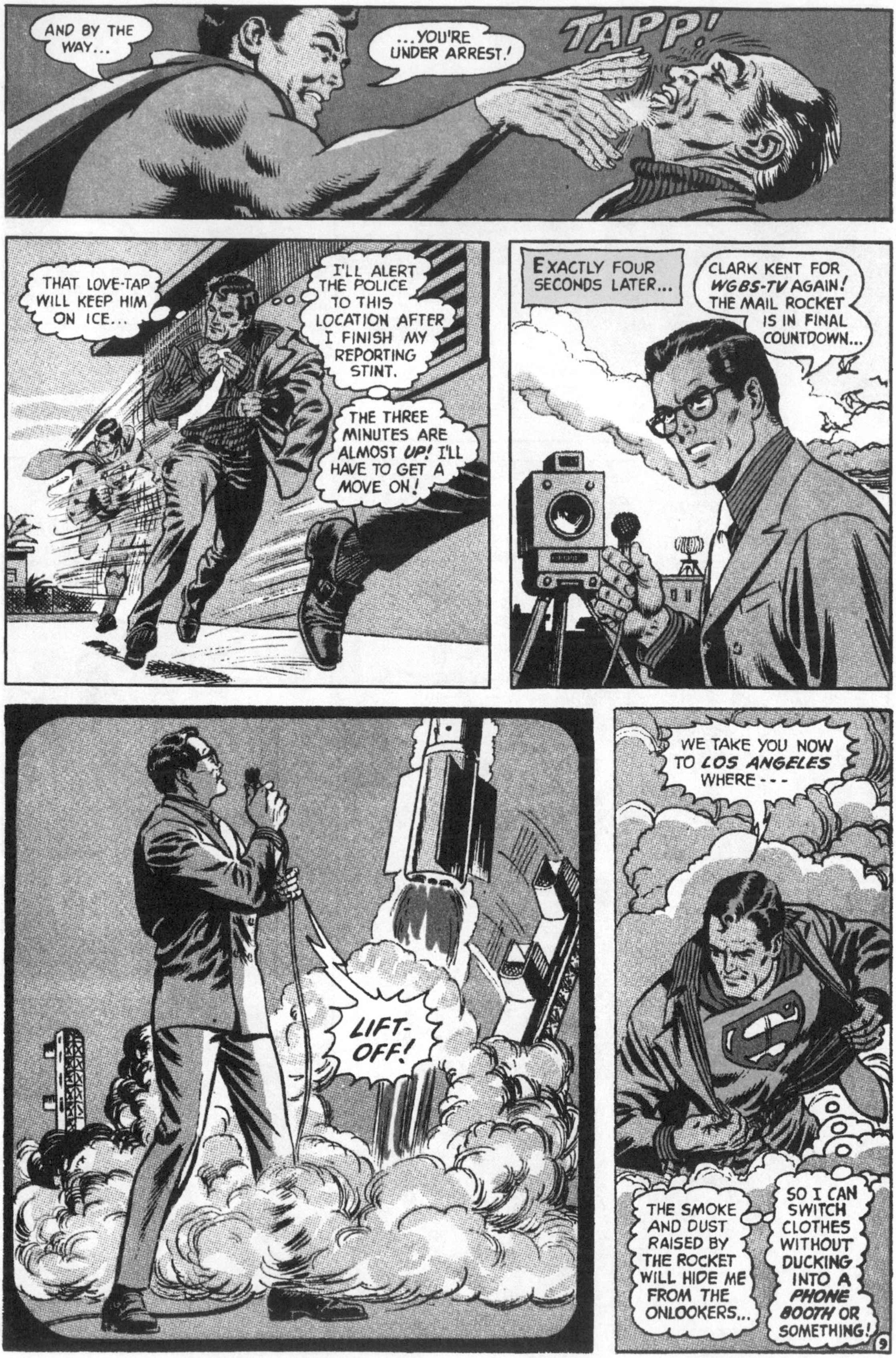
AND BY THE WAY...
...YOU'RE UNDER ARREST!
TAPP!
THAT LOVE-TAP WILL KEEP HIM ON ICE...
I'LL ALERT THE POLICE TO THIS LOCATION AFTER I FINISH MY REPORTING STINT.
THE THREE MINUTES ARE ALMOST UP! I'LL HAVE TO GET A MOVE ON!
EXACTLY FOUR SECONDS LATER...
CLARK KENT FOR WGBS-TV AGAIN! THE MAIL ROCKET IS IN FINAL COUNTDOWN...
LIFT-OFF!
WE TAKE YOU NOW TO LOS ANGELES WHERE---
THE SMOKE AND DUST RAISED BY THE ROCKET WILL HIDE ME FROM THE ONLOOKERS...
SO I CAN SWITCH CLOTHES WITHOUT DUCKING INTO A PHONE BOOTH OR SOMETHING!
9

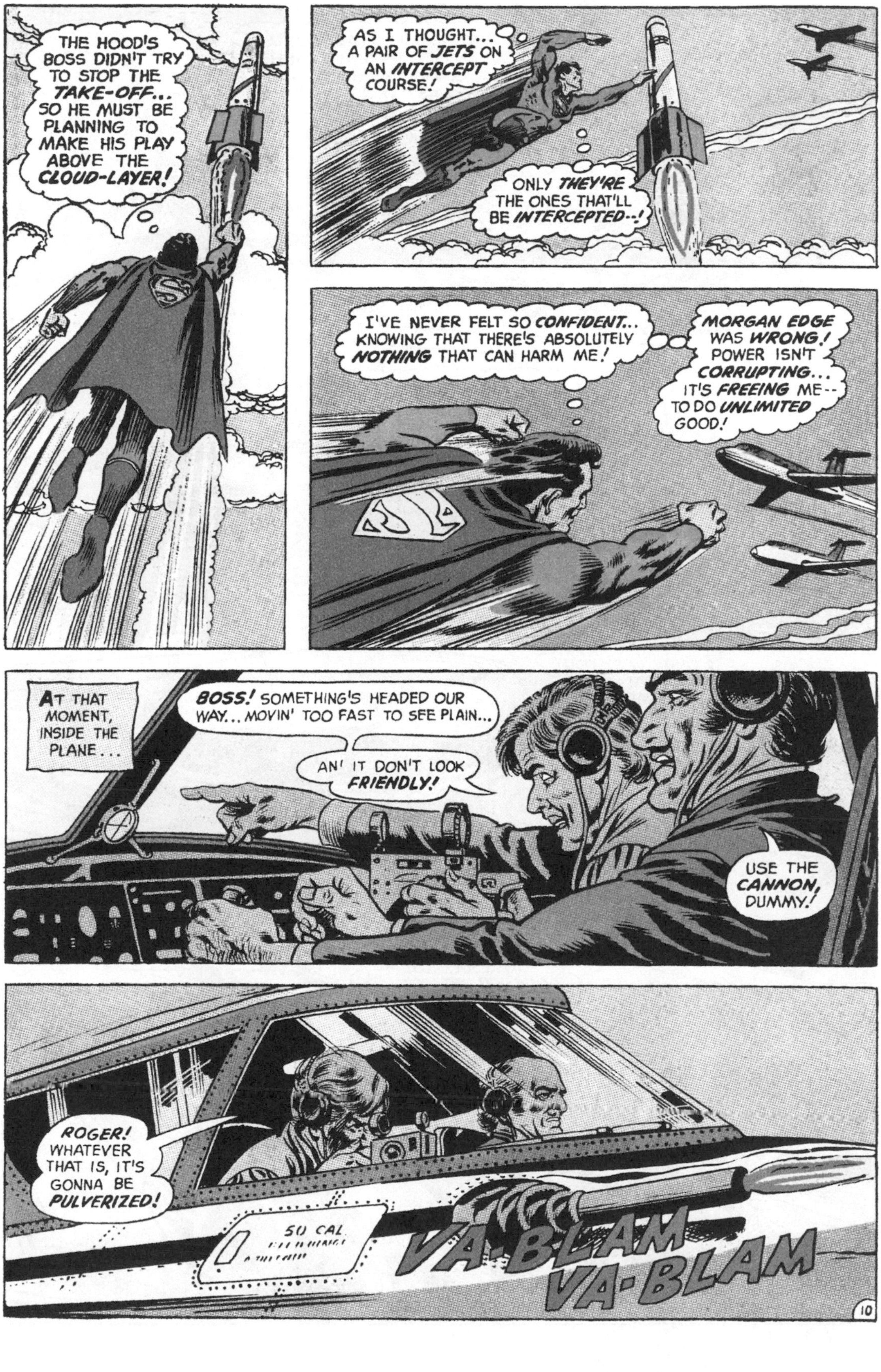
THE HOOD'S BOSS DIDN'T TRY TO STOP THE TAKE-OFF... SO HE MUST BE PLANNING TO MAKE HIS PLAY ABOVE THE CLOUD-LAYER!
AS I THOUGHT... A PAIR OF JETS ON AN INTERCEPT COURSE!
ONLY THEY'RE THE ONES THAT'LL BE INTERCEPTED--!
I'VE NEVER FELT SO CONFIDENT... KNOWING THAT THERE'S ABSOLUTELY NOTHING THAT CAN HARM ME!
MORGAN EDGE WAS WRONG! POWER ISN'T CORRUPTING... IT'S FREEING ME--TO DO UNLIMITED GOOD!
AT THAT MOMENT, INSIDE THE PLANE...
BOSS! SOMETHING'S HEADED OUR WAY... MOVIN' TOO FAST TO SEE PLAIN...
AN' IT DON'T LOOK FRIENDLY!
USE THE CANNON, DUMMY!
ROGER! WHATEVER THAT IS, IT'S GONNA BE PULVERIZED!
50 CAL.
VA-BLAM
VA-BLAM
10

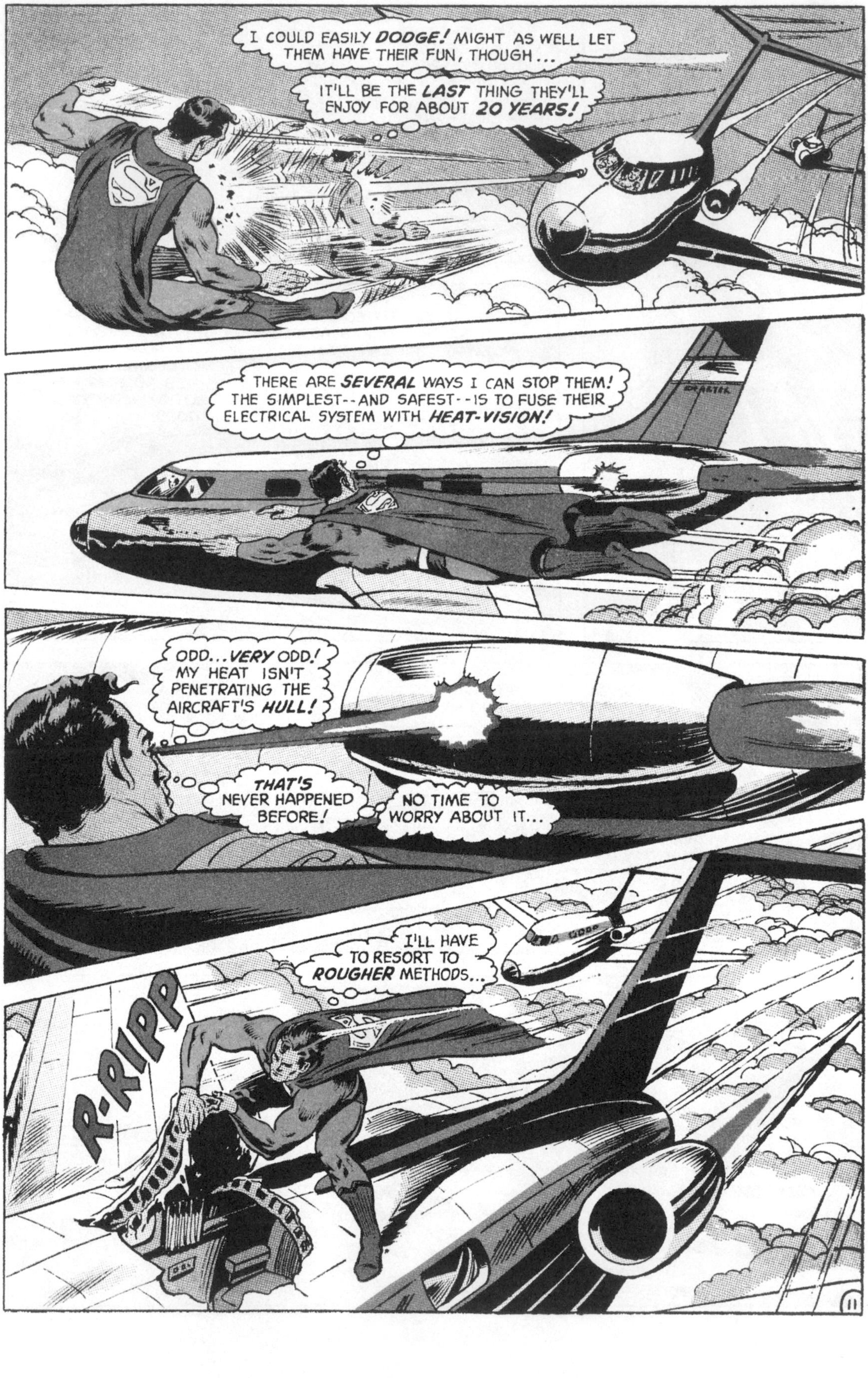
I COULD EASILY DODGE! MIGHT AS WELL LET THEM HAVE THEIR FUN, THOUGH...
IT'LL BE THE LAST THING THEY'LL ENJOY FOR ABOUT 20 YEARS!
THERE ARE SEVERAL WAYS I CAN STOP THEM! THE SIMPLEST--AND SAFEST--IS TO FUSE THEIR ELECTRICAL SYSTEM WITH HEAT-VISION!
ODD...VERY ODD! MY HEAT ISN'T PENETRATING THE AIRCRAFT'S HULL!
THAT'S NEVER HAPPENED BEFORE!
NO TIME TO WORRY ABOUT IT...
I'LL HAVE TO RESORT TO ROUGHER METHODS...
R-RIPP
11

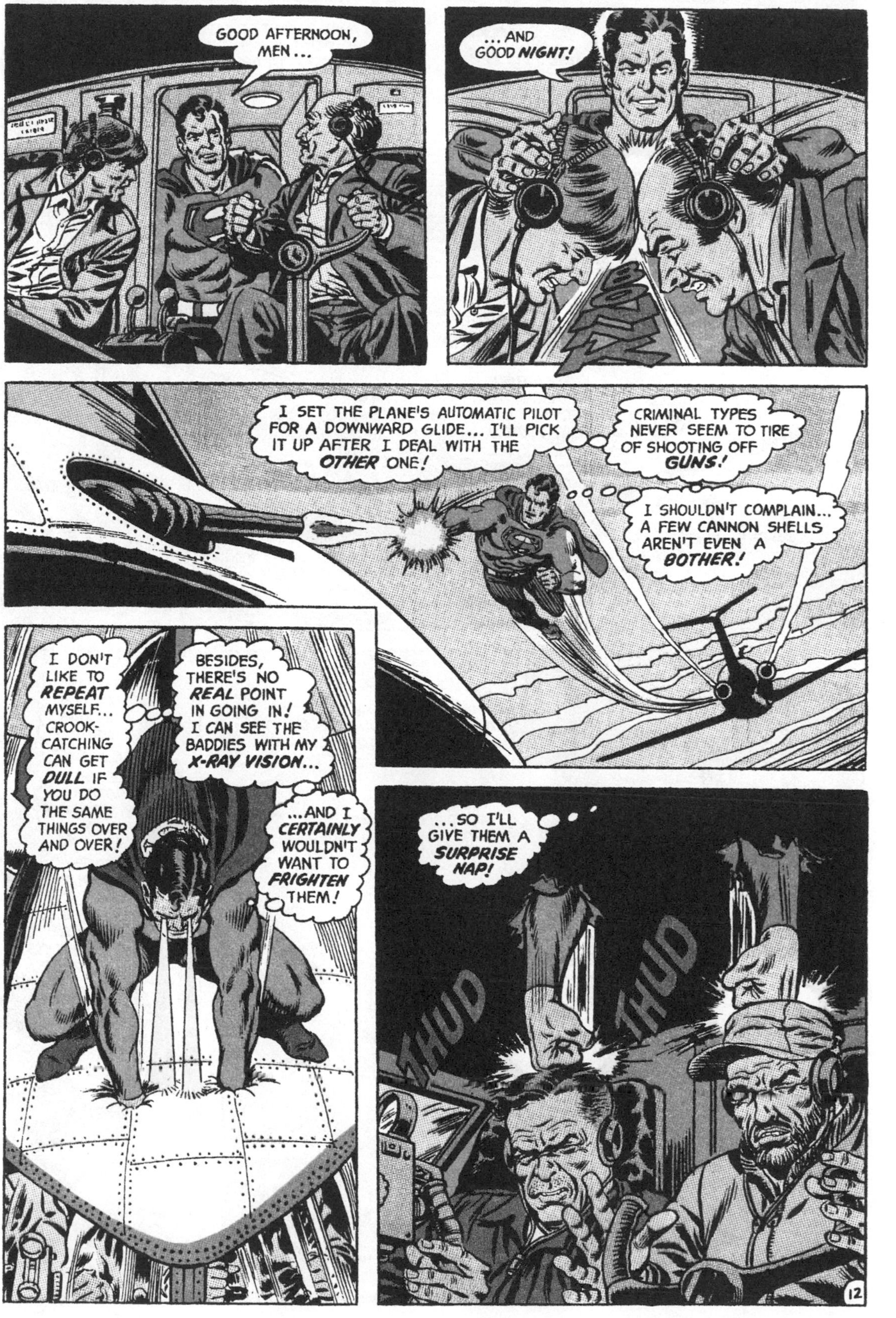
GOOD AFTERNOON, MEN...
...AND GOOD NIGHT!
I SET THE PLANE'S AUTOMATIC PILOT FOR A DOWNWARD GLIDE... I'LL PICK IT UP AFTER I DEAL WITH THE OTHER ONE!
CRIMINAL TYPES NEVER SEEM TO TIRE OF SHOOTING OFF GUNS!
I SHOULDN'T COMPLAIN... A FEW CANNON SHELLS AREN'T EVEN A BOTHER!
I DON'T LIKE TO REPEAT MYSELF... CROOK-CATCHING CAN GET DULL IF YOU DO THE SAME THINGS OVER AND OVER!
BESIDES, THERE'S NO REAL POINT IN GOING IN! I CAN SEE THE BADDIES WITH MY X-RAY VISION...
...AND I CERTAINLY WOULDN'T WANT TO FRIGHTEN THEM!
...SO I'LL GIVE THEM A SURPRISE NAP!
THUD
THUD
12

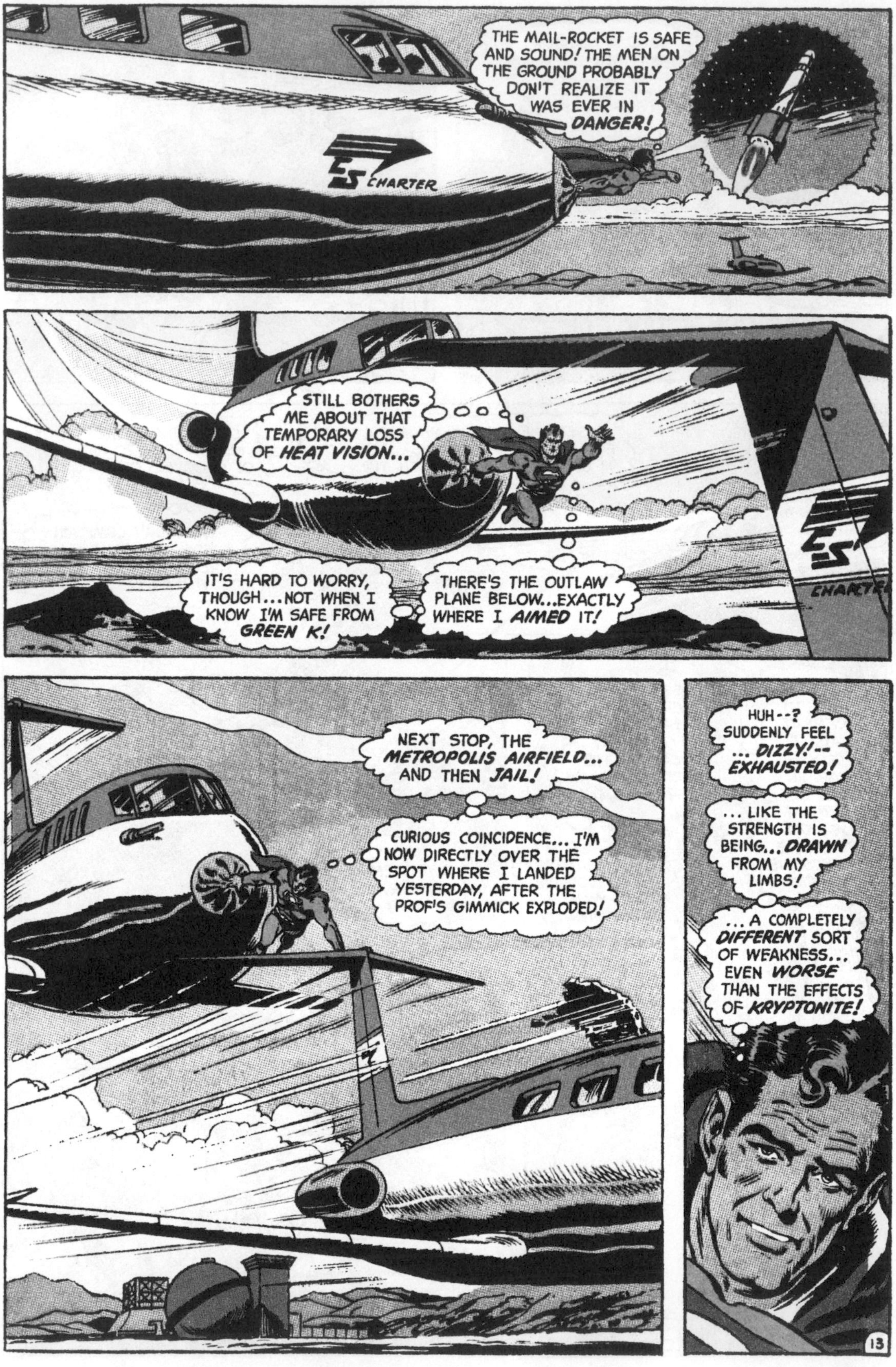
THE MAIL-ROCKET IS SAFE AND SOUND! THE MEN ON THE GROUND PROBABLY DON'T REALIZE IT WAS EVER IN DANGER!
CHARTER
STILL BOTHERS ME ABOUT THAT TEMPORARY LOSS OF HEAT VISION...
IT'S HARD TO WORRY, THOUGH...NOT WHEN I KNOW I'M SAFE FROM GREEN K!
THERE'S THE OUTLAW PLANE BELOW...EXACTLY WHERE I AIMED IT!
NEXT STOP, THE METROPOLIS AIRFIELD... AND THEN JAIL!
CURIOUS COINCIDENCE... I'M NOW DIRECTLY OVER THE SPOT WHERE I LANDED YESTERDAY, AFTER THE PROF'S GIMMICK EXPLODED!
HUH--? SUDDENLY FEEL ... DIZZY!-- EXHAUSTED!
... LIKE THE STRENGTH IS BEING... DRAWN FROM MY LIMBS!
... A COMPLETELY DIFFERENT SORT OF WEAKNESS... EVEN WORSE THAN THE EFFECTS OF KRYPTONITE!
13

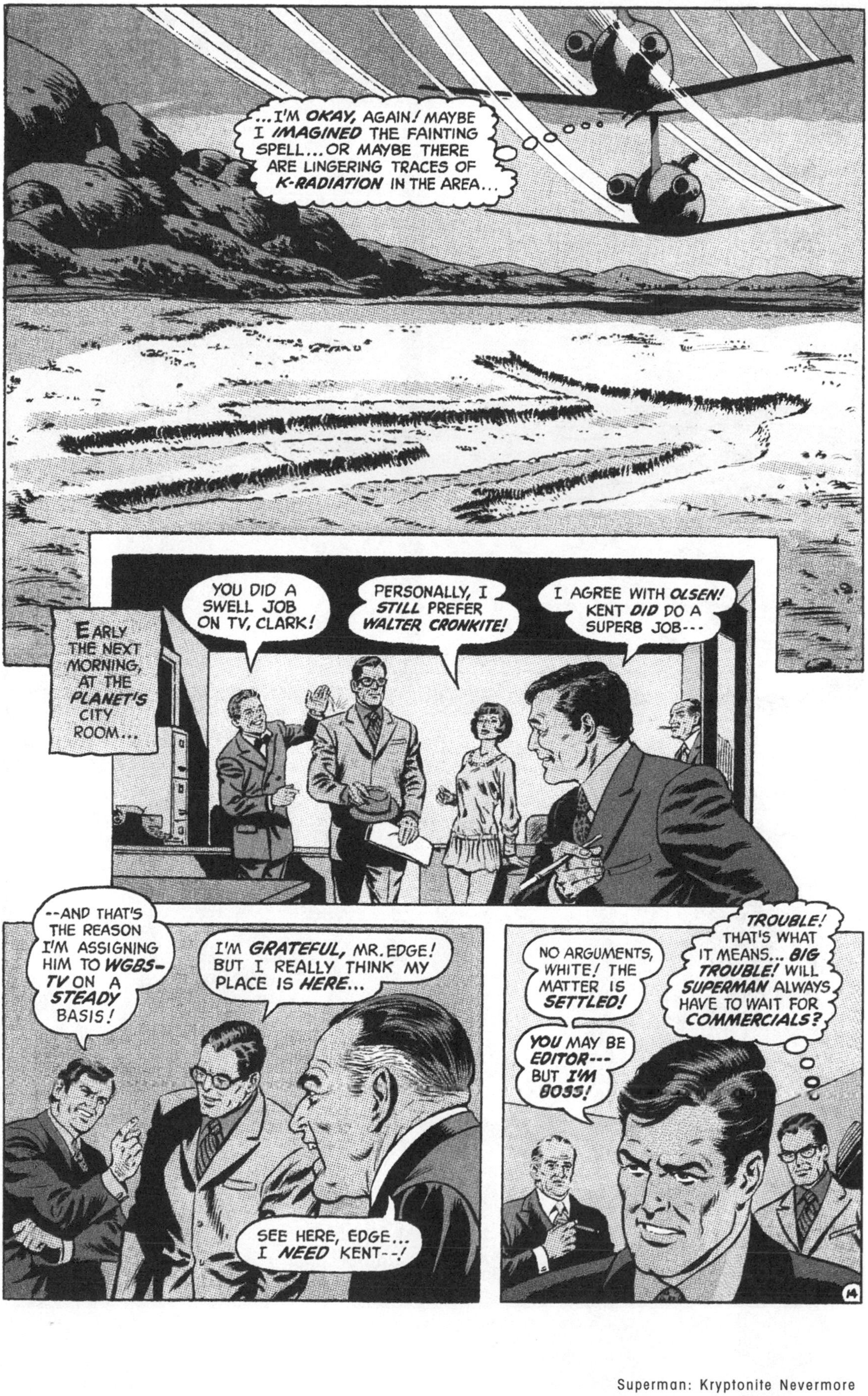
...I'M OKAY, AGAIN! MAYBE I IMAGINED THE FAINTING SPELL...OR MAYBE THERE ARE LINGERING TRACES OF K-RADIATION IN THE AREA...
EARLY THE NEXT MORNING, AT THE PLANET'S CITY ROOM...
YOU DID A SWELL JOB ON TV, CLARK!
PERSONALLY, I STILL PREFER WALTER CRONKITE!
I AGREE WITH OLSEN! KENT DID DO A SUPERB JOB---
--AND THAT'S THE REASON I'M ASSIGNING HIM TO WGBS-TV ON A STEADY BASIS!
I'M GRATEFUL, MR. EDGE! BUT I REALLY THINK MY PLACE IS HERE...
SEE HERE, EDGE... I NEED KENT--!
NO ARGUMENTS, WHITE! THE MATTER IS SETTLED!
YOU MAY BE EDITOR--- BUT I'M BOSS!
TROUBLE! THAT'S WHAT IT MEANS... BIG TROUBLE! WILL SUPERMAN ALWAYS HAVE TO WAIT FOR COMMERCIALS?
14

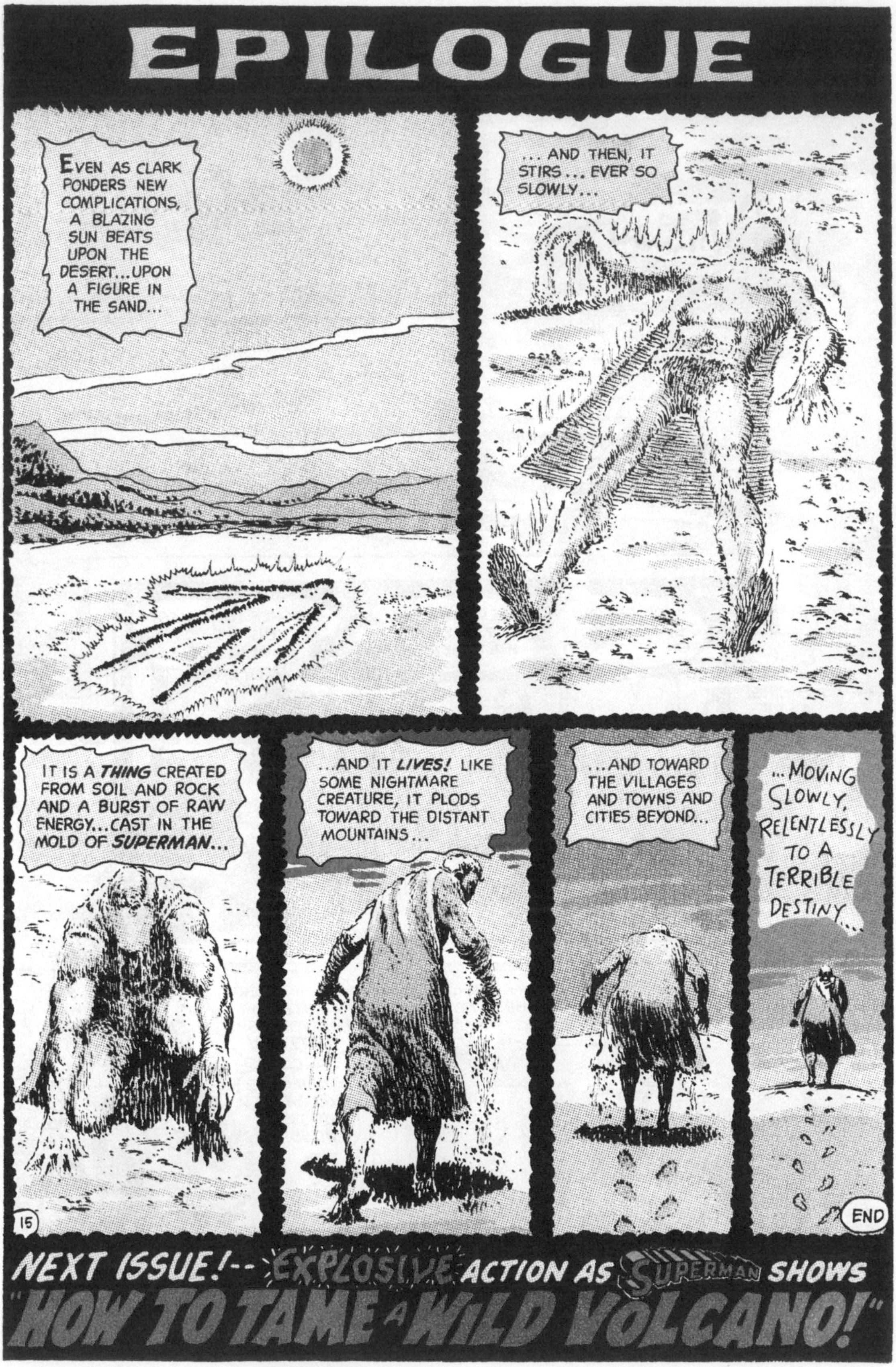
EPILOGUE
EVEN AS CLARK PONDERS NEW COMPLICATIONS, A BLAZING SUN BEATS UPON THE DESERT...UPON A FIGURE IN THE SAND...
...AND THEN, IT STIRS...EVER SO SLOWLY...
IT IS A THING CREATED FROM SOIL AND ROCK AND A BURST OF RAW ENERGY...CAST IN THE MOLD OF SUPERMAN...
15
...AND IT LIVES! LIKE SOME NIGHTMARE CREATURE, IT PLODS TOWARD THE DISTANT MOUNTAINS...
...AND TOWARD THE VILLAGES AND TOWNS AND CITIES BEYOND...
...MOVING SLOWLY, RELENTLESSLY TO A TERRIBLE DESTINY.
END
NEXT ISSUE!-- EXPLOSIVE ACTION AS SUPERMAN SHOWS
"HOW TO TAME A WILD VOLCANO!"

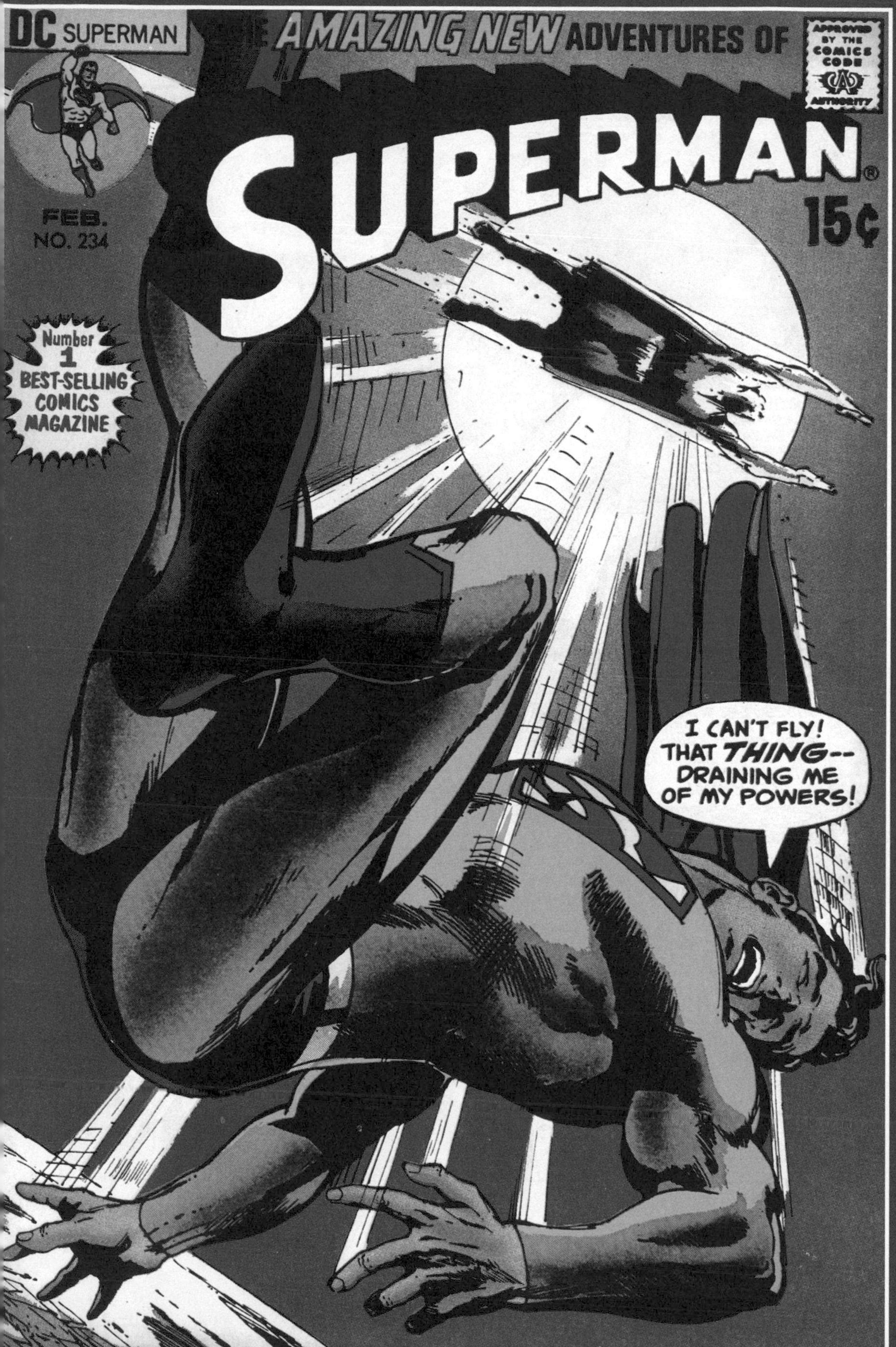
DC SUPERMAN
THE AMAZING NEW ADVENTURES OF
APPROVED BY THE COMICS CODE AUTHORITY
SUPERMAN®
FEB.
NO. 234
15¢
Number 1 BEST-SELLING COMICS MAGAZINE
I CAN'T FLY! THAT THING-- DRAINING ME OF MY POWERS!

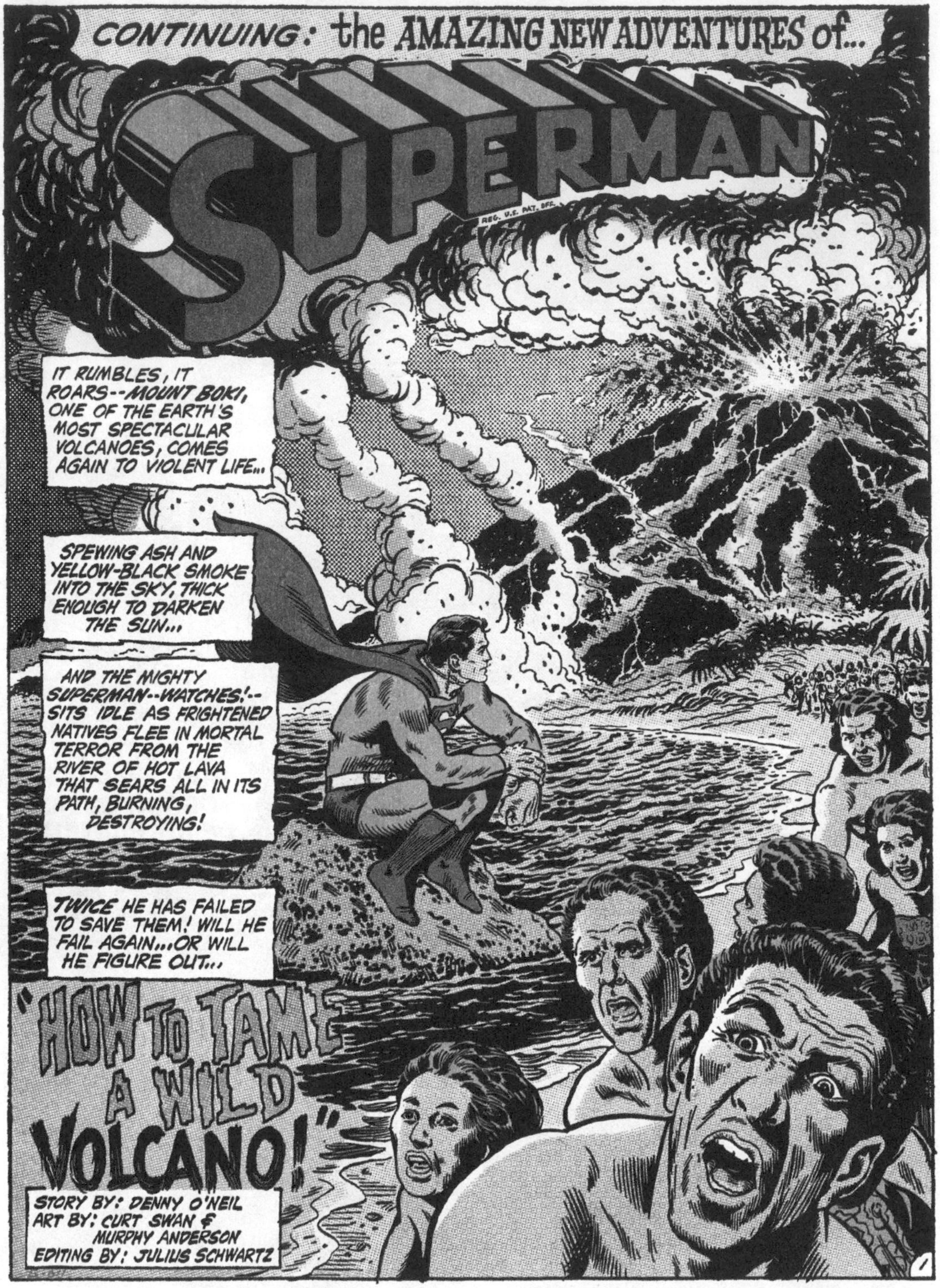
CONTINUING: the AMAZING NEW ADVENTURES of...
SUPERMAN
REG. U.S. PAT. OFF.
IT RUMBLES, IT ROARS--MOUNT BOKI, ONE OF THE EARTH'S MOST SPECTACULAR VOLCANOES, COMES AGAIN TO VIOLENT LIFE...
SPEWING ASH AND YELLOW-BLACK SMOKE INTO THE SKY, THICK ENOUGH TO DARKEN THE SUN...
AND THE MIGHTY SUPERMAN--WATCHES!--SITS IDLE AS FRIGHTENED NATIVES FLEE IN MORTAL TERROR FROM THE RIVER OF HOT LAVA THAT SEARS ALL IN ITS PATH, BURNING, DESTROYING!
TWICE HE HAS FAILED TO SAVE THEM! WILL HE FAIL AGAIN...OR WILL HE FIGURE OUT...
"HOW TO TAME A WILD VOLCANO!"
STORY BY: DENNY O'NEIL
ART BY: CURT SWAN & MURPHY ANDERSON
EDITING BY: JULIUS SCHWARTZ
1

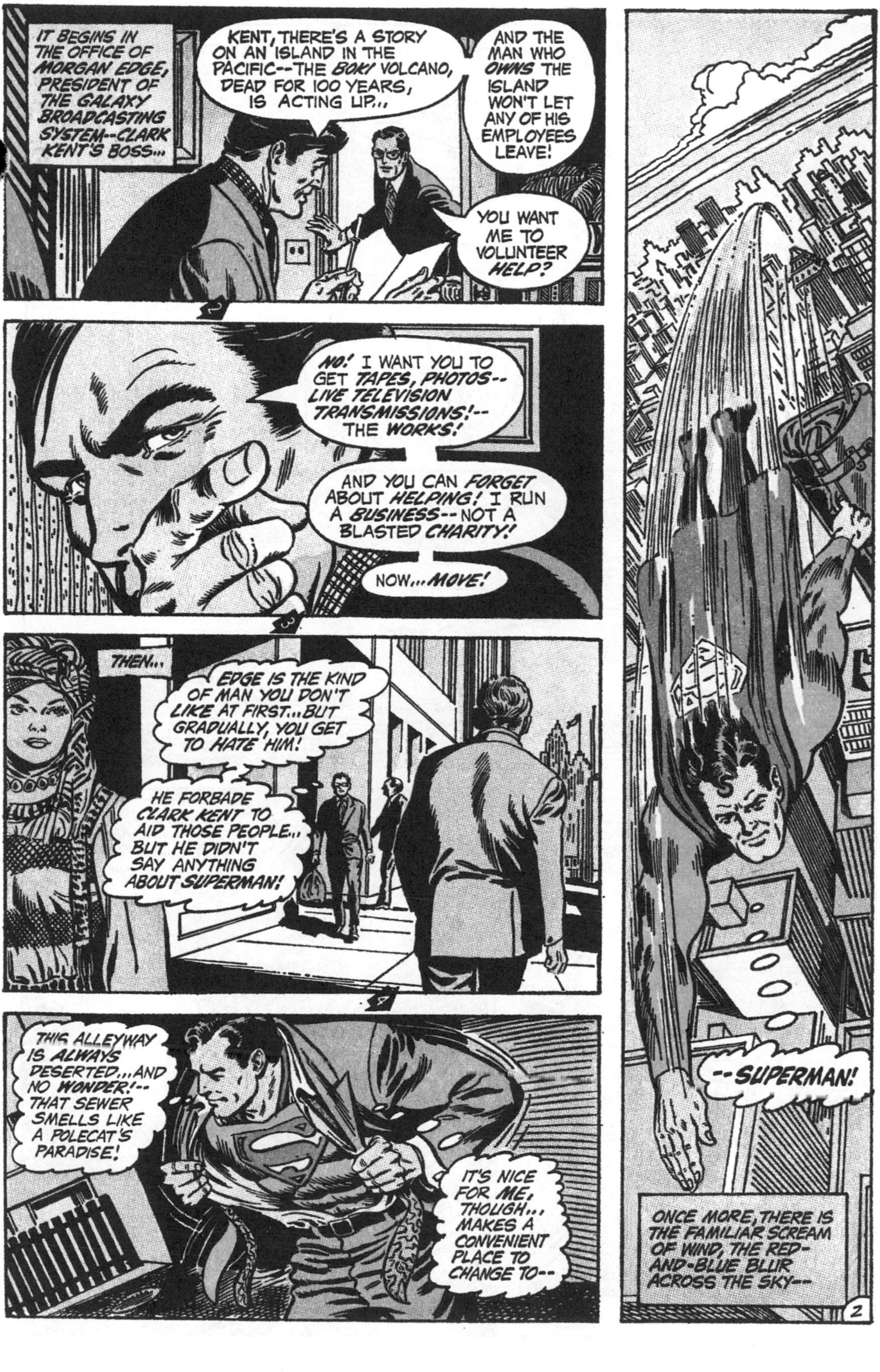
IT BEGINS IN THE OFFICE OF MORGAN EDGE, PRESIDENT OF THE GALAXY BROADCASTING SYSTEM--CLARK KENT'S BOSS...
KENT, THERE'S A STORY ON AN ISLAND IN THE PACIFIC--THE BOKI VOLCANO, DEAD FOR 100 YEARS, IS ACTING UP...
AND THE MAN WHO OWNS THE ISLAND WON'T LET ANY OF HIS EMPLOYEES LEAVE!
YOU WANT ME TO VOLUNTEER HELP?
NO! I WANT YOU TO GET TAPES, PHOTOS--LIVE TELEVISION TRANSMISSIONS!--THE WORKS!
AND YOU CAN FORGET ABOUT HELPING! I RUN A BUSINESS--NOT A BLASTED CHARITY!
NOW...MOVE!
THEN...
EDGE IS THE KIND OF MAN YOU DON'T LIKE AT FIRST...BUT GRADUALLY, YOU GET TO HATE HIM!
HE FORBADE CLARK KENT TO AID THOSE PEOPLE...BUT HE DIDN'T SAY ANYTHING ABOUT SUPERMAN!
THIS ALLEYWAY IS ALWAYS DESERTED...AND NO WONDER!--THAT SEWER SMELLS LIKE A POLECAT'S PARADISE!
IT'S NICE FOR ME, THOUGH... MAKES A CONVENIENT PLACE TO CHANGE TO--
--SUPERMAN!
ONCE MORE, THERE IS THE FAMILIAR SCREAM OF WIND, THE RED-AND-BLUE BLUR ACROSS THE SKY--
2

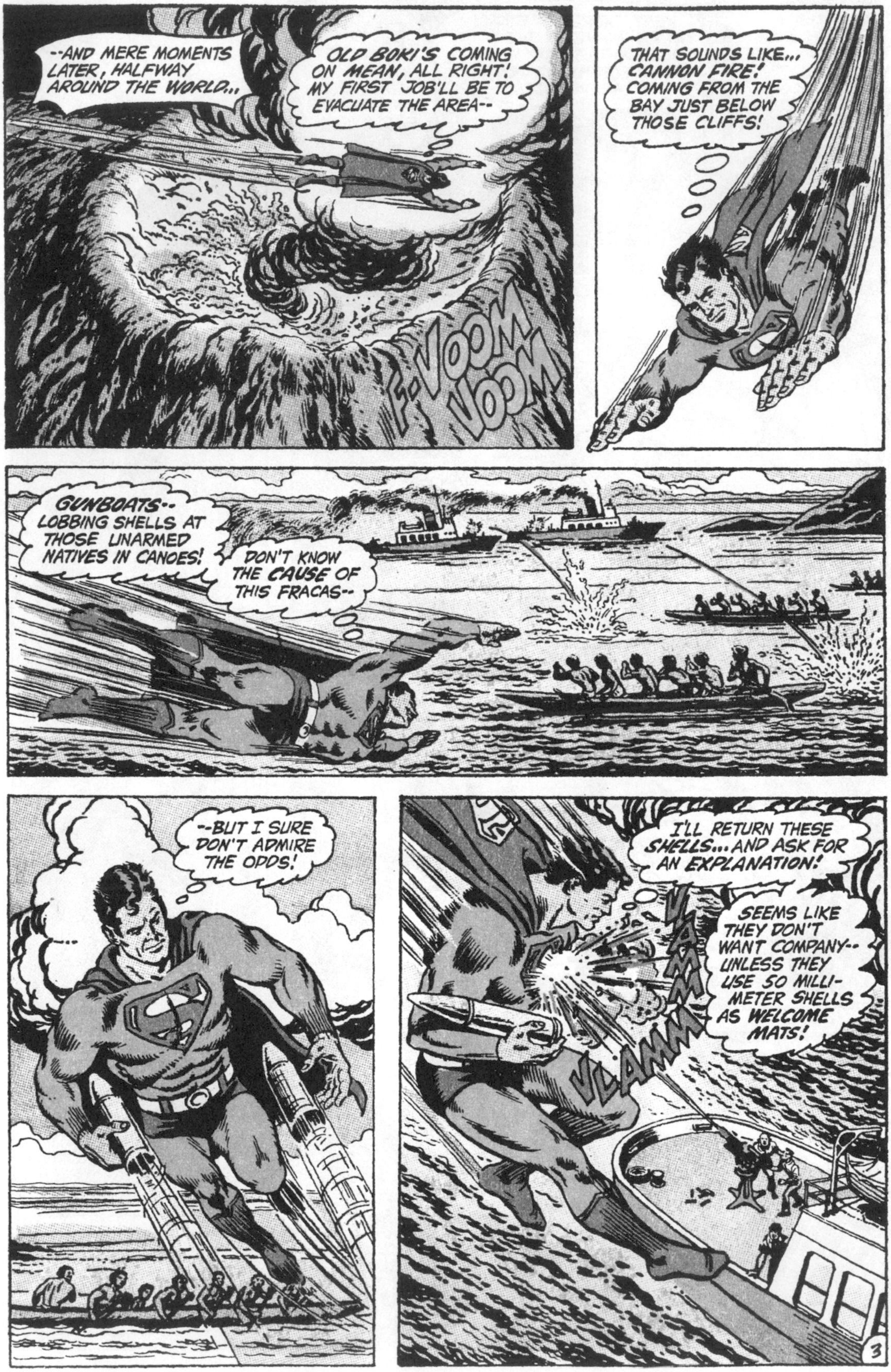
--AND MERE MOMENTS LATER, HALFWAY AROUND THE WORLD...
OLD BOKI'S COMING ON MEAN, ALL RIGHT! MY FIRST JOB'LL BE TO EVACUATE THE AREA--
F-VOOM VOOM
THAT SOUNDS LIKE... CANNON FIRE! COMING FROM THE BAY JUST BELOW THOSE CLIFFS!
GUNBOATS-- LOBBING SHELLS AT THOSE UNARMED NATIVES IN CANOES!
DON'T KNOW THE CAUSE OF THIS FRACAS--
--BUT I SURE DON'T ADMIRE THE ODDS!
I'LL RETURN THESE SHELLS... AND ASK FOR AN EXPLANATION!
SEEMS LIKE THEY DON'T WANT COMPANY-- UNLESS THEY USE 50 MILLI-METER SHELLS AS WELCOME MATS!
VLAAM
JLAMM
3

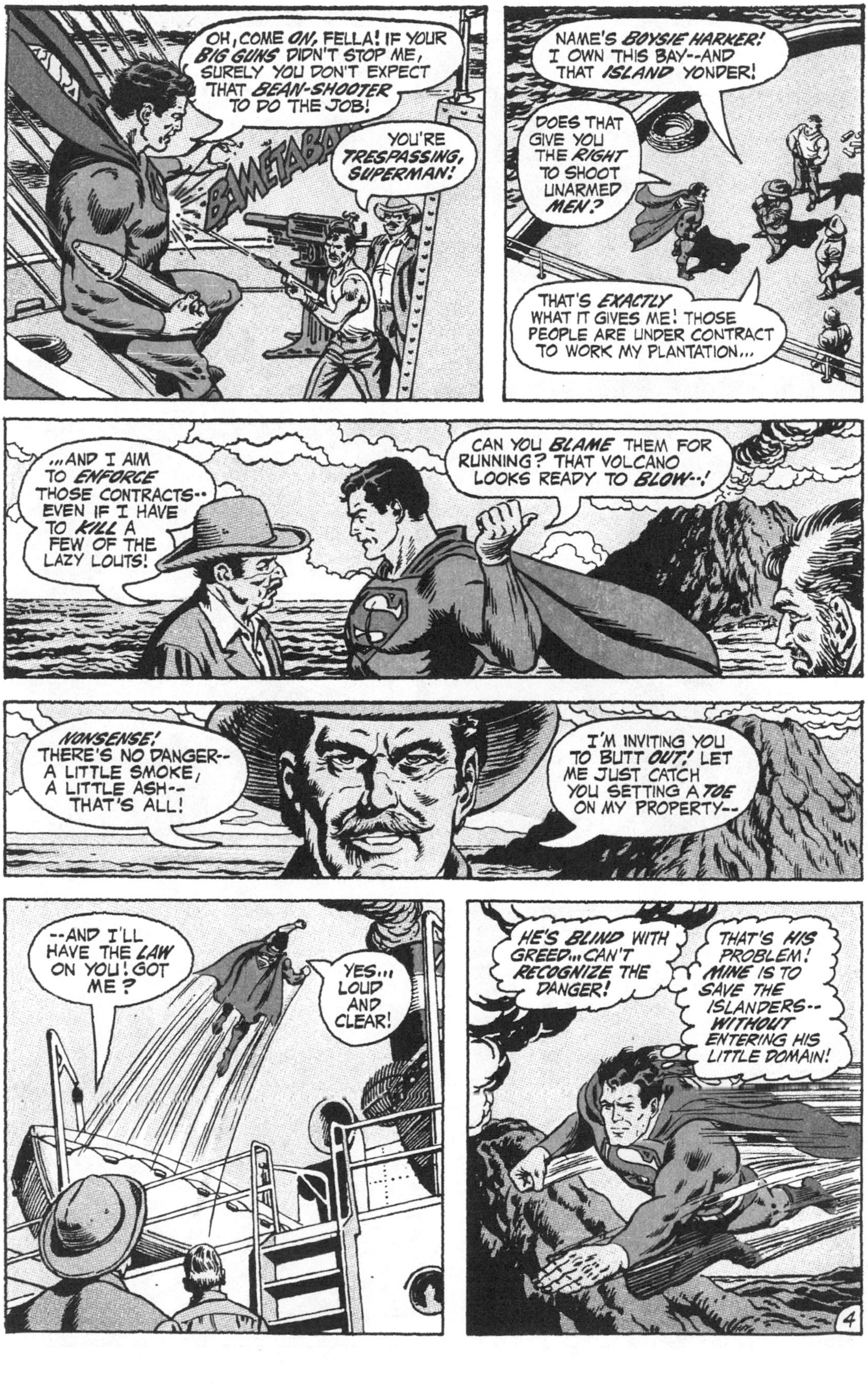
OH, COME ON, FELLA! IF YOUR BIG GUNS DIDN'T STOP ME, SURELY YOU DON'T EXPECT THAT BEAN-SHOOTER TO DO THE JOB!
YOU'RE TRESPASSING, SUPERMAN!
NAME'S BOYSIE HARKER! I OWN THIS BAY--AND THAT ISLAND YONDER!
DOES THAT GIVE YOU THE RIGHT TO SHOOT UNARMED MEN?
THAT'S EXACTLY WHAT IT GIVES ME! THOSE PEOPLE ARE UNDER CONTRACT TO WORK MY PLANTATION...
...AND I AIM TO ENFORCE THOSE CONTRACTS-- EVEN IF I HAVE TO KILL A FEW OF THE LAZY LOUTS!
CAN YOU BLAME THEM FOR RUNNING? THAT VOLCANO LOOKS READY TO BLOW--!
NONSENSE! THERE'S NO DANGER-- A LITTLE SMOKE, A LITTLE ASH-- THAT'S ALL!
I'M INVITING YOU TO BUTT OUT! LET ME JUST CATCH YOU SETTING A TOE ON MY PROPERTY--
--AND I'LL HAVE THE LAW ON YOU! GOT ME?
YES... LOUD AND CLEAR!
HE'S BLIND WITH GREED... CAN'T RECOGNIZE THE DANGER!
THAT'S HIS PROBLEM! MINE IS TO SAVE THE ISLANDERS-- WITHOUT ENTERING HIS LITTLE DOMAIN!
4

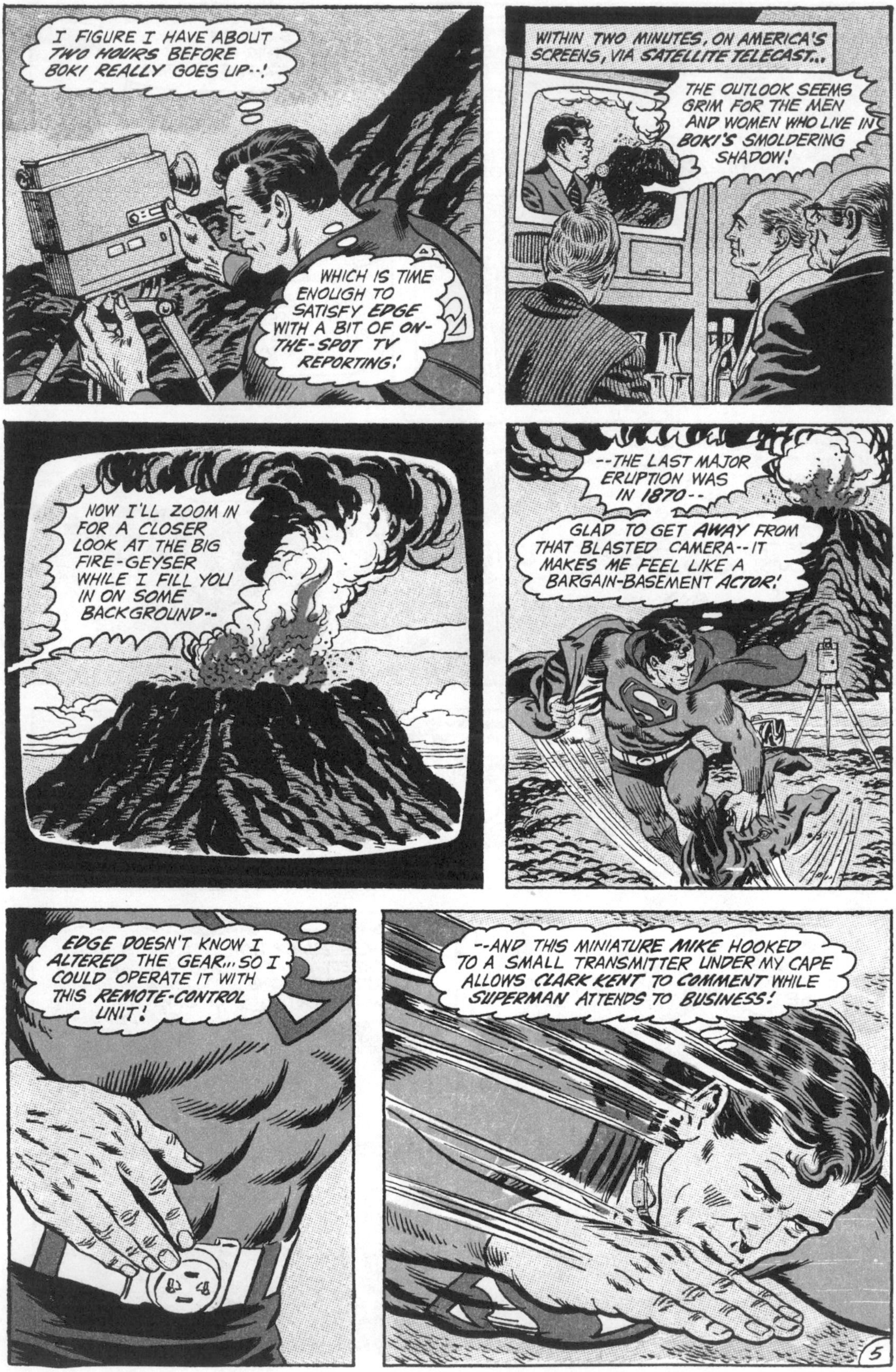
I FIGURE I HAVE ABOUT TWO HOURS BEFORE BOKI REALLY GOES UP--!
WHICH IS TIME ENOUGH TO SATISFY EDGE WITH A BIT OF ON-THE-SPOT TV REPORTING!
WITHIN TWO MINUTES, ON AMERICA'S SCREENS, VIA SATELLITE TELECAST...
THE OUTLOOK SEEMS GRIM FOR THE MEN AND WOMEN WHO LIVE IN BOKI'S SMOLDERING SHADOW!
NOW I'LL ZOOM IN FOR A CLOSER LOOK AT THE BIG FIRE-GEYSER WHILE I FILL YOU IN ON SOME BACKGROUND--
--THE LAST MAJOR ERUPTION WAS IN 1870--
GLAD TO GET AWAY FROM THAT BLASTED CAMERA--IT MAKES ME FEEL LIKE A BARGAIN-BASEMENT ACTOR!
EDGE DOESN'T KNOW I ALTERED THE GEAR... SO I COULD OPERATE IT WITH THIS REMOTE-CONTROL UNIT!
--AND THIS MINIATURE MIKE HOOKED TO A SMALL TRANSMITTER UNDER MY CAPE ALLOWS CLARK KENT TO COMMENT WHILE SUPERMAN ATTENDS TO BUSINESS!
5

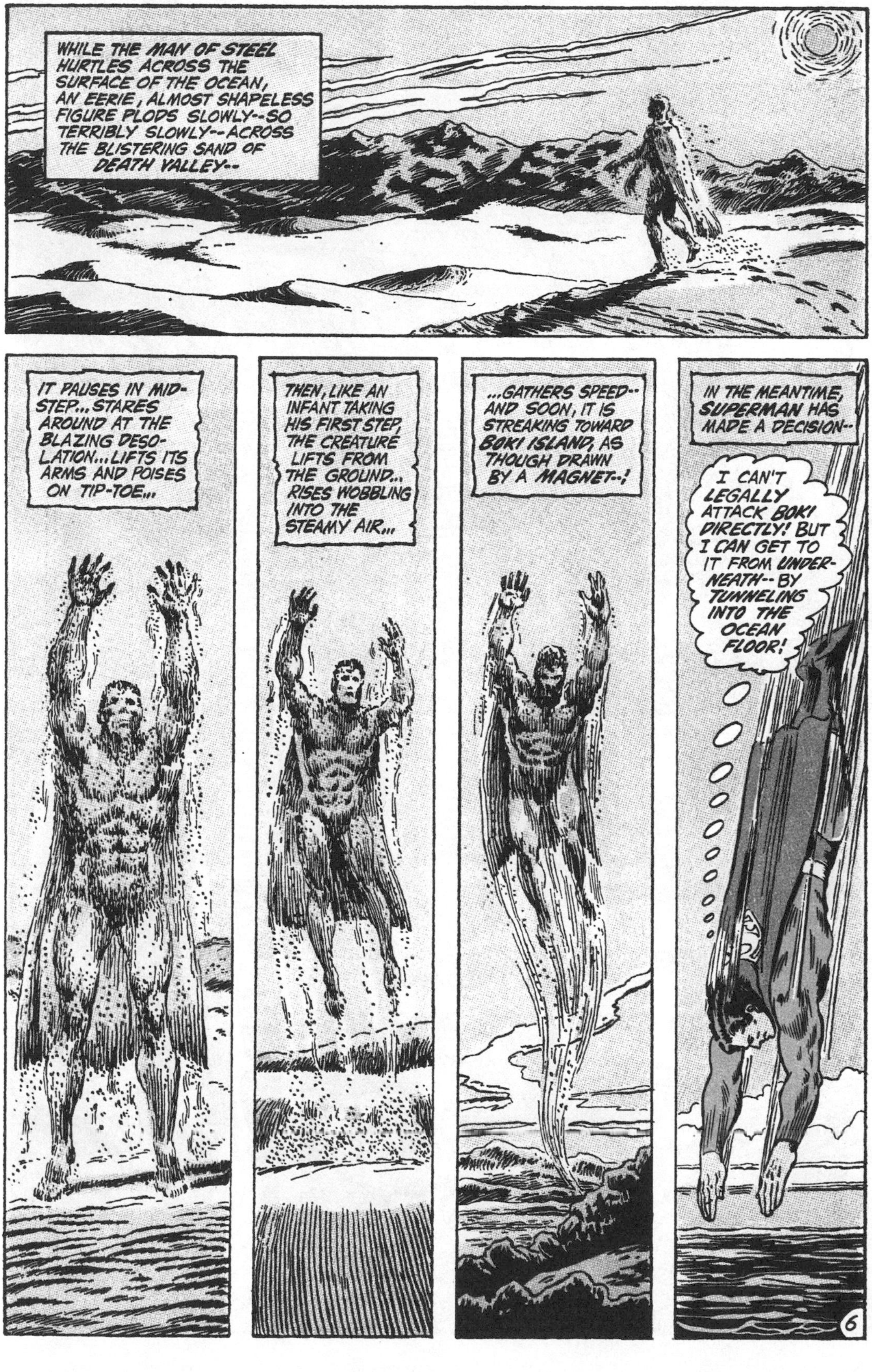
WHILE THE MAN OF STEEL HURTLES ACROSS THE SURFACE OF THE OCEAN, AN EERIE, ALMOST SHAPELESS FIGURE PLODS SLOWLY--SO TERRIBLY SLOWLY--ACROSS THE BLISTERING SAND OF DEATH VALLEY--
IT PAUSES IN MID-STEP...STARES AROUND AT THE BLAZING DESOLATION...LIFTS ITS ARMS AND POISES ON TIP-TOE...
THEN, LIKE AN INFANT TAKING HIS FIRST STEP, THE CREATURE LIFTS FROM THE GROUND...RISES WOBBLING INTO THE STEAMY AIR...
...GATHERS SPEED--AND SOON, IT IS STREAKING TOWARD BOKI ISLAND, AS THOUGH DRAWN BY A MAGNET--!
IN THE MEANTIME, SUPERMAN HAS MADE A DECISION--
I CAN'T LEGALLY ATTACK BOKI DIRECTLY! BUT I CAN GET TO IT FROM UNDERNEATH--BY TUNNELING INTO THE OCEAN FLOOR!
6

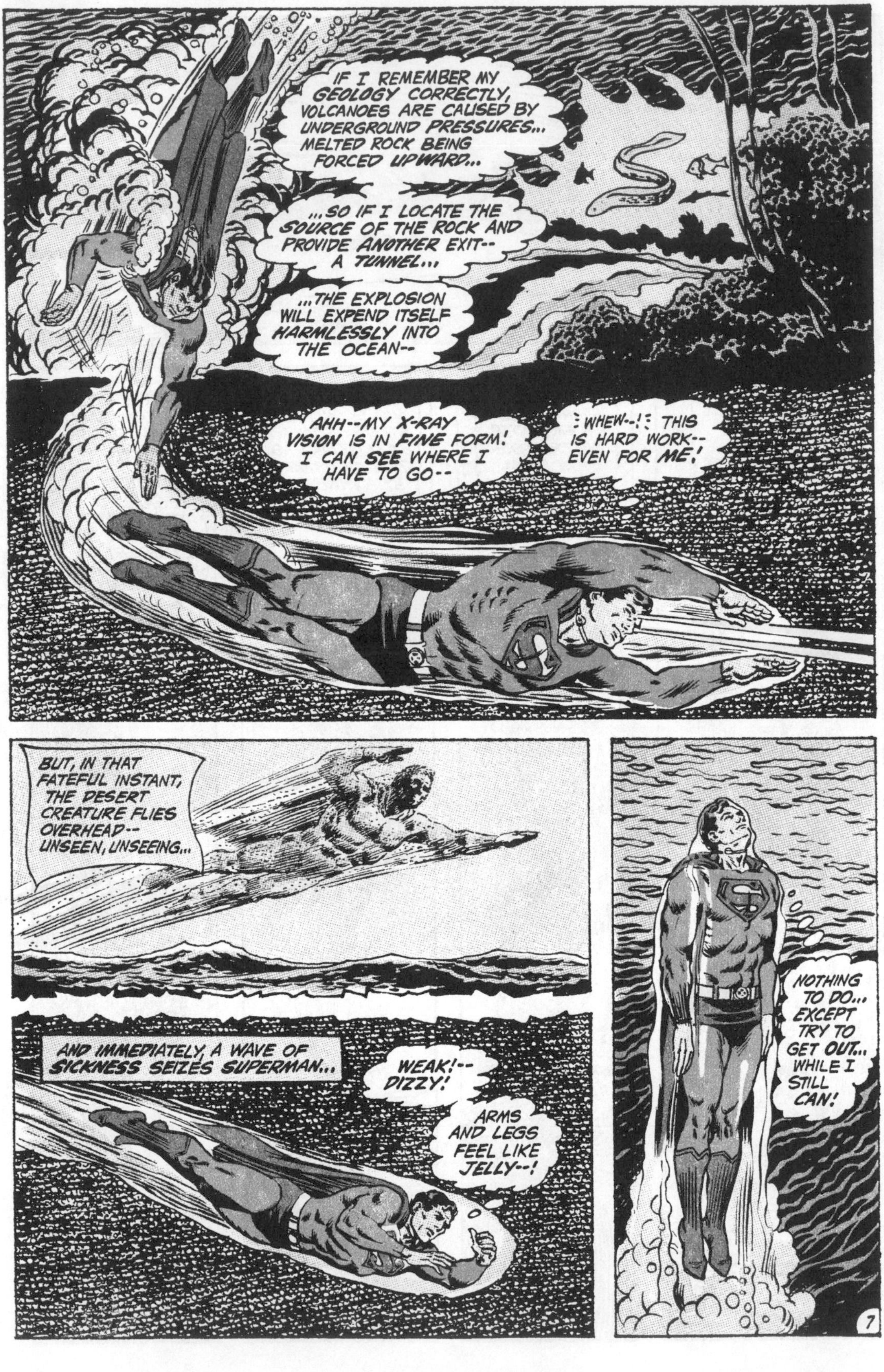
IF I REMEMBER MY GEOLOGY CORRECTLY, VOLCANOES ARE CAUSED BY UNDERGROUND PRESSURES... MELTED ROCK BEING FORCED UPWARD...
...SO IF I LOCATE THE SOURCE OF THE ROCK AND PROVIDE ANOTHER EXIT-- A TUNNEL...
...THE EXPLOSION WILL EXPEND ITSELF HARMLESSLY INTO THE OCEAN--
AHH--MY X-RAY VISION IS IN FINE FORM! I CAN SEE WHERE I HAVE TO GO--
WHEW--! THIS IS HARD WORK-- EVEN FOR ME!
BUT, IN THAT FATEFUL INSTANT, THE DESERT CREATURE FLIES OVERHEAD-- UNSEEN, UNSEEING...
AND IMMEDIATELY, A WAVE OF SICKNESS SEIZES SUPERMAN...
WEAK!-- DIZZY!
ARMS AND LEGS FEEL LIKE JELLY--!
NOTHING TO DO... EXCEPT TRY TO GET OUT... WHILE I STILL CAN!
7

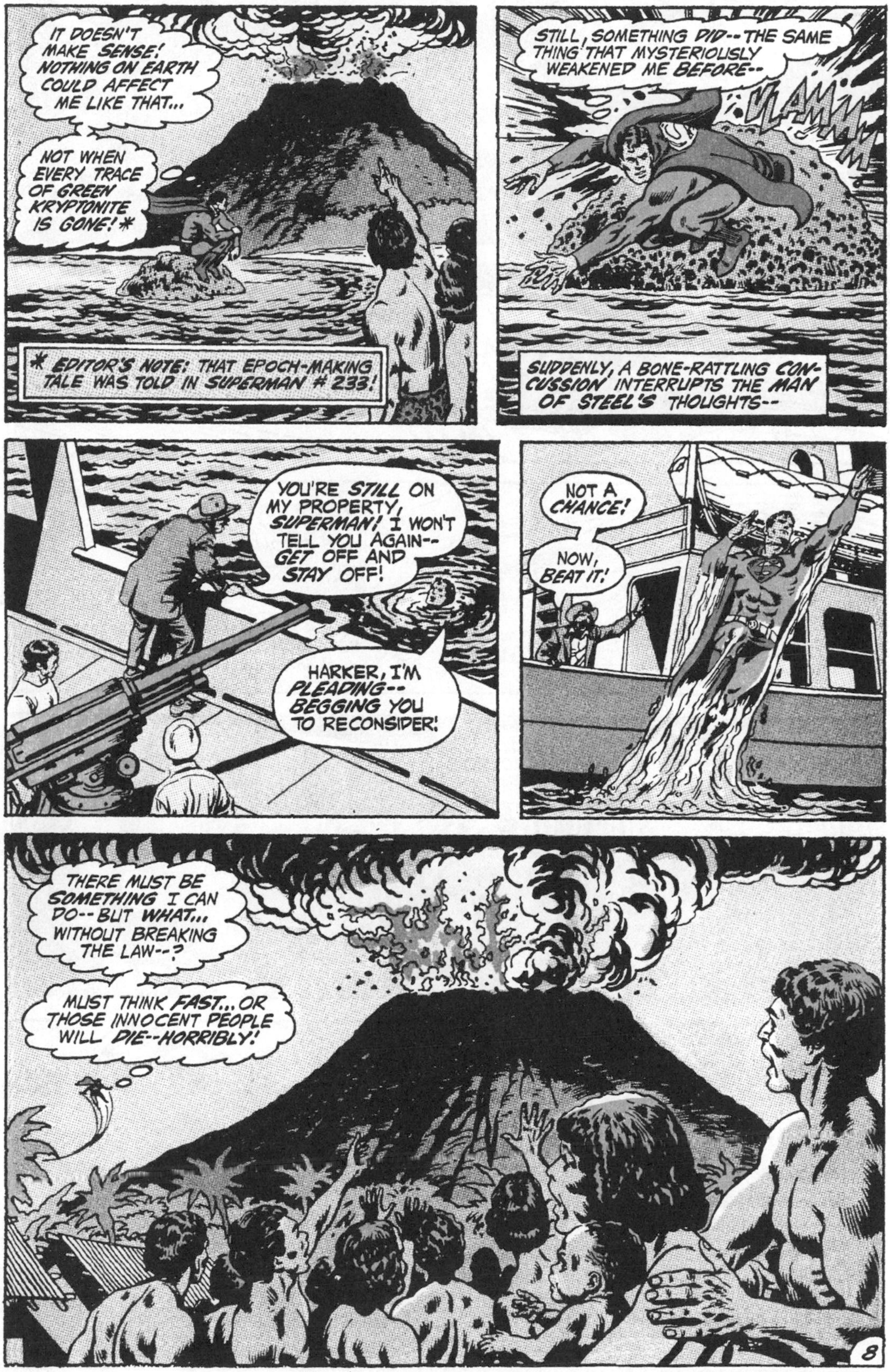
IT DOESN'T MAKE SENSE! NOTHING ON EARTH COULD AFFECT ME LIKE THAT...
NOT WHEN EVERY TRACE OF GREEN KRYPTONITE IS GONE! *
* EDITOR'S NOTE: THAT EPOCH-MAKING TALE WAS TOLD IN SUPERMAN # 233!
STILL, SOMETHING DID--THE SAME THING THAT MYSTERIOUSLY WEAKENED ME BEFORE--
VLAMM
SUDDENLY, A BONE-RATTLING CONCUSSION INTERRUPTS THE MAN OF STEEL'S THOUGHTS--
YOU'RE STILL ON MY PROPERTY, SUPERMAN! I WON'T TELL YOU AGAIN--GET OFF AND STAY OFF!
HARKER, I'M PLEADING--BEGGING YOU TO RECONSIDER!
NOT A CHANCE!
NOW, BEAT IT!
THERE MUST BE SOMETHING I CAN DO--BUT WHAT... WITHOUT BREAKING THE LAW--?
MUST THINK FAST...OR THOSE INNOCENT PEOPLE WILL DIE--HORRIBLY!
8

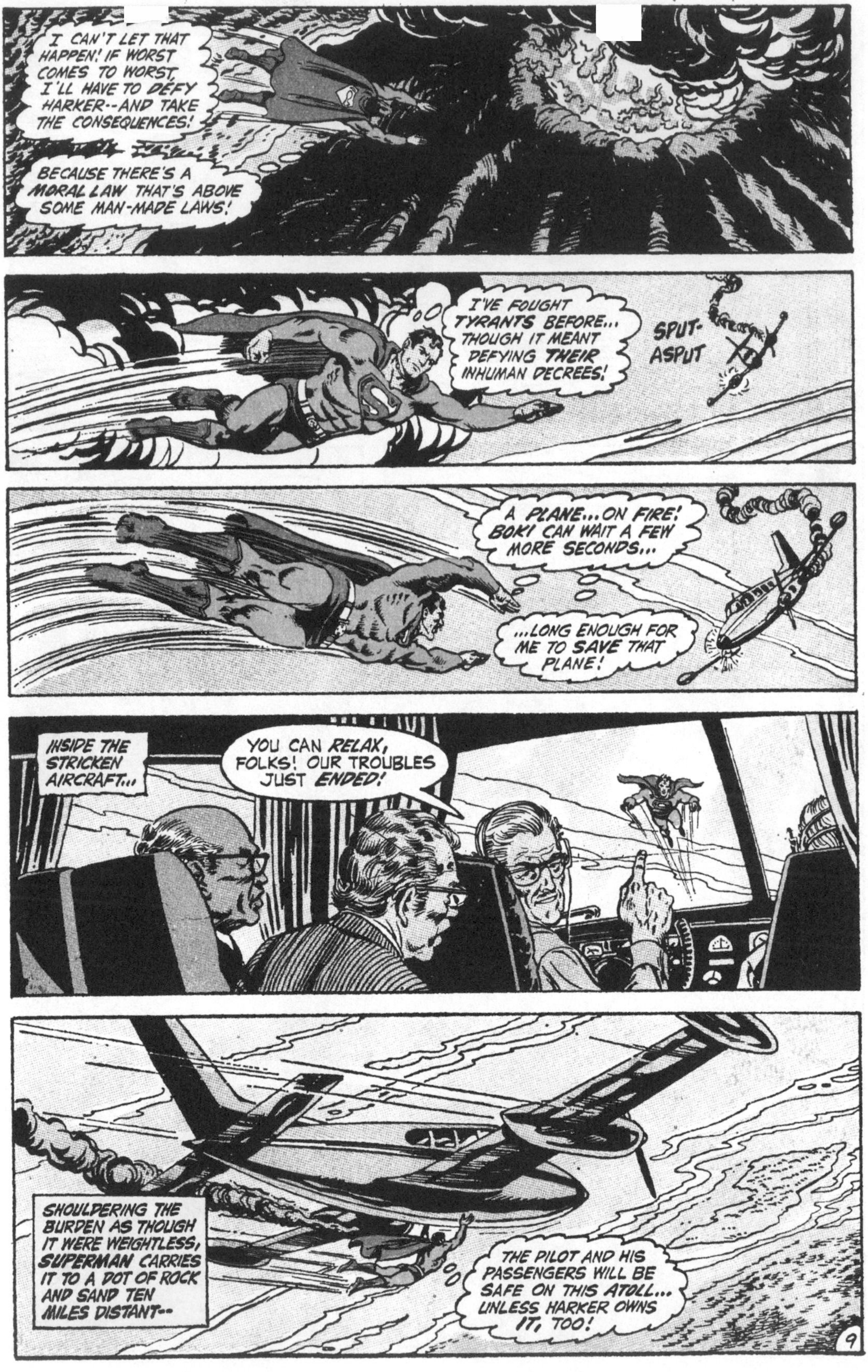

I CAN'T LET THAT HAPPEN! IF WORST COMES TO WORST, I'LL HAVE TO DEFY HARKER--AND TAKE THE CONSEQUENCES!
BECAUSE THERE'S A MORAL LAW THAT'S ABOVE SOME MAN-MADE LAWS!
I'VE FOUGHT TYRANTS BEFORE... THOUGH IT MEANT DEFYING THEIR INHUMAN DECREES!
SPUT-ASPUT
A PLANE...ON FIRE! BOKI CAN WAIT A FEW MORE SECONDS...
...LONG ENOUGH FOR ME TO SAVE THAT PLANE!
INSIDE THE STRICKEN AIRCRAFT...
YOU CAN RELAX, FOLKS! OUR TROUBLES JUST ENDED!
SHOULDERING THE BURDEN AS THOUGH IT WERE WEIGHTLESS, SUPERMAN CARRIES IT TO A DOT OF ROCK AND SAND TEN MILES DISTANT--
THE PILOT AND HIS PASSENGERS WILL BE SAFE ON THIS ATOLL... UNLESS HARKER OWNS IT, TOO!
9

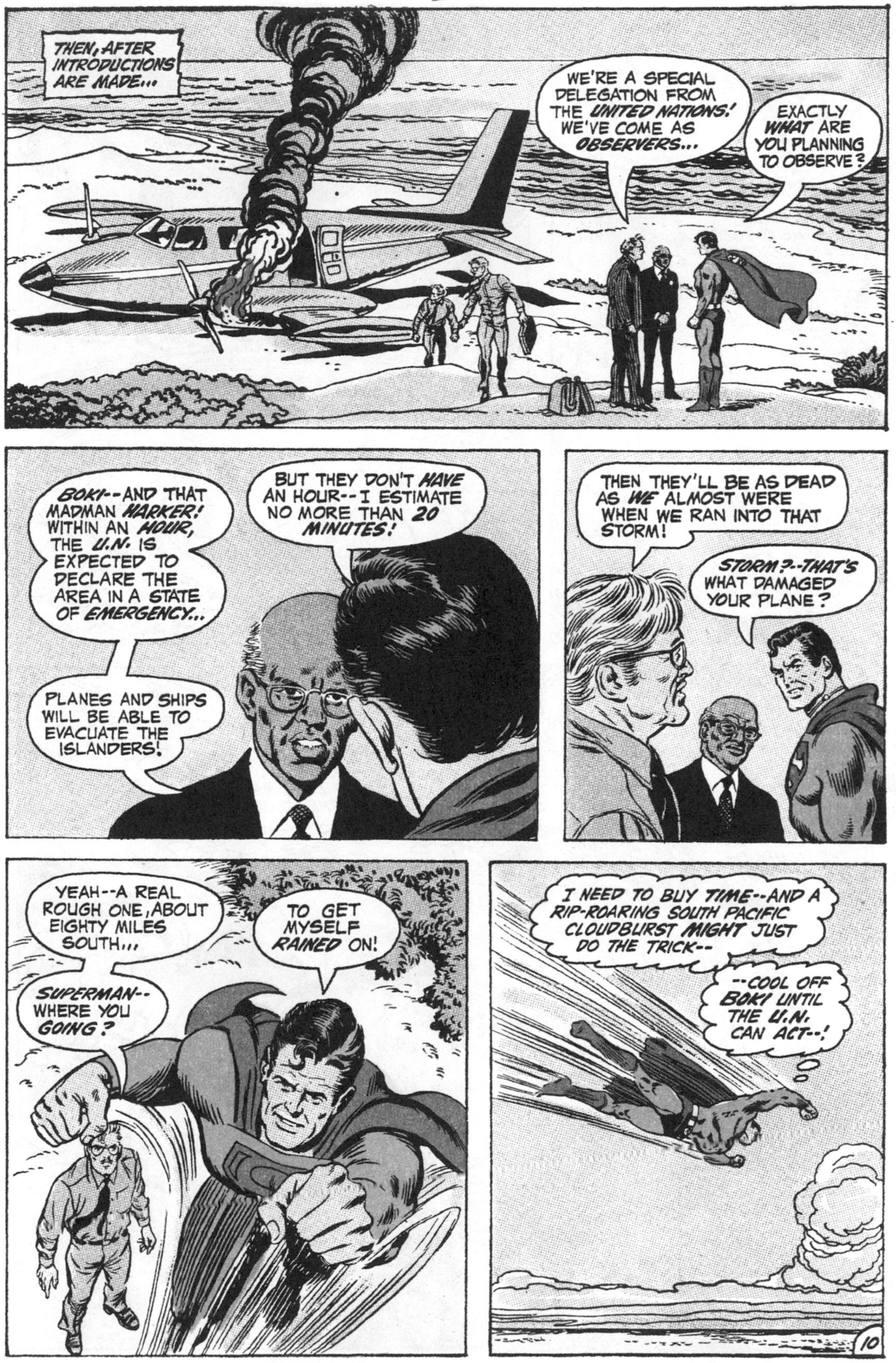
THEN, AFTER INTRODUCTIONS ARE MADE...
WE'RE A SPECIAL DELEGATION FROM THE UNITED NATIONS! WE'VE COME AS OBSERVERS...
EXACTLY WHAT ARE YOU PLANNING TO OBSERVE?
BOKI--AND THAT MADMAN HARKER! WITHIN AN HOUR, THE U.N. IS EXPECTED TO DECLARE THE AREA IN A STATE OF EMERGENCY...
PLANES AND SHIPS WILL BE ABLE TO EVACUATE THE ISLANDERS!
BUT THEY DON'T HAVE AN HOUR--I ESTIMATE NO MORE THAN 20 MINUTES!
THEN THEY'LL BE AS DEAD AS WE ALMOST WERE WHEN WE RAN INTO THAT STORM!
STORM?--THAT'S WHAT DAMAGED YOUR PLANE?
YEAH--A REAL ROUGH ONE, ABOUT EIGHTY MILES SOUTH...
SUPERMAN--WHERE YOU GOING?
TO GET MYSELF RAINED ON!
I NEED TO BUY TIME--AND A RIP-ROARING SOUTH PACIFIC CLOUDBURST MIGHT JUST DO THE TRICK--
--COOL OFF BOKI UNTIL THE U.N. CAN ACT--!
10

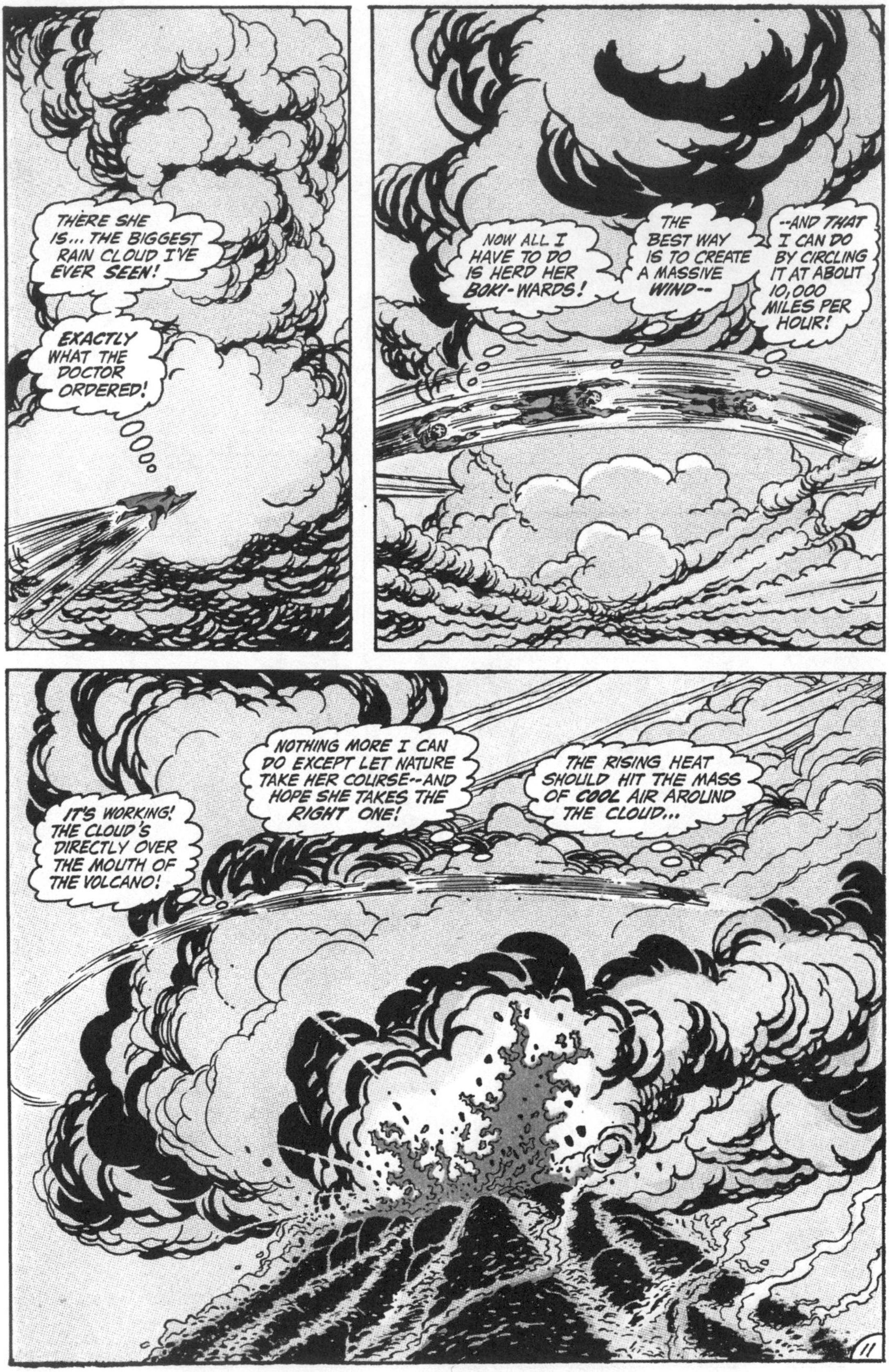
THERE SHE IS... THE BIGGEST RAIN CLOUD I'VE EVER SEEN!
EXACTLY WHAT THE DOCTOR ORDERED!
NOW ALL I HAVE TO DO IS HERD HER BOKI-WARDS!
THE BEST WAY IS TO CREATE A MASSIVE WIND--
--AND THAT I CAN DO BY CIRCLING IT AT ABOUT 10,000 MILES PER HOUR!
IT'S WORKING! THE CLOUD'S DIRECTLY OVER THE MOUTH OF THE VOLCANO!
NOTHING MORE I CAN DO EXCEPT LET NATURE TAKE HER COURSE--AND HOPE SHE TAKES THE RIGHT ONE!
THE RISING HEAT SHOULD HIT THE MASS OF COOL AIR AROUND THE CLOUD...
11

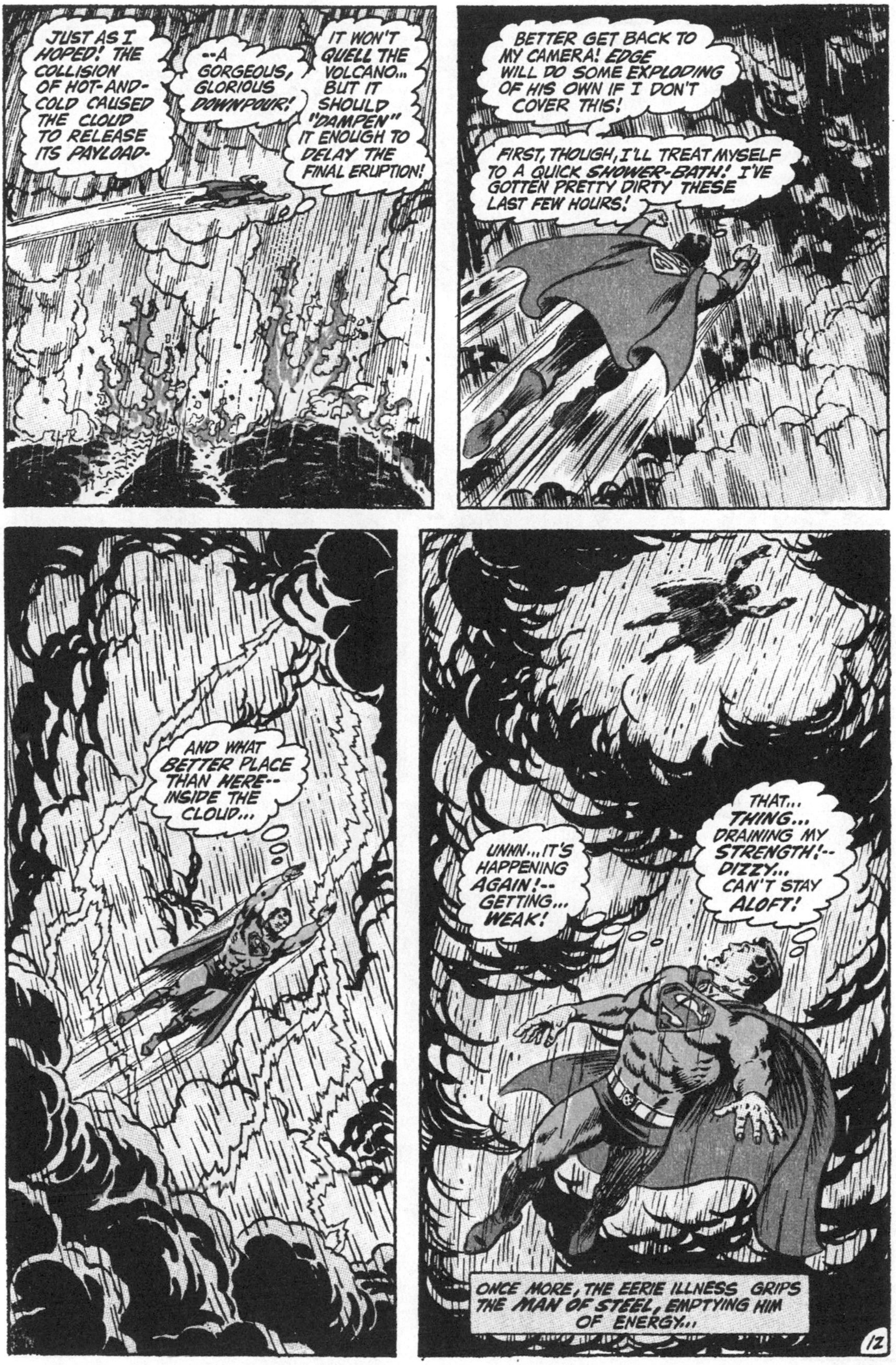
JUST AS I HOPED! THE COLLISION OF HOT-AND-COLD CAUSED THE CLOUD TO RELEASE ITS PAYLOAD-
--A GORGEOUS, GLORIOUS DOWNPOUR!
IT WON'T QUELL THE VOLCANO... BUT IT SHOULD "DAMPEN" IT ENOUGH TO DELAY THE FINAL ERUPTION!
BETTER GET BACK TO MY CAMERA! EDGE WILL DO SOME EXPLODING OF HIS OWN IF I DON'T COVER THIS!
FIRST, THOUGH, I'LL TREAT MYSELF TO A QUICK SHOWER-BATH! I'VE GOTTEN PRETTY DIRTY THESE LAST FEW HOURS!
AND WHAT BETTER PLACE THAN HERE-- INSIDE THE CLOUD...
UNNN... IT'S HAPPENING AGAIN!-- GETTING... WEAK!
THAT... THING... DRAINING MY STRENGTH!-- DIZZY... CAN'T STAY ALOFT!
ONCE MORE, THE EERIE ILLNESS GRIPS THE MAN OF STEEL, EMPTYING HIM OF ENERGY...
12

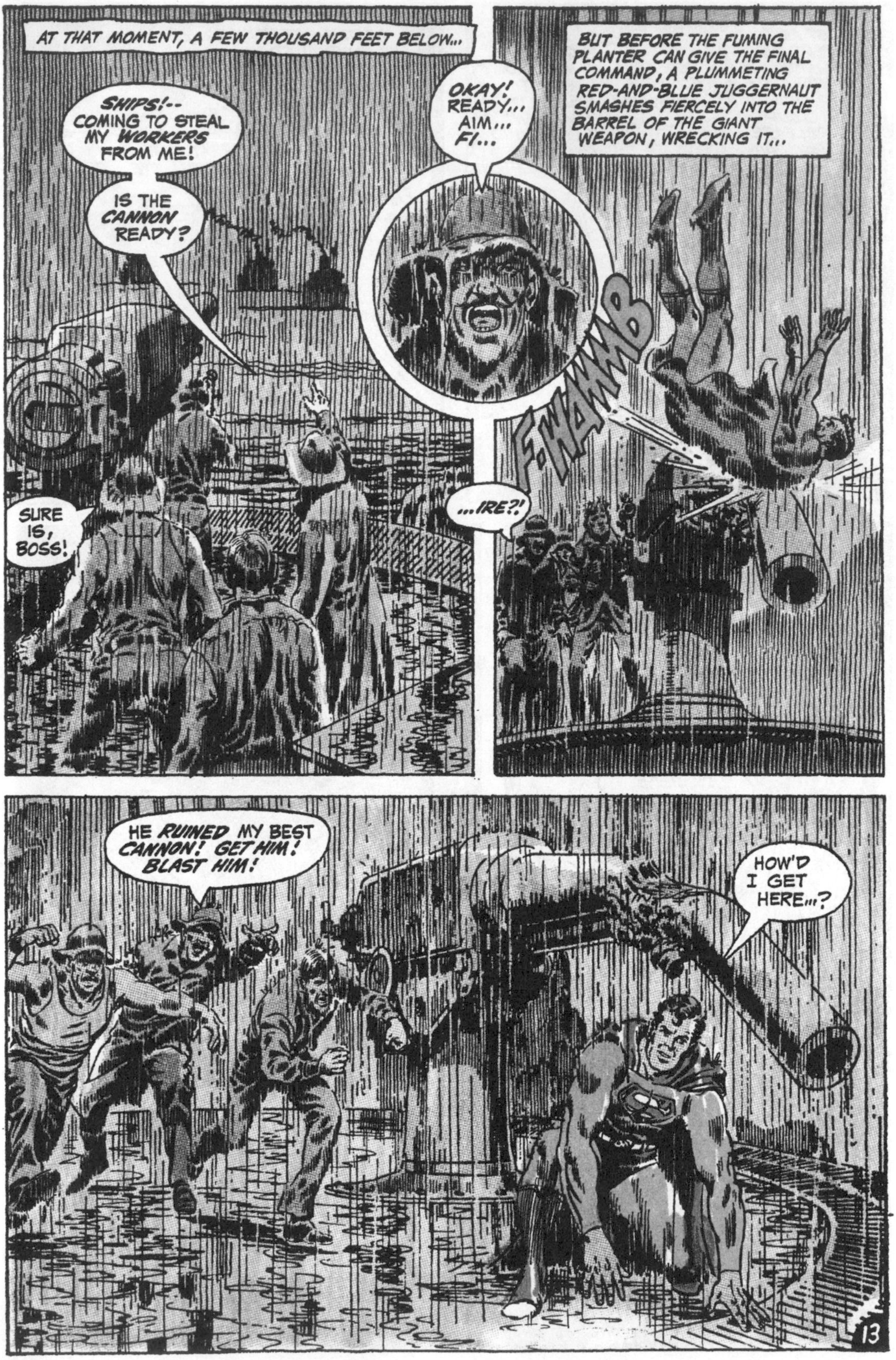
AT THAT MOMENT, A FEW THOUSAND FEET BELOW...
SHIPS!-- COMING TO STEAL MY WORKERS FROM ME!
IS THE CANNON READY?
SURE IS, BOSS!
OKAY! READY... AIM... FI...
BUT BEFORE THE FUMING PLANTER CAN GIVE THE FINAL COMMAND, A PLUMMETING RED-AND-BLUE JUGGERNAUT SMASHES FIERCELY INTO THE BARREL OF THE GIANT WEAPON, WRECKING IT...
F-WHAMB
...IRE?!
HE RUINED MY BEST CANNON! GET HIM! BLAST HIM!
HOW'D I GET HERE...?
13

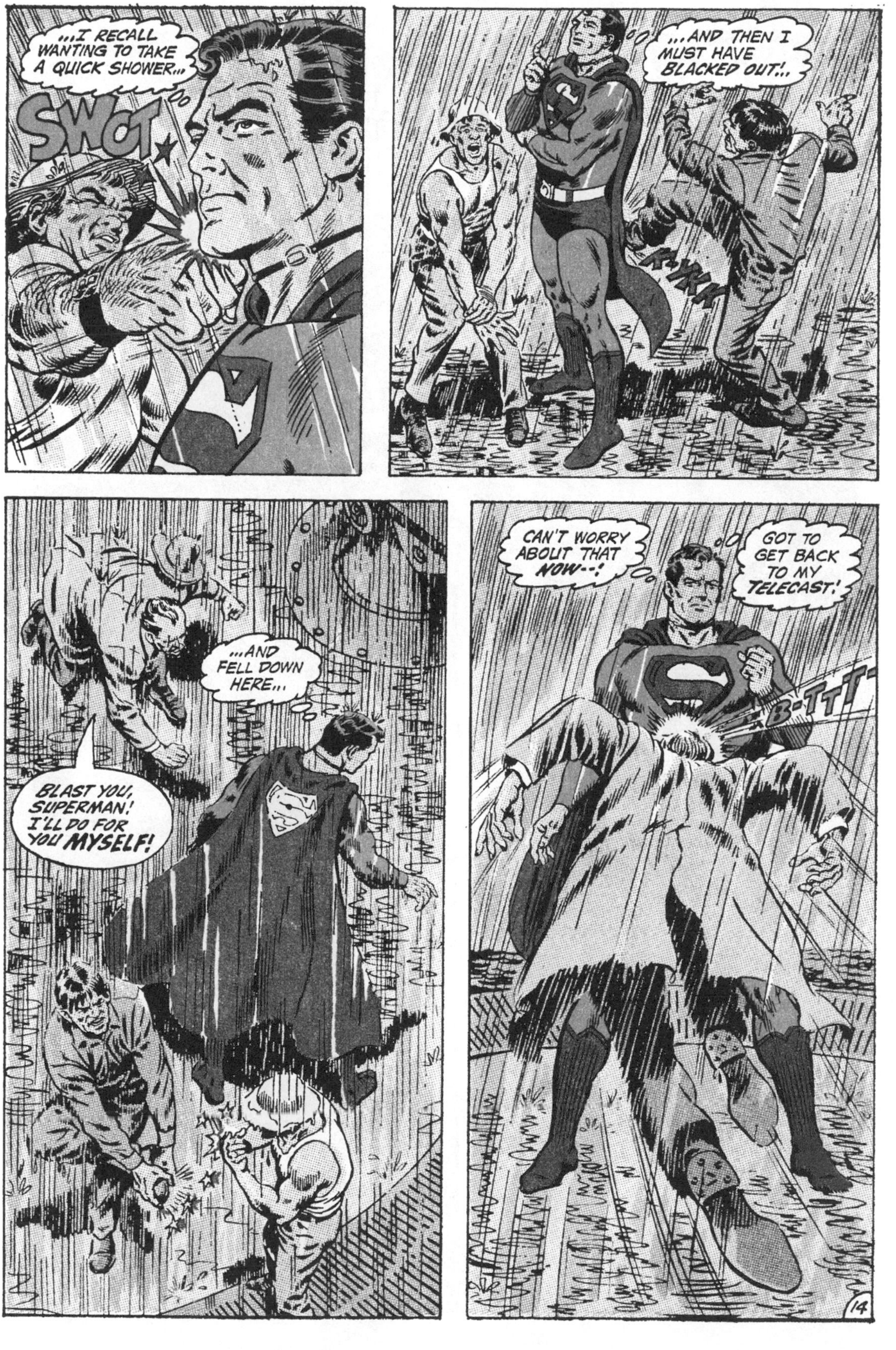
...I RECALL WANTING TO TAKE A QUICK SHOWER...
SWOT
...AND THEN I MUST HAVE BLACKED OUT!..
...AND FELL DOWN HERE...
BLAST YOU, SUPERMAN! I'LL DO FOR YOU MYSELF!
CAN'T WORRY ABOUT THAT NOW--!
GOT TO GET BACK TO MY TELECAST!
B-TTT-
14

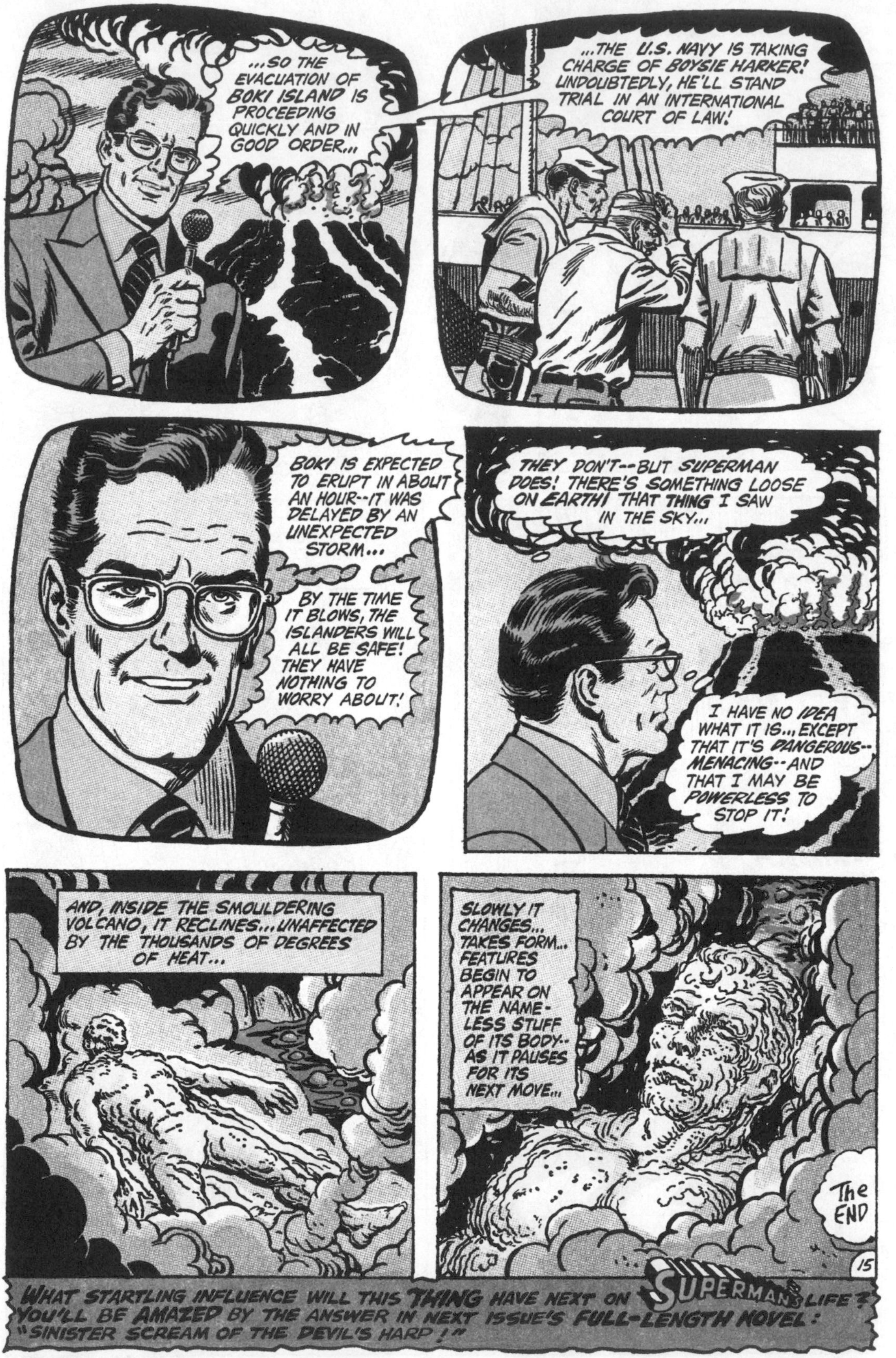
...SO THE EVACUATION OF BOKI ISLAND IS PROCEEDING QUICKLY AND IN GOOD ORDER...
...THE U.S. NAVY IS TAKING CHARGE OF BOYSIE HARKER! UNDOUBTEDLY, HE'LL STAND TRIAL IN AN INTERNATIONAL COURT OF LAW!
BOKI IS EXPECTED TO ERUPT IN ABOUT AN HOUR--IT WAS DELAYED BY AN UNEXPECTED STORM...
BY THE TIME IT BLOWS, THE ISLANDERS WILL ALL BE SAFE! THEY HAVE NOTHING TO WORRY ABOUT!
THEY DON'T--BUT SUPERMAN DOES! THERE'S SOMETHING LOOSE ON EARTH! THAT THING I SAW IN THE SKY...
I HAVE NO IDEA WHAT IT IS... EXCEPT THAT IT'S DANGEROUS--MENACING--AND THAT I MAY BE POWERLESS TO STOP IT!
AND, INSIDE THE SMOULDERING VOLCANO, IT RECLINES... UNAFFECTED BY THE THOUSANDS OF DEGREES OF HEAT...
SLOWLY IT CHANGES... TAKES FORM... FEATURES BEGIN TO APPEAR ON THE NAMELESS STUFF OF ITS BODY.. AS IT PAUSES FOR ITS NEXT MOVE...
The END
15
WHAT STARTLING INFLUENCE WILL THIS THING HAVE NEXT ON SUPERMAN'S LIFE? YOU'LL BE AMAZED BY THE ANSWER IN NEXT ISSUE'S FULL-LENGTH NOVEL: "SINISTER SCREAM OF THE DEVIL'S HARP!"

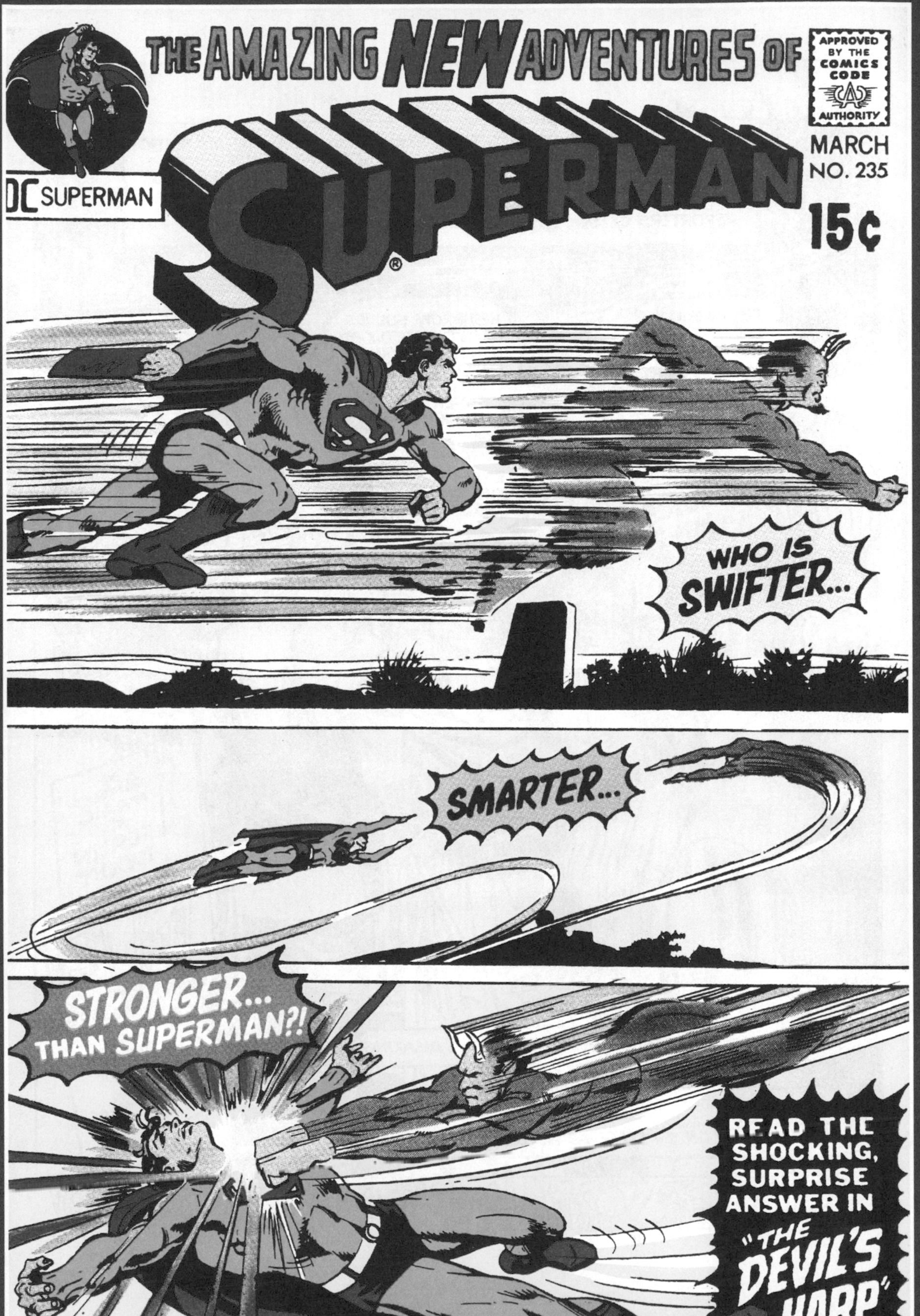
THE AMAZING NEW ADVENTURES OF
SUPERMAN
DC SUPERMAN
APPROVED BY THE COMICS CODE AUTHORITY
MARCH
NO. 235
15¢
WHO IS SWIFTER...
SMARTER...
STRONGER... THAN SUPERMAN?!
READ THE SHOCKING, SURPRISE ANSWER IN "THE DEVIL'S HARP"

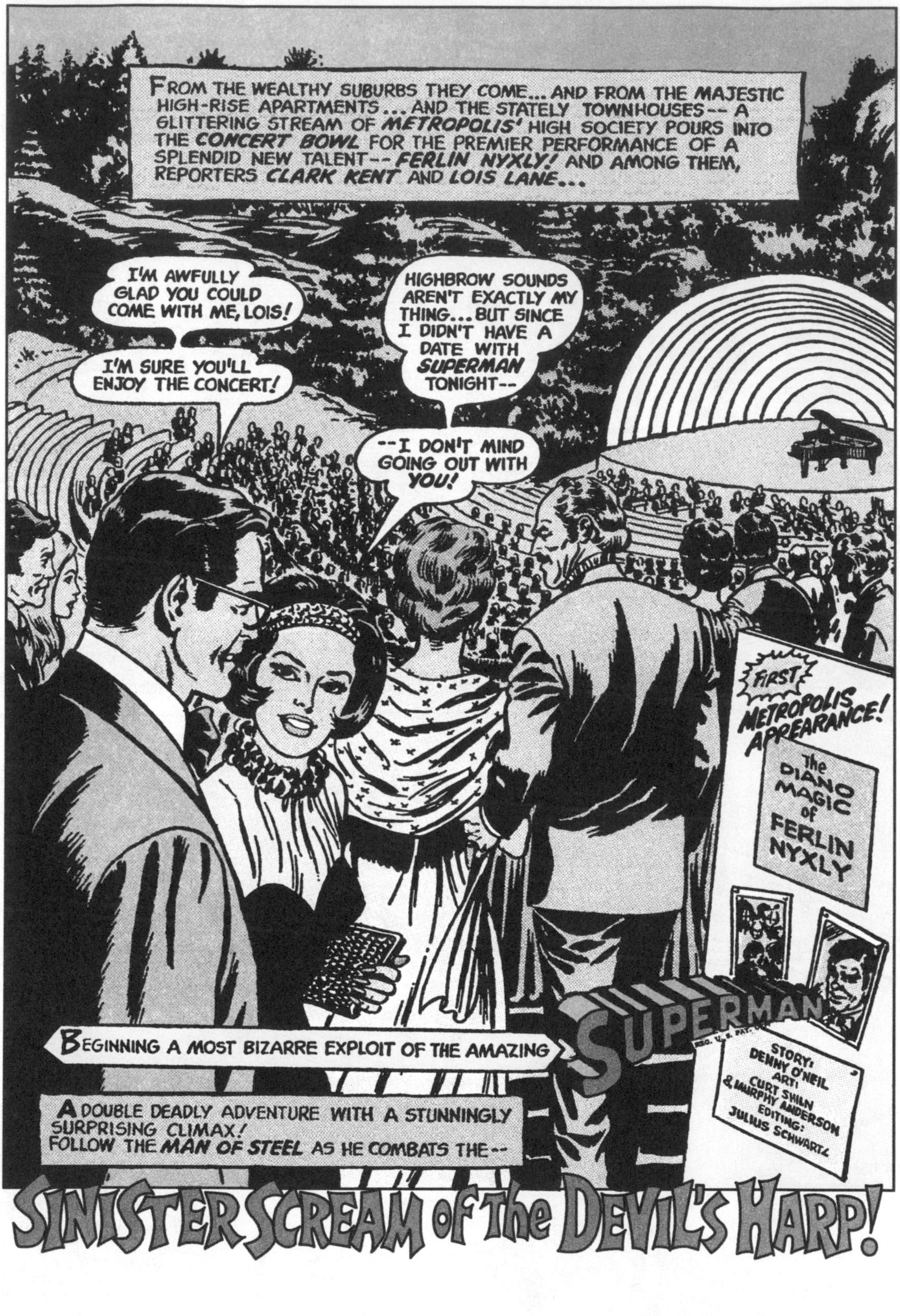
FROM THE WEALTHY SUBURBS THEY COME... AND FROM THE MAJESTIC HIGH-RISE APARTMENTS... AND THE STATELY TOWNHOUSES-- A GLITTERING STREAM OF METROPOLIS' HIGH SOCIETY POURS INTO THE CONCERT BOWL FOR THE PREMIER PERFORMANCE OF A SPLENDID NEW TALENT-- FERLIN NYXLY! AND AMONG THEM, REPORTERS CLARK KENT AND LOIS LANE...
I'M AWFULLY GLAD YOU COULD COME WITH ME, LOIS!
I'M SURE YOU'LL ENJOY THE CONCERT!
HIGHBROW SOUNDS AREN'T EXACTLY MY THING... BUT SINCE I DIDN'T HAVE A DATE WITH SUPERMAN TONIGHT--
--I DON'T MIND GOING OUT WITH YOU!
FIRST METROPOLIS APPEARANCE!
The PIANO MAGIC of FERLIN NYXLY
BEGINNING A MOST BIZARRE EXPLOIT OF THE AMAZING
SUPERMAN
STORY: DENNY O'NEIL
ART: CURT SWAN & MURPHY ANDERSON
EDITING: JULIUS SCHWARTZ
A DOUBLE DEADLY ADVENTURE WITH A STUNNINGLY SURPRISING CLIMAX! FOLLOW THE MAN OF STEEL AS HE COMBATS THE--
SINISTER SCREAM of the DEVIL'S HARP!

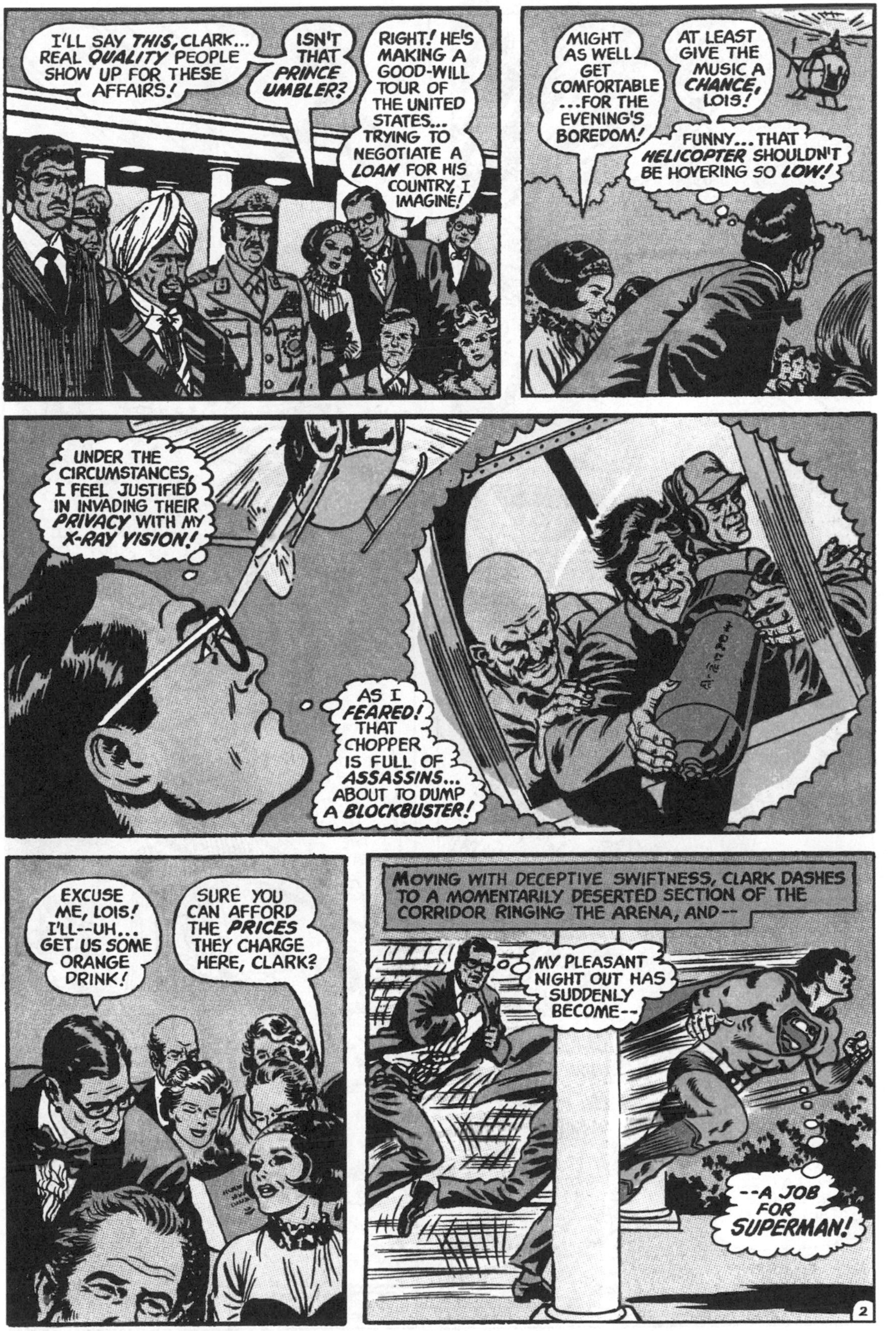
I'LL SAY THIS, CLARK... REAL QUALITY PEOPLE SHOW UP FOR THESE AFFAIRS!
ISN'T THAT PRINCE UMBLER?
RIGHT! HE'S MAKING A GOOD-WILL TOUR OF THE UNITED STATES... TRYING TO NEGOTIATE A LOAN FOR HIS COUNTRY, I IMAGINE!
MIGHT AS WELL GET COMFORTABLE ...FOR THE EVENING'S BOREDOM!
AT LEAST GIVE THE MUSIC A CHANCE, LOIS!
FUNNY... THAT HELICOPTER SHOULDN'T BE HOVERING SO LOW!
UNDER THE CIRCUMSTANCES, I FEEL JUSTIFIED IN INVADING THEIR PRIVACY WITH MY X-RAY VISION!
AS I FEARED! THAT CHOPPER IS FULL OF ASSASSINS... ABOUT TO DUMP A BLOCKBUSTER!
EXCUSE ME, LOIS! I'LL--UH... GET US SOME ORANGE DRINK!
SURE YOU CAN AFFORD THE PRICES THEY CHARGE HERE, CLARK?
MOVING WITH DECEPTIVE SWIFTNESS, CLARK DASHES TO A MOMENTARILY DESERTED SECTION OF THE CORRIDOR RINGING THE ARENA, AND--
MY PLEASANT NIGHT OUT HAS SUDDENLY BECOME--
--A JOB FOR SUPERMAN!
2

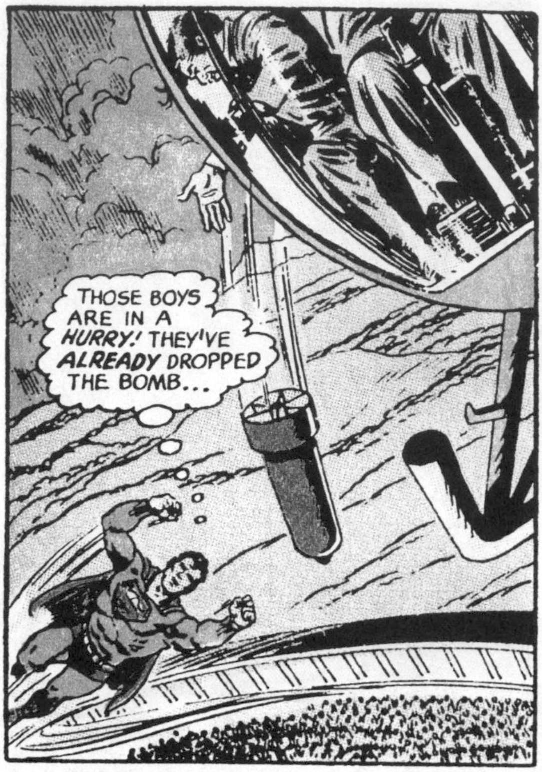
THOSE BOYS ARE IN A HURRY! THEY'VE ALREADY DROPPED THE BOMB...

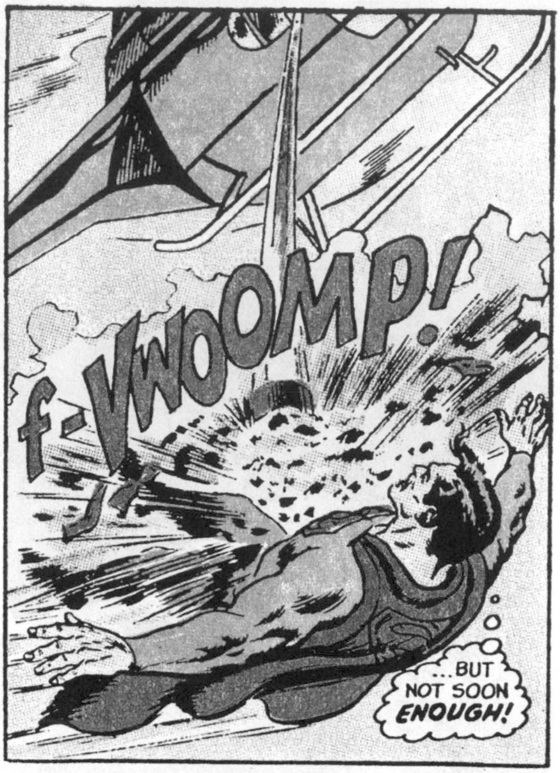
f-VWOOMP!
...BUT NOT SOON ENOUGH!

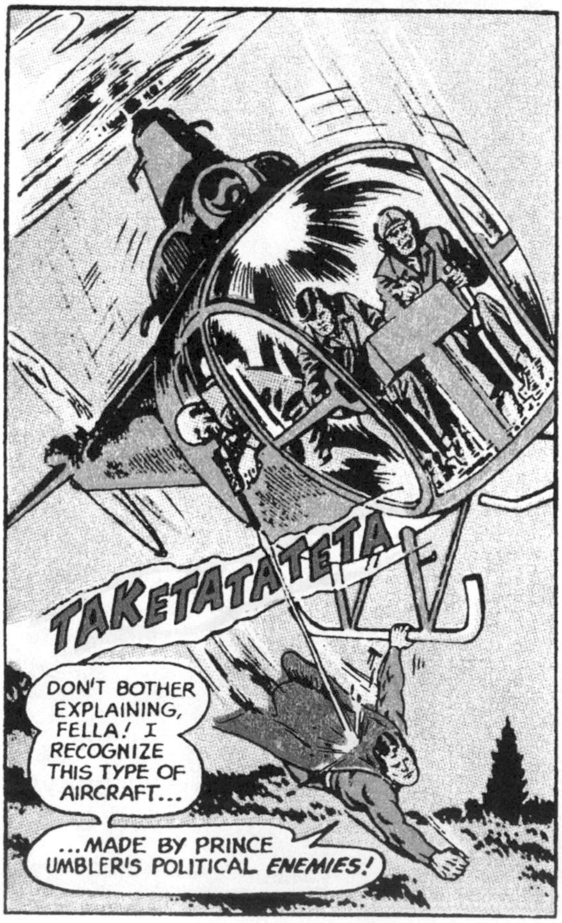
TAKETATATETA
DON'T BOTHER EXPLAINING, FELLA! I RECOGNIZE THIS TYPE OF AIRCRAFT...
...MADE BY PRINCE UMBLER'S POLITICAL ENEMIES!

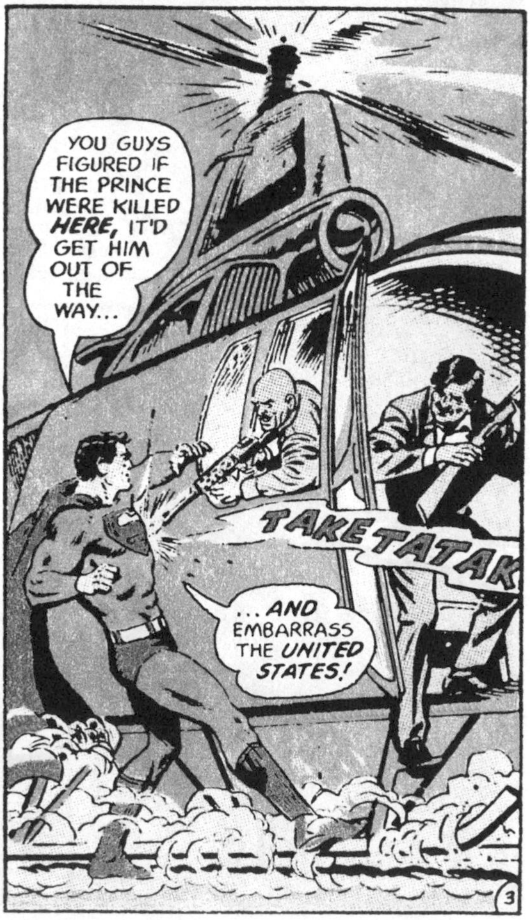
YOU GUYS FIGURED IF THE PRINCE WERE KILLED HERE, IT'D GET HIM OUT OF THE WAY...
TAKETATAK
...AND EMBARRASS THE UNITED STATES!
3

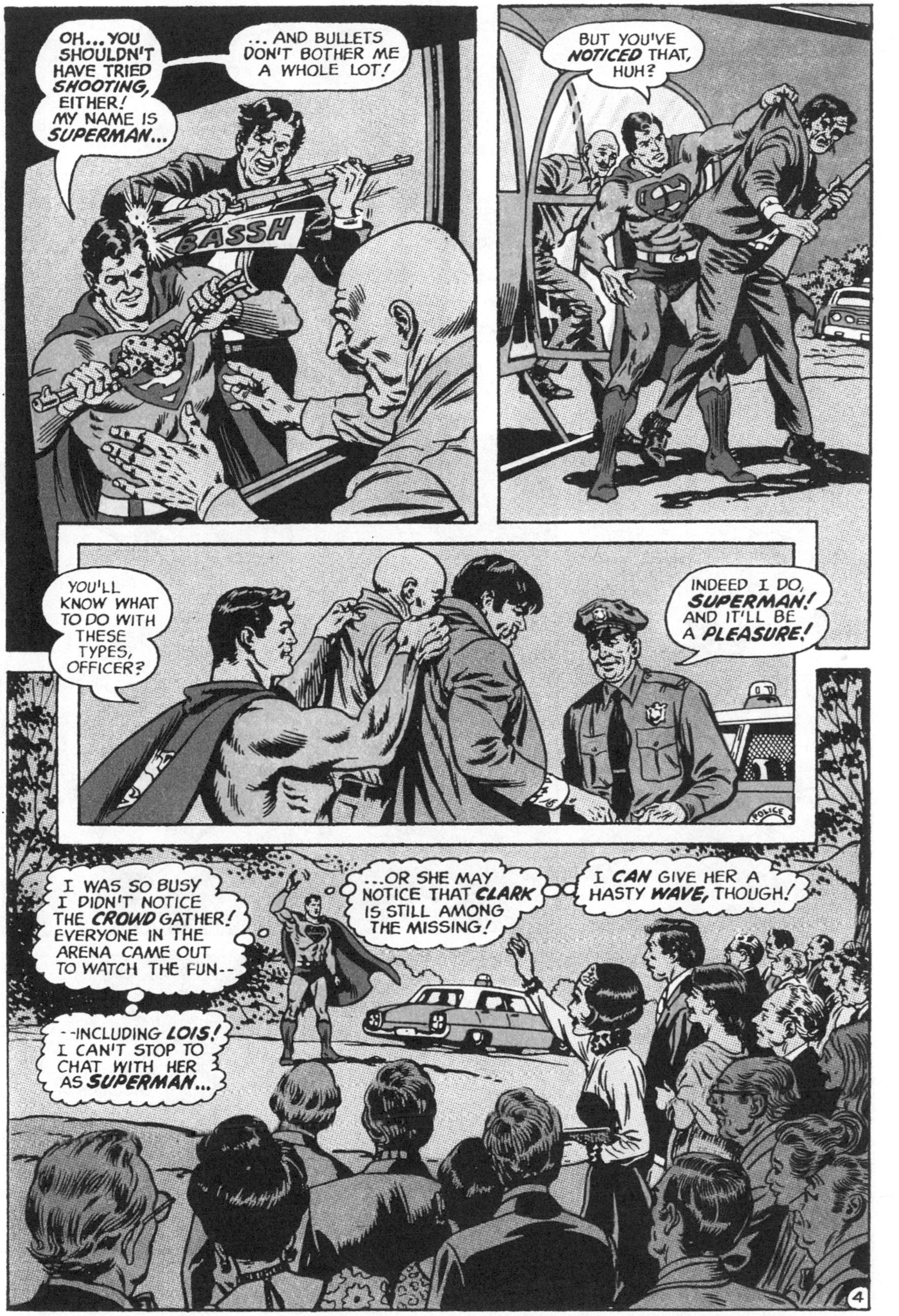
OH... YOU SHOULDN'T HAVE TRIED SHOOTING, EITHER! MY NAME IS SUPERMAN...
... AND BULLETS DON'T BOTHER ME A WHOLE LOT!
BASSH
BUT YOU'VE NOTICED THAT, HUH?
YOU'LL KNOW WHAT TO DO WITH THESE TYPES, OFFICER?
INDEED I DO, SUPERMAN! AND IT'LL BE A PLEASURE!
POLICE
I WAS SO BUSY I DIDN'T NOTICE THE CROWD GATHER! EVERYONE IN THE ARENA CAME OUT TO WATCH THE FUN--
--INCLUDING LOIS! I CAN'T STOP TO CHAT WITH HER AS SUPERMAN...
...OR SHE MAY NOTICE THAT CLARK IS STILL AMONG THE MISSING!
I CAN GIVE HER A HASTY WAVE, THOUGH!
4

MOMENTS LATER...

SORRY I'M LATE, LOIS... I WAS CAUGHT IN THE MOB!

DON'T BOTHER APOLOGIZING! I CAN'T HEAR YOU ANYWAY...

...AFTER WATCHING *HIM* IN ACTION, ANYONE ELSE HAS THE PERSONALITY OF A SUIT OF CLOTHES HANGING IN AN EMPTY CLOSET!

THEN, *FERLIN NYXLY* TAKES HIS SEAT AT THE GRAND PIANO AND LAUNCHES HIS CONCERT...

THEY AREN'T PAYING *ATTENTION!* THEY'RE *CHATTERING* WHILE I PLAY! THEY'RE STILL TALKING ABOUT *SUPERMAN!*

FOR *YEARS* I'VE DREAMED OF THIS PERFORMANCE... ONLY TO HAVE IT *RUINED!*

I'M A *LOSER!*

I'VE *ALWAYS* BEEN A LOSER...A WEAK, FORCELESS SCHOLAR!

THAT NIGHT, SIX MONTHS AGO, I THOUGHT MY LUCK HAD *CHANGED...*

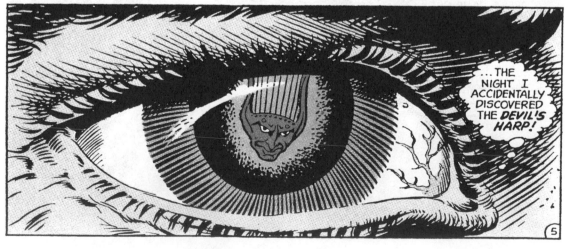

...THE NIGHT I ACCIDENTALLY DISCOVERED THE *DEVIL'S HARP!*

5

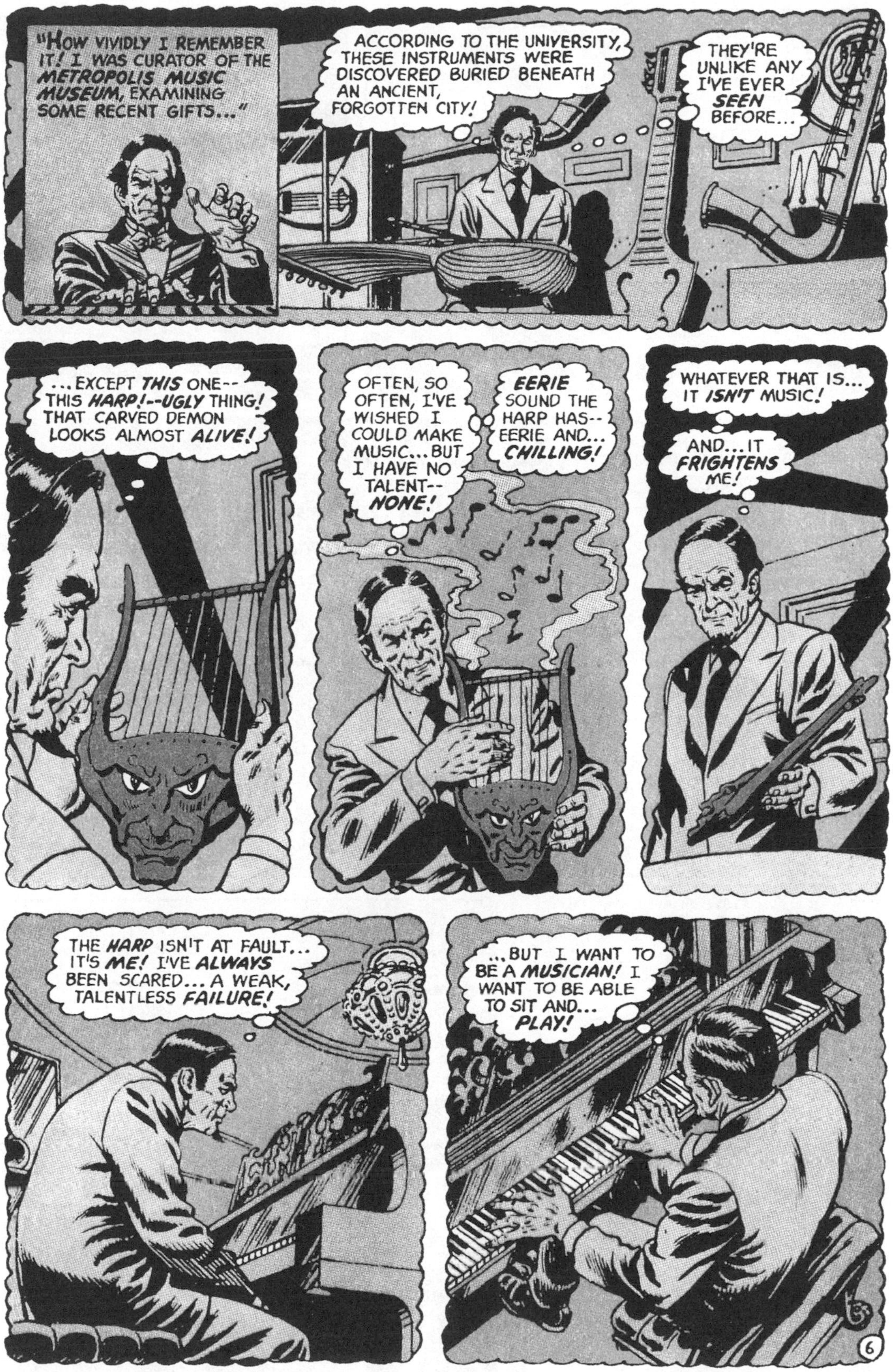
"HOW VIVIDLY I REMEMBER IT! I WAS CURATOR OF THE METROPOLIS MUSIC MUSEUM, EXAMINING SOME RECENT GIFTS..."
ACCORDING TO THE UNIVERSITY, THESE INSTRUMENTS WERE DISCOVERED BURIED BENEATH AN ANCIENT, FORGOTTEN CITY!
THEY'RE UNLIKE ANY I'VE EVER SEEN BEFORE...
...EXCEPT THIS ONE-- THIS HARP!--UGLY THING! THAT CARVED DEMON LOOKS ALMOST ALIVE!
OFTEN, SO OFTEN, I'VE WISHED I COULD MAKE MUSIC...BUT I HAVE NO TALENT-- NONE!
EERIE SOUND THE HARP HAS-- EERIE AND... CHILLING!
WHATEVER THAT IS... IT ISN'T MUSIC!
AND...IT FRIGHTENS ME!
THE HARP ISN'T AT FAULT... IT'S ME! I'VE ALWAYS BEEN SCARED... A WEAK, TALENTLESS FAILURE!
...BUT I WANT TO BE A MUSICIAN! I WANT TO BE ABLE TO SIT AND... PLAY!
6

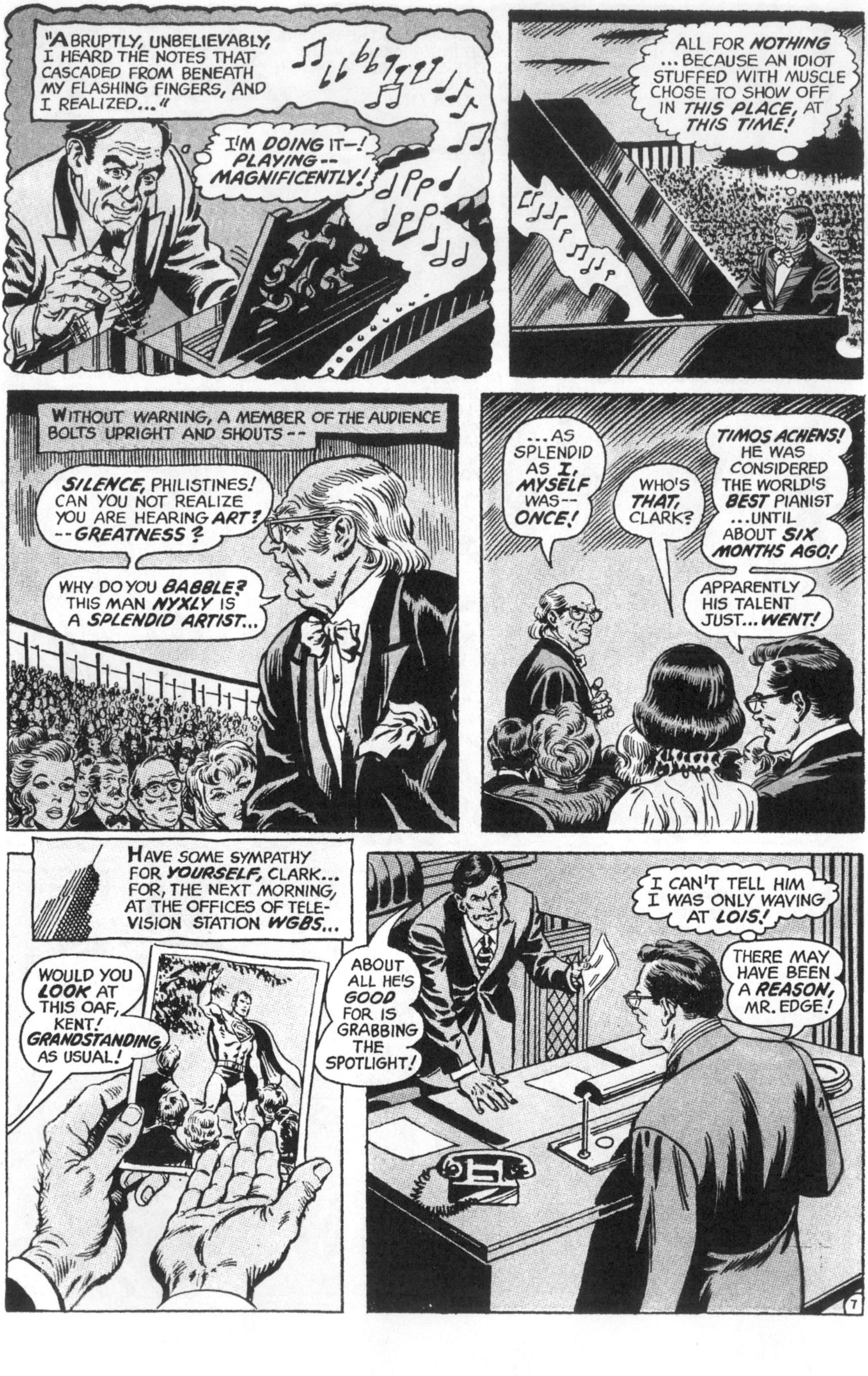
"ABRUPTLY, UNBELIEVABLY, I HEARD THE NOTES THAT CASCADED FROM BENEATH MY FLASHING FINGERS, AND I REALIZED..."
I'M DOING IT--! PLAYING-- MAGNIFICENTLY!
ALL FOR NOTHING ...BECAUSE AN IDIOT STUFFED WITH MUSCLE CHOSE TO SHOW OFF IN THIS PLACE, AT THIS TIME!
WITHOUT WARNING, A MEMBER OF THE AUDIENCE BOLTS UPRIGHT AND SHOUTS--
SILENCE, PHILISTINES! CAN YOU NOT REALIZE YOU ARE HEARING ART? --GREATNESS?
WHY DO YOU BABBLE? THIS MAN NYXLY IS A SPLENDID ARTIST...
...AS SPLENDID AS I, MYSELF WAS-- ONCE!
WHO'S THAT, CLARK?
TIMOS ACHENS! HE WAS CONSIDERED THE WORLD'S BEST PIANIST ...UNTIL ABOUT SIX MONTHS AGO!
APPARENTLY HIS TALENT JUST...WENT!
HAVE SOME SYMPATHY FOR YOURSELF, CLARK... FOR, THE NEXT MORNING, AT THE OFFICES OF TELE-VISION STATION WGBS...
WOULD YOU LOOK AT THIS OAF, KENT! GRANDSTANDING AS USUAL!
ABOUT ALL HE'S GOOD FOR IS GRABBING THE SPOTLIGHT!
I CAN'T TELL HIM I WAS ONLY WAVING AT LOIS!
THERE MAY HAVE BEEN A REASON, MR. EDGE!
7

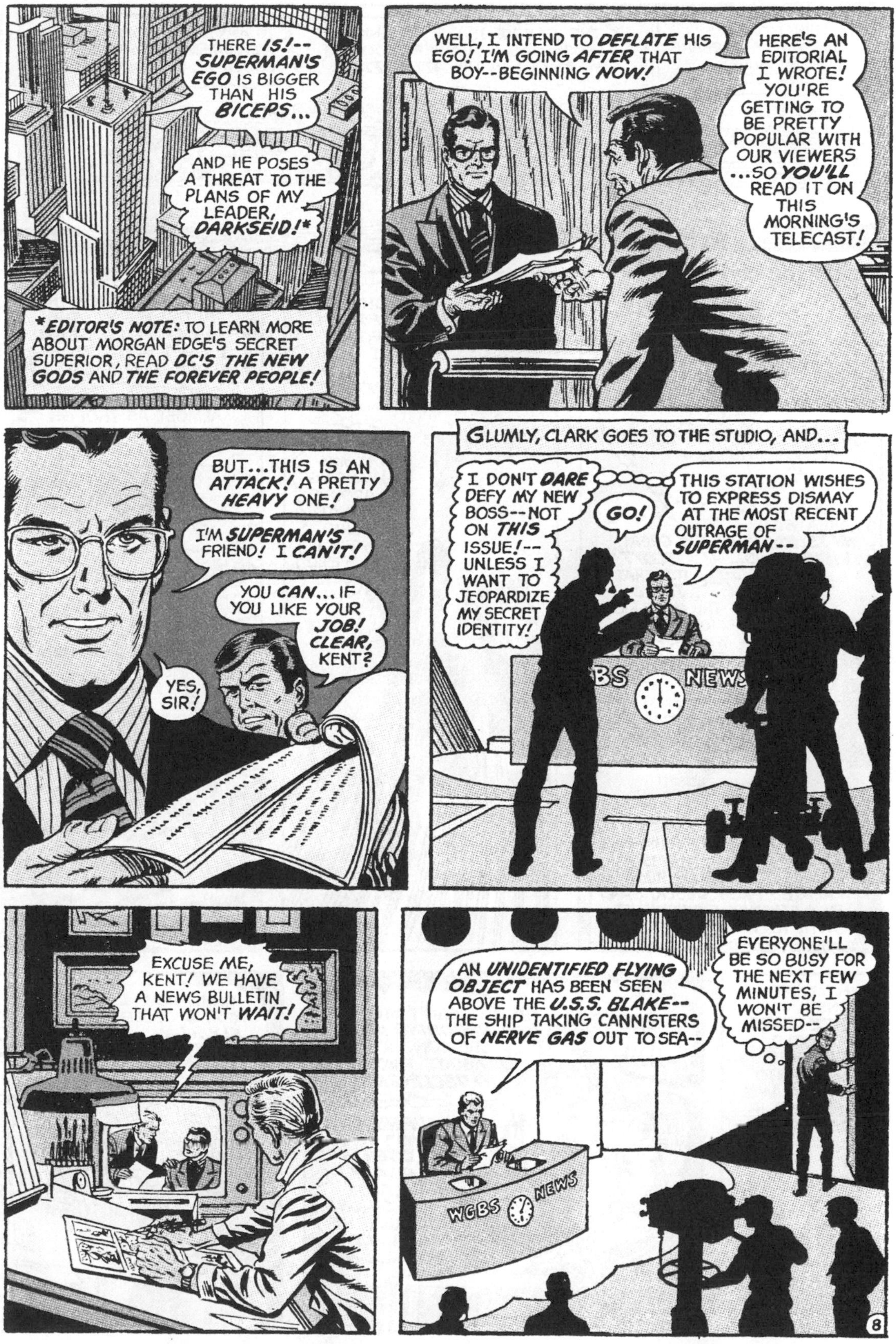
THERE IS!-- SUPERMAN'S EGO IS BIGGER THAN HIS BICEPS...
AND HE POSES A THREAT TO THE PLANS OF MY LEADER, DARKSEID!*
*EDITOR'S NOTE: TO LEARN MORE ABOUT MORGAN EDGE'S SECRET SUPERIOR, READ DC'S THE NEW GODS AND THE FOREVER PEOPLE!
WELL, I INTEND TO DEFLATE HIS EGO! I'M GOING AFTER THAT BOY--BEGINNING NOW!
HERE'S AN EDITORIAL I WROTE! YOU'RE GETTING TO BE PRETTY POPULAR WITH OUR VIEWERS ...SO YOU'LL READ IT ON THIS MORNING'S TELECAST!
BUT...THIS IS AN ATTACK! A PRETTY HEAVY ONE!
I'M SUPERMAN'S FRIEND! I CAN'T!
YOU CAN... IF YOU LIKE YOUR JOB! CLEAR, KENT?
YES, SIR!
GLUMLY, CLARK GOES TO THE STUDIO, AND...
I DON'T DARE DEFY MY NEW BOSS--NOT ON THIS ISSUE!-- UNLESS I WANT TO JEOPARDIZE MY SECRET IDENTITY!
GO!
THIS STATION WISHES TO EXPRESS DISMAY AT THE MOST RECENT OUTRAGE OF SUPERMAN--
NEWS
EXCUSE ME, KENT! WE HAVE A NEWS BULLETIN THAT WON'T WAIT!
AN UNIDENTIFIED FLYING OBJECT HAS BEEN SEEN ABOVE THE U.S.S. BLAKE-- THE SHIP TAKING CANNISTERS OF NERVE GAS OUT TO SEA--
EVERYONE'LL BE SO BUSY FOR THE NEXT FEW MINUTES, I WON'T BE MISSED--
WGBS NEWS
8

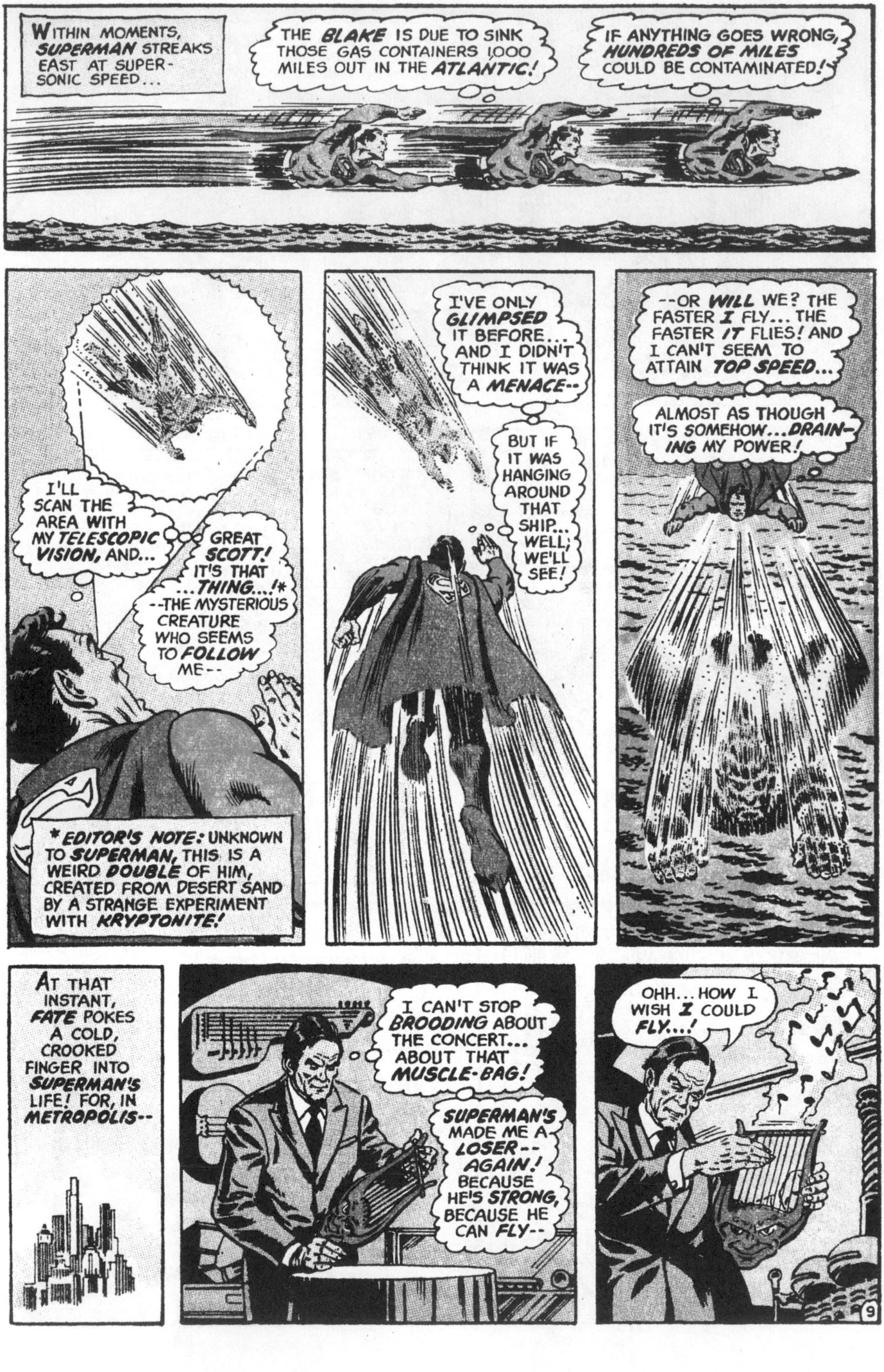

WITHIN MOMENTS, SUPERMAN STREAKS EAST AT SUPER-SONIC SPEED...
THE BLAKE IS DUE TO SINK THOSE GAS CONTAINERS 1,000 MILES OUT IN THE ATLANTIC!
IF ANYTHING GOES WRONG, HUNDREDS OF MILES COULD BE CONTAMINATED!
I'LL SCAN THE AREA WITH MY TELESCOPIC VISION, AND...
GREAT SCOTT! IT'S THAT ...THING...!* --THE MYSTERIOUS CREATURE WHO SEEMS TO FOLLOW ME--
*EDITOR'S NOTE: UNKNOWN TO SUPERMAN, THIS IS A WEIRD DOUBLE OF HIM, CREATED FROM DESERT SAND BY A STRANGE EXPERIMENT WITH KRYPTONITE!
I'VE ONLY GLIMPSED IT BEFORE... AND I DIDN'T THINK IT WAS A MENACE--
BUT IF IT WAS HANGING AROUND THAT SHIP... WELL; WE'LL SEE!
--OR WILL WE? THE FASTER I FLY... THE FASTER IT FLIES! AND I CAN'T SEEM TO ATTAIN TOP SPEED...
ALMOST AS THOUGH IT'S SOMEHOW...DRAINING MY POWER!
AT THAT INSTANT, FATE POKES A COLD, CROOKED FINGER INTO SUPERMAN'S LIFE! FOR, IN METROPOLIS--
I CAN'T STOP BROODING ABOUT THE CONCERT... ABOUT THAT MUSCLE-BAG!
SUPERMAN'S MADE ME A LOSER--AGAIN! BECAUSE HE'S STRONG, BECAUSE HE CAN FLY--
OHH...HOW I WISH I COULD FLY...!
9

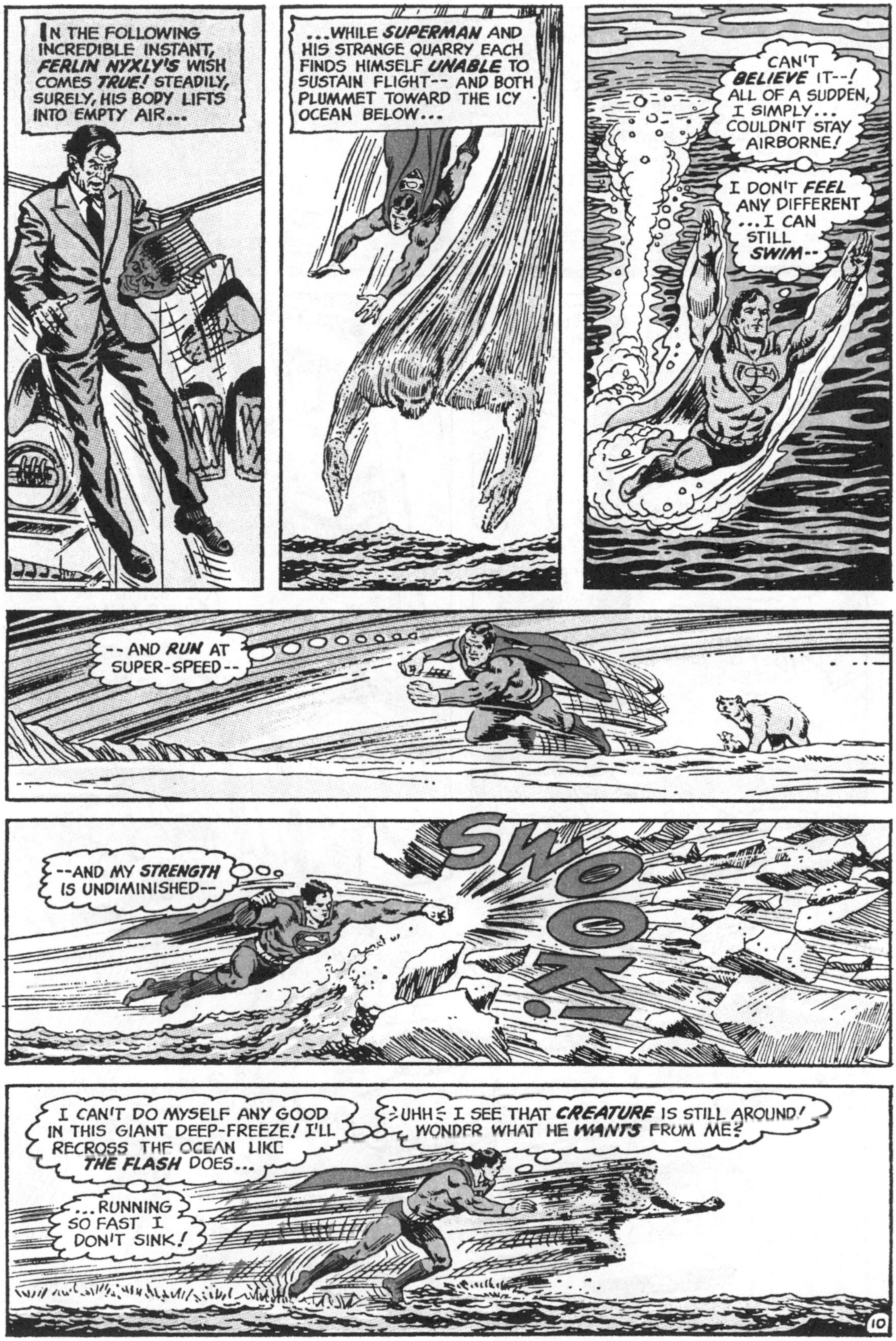
IN THE FOLLOWING INCREDIBLE INSTANT, FERLIN NYXLY'S WISH COMES TRUE! STEADILY, SURELY, HIS BODY LIFTS INTO EMPTY AIR...
...WHILE SUPERMAN AND HIS STRANGE QUARRY EACH FINDS HIMSELF UNABLE TO SUSTAIN FLIGHT-- AND BOTH PLUMMET TOWARD THE ICY OCEAN BELOW...
CAN'T BELIEVE IT--! ALL OF A SUDDEN, I SIMPLY... COULDN'T STAY AIRBORNE!
I DON'T FEEL ANY DIFFERENT ...I CAN STILL SWIM--
--AND RUN AT SUPER-SPEED--
--AND MY STRENGTH IS UNDIMINISHED--
SWOOK!
I CAN'T DO MYSELF ANY GOOD IN THIS GIANT DEEP-FREEZE! I'LL RECROSS THE OCEAN LIKE THE FLASH DOES...
...RUNNING SO FAST I DON'T SINK!
UHH-- I SEE THAT CREATURE IS STILL AROUND! WONDER WHAT HE WANTS FROM ME?
10

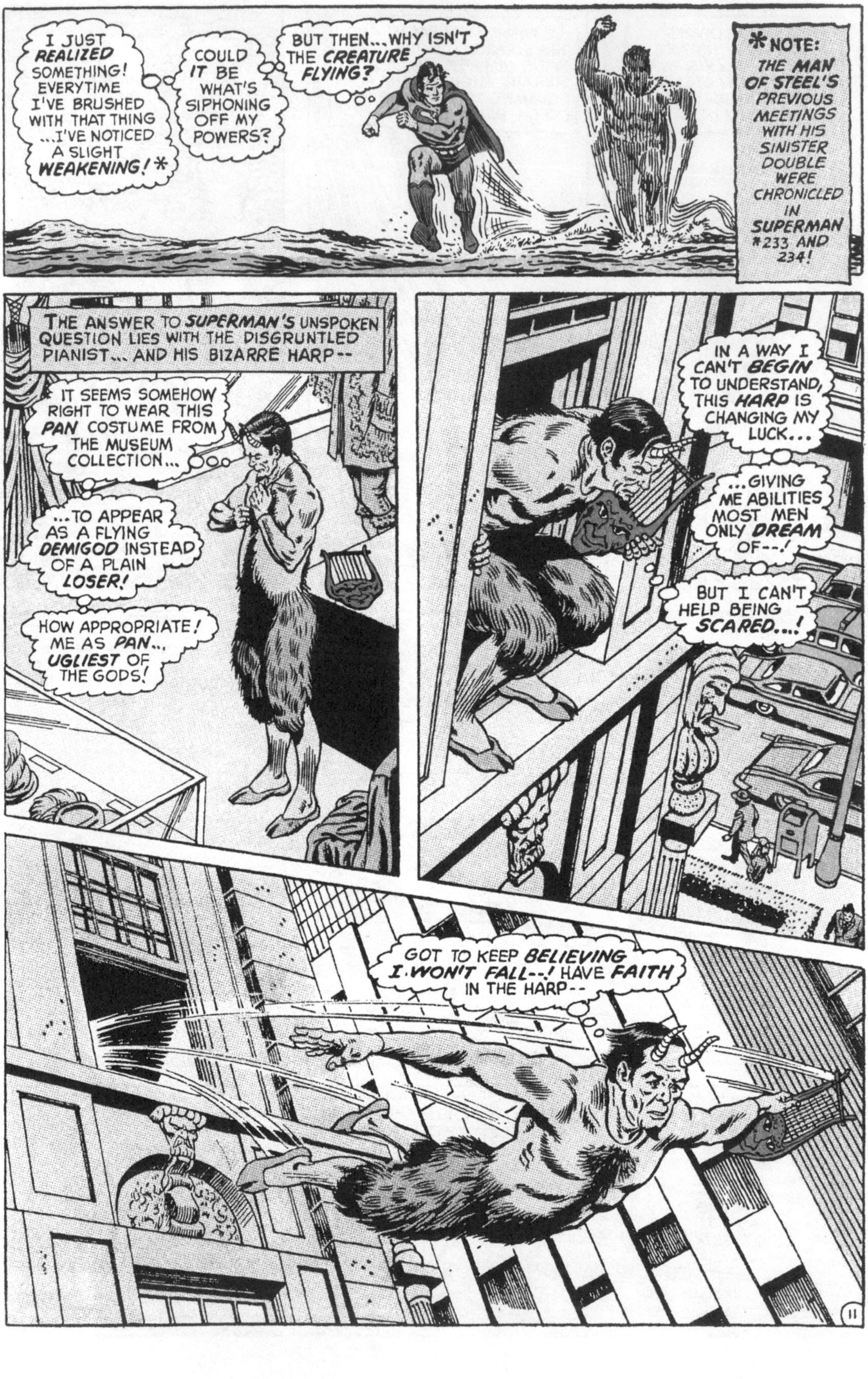
I JUST REALIZED SOMETHING! EVERYTIME I'VE BRUSHED WITH THAT THING ...I'VE NOTICED A SLIGHT WEAKENING! *
COULD IT BE WHAT'S SIPHONING OFF MY POWERS?
BUT THEN...WHY ISN'T THE CREATURE FLYING?
* NOTE: THE MAN OF STEEL'S PREVIOUS MEETINGS WITH HIS SINISTER DOUBLE WERE CHRONICLED IN SUPERMAN #233 AND 234!
THE ANSWER TO SUPERMAN'S UNSPOKEN QUESTION LIES WITH THE DISGRUNTLED PIANIST... AND HIS BIZARRE HARP--
IT SEEMS SOMEHOW RIGHT TO WEAR THIS PAN COSTUME FROM THE MUSEUM COLLECTION...
...TO APPEAR AS A FLYING DEMIGOD INSTEAD OF A PLAIN LOSER!
HOW APPROPRIATE! ME AS PAN... UGLIEST OF THE GODS!
IN A WAY I CAN'T BEGIN TO UNDERSTAND, THIS HARP IS CHANGING MY LUCK...
...GIVING ME ABILITIES MOST MEN ONLY DREAM OF--!
BUT I CAN'T HELP BEING SCARED...!
GOT TO KEEP BELIEVING I WON'T FALL--! HAVE FAITH IN THE HARP--
11

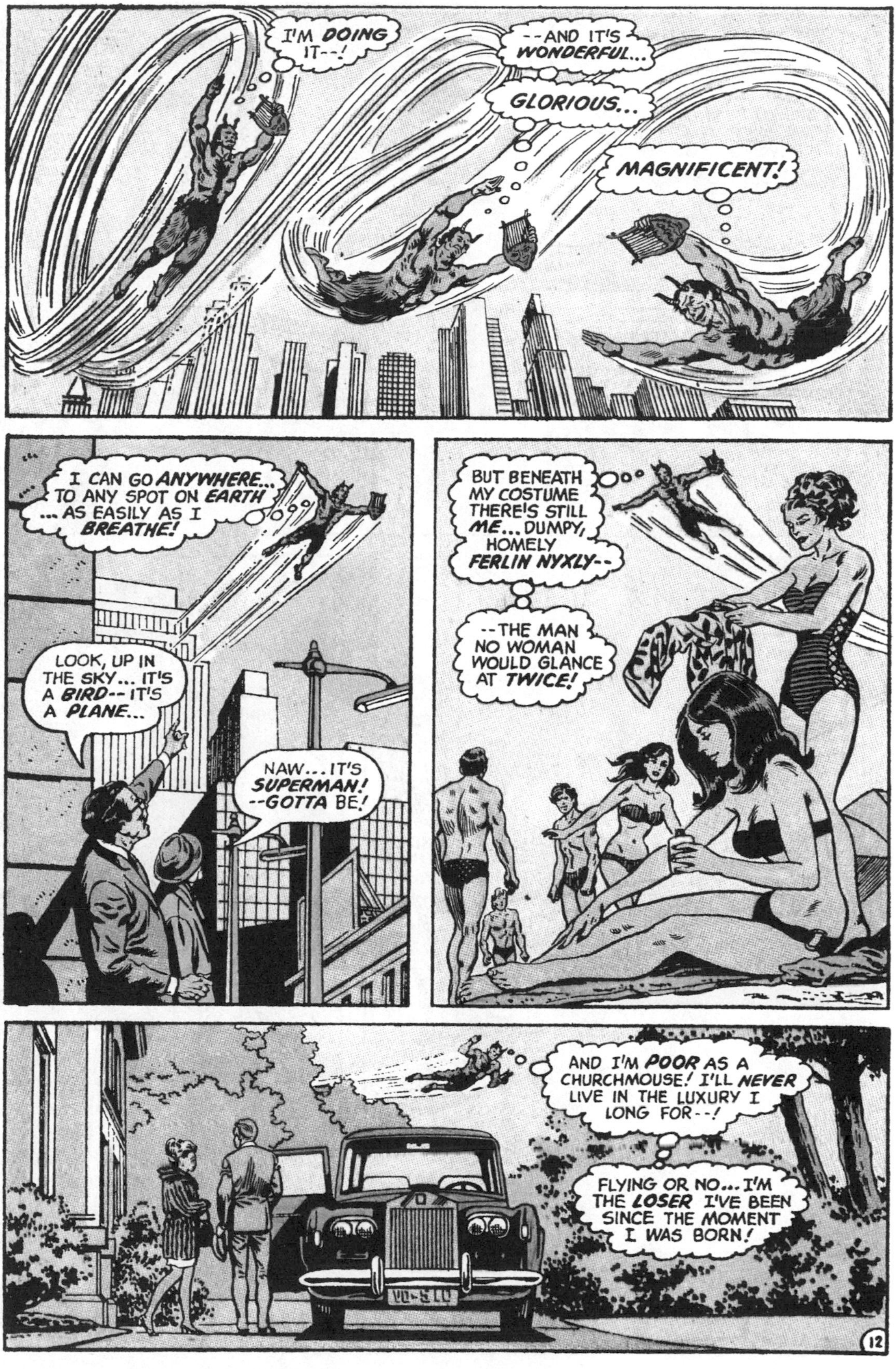
I'M DOING IT--!
--AND IT'S WONDERFUL...
GLORIOUS...
MAGNIFICENT!
I CAN GO ANYWHERE... TO ANY SPOT ON EARTH ... AS EASILY AS I BREATHE!
LOOK, UP IN THE SKY... IT'S A BIRD-- IT'S A PLANE...
NAW... IT'S SUPERMAN! --GOTTA BE!
BUT BENEATH MY COSTUME THERE'S STILL ME... DUMPY, HOMELY FERLIN NYXLY--
--THE MAN NO WOMAN WOULD GLANCE AT TWICE!
AND I'M POOR AS A CHURCHMOUSE! I'LL NEVER LIVE IN THE LUXURY I LONG FOR--!
FLYING OR NO... I'M THE LOSER I'VE BEEN SINCE THE MOMENT I WAS BORN!
12

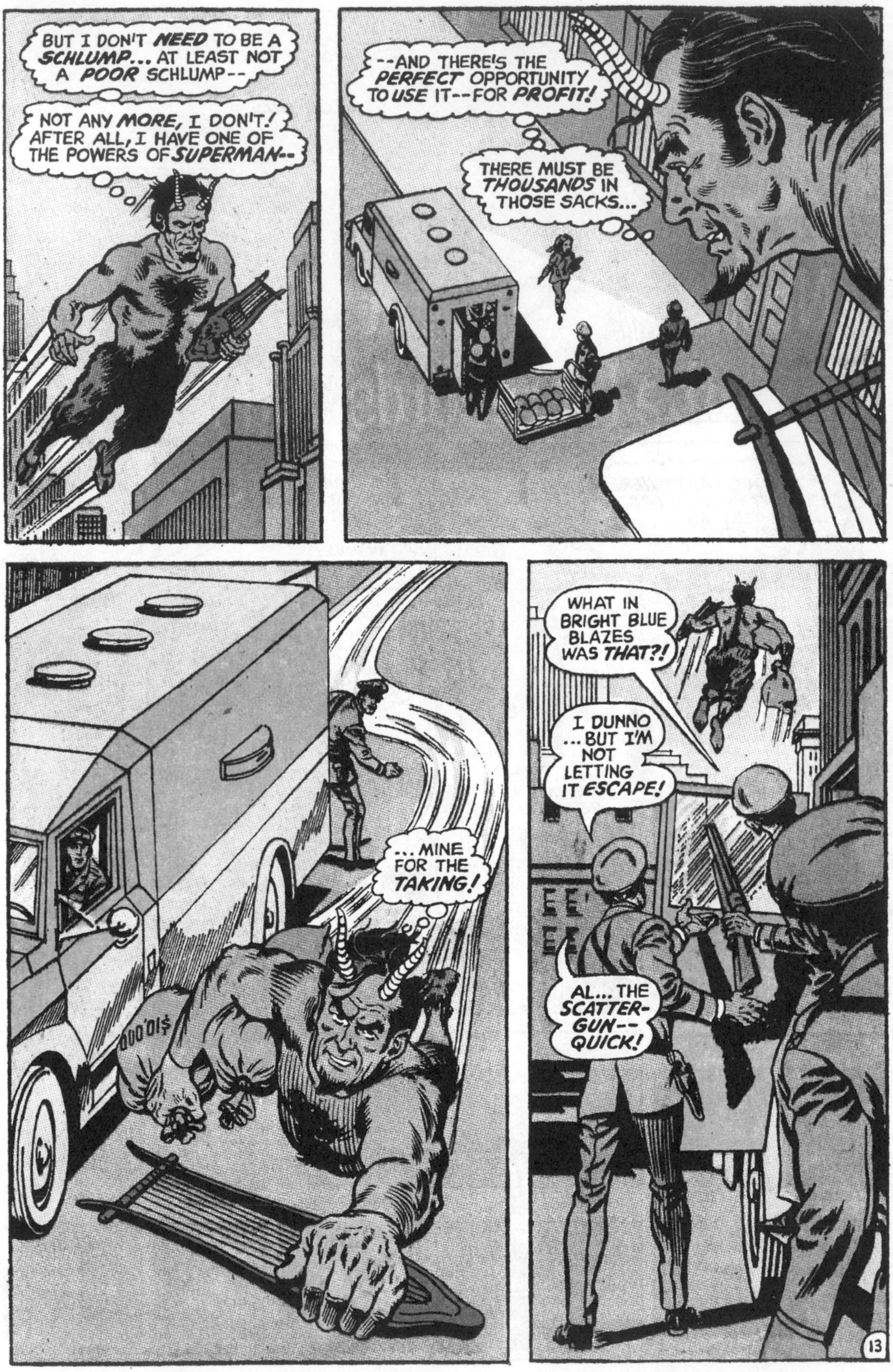
BUT I DON'T NEED TO BE A SCHLUMP... AT LEAST NOT A POOR SCHLUMP--
NOT ANY MORE, I DON'T! AFTER ALL, I HAVE ONE OF THE POWERS OF SUPERMAN--
--AND THERE'S THE PERFECT OPPORTUNITY TO USE IT--FOR PROFIT!
THERE MUST BE THOUSANDS IN THOSE SACKS...
...MINE FOR THE TAKING!
$10,000
WHAT IN BRIGHT BLUE BLAZES WAS THAT?!
I DUNNO ...BUT I'M NOT LETTING IT ESCAPE!
AL... THE SCATTER-GUN-- QUICK!
13

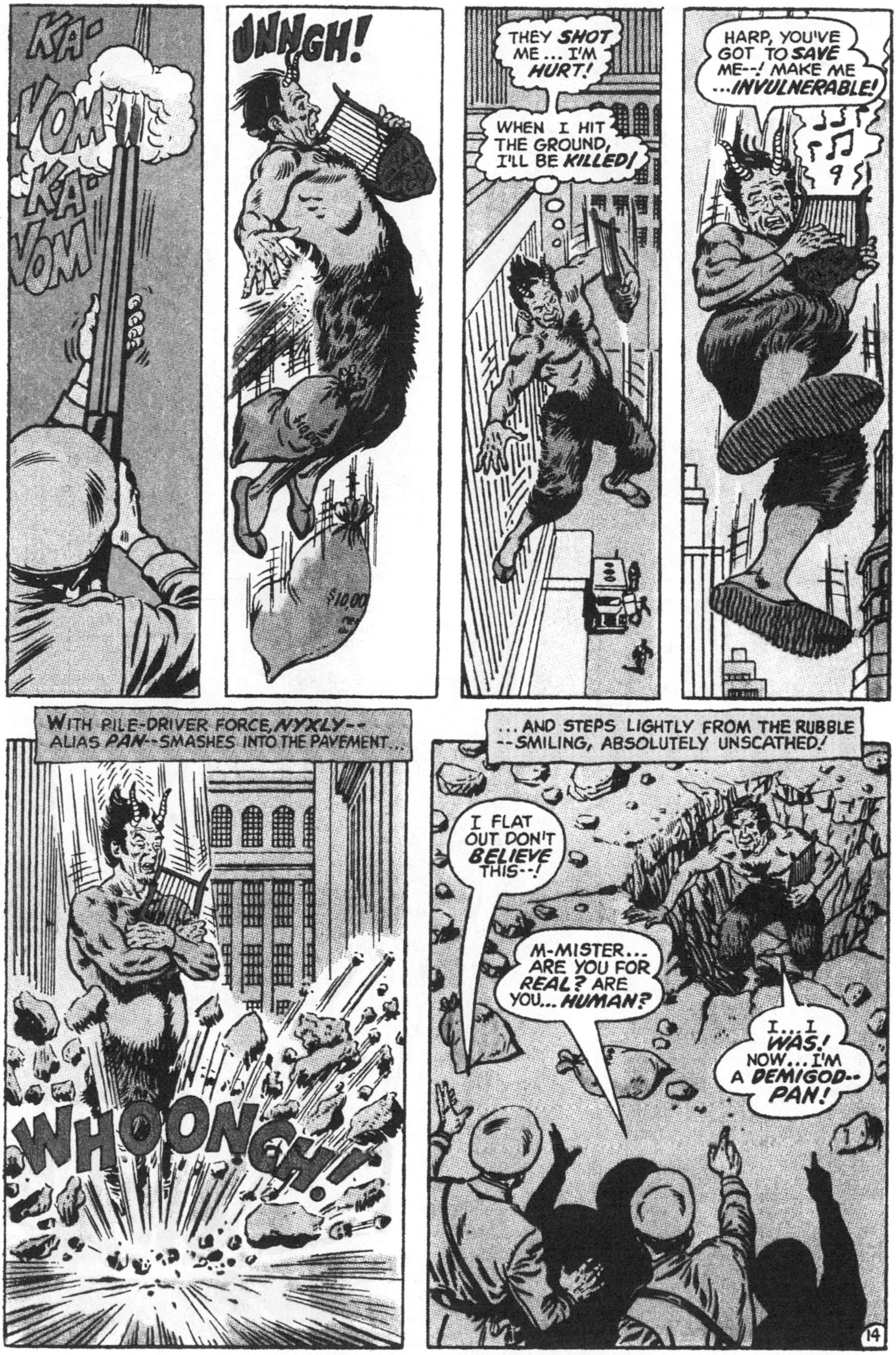
KA-VOM KA-VOM KA-VOM
UNNGH!
THEY SHOT ME... I'M HURT!
WHEN I HIT THE GROUND, I'LL BE KILLED!
HARP, YOU'VE GOT TO SAVE ME--! MAKE ME ...INVULNERABLE!
WITH PILE-DRIVER FORCE, NYXLY-- ALIAS PAN--SMASHES INTO THE PAVEMENT...
WHOONCH!
...AND STEPS LIGHTLY FROM THE RUBBLE --SMILING, ABSOLUTELY UNSCATHED!
I FLAT OUT DON'T BELIEVE THIS--!
M-MISTER... ARE YOU FOR REAL? ARE YOU... HUMAN?
I... I WAS! NOW... I'M A DEMIGOD-- PAN!
14

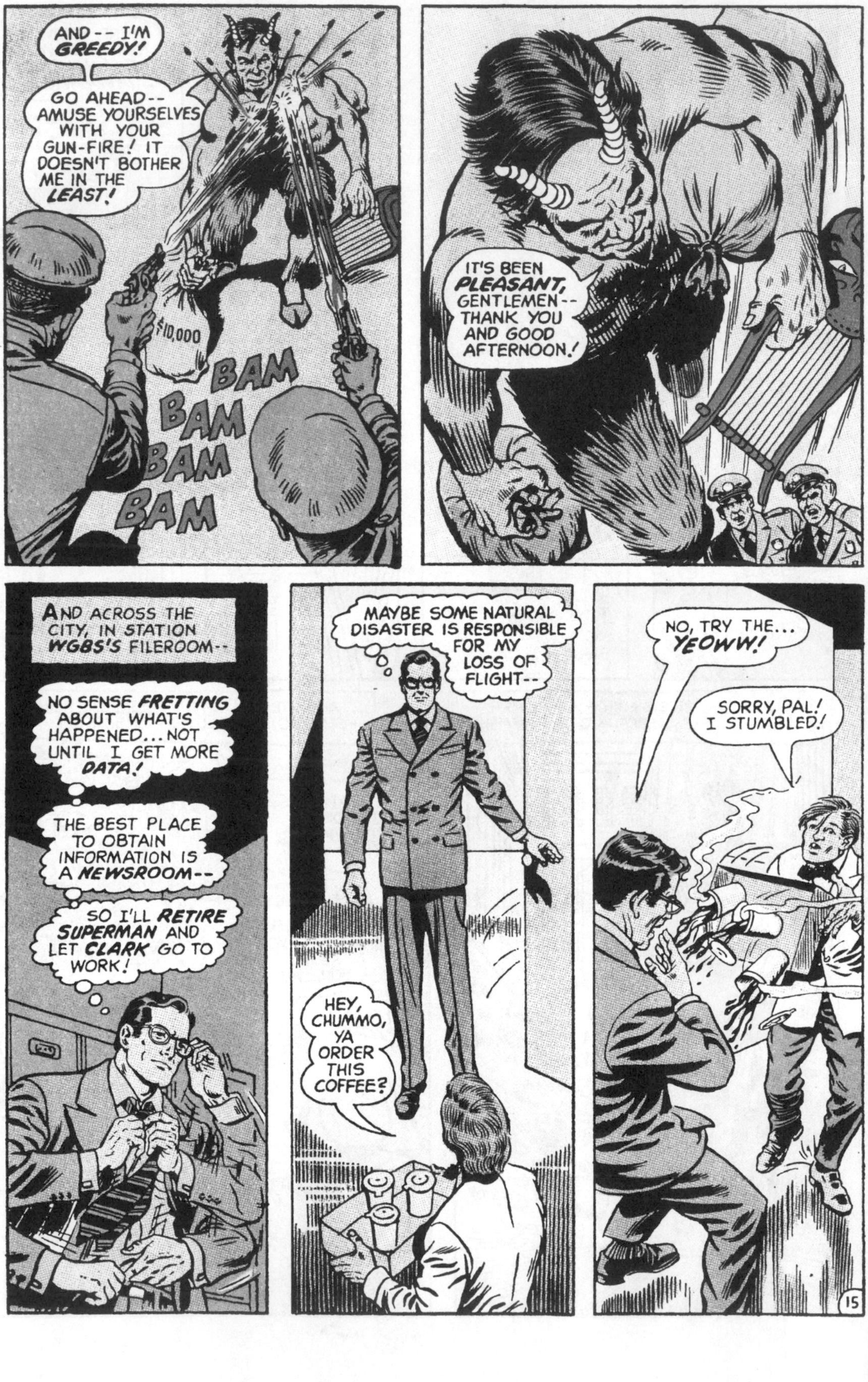
AND -- I'M GREEDY!
GO AHEAD -- AMUSE YOURSELVES WITH YOUR GUN-FIRE! IT DOESN'T BOTHER ME IN THE LEAST!
$10,000
BAM
BAM
BAM
BAM
IT'S BEEN PLEASANT, GENTLEMEN -- THANK YOU AND GOOD AFTERNOON!
AND ACROSS THE CITY, IN STATION WGBS'S FILEROOM --
NO SENSE FRETTING ABOUT WHAT'S HAPPENED... NOT UNTIL I GET MORE DATA!
THE BEST PLACE TO OBTAIN INFORMATION IS A NEWSROOM --
SO I'LL RETIRE SUPERMAN AND LET CLARK GO TO WORK!
MAYBE SOME NATURAL DISASTER IS RESPONSIBLE FOR MY LOSS OF FLIGHT --
HEY, CHUMMO, YA ORDER THIS COFFEE?
NO, TRY THE... YEOWW!
SORRY, PAL! I STUMBLED!
15

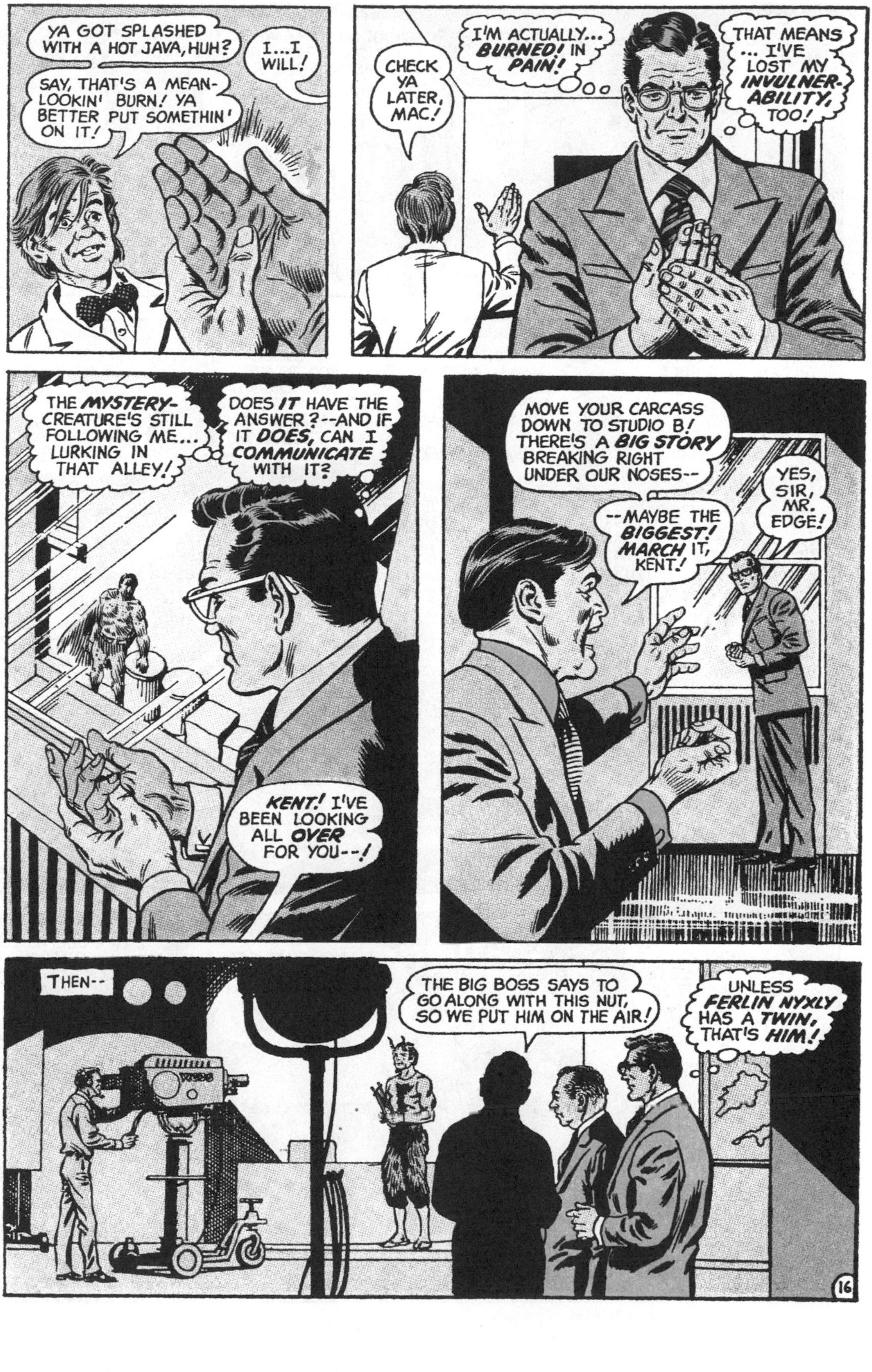
YA GOT SPLASHED WITH A HOT JAVA, HUH?
SAY, THAT'S A MEAN-LOOKIN' BURN! YA BETTER PUT SOMETHIN' ON IT!
I...I WILL!
CHECK YA LATER, MAC!
I'M ACTUALLY... BURNED! IN PAIN!
THAT MEANS ... I'VE LOST MY INVULNERABILITY, TOO!
THE MYSTERY-CREATURE'S STILL FOLLOWING ME... LURKING IN THAT ALLEY!
DOES IT HAVE THE ANSWER?--AND IF IT DOES, CAN I COMMUNICATE WITH IT?
KENT! I'VE BEEN LOOKING ALL OVER FOR YOU--!
MOVE YOUR CARCASS DOWN TO STUDIO B! THERE'S A BIG STORY BREAKING RIGHT UNDER OUR NOSES--
--MAYBE THE BIGGEST! MARCH IT, KENT!
YES, SIR, MR. EDGE!
THEN--
THE BIG BOSS SAYS TO GO ALONG WITH THIS NUT, SO WE PUT HIM ON THE AIR!
UNLESS FERLIN NYXLY HAS A TWIN, THAT'S HIM!
16

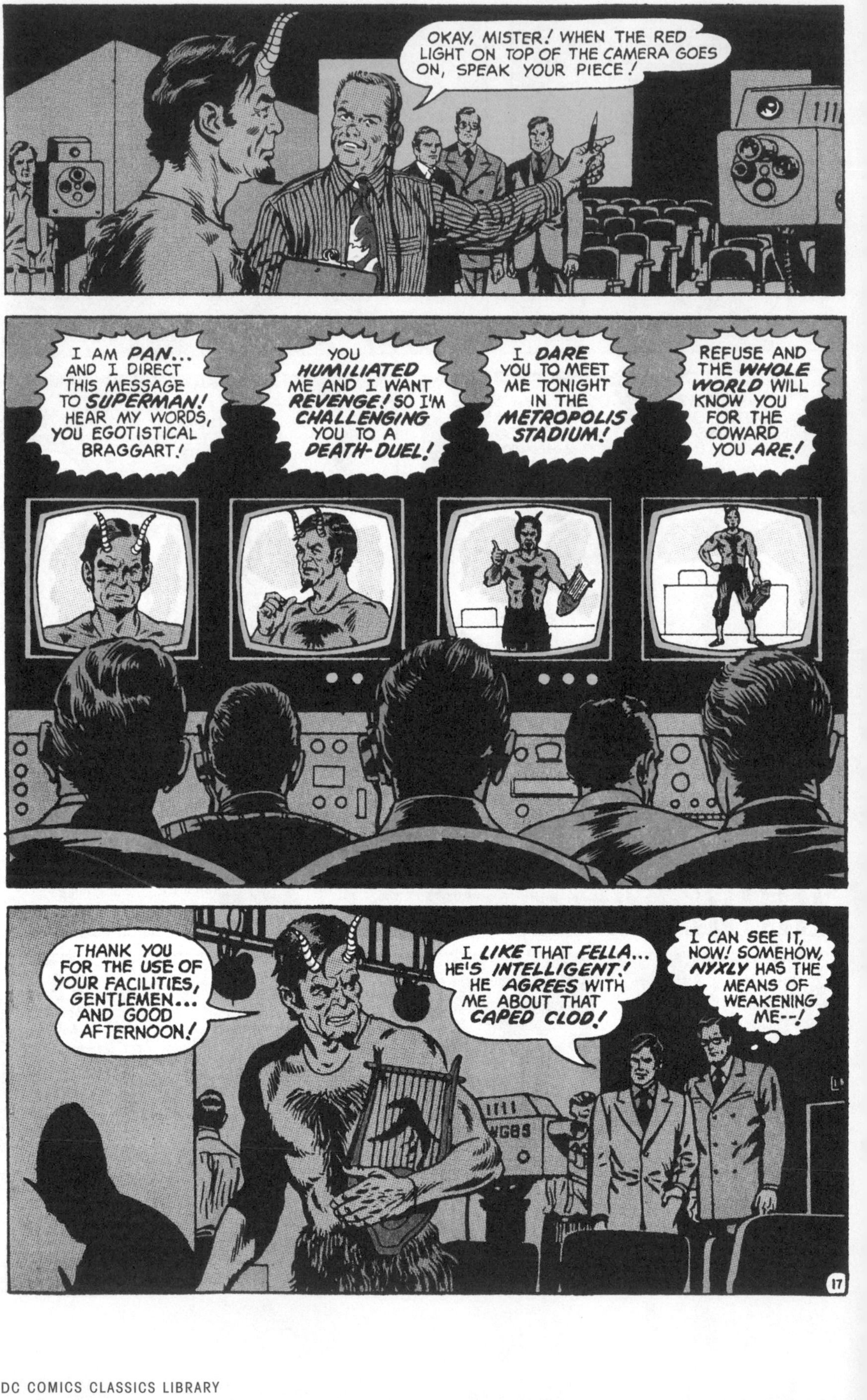
OKAY, MISTER! WHEN THE RED LIGHT ON TOP OF THE CAMERA GOES ON, SPEAK YOUR PIECE!
I AM PAN... AND I DIRECT THIS MESSAGE TO SUPERMAN! HEAR MY WORDS, YOU EGOTISTICAL BRAGGART!
YOU HUMILIATED ME AND I WANT REVENGE! SO I'M CHALLENGING YOU TO A DEATH-DUEL!
I DARE YOU TO MEET ME TONIGHT IN THE METROPOLIS STADIUM!
REFUSE AND THE WHOLE WORLD WILL KNOW YOU FOR THE COWARD YOU ARE!
THANK YOU FOR THE USE OF YOUR FACILITIES, GENTLEMEN... AND GOOD AFTERNOON!
I LIKE THAT FELLA... HE'S INTELLIGENT! HE AGREES WITH ME ABOUT THAT CAPED CLOD!
I CAN SEE IT, NOW! SOMEHOW, NYXLY HAS THE MEANS OF WEAKENING ME--!
17

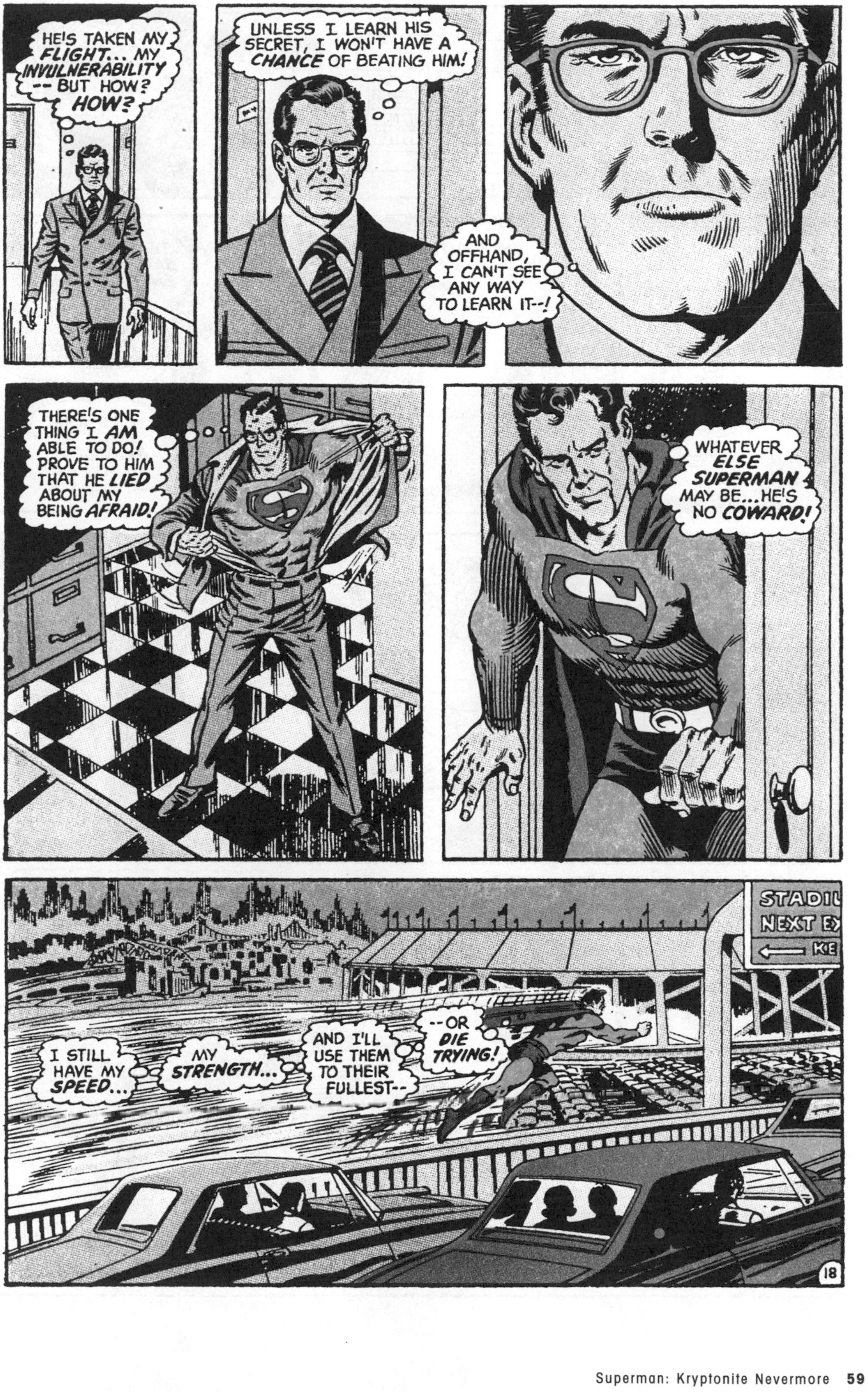
HE'S TAKEN MY FLIGHT... MY INVULNERABILITY -- BUT HOW? HOW?
UNLESS I LEARN HIS SECRET, I WON'T HAVE A CHANCE OF BEATING HIM!
AND OFFHAND, I CAN'T SEE ANY WAY TO LEARN IT--!
THERE'S ONE THING I AM ABLE TO DO! PROVE TO HIM THAT HE LIED ABOUT MY BEING AFRAID!
WHATEVER ELSE SUPERMAN MAY BE...HE'S NO COWARD!
STADIU
NEXT EX
KE
I STILL HAVE MY SPEED...
MY STRENGTH...
AND I'LL USE THEM TO THEIR FULLEST--
--OR DIE TRYING!
18

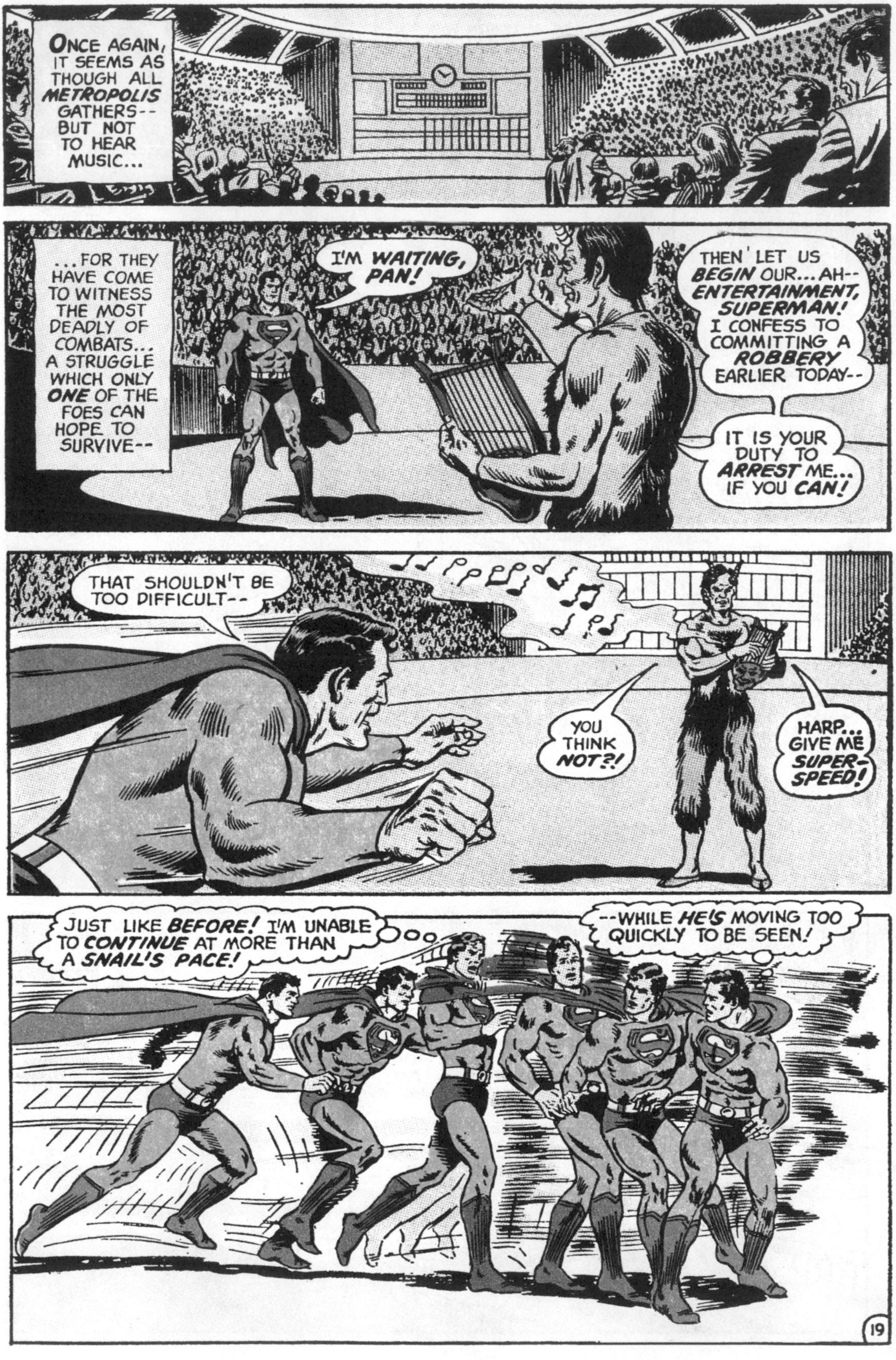
ONCE AGAIN, IT SEEMS AS THOUGH ALL METROPOLIS GATHERS-- BUT NOT TO HEAR MUSIC...
...FOR THEY HAVE COME TO WITNESS THE MOST DEADLY OF COMBATS... A STRUGGLE WHICH ONLY ONE OF THE FOES CAN HOPE TO SURVIVE--
I'M WAITING, PAN!
THEN LET US BEGIN OUR...AH-- ENTERTAINMENT, SUPERMAN! I CONFESS TO COMMITTING A ROBBERY EARLIER TODAY--
IT IS YOUR DUTY TO ARREST ME... IF YOU CAN!
THAT SHOULDN'T BE TOO DIFFICULT--
YOU THINK NOT?!
HARP... GIVE ME SUPER-SPEED!
JUST LIKE BEFORE! I'M UNABLE TO CONTINUE AT MORE THAN A SNAIL'S PACE!
--WHILE HE'S MOVING TOO QUICKLY TO BE SEEN!
19

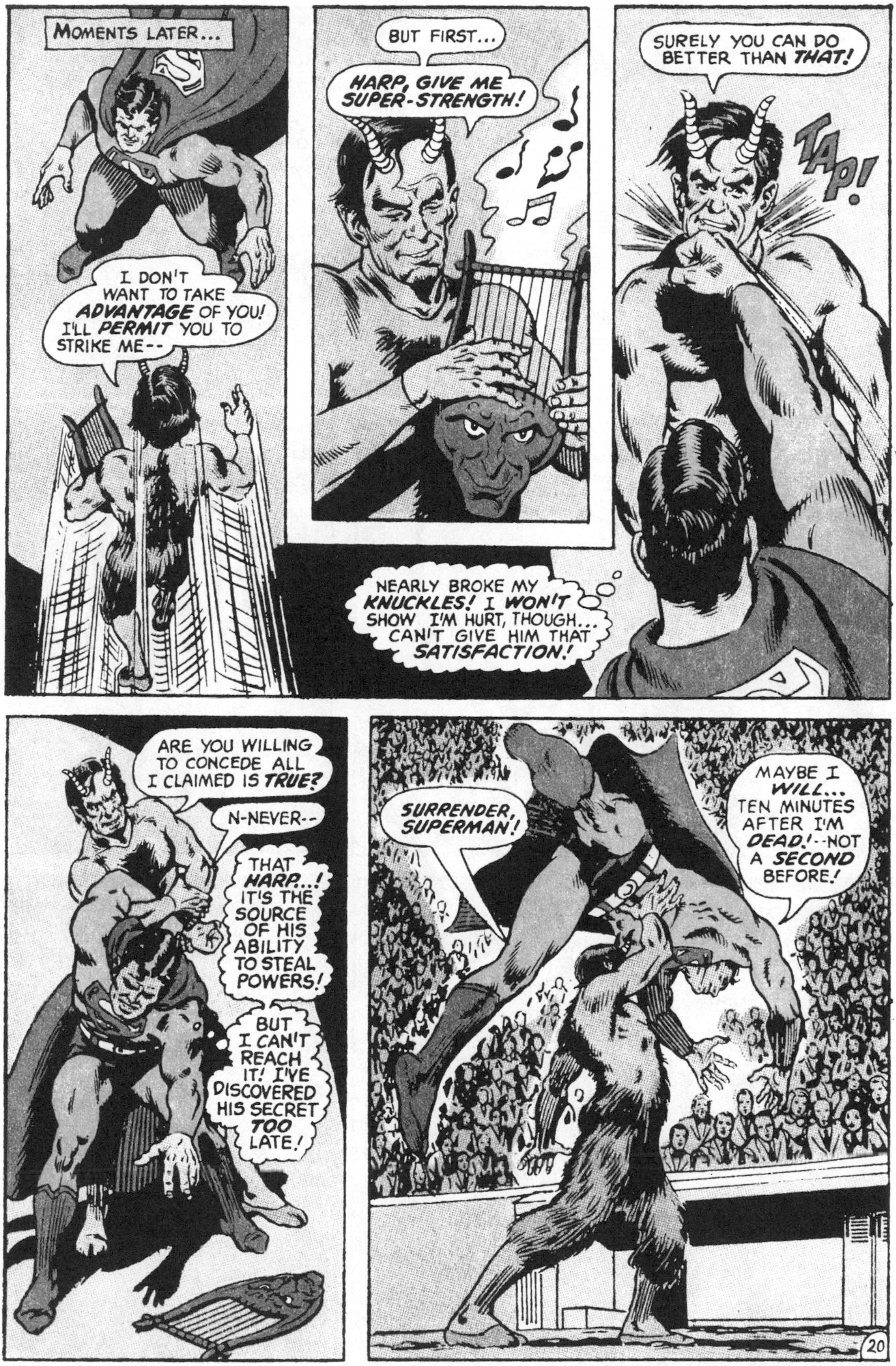
MOMENTS LATER...
I DON'T WANT TO TAKE ADVANTAGE OF YOU! I'LL PERMIT YOU TO STRIKE ME--
BUT FIRST...
HARP, GIVE ME SUPER-STRENGTH!
SURELY YOU CAN DO BETTER THAN THAT!
TAP!
NEARLY BROKE MY KNUCKLES! I WON'T SHOW I'M HURT, THOUGH... CAN'T GIVE HIM THAT SATISFACTION!
ARE YOU WILLING TO CONCEDE ALL I CLAIMED IS TRUE?
N-NEVER--
THAT HARP...! IT'S THE SOURCE OF HIS ABILITY TO STEAL POWERS!
BUT I CAN'T REACH IT! I'VE DISCOVERED HIS SECRET TOO LATE!
SURRENDER, SUPERMAN!
MAYBE I WILL... TEN MINUTES AFTER I'M DEAD!--NOT A SECOND BEFORE!
20

Kr-ASSH!

YOUR FINAL OPPORTUNITY... TO ADMIT THAT YOUR SOUL IS FILLED WITH *PETTINESS*... WITH *COWARDICE!*

N-NEVER--

SOME-THING... MOVING IN THE SHADOWS--

THEN... DIE-- *DIE!*

GHHH... GET THE *HARP!*

DESTROY IT... *QUICKLY!*

NO! GIVE IT *BACK!*

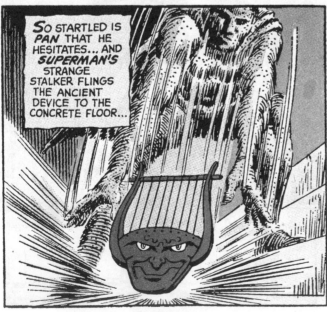

SO STARTLED IS *PAN* THAT HE HESITATES... AND *SUPERMAN'S* STRANGE STALKER FLINGS THE ANCIENT DEVICE TO THE CONCRETE FLOOR...

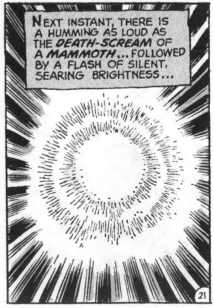

NEXT INSTANT, THERE IS A HUMMING AS LOUD AS THE *DEATH-SCREAM* OF A *MAMMOTH*... FOLLOWED BY A FLASH OF SILENT, SEARING BRIGHTNESS...

21

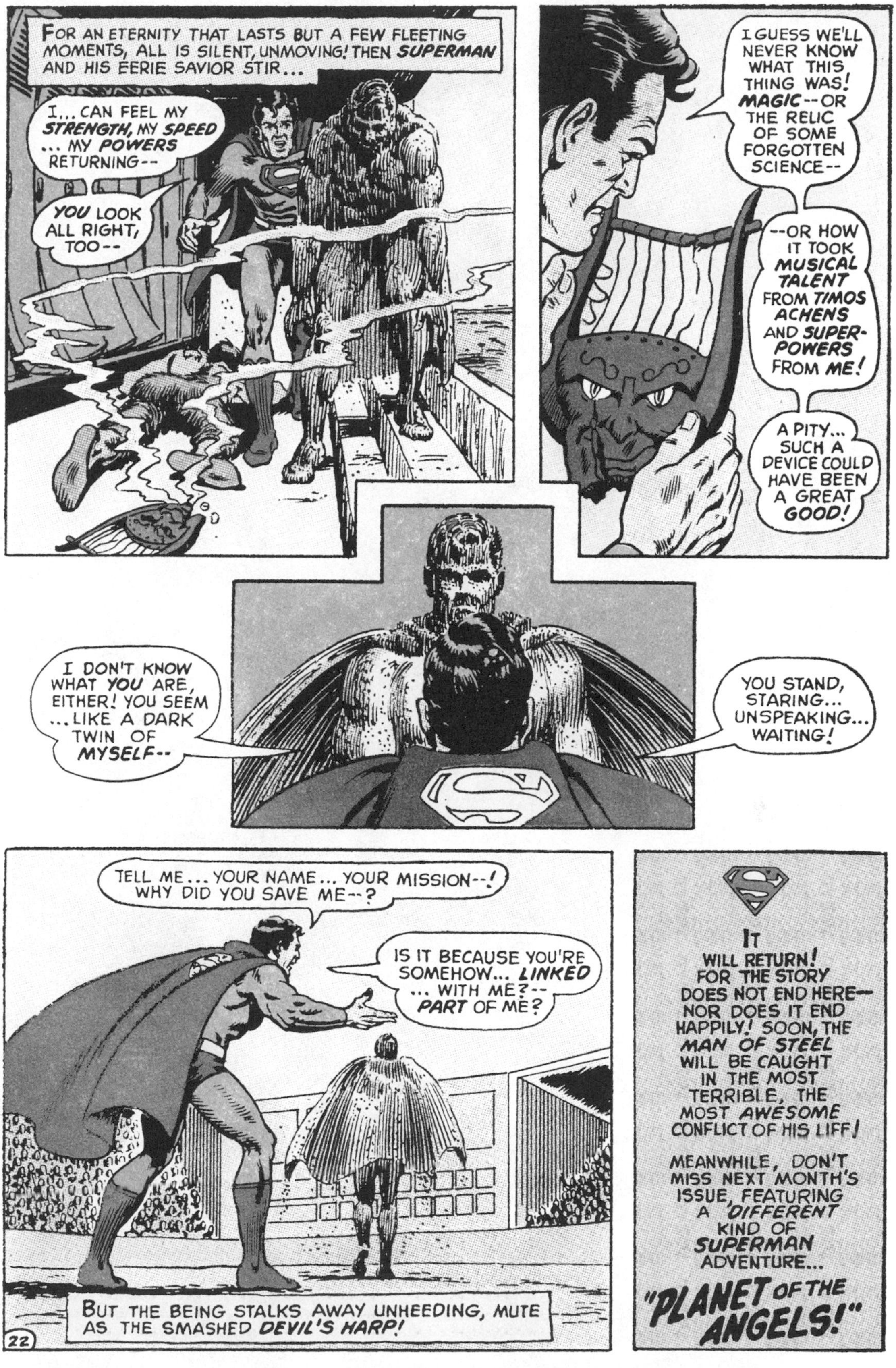

FOR AN ETERNITY THAT LASTS BUT A FEW FLEETING MOMENTS, ALL IS SILENT, UNMOVING! THEN SUPERMAN AND HIS EERIE SAVIOR STIR...
I... CAN FEEL MY STRENGTH, MY SPEED ... MY POWERS RETURNING--
YOU LOOK ALL RIGHT, TOO--
I GUESS WE'LL NEVER KNOW WHAT THIS THING WAS! MAGIC--OR THE RELIC OF SOME FORGOTTEN SCIENCE--
--OR HOW IT TOOK MUSICAL TALENT FROM TIMOS ACHENS AND SUPER-POWERS FROM ME!
A PITY... SUCH A DEVICE COULD HAVE BEEN A GREAT GOOD!
I DON'T KNOW WHAT YOU ARE, EITHER! YOU SEEM ...LIKE A DARK TWIN OF MYSELF--
YOU STAND, STARING... UNSPEAKING... WAITING!
TELL ME... YOUR NAME... YOUR MISSION--! WHY DID YOU SAVE ME--?
IS IT BECAUSE YOU'RE SOMEHOW... LINKED ... WITH ME?-- PART OF ME?
BUT THE BEING STALKS AWAY UNHEEDING, MUTE AS THE SMASHED DEVIL'S HARP!
22
IT WILL RETURN! FOR THE STORY DOES NOT END HERE-- NOR DOES IT END HAPPILY! SOON, THE MAN OF STEEL WILL BE CAUGHT IN THE MOST TERRIBLE, THE MOST AWESOME CONFLICT OF HIS LIFE!
MEANWHILE, DON'T MISS NEXT MONTH'S ISSUE, FEATURING A 'DIFFERENT' KIND OF SUPERMAN ADVENTURE...
"PLANET OF THE ANGELS!"

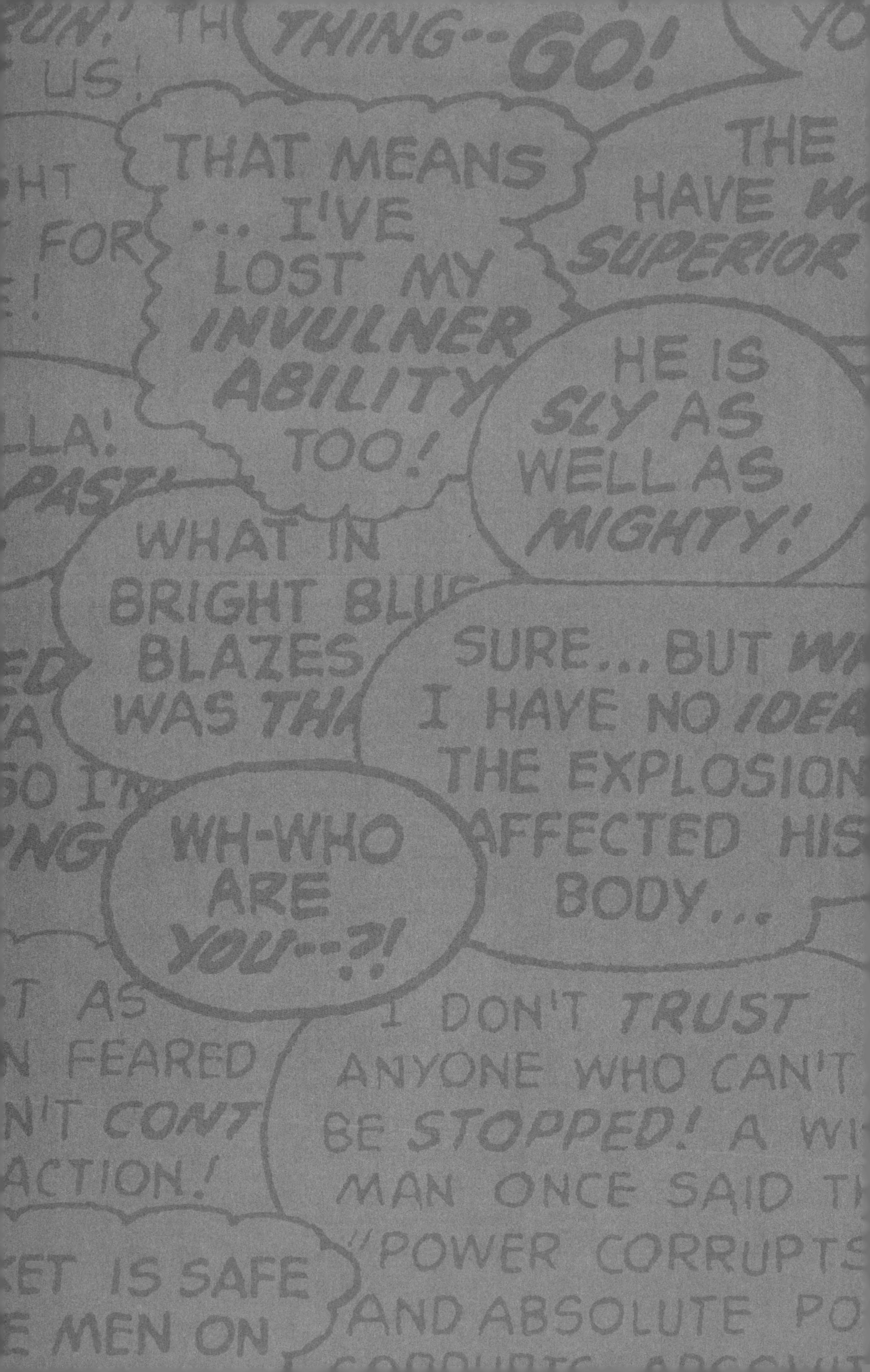

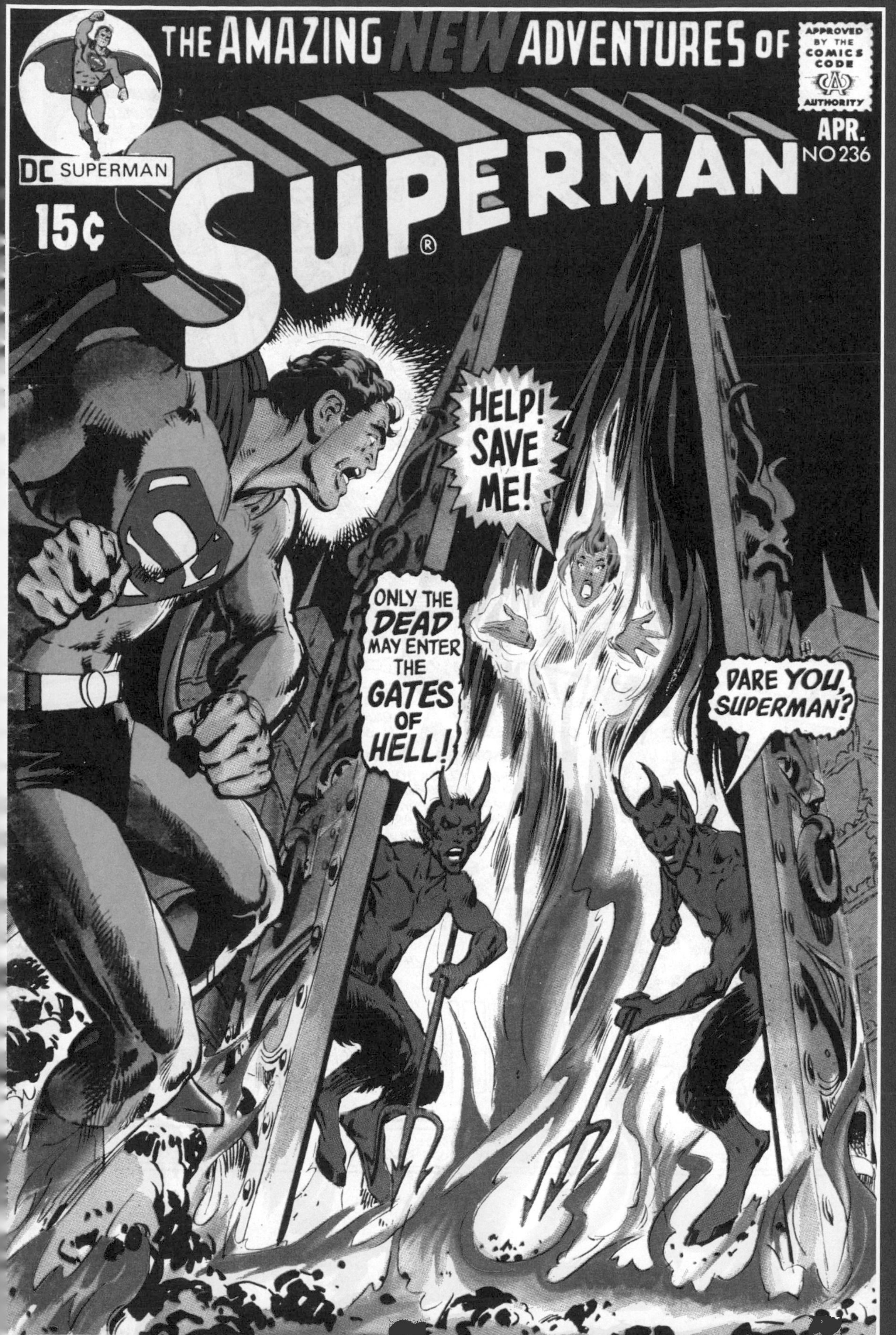
THE AMAZING NEW ADVENTURES OF
SUPERMAN
APPROVED BY THE COMICS CODE AUTHORITY
APR. NO 236
DC SUPERMAN
15¢
HELP! SAVE ME!
ONLY THE DEAD MAY ENTER THE GATES OF HELL!
DARE YOU, SUPERMAN?

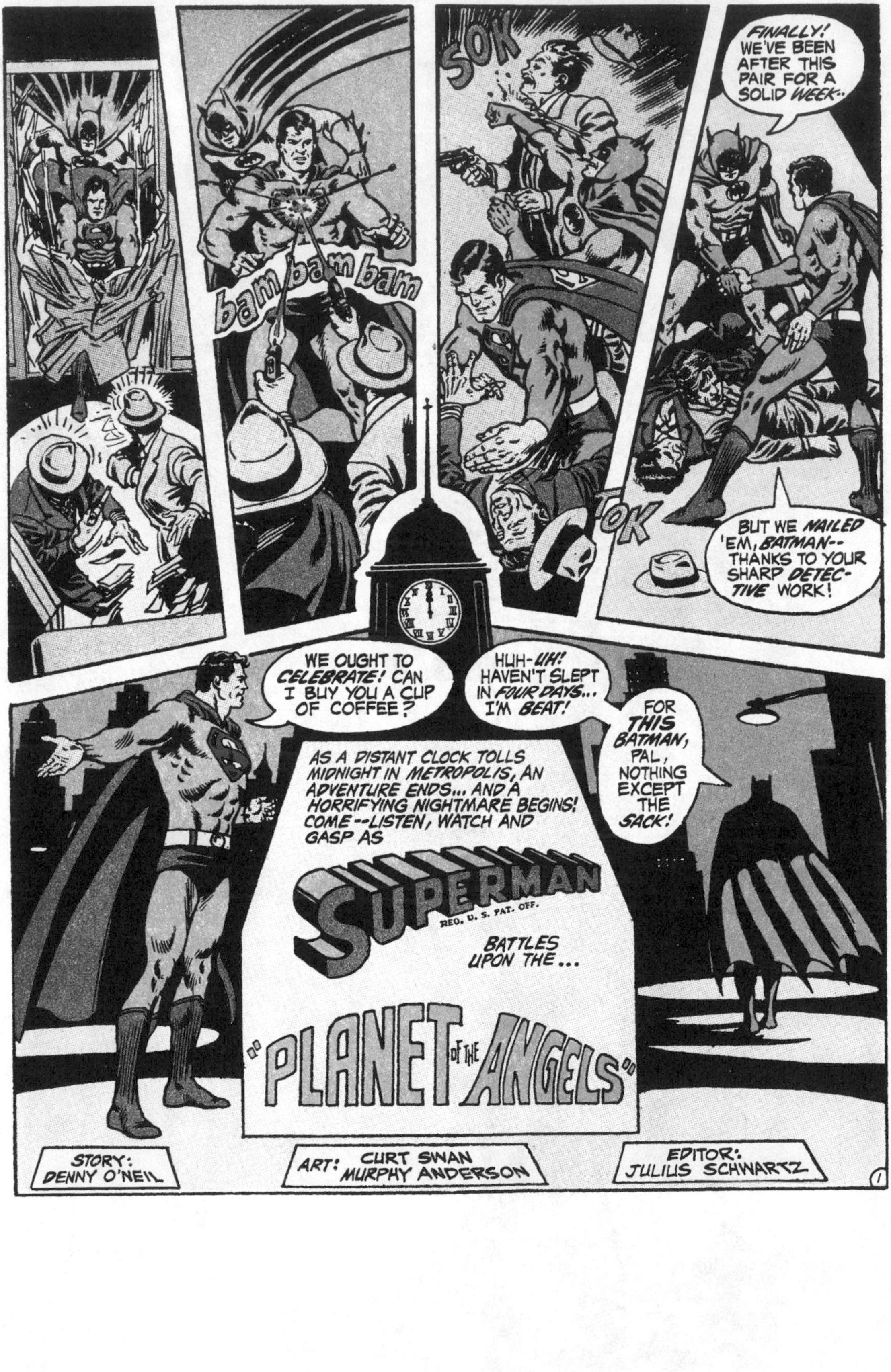
SOK
bam bam bam
FINALLY! WE'VE BEEN AFTER THIS PAIR FOR A SOLID WEEK..
TOK
BUT WE NAILED 'EM, BATMAN-- THANKS TO YOUR SHARP DETECTIVE WORK!
WE OUGHT TO CELEBRATE! CAN I BUY YOU A CUP OF COFFEE?
HUH-UH! HAVEN'T SLEPT IN FOUR DAYS... I'M BEAT!
FOR THIS BATMAN, PAL, NOTHING EXCEPT THE SACK!
AS A DISTANT CLOCK TOLLS MIDNIGHT IN METROPOLIS, AN ADVENTURE ENDS... AND A HORRIFYING NIGHTMARE BEGINS! COME--LISTEN, WATCH AND GASP AS
SUPERMAN
REG. U. S. PAT. OFF.
BATTLES UPON THE...
"PLANET OF THE ANGELS"
STORY: DENNY O'NEIL
ART: CURT SWAN MURPHY ANDERSON
EDITOR: JULIUS SCHWARTZ
1

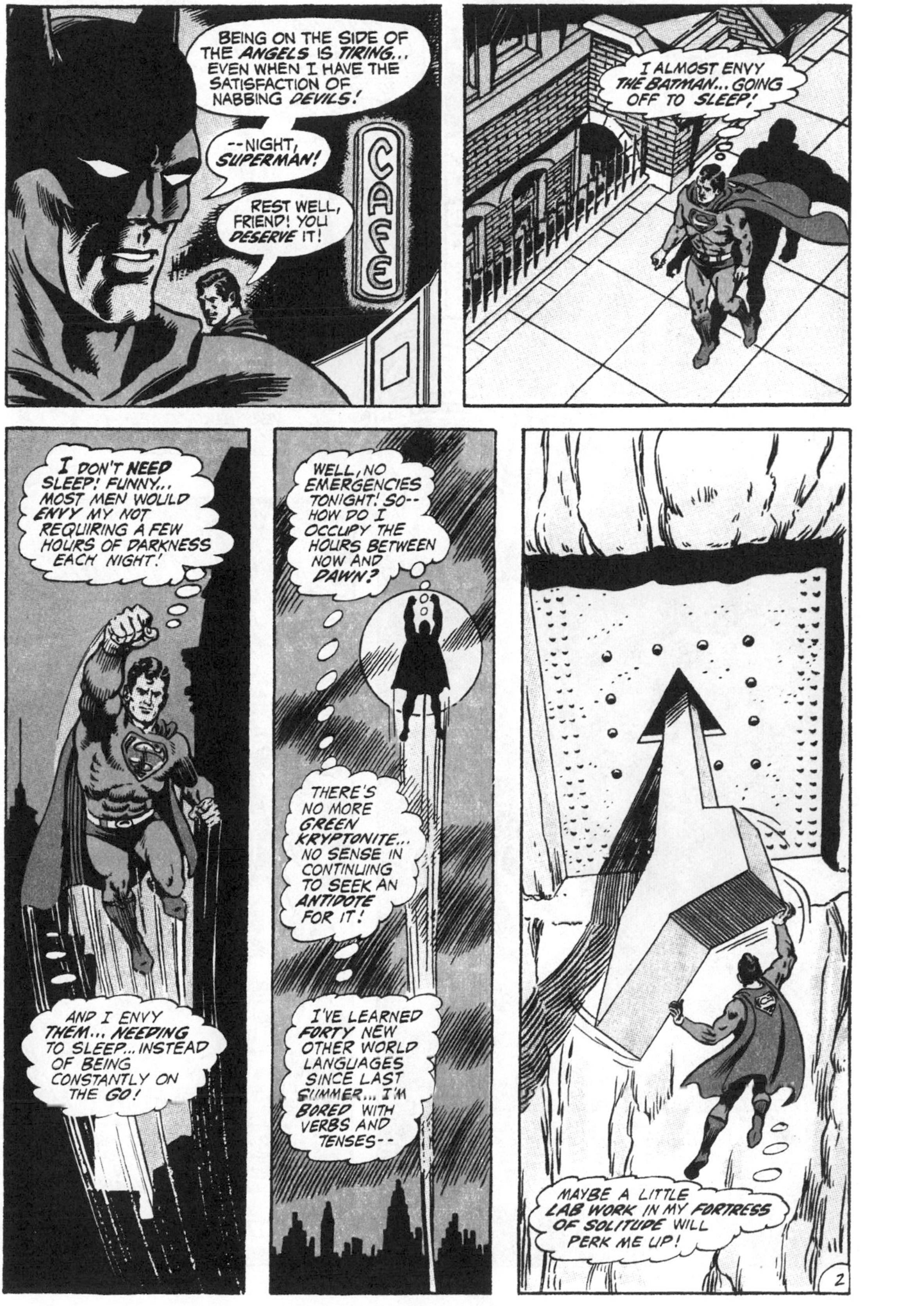
BEING ON THE SIDE OF THE ANGELS IS TIRING... EVEN WHEN I HAVE THE SATISFACTION OF NABBING DEVILS!
--NIGHT, SUPERMAN!
REST WELL, FRIEND! YOU DESERVE IT!
CAFE
I ALMOST ENVY THE BATMAN... GOING OFF TO SLEEP!
I DON'T NEED SLEEP! FUNNY... MOST MEN WOULD ENVY MY NOT REQUIRING A FEW HOURS OF DARKNESS EACH NIGHT!
AND I ENVY THEM... NEEDING TO SLEEP... INSTEAD OF BEING CONSTANTLY ON THE GO!
WELL, NO EMERGENCIES TONIGHT! SO--HOW DO I OCCUPY THE HOURS BETWEEN NOW AND DAWN?
THERE'S NO MORE GREEN KRYPTONITE... NO SENSE IN CONTINUING TO SEEK AN ANTIDOTE FOR IT!
I'VE LEARNED FORTY NEW OTHER WORLD LANGUAGES SINCE LAST SUMMER... I'M BORED WITH VERBS AND TENSES--
MAYBE A LITTLE LAB WORK IN MY FORTRESS OF SOLITUDE WILL PERK ME UP!
2

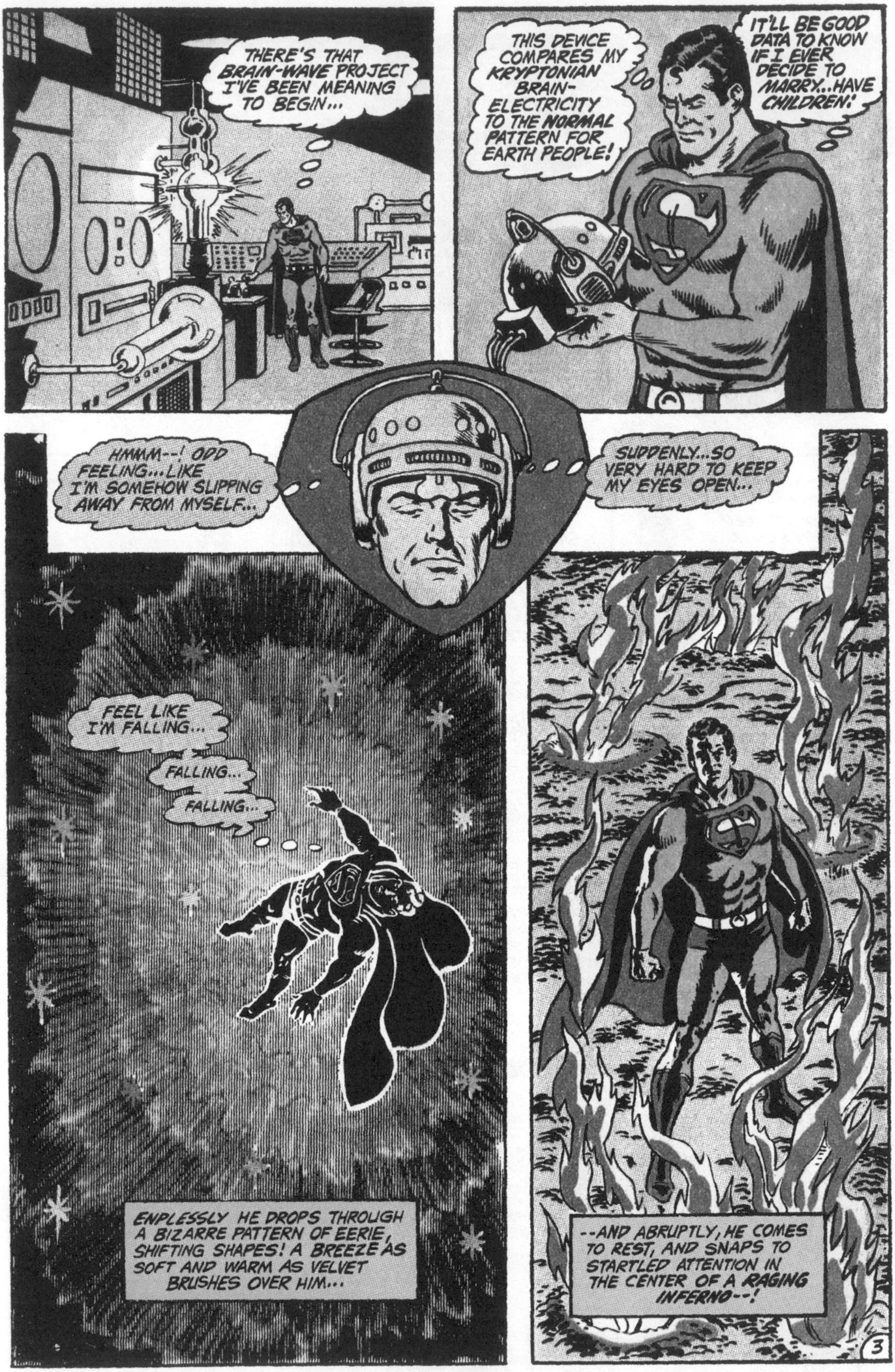
THERE'S THAT BRAIN-WAVE PROJECT I'VE BEEN MEANING TO BEGIN...
THIS DEVICE COMPARES MY KRYPTONIAN BRAIN-ELECTRICITY TO THE NORMAL PATTERN FOR EARTH PEOPLE!
IT'LL BE GOOD DATA TO KNOW IF I EVER DECIDE TO MARRY..HAVE CHILDREN!
HMMM--! ODD FEELING...LIKE I'M SOMEHOW SLIPPING AWAY FROM MYSELF...
SUDDENLY...SO VERY HARD TO KEEP MY EYES OPEN...
FEEL LIKE I'M FALLING...
FALLING...
FALLING...
ENDLESSLY HE DROPS THROUGH A BIZARRE PATTERN OF EERIE, SHIFTING SHAPES! A BREEZE AS SOFT AND WARM AS VELVET BRUSHES OVER HIM...
--AND ABRUPTLY, HE COMES TO REST, AND SNAPS TO STARTLED ATTENTION IN THE CENTER OF A RAGING INFERNO--!
3

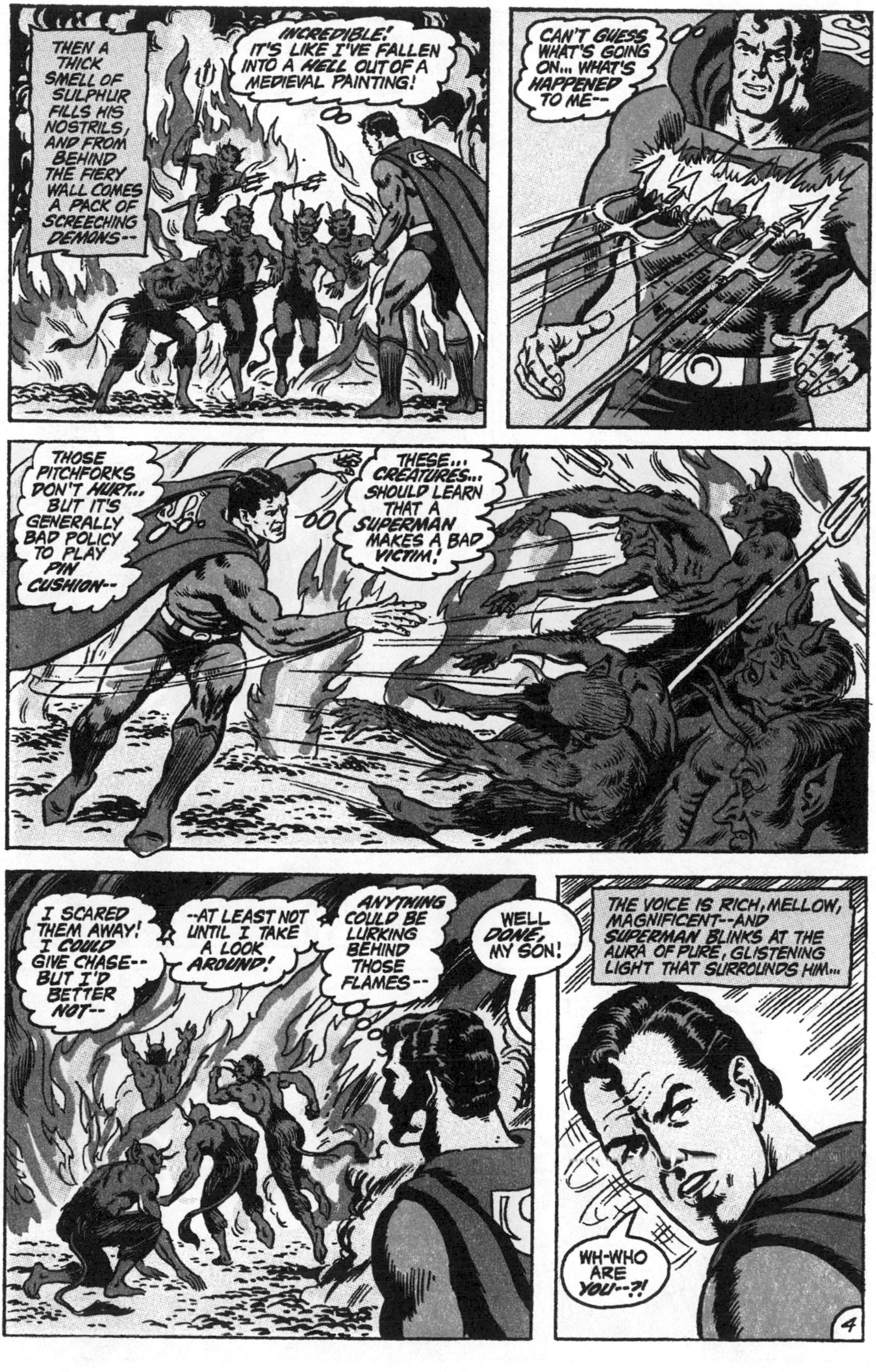

THEN A THICK SMELL OF SULPHUR FILLS HIS NOSTRILS, AND FROM BEHIND THE FIERY WALL COMES A PACK OF SCREECHING DEMONS--
INCREDIBLE! IT'S LIKE I'VE FALLEN INTO A HELL OUT OF A MEDIEVAL PAINTING!
CAN'T GUESS WHAT'S GOING ON... WHAT'S HAPPENED TO ME--
THOSE PITCHFORKS DON'T HURT... BUT IT'S GENERALLY BAD POLICY TO PLAY PIN CUSHION--
THESE... CREATURES... SHOULD LEARN THAT A SUPERMAN MAKES A BAD VICTIM!
I SCARED THEM AWAY! I COULD GIVE CHASE-- BUT I'D BETTER NOT--
--AT LEAST NOT UNTIL I TAKE A LOOK AROUND!
ANYTHING COULD BE LURKING BEHIND THOSE FLAMES--
WELL DONE, MY SON!
THE VOICE IS RICH, MELLOW, MAGNIFICENT--AND SUPERMAN BLINKS AT THE AURA OF PURE, GLISTENING LIGHT THAT SURROUNDS HIM...
WH-WHO ARE YOU--?!
4

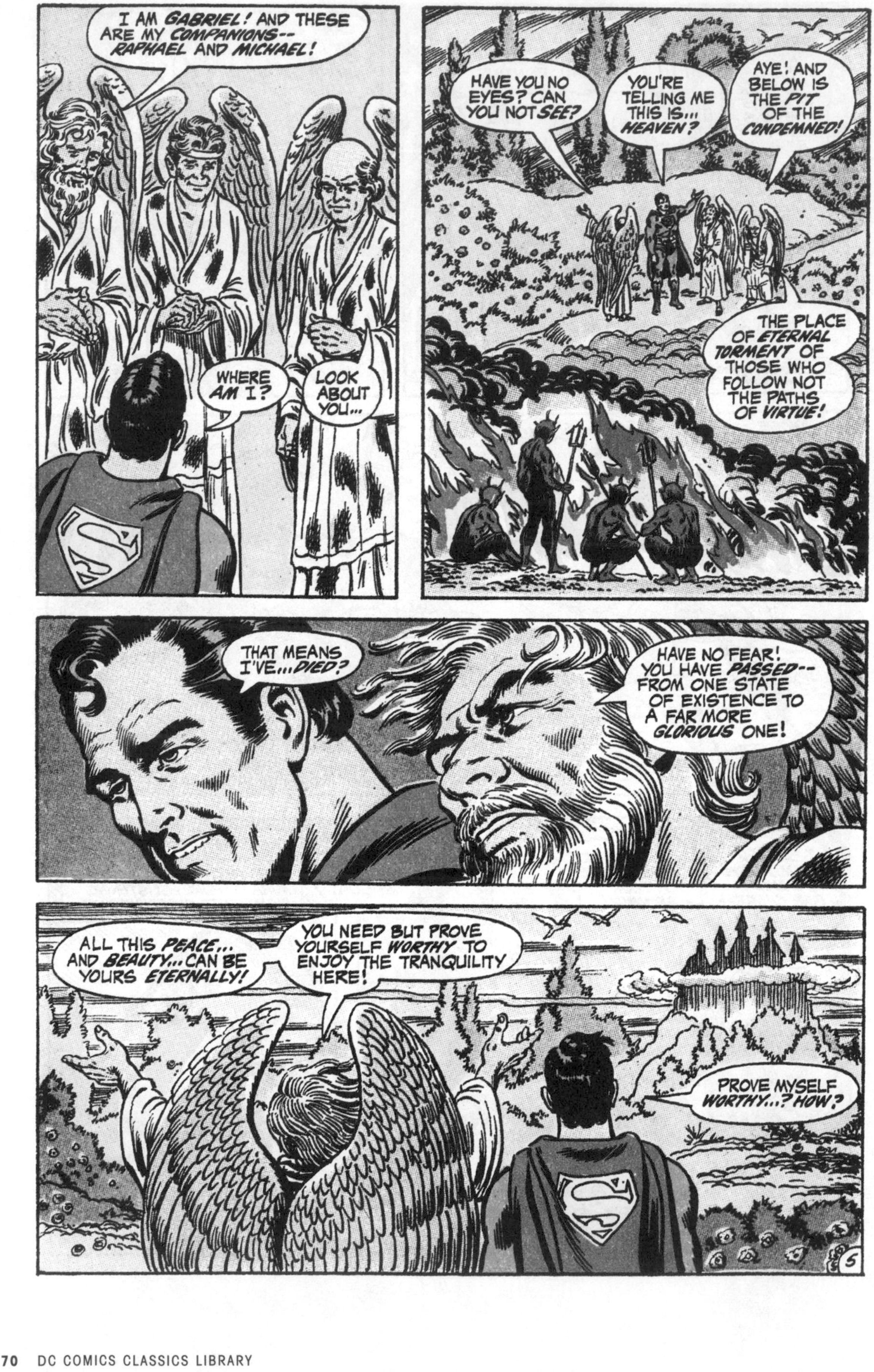
I AM GABRIEL! AND THESE ARE MY COMPANIONS-- RAPHAEL AND MICHAEL!
WHERE AM I?
LOOK ABOUT YOU...
HAVE YOU NO EYES? CAN YOU NOT SEE?
YOU'RE TELLING ME THIS IS... HEAVEN?
AYE! AND BELOW IS THE PIT OF THE CONDEMNED!
THE PLACE OF ETERNAL TORMENT OF THOSE WHO FOLLOW NOT THE PATHS OF VIRTUE!
THAT MEANS I'VE...DIED?
HAVE NO FEAR! YOU HAVE PASSED-- FROM ONE STATE OF EXISTENCE TO A FAR MORE GLORIOUS ONE!
ALL THIS PEACE... AND BEAUTY...CAN BE YOURS ETERNALLY!
YOU NEED BUT PROVE YOURSELF WORTHY TO ENJOY THE TRANQUILITY HERE!
PROVE MYSELF WORTHY...? HOW?
5

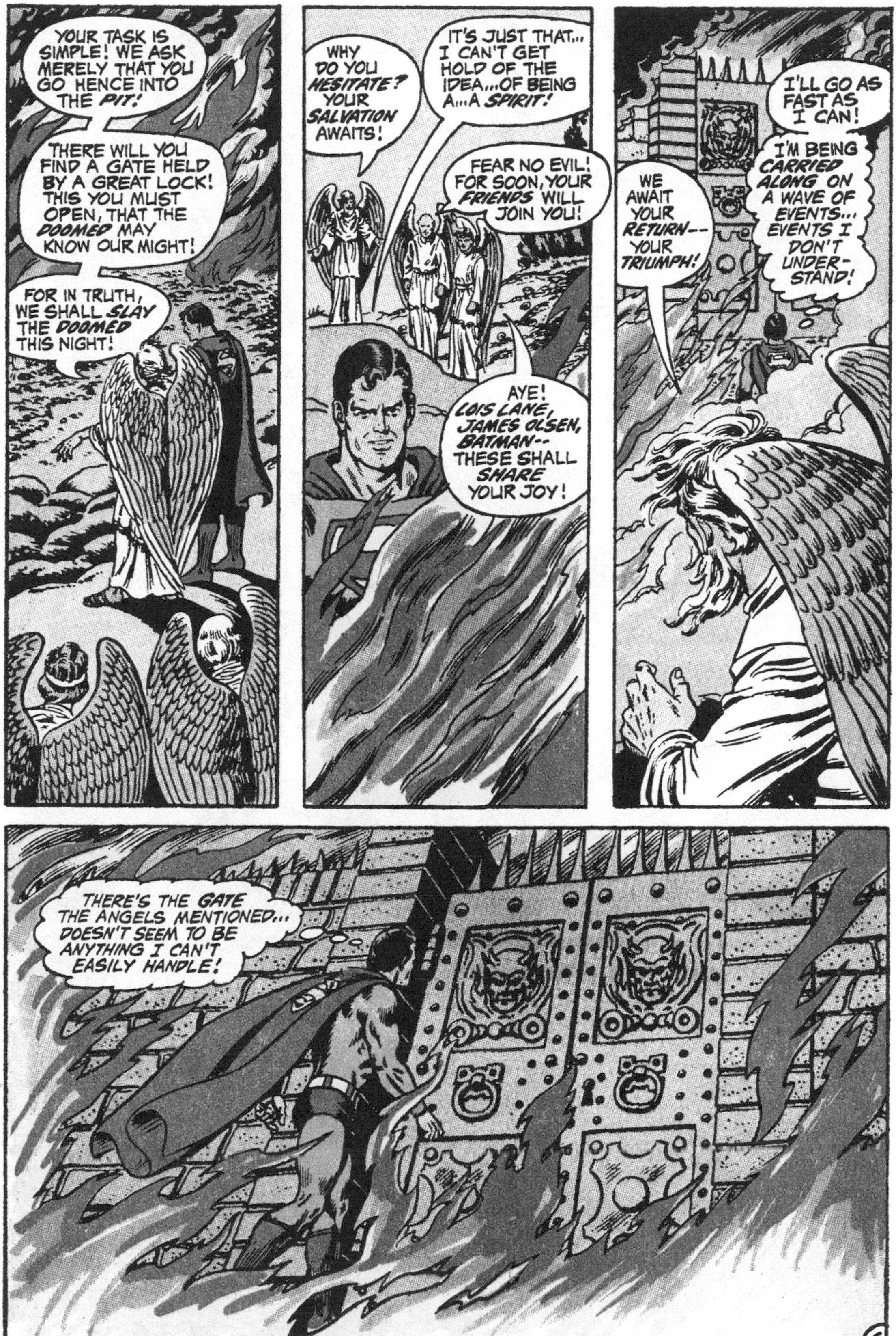
YOUR TASK IS SIMPLE! WE ASK MERELY THAT YOU GO HENCE INTO THE PIT!
THERE WILL YOU FIND A GATE HELD BY A GREAT LOCK! THIS YOU MUST OPEN, THAT THE DOOMED MAY KNOW OUR MIGHT!
FOR IN TRUTH, WE SHALL SLAY THE DOOMED THIS NIGHT!
WHY DO YOU HESITATE? YOUR SALVATION AWAITS!
IT'S JUST THAT... I CAN'T GET HOLD OF THE IDEA...OF BEING A...A SPIRIT!
FEAR NO EVIL! FOR SOON, YOUR FRIENDS WILL JOIN YOU!
AYE! LOIS LANE, JAMES OLSEN, BATMAN-- THESE SHALL SHARE YOUR JOY!
I'LL GO AS FAST AS I CAN!
I'M BEING CARRIED ALONG ON A WAVE OF EVENTS... EVENTS I DON'T UNDER-STAND!
WE AWAIT YOUR RETURN-- YOUR TRIUMPH!
THERE'S THE GATE THE ANGELS MENTIONED... DOESN'T SEEM TO BE ANYTHING I CAN'T EASILY HANDLE!
6

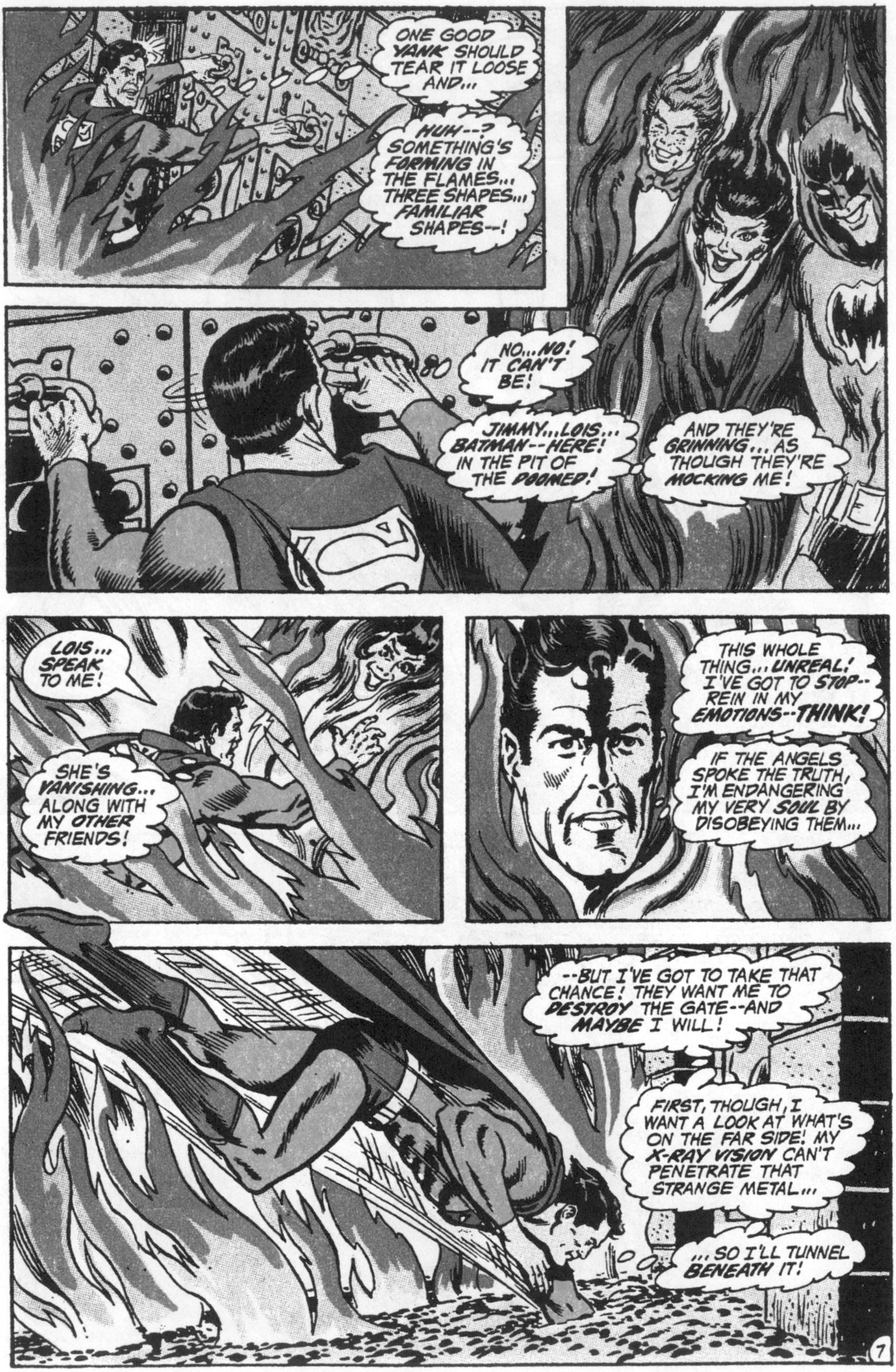
ONE GOOD YANK SHOULD TEAR IT LOOSE AND...
HUH--? SOMETHING'S FORMING IN THE FLAMES... THREE SHAPES... FAMILIAR SHAPES--!
NO...NO! IT CAN'T BE!
JIMMY...LOIS... BATMAN--HERE! IN THE PIT OF THE DOOMED!
AND THEY'RE GRINNING... AS THOUGH THEY'RE MOCKING ME!
LOIS... SPEAK TO ME!
SHE'S VANISHING... ALONG WITH MY OTHER FRIENDS!
THIS WHOLE THING... UNREAL! I'VE GOT TO STOP-- REIN IN MY EMOTIONS--THINK!
IF THE ANGELS SPOKE THE TRUTH, I'M ENDANGERING MY VERY SOUL BY DISOBEYING THEM...
--BUT I'VE GOT TO TAKE THAT CHANCE! THEY WANT ME TO DESTROY THE GATE--AND MAYBE I WILL!
FIRST, THOUGH, I WANT A LOOK AT WHAT'S ON THE FAR SIDE! MY X-RAY VISION CAN'T PENETRATE THAT STRANGE METAL...
...SO I'LL TUNNEL BENEATH IT!
7

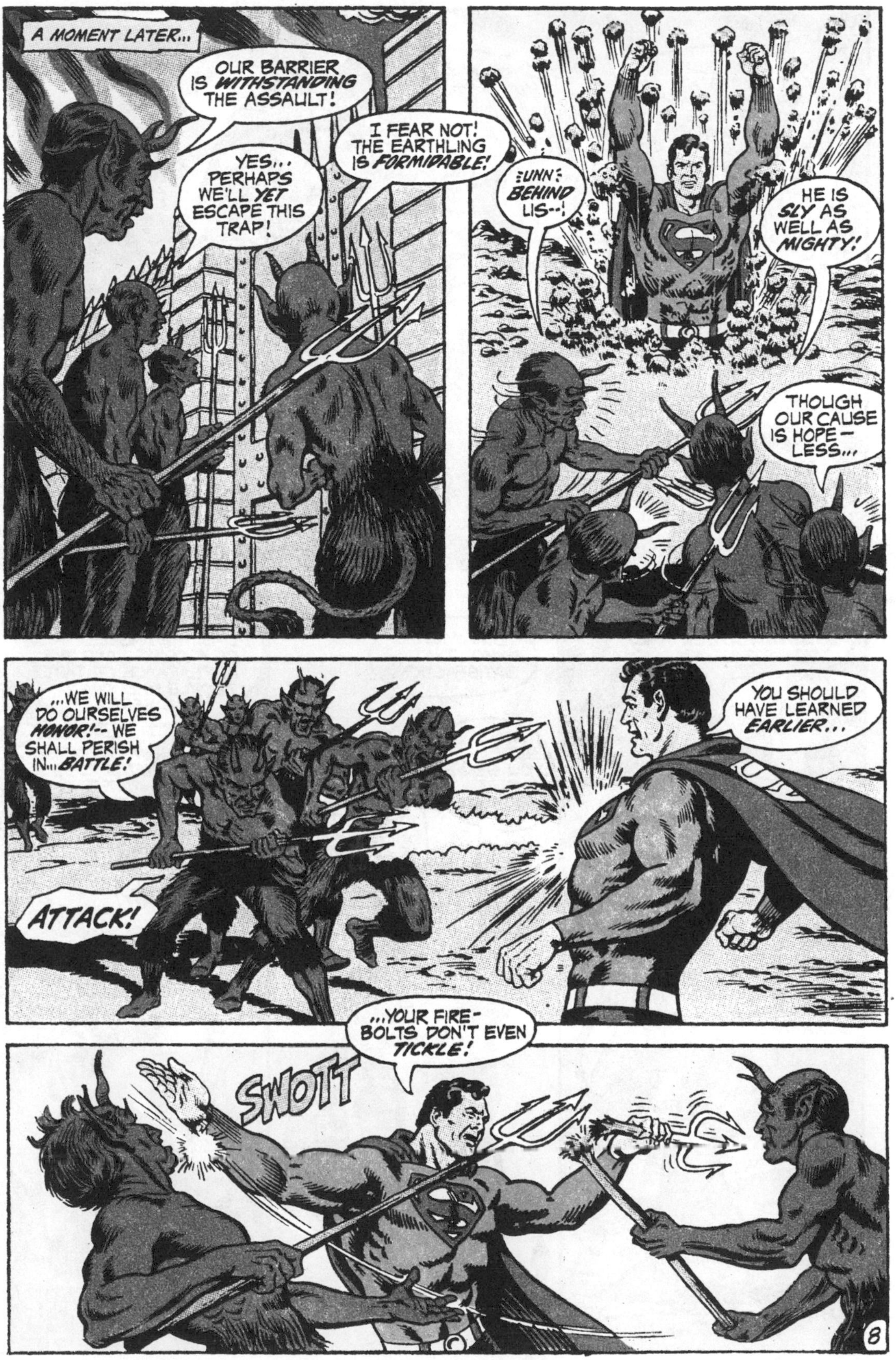
A MOMENT LATER...
OUR BARRIER IS WITHSTANDING THE ASSAULT!
YES... PERHAPS WE'LL YET ESCAPE THIS TRAP!
I FEAR NOT! THE EARTHLING IS FORMIDABLE!
UNN! BEHIND US--!
HE IS SLY AS WELL AS MIGHTY!
THOUGH OUR CAUSE IS HOPE-LESS...
...WE WILL DO OURSELVES HONOR!-- WE SHALL PERISH IN... BATTLE!
ATTACK!
YOU SHOULD HAVE LEARNED EARLIER...
...YOUR FIRE-BOLTS DON'T EVEN TICKLE!
SWOTT
8

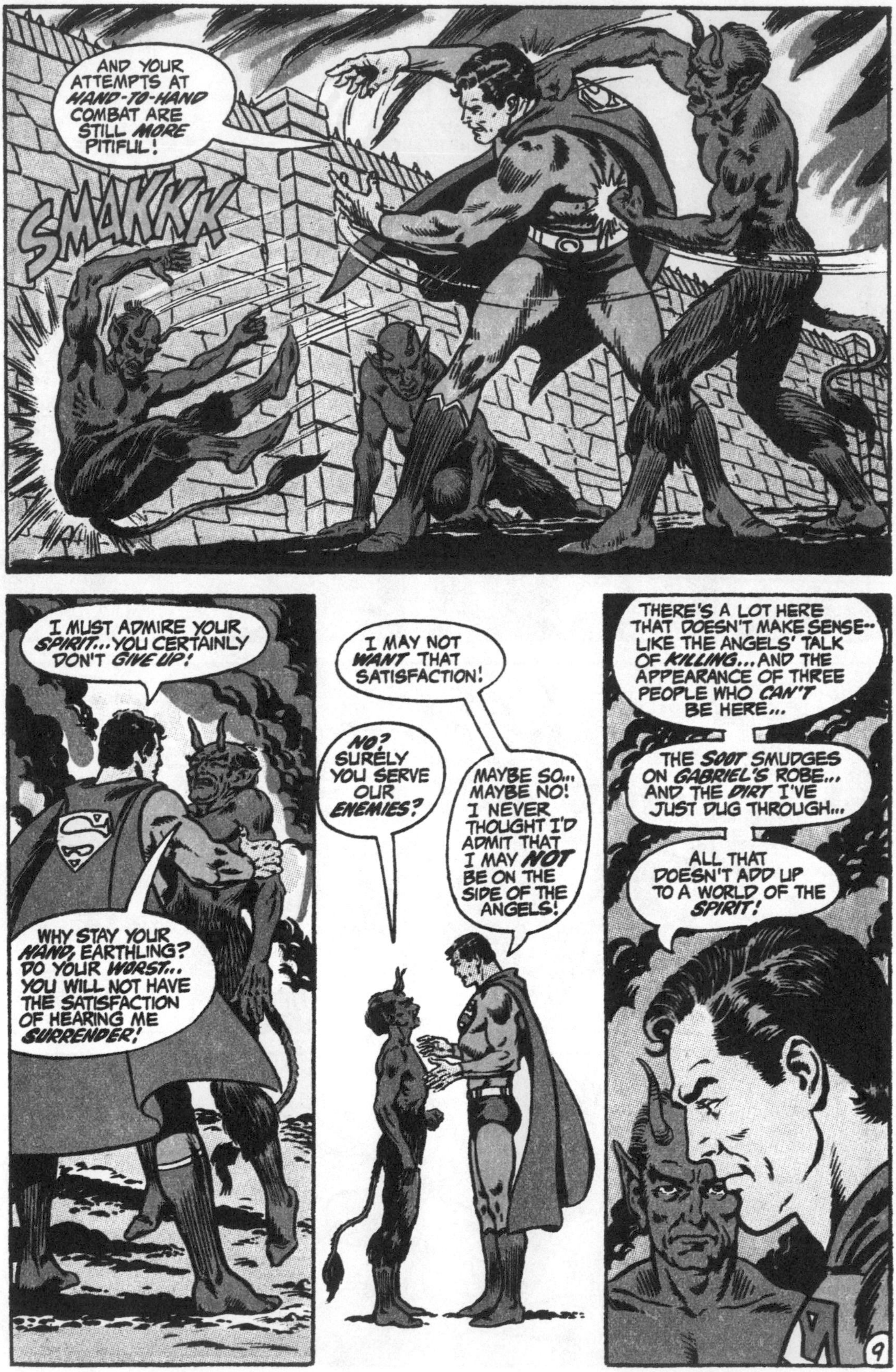
AND YOUR ATTEMPTS AT HAND-TO-HAND COMBAT ARE STILL MORE PITIFUL!
SMAKKK
I MUST ADMIRE YOUR SPIRIT... YOU CERTAINLY DON'T GIVE UP!
WHY STAY YOUR HAND, EARTHLING? DO YOUR WORST... YOU WILL NOT HAVE THE SATISFACTION OF HEARING ME SURRENDER!
I MAY NOT WANT THAT SATISFACTION!
NO? SURELY YOU SERVE OUR ENEMIES?
MAYBE SO... MAYBE NO! I NEVER THOUGHT I'D ADMIT THAT I MAY NOT BE ON THE SIDE OF THE ANGELS!
THERE'S A LOT HERE THAT DOESN'T MAKE SENSE-- LIKE THE ANGELS' TALK OF KILLING... AND THE APPEARANCE OF THREE PEOPLE WHO CAN'T BE HERE...
THE SOOT SMUDGES ON GABRIEL'S ROBE... AND THE DIRT I'VE JUST DUG THROUGH...
ALL THAT DOESN'T ADD UP TO A WORLD OF THE SPIRIT!
9

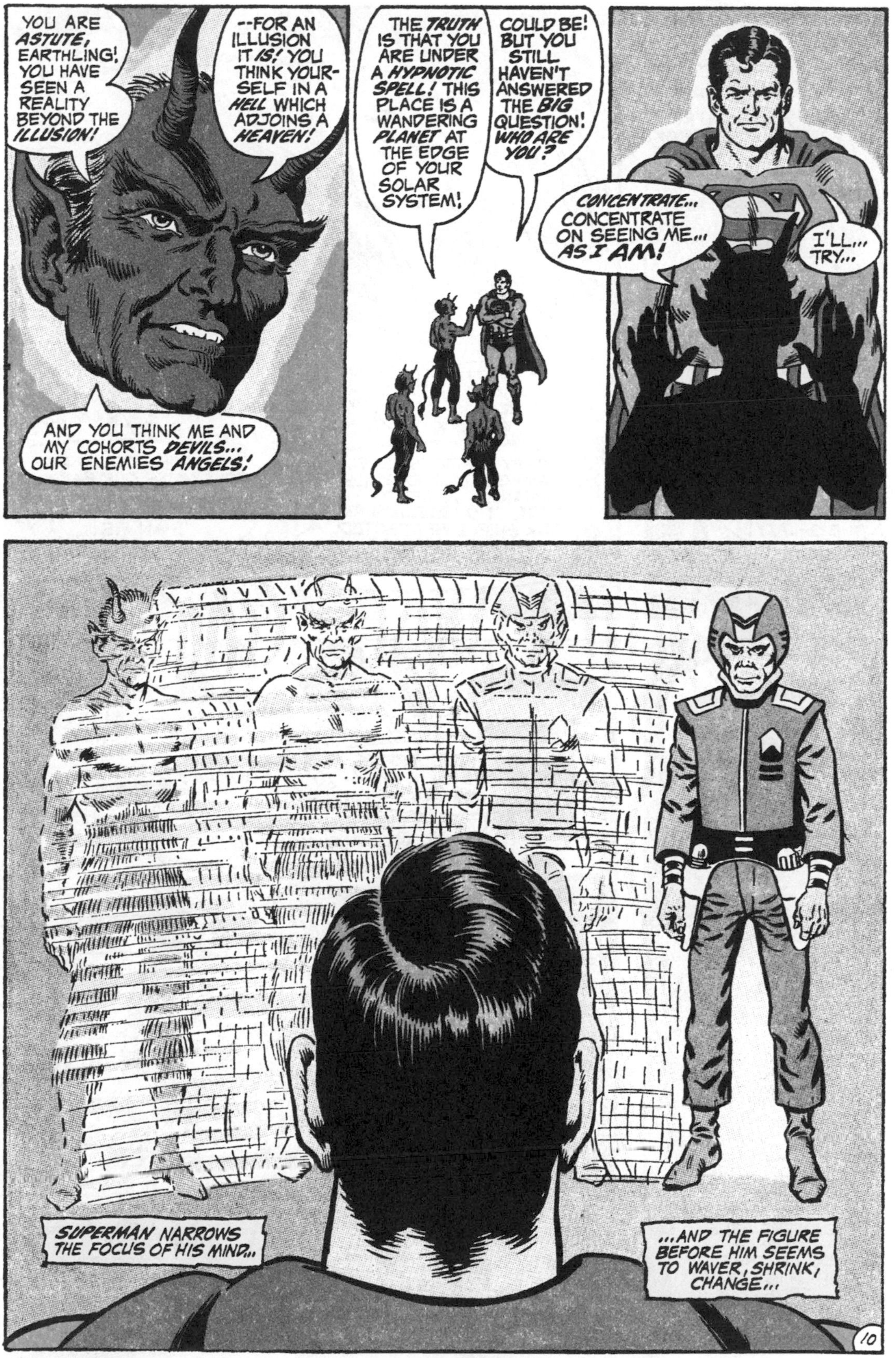
YOU ARE ASTUTE, EARTHLING! YOU HAVE SEEN A REALITY BEYOND THE ILLUSION!
--FOR AN ILLUSION IT IS! YOU THINK YOURSELF IN A HELL WHICH ADJOINS A HEAVEN!
AND YOU THINK ME AND MY COHORTS DEVILS... OUR ENEMIES ANGELS!
THE TRUTH IS THAT YOU ARE UNDER A HYPNOTIC SPELL! THIS PLACE IS A WANDERING PLANET AT THE EDGE OF YOUR SOLAR SYSTEM!
COULD BE! BUT YOU STILL HAVEN'T ANSWERED THE BIG QUESTION! WHO ARE YOU?
CONCENTRATE... CONCENTRATE ON SEEING ME... AS I AM!
I'LL... TRY...
SUPERMAN NARROWS THE FOCUS OF HIS MIND...
...AND THE FIGURE BEFORE HIM SEEMS TO WAVER, SHRINK, CHANGE...
10

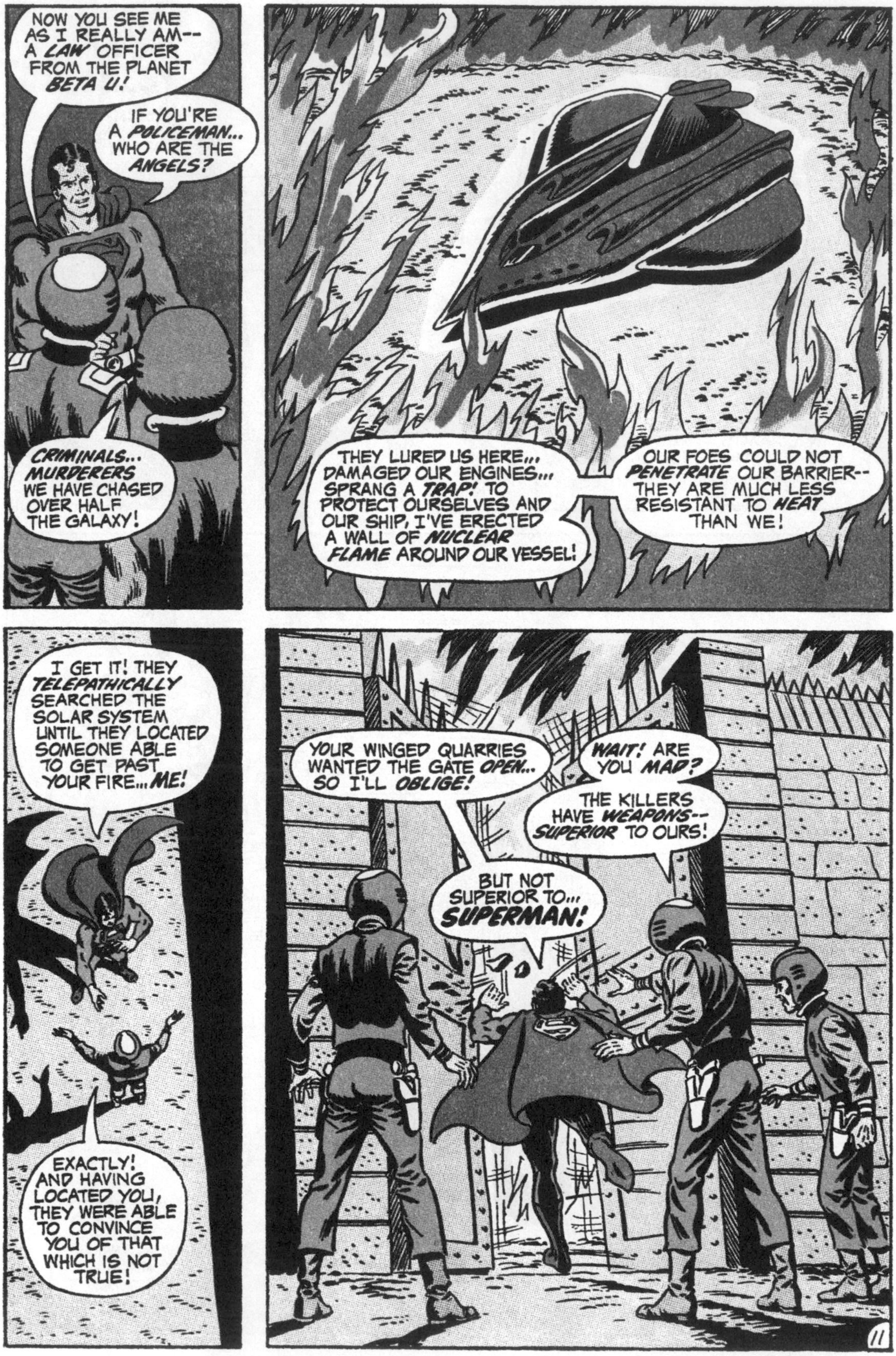

NOW YOU SEE ME AS I REALLY AM-- A LAW OFFICER FROM THE PLANET BETA U!
IF YOU'RE A POLICEMAN... WHO ARE THE ANGELS?
CRIMINALS... MURDERERS WE HAVE CHASED OVER HALF THE GALAXY!
THEY LURED US HERE... DAMAGED OUR ENGINES... SPRANG A TRAP! TO PROTECT OURSELVES AND OUR SHIP, I'VE ERECTED A WALL OF NUCLEAR FLAME AROUND OUR VESSEL!
OUR FOES COULD NOT PENETRATE OUR BARRIER-- THEY ARE MUCH LESS RESISTANT TO HEAT THAN WE!
I GET IT! THEY TELEPATHICALLY SEARCHED THE SOLAR SYSTEM UNTIL THEY LOCATED SOMEONE ABLE TO GET PAST YOUR FIRE...ME!
EXACTLY! AND HAVING LOCATED YOU, THEY WERE ABLE TO CONVINCE YOU OF THAT WHICH IS NOT TRUE!
YOUR WINGED QUARRIES WANTED THE GATE OPEN... SO I'LL OBLIGE!
WAIT! ARE YOU MAD?
THE KILLERS HAVE WEAPONS-- SUPERIOR TO OURS!
BUT NOT SUPERIOR TO... SUPERMAN!
11

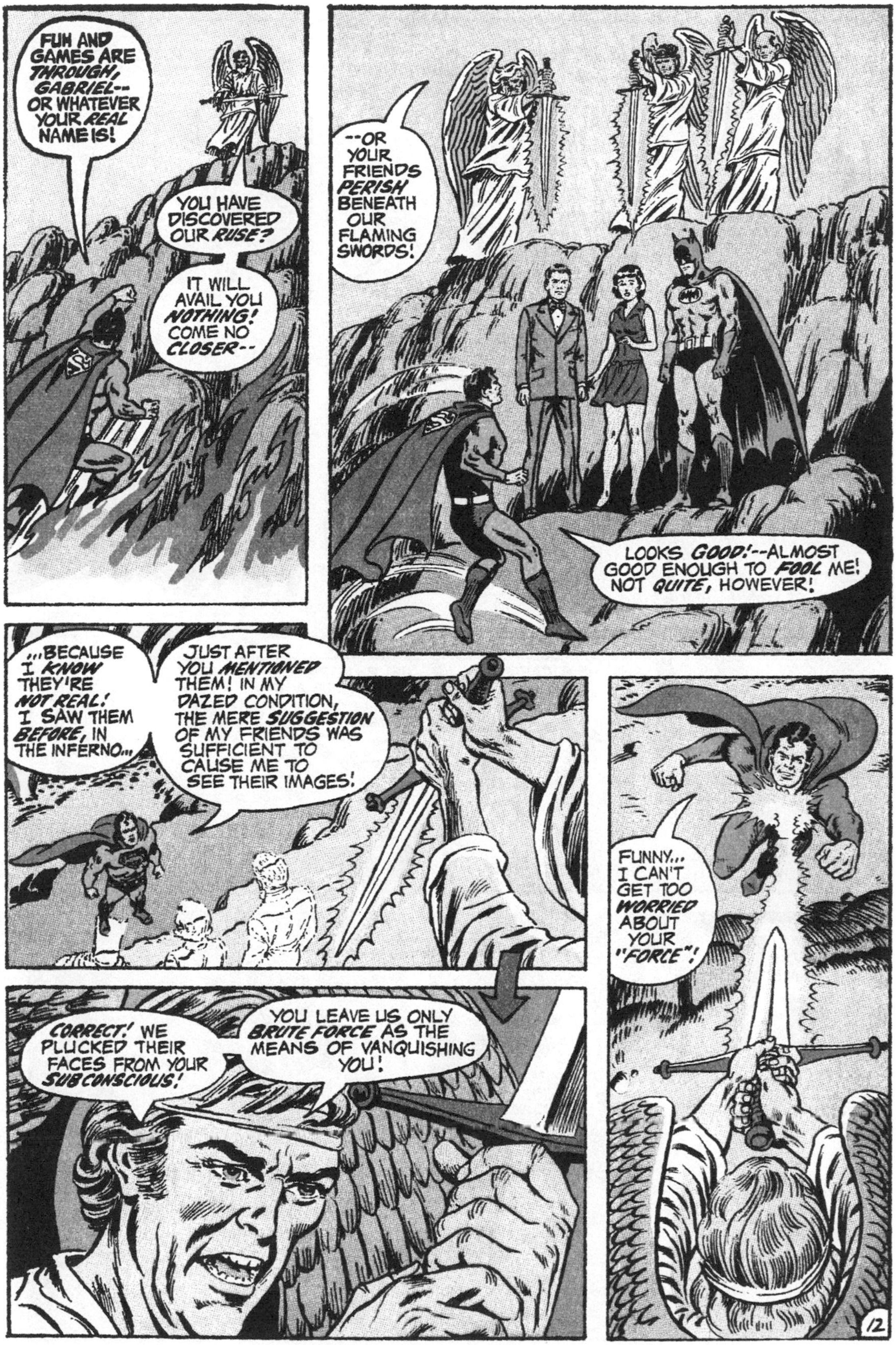
FUN AND GAMES ARE THROUGH, GABRIEL-- OR WHATEVER YOUR REAL NAME IS!
YOU HAVE DISCOVERED OUR RUSE?
IT WILL AVAIL YOU NOTHING! COME NO CLOSER--
--OR YOUR FRIENDS PERISH BENEATH OUR FLAMING SWORDS!
LOOKS GOOD!--ALMOST GOOD ENOUGH TO FOOL ME! NOT QUITE, HOWEVER!
...BECAUSE I KNOW THEY'RE NOT REAL! I SAW THEM BEFORE, IN THE INFERNO...
JUST AFTER YOU MENTIONED THEM! IN MY DAZED CONDITION, THE MERE SUGGESTION OF MY FRIENDS WAS SUFFICIENT TO CAUSE ME TO SEE THEIR IMAGES!
CORRECT! WE PLUCKED THEIR FACES FROM YOUR SUBCONSCIOUS!
YOU LEAVE US ONLY BRUTE FORCE AS THE MEANS OF VANQUISHING YOU!
FUNNY... I CAN'T GET TOO WORRIED ABOUT YOUR "FORCE"!
12

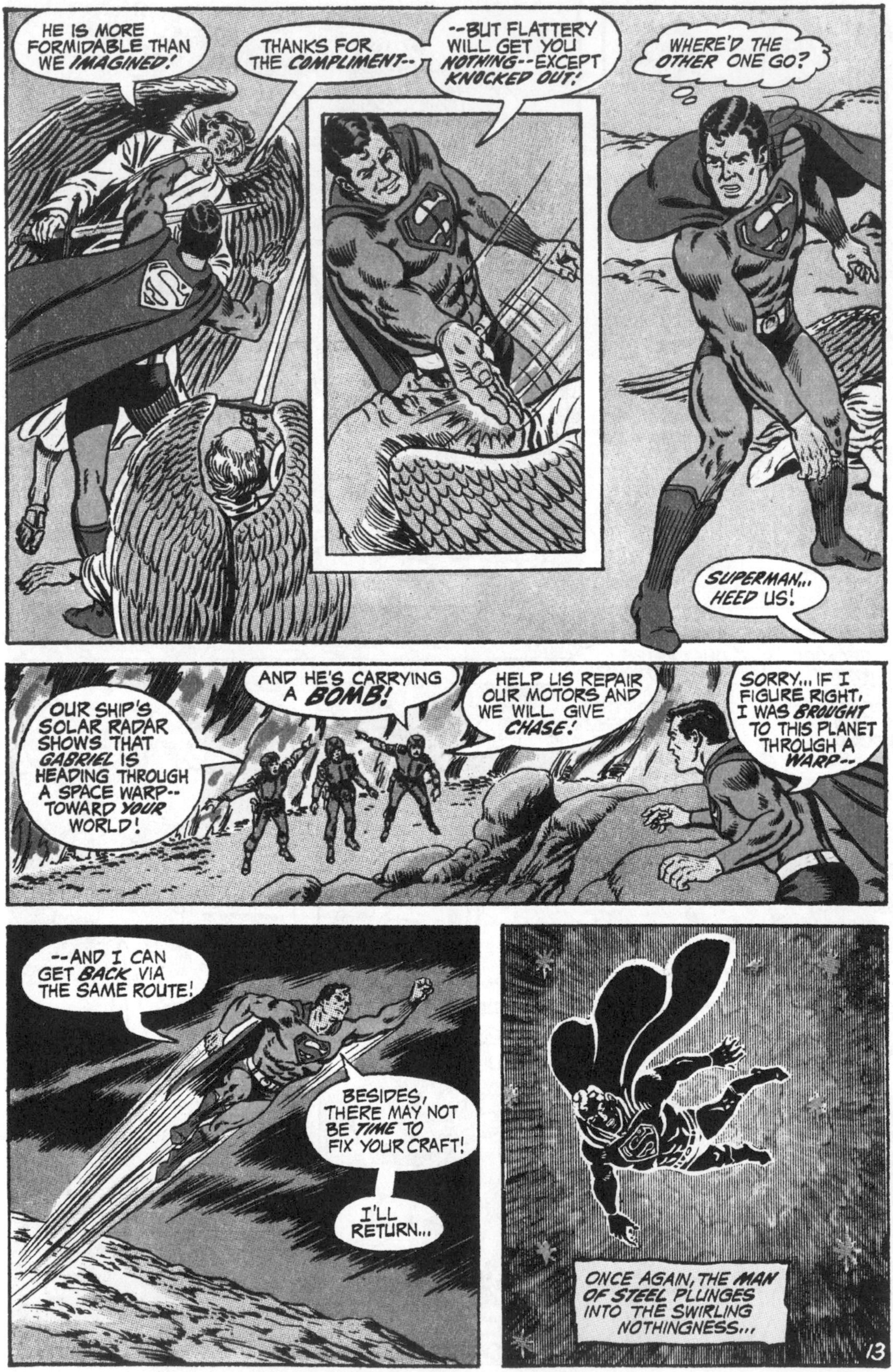
HE IS MORE FORMIDABLE THAN WE IMAGINED!
THANKS FOR THE COMPLIMENT--
--BUT FLATTERY WILL GET YOU NOTHING--EXCEPT KNOCKED OUT!
WHERE'D THE OTHER ONE GO?
SUPERMAN... HEED US!
OUR SHIP'S SOLAR RADAR SHOWS THAT GABRIEL IS HEADING THROUGH A SPACE WARP--TOWARD YOUR WORLD!
AND HE'S CARRYING A BOMB!
HELP US REPAIR OUR MOTORS AND WE WILL GIVE CHASE!
SORRY... IF I FIGURE RIGHT, I WAS BROUGHT TO THIS PLANET THROUGH A WARP--
--AND I CAN GET BACK VIA THE SAME ROUTE!
BESIDES, THERE MAY NOT BE TIME TO FIX YOUR CRAFT!
I'LL RETURN...
ONCE AGAIN, THE MAN OF STEEL PLUNGES INTO THE SWIRLING NOTHINGNESS...
13

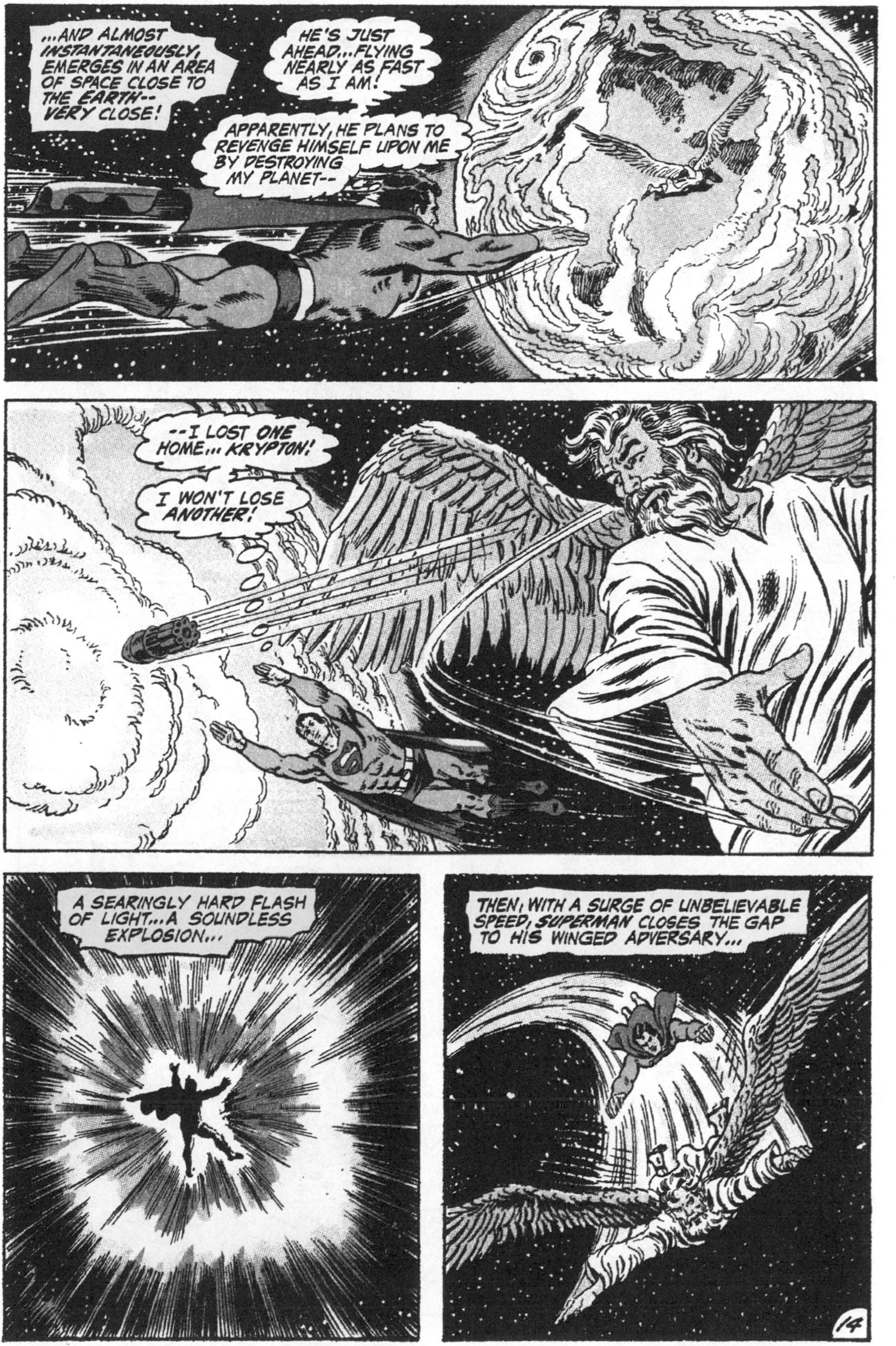
...AND ALMOST INSTANTANEOUSLY, EMERGES IN AN AREA OF SPACE CLOSE TO THE EARTH-- VERY CLOSE!
HE'S JUST AHEAD...FLYING NEARLY AS FAST AS I AM!
APPARENTLY, HE PLANS TO REVENGE HIMSELF UPON ME BY DESTROYING MY PLANET--
--I LOST ONE HOME... KRYPTON!
I WON'T LOSE ANOTHER!
A SEARINGLY HARD FLASH OF LIGHT...A SOUNDLESS EXPLOSION...
THEN, WITH A SURGE OF UNBELIEVABLE SPEED, SUPERMAN CLOSES THE GAP TO HIS WINGED ADVERSARY...
14

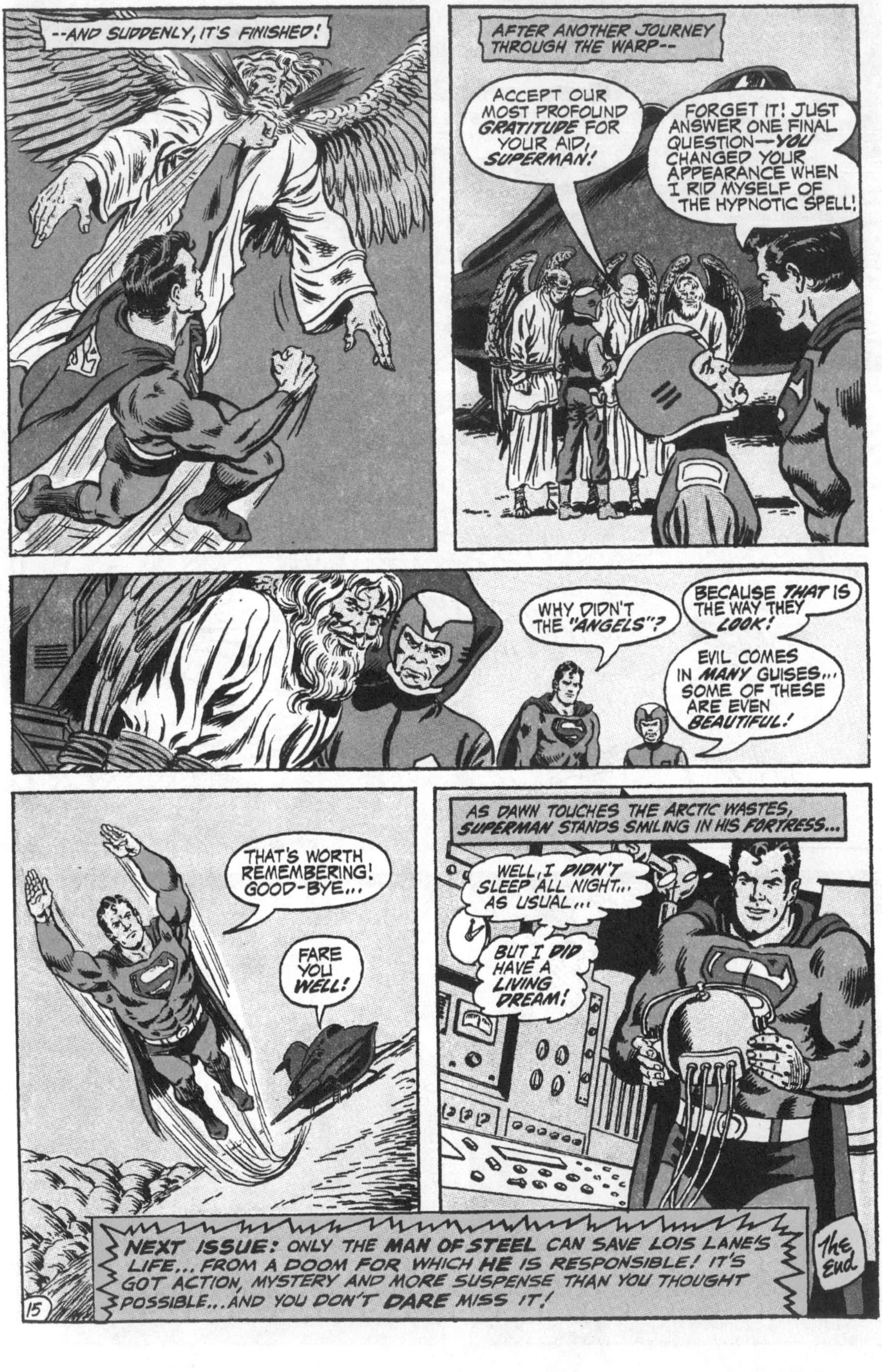
--AND SUDDENLY, IT'S FINISHED!
AFTER ANOTHER JOURNEY THROUGH THE WARP--
ACCEPT OUR MOST PROFOUND GRATITUDE FOR YOUR AID, SUPERMAN!
FORGET IT! JUST ANSWER ONE FINAL QUESTION--YOU CHANGED YOUR APPEARANCE WHEN I RID MYSELF OF THE HYPNOTIC SPELL!
WHY DIDN'T THE "ANGELS"?
BECAUSE THAT IS THE WAY THEY LOOK!
EVIL COMES IN MANY GUISES... SOME OF THESE ARE EVEN BEAUTIFUL!
THAT'S WORTH REMEMBERING! GOOD-BYE...
FARE YOU WELL!
AS DAWN TOUCHES THE ARCTIC WASTES, SUPERMAN STANDS SMILING IN HIS FORTRESS...
WELL, I DIDN'T SLEEP ALL NIGHT... AS USUAL...
BUT I DID HAVE A LIVING DREAM!
NEXT ISSUE: ONLY THE MAN OF STEEL CAN SAVE LOIS LANE'S LIFE... FROM A DOOM FOR WHICH HE IS RESPONSIBLE! IT'S GOT ACTION, MYSTERY AND MORE SUSPENSE THAN YOU THOUGHT POSSIBLE... AND YOU DON'T DARE MISS IT!
The End
15

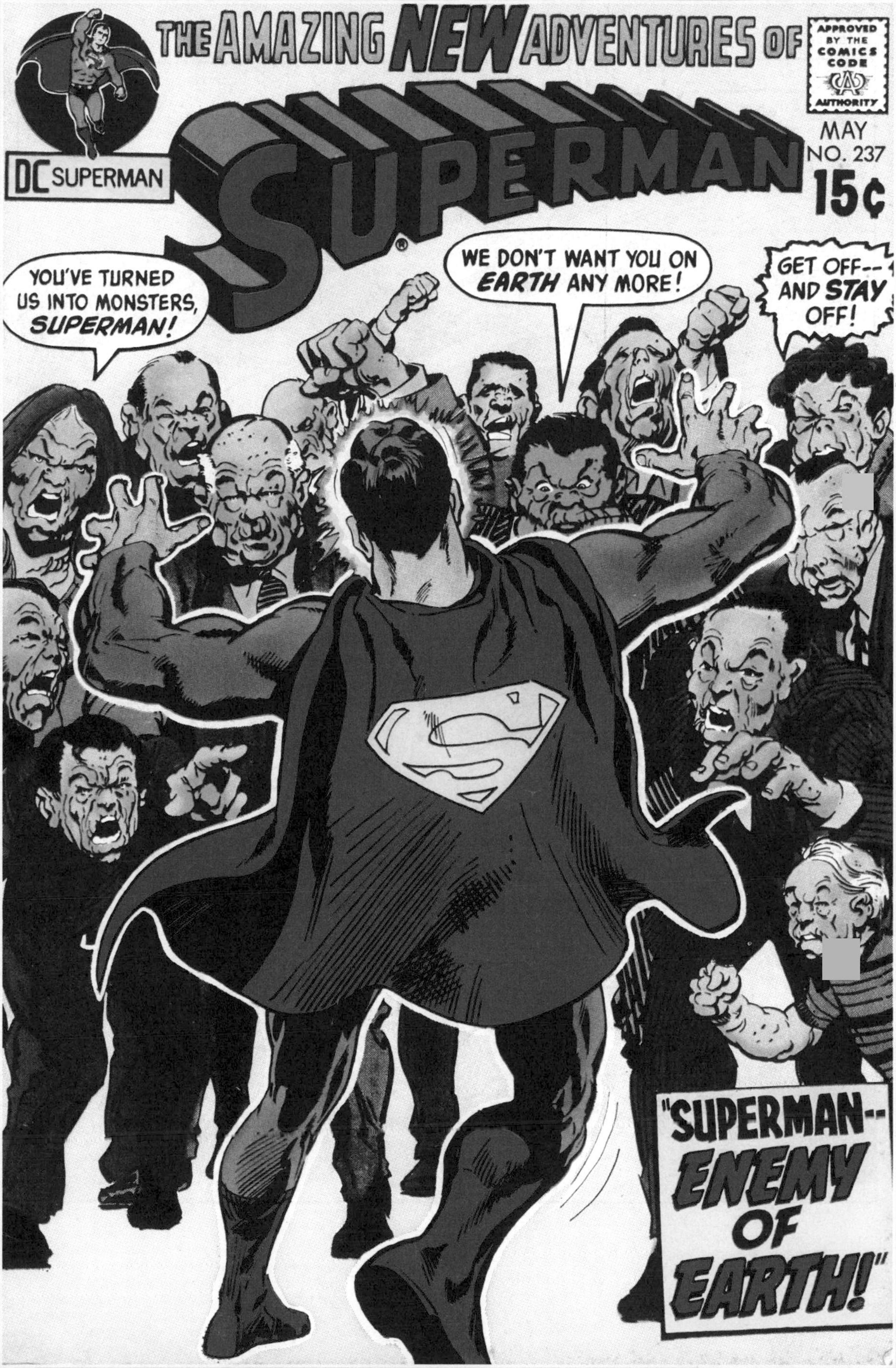
THE AMAZING NEW ADVENTURES OF
SUPERMAN
DC SUPERMAN
APPROVED BY THE COMICS CODE AUTHORITY
MAY
NO. 237
15¢
YOU'VE TURNED US INTO MONSTERS, SUPERMAN!
WE DON'T WANT YOU ON EARTH ANY MORE!
GET OFF-- AND STAY OFF!
"SUPERMAN-- ENEMY OF EARTH!"

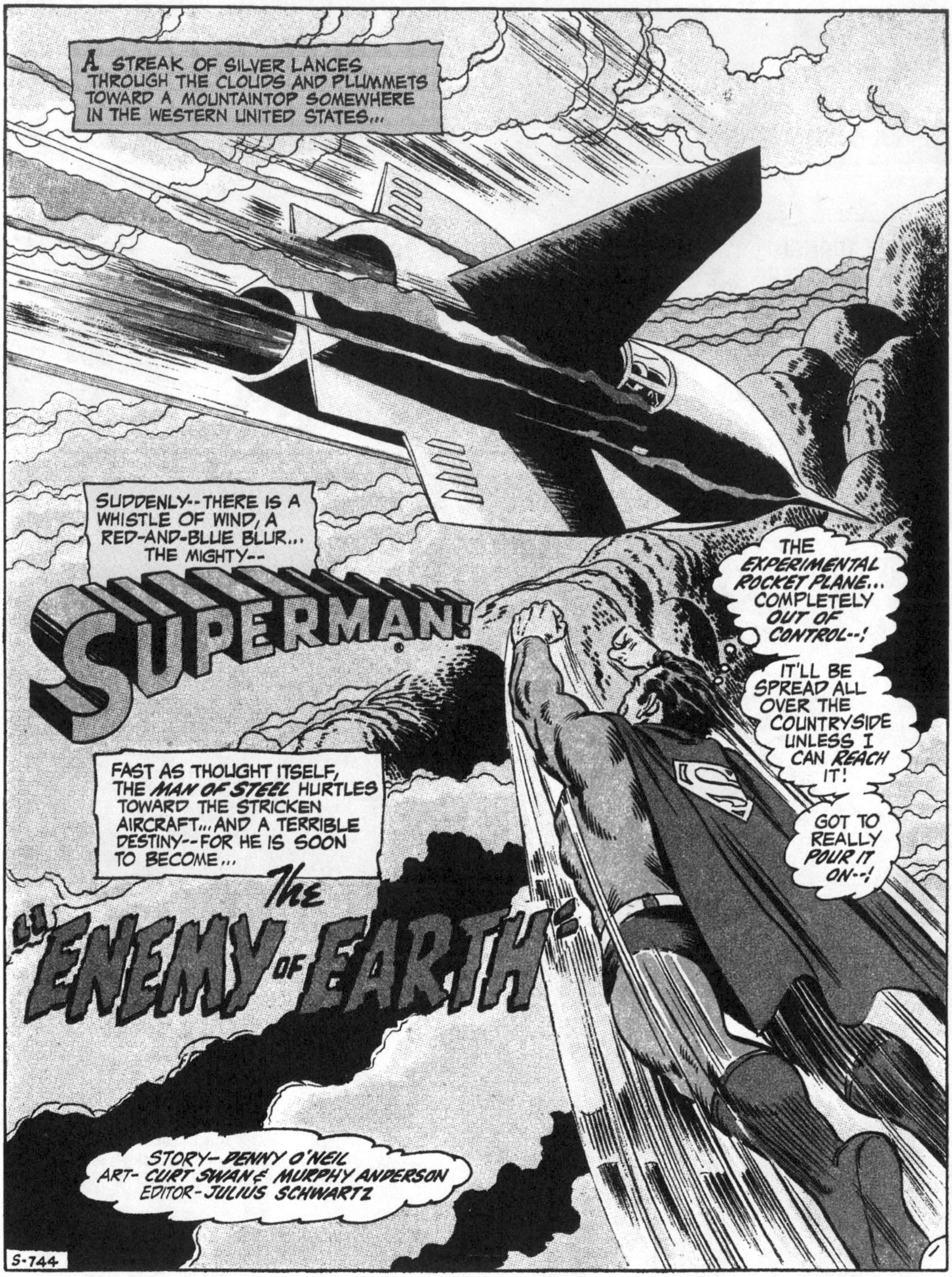
A STREAK OF SILVER LANCES THROUGH THE CLOUDS AND PLUMMETS TOWARD A MOUNTAINTOP SOMEWHERE IN THE WESTERN UNITED STATES...
SUDDENLY--THERE IS A WHISTLE OF WIND, A RED-AND-BLUE BLUR... THE MIGHTY--
SUPERMAN!
THE EXPERIMENTAL ROCKET PLANE... COMPLETELY OUT OF CONTROL--!
IT'LL BE SPREAD ALL OVER THE COUNTRYSIDE UNLESS I CAN REACH IT!
GOT TO REALLY POUR IT ON--!
FAST AS THOUGHT ITSELF, THE MAN OF STEEL HURTLES TOWARD THE STRICKEN AIRCRAFT... AND A TERRIBLE DESTINY--FOR HE IS SOON TO BECOME...
The "ENEMY of EARTH"
STORY-DENNY O'NEIL
ART-CURT SWAN & MURPHY ANDERSON
EDITOR-JULIUS SCHWARTZ
S-744
1

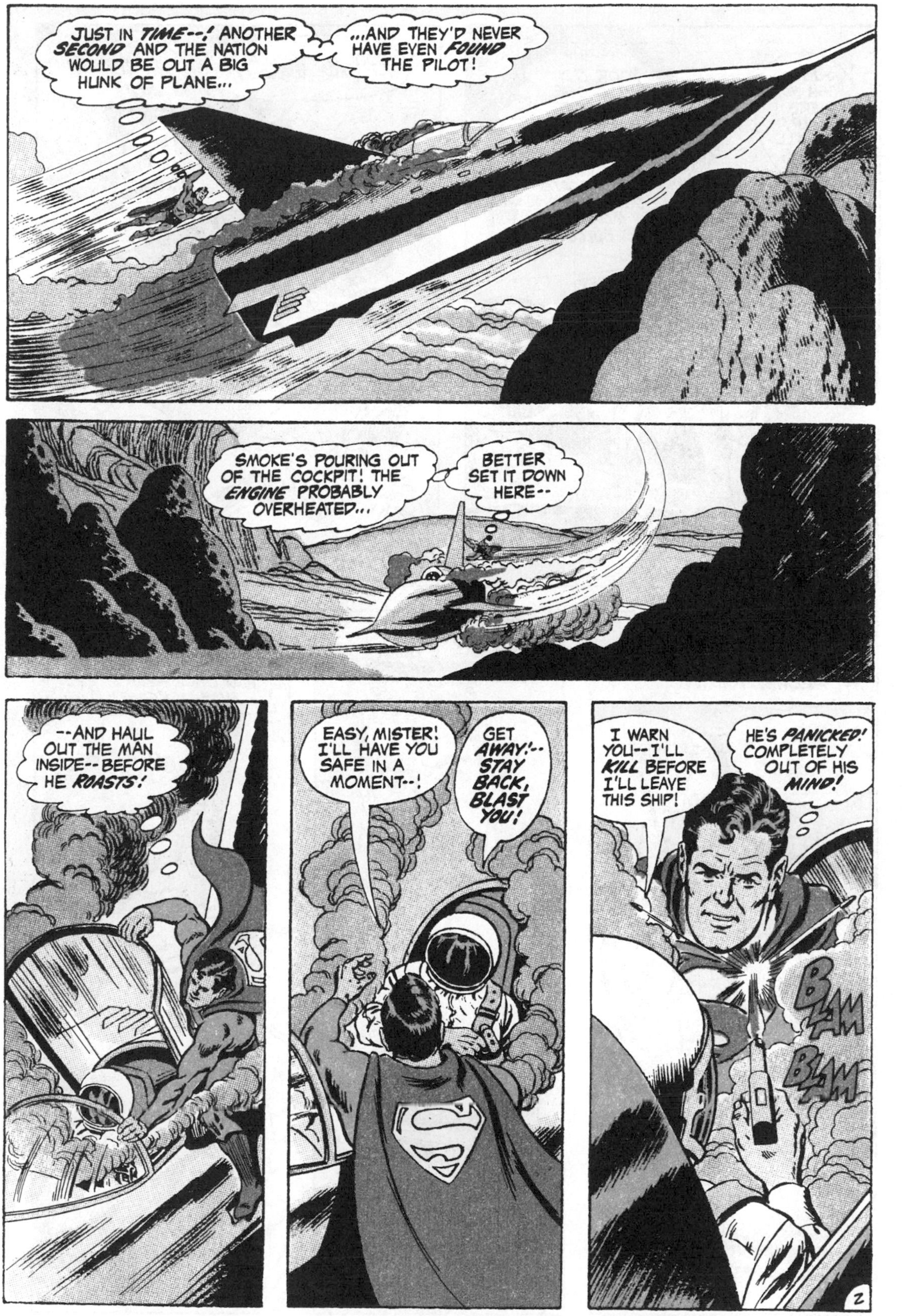
JUST IN TIME--! ANOTHER SECOND AND THE NATION WOULD BE OUT A BIG HUNK OF PLANE...
...AND THEY'D NEVER HAVE EVEN FOUND THE PILOT!
SMOKE'S POURING OUT OF THE COCKPIT! THE ENGINE PROBABLY OVERHEATED...
BETTER SET IT DOWN HERE--
--AND HAUL OUT THE MAN INSIDE--BEFORE HE ROASTS!
EASY, MISTER! I'LL HAVE YOU SAFE IN A MOMENT--!
GET AWAY!--STAY BACK, BLAST YOU!
I WARN YOU--I'LL KILL BEFORE I'LL LEAVE THIS SHIP!
HE'S PANICKED! COMPLETELY OUT OF HIS MIND!
BLAM
BLAM
2

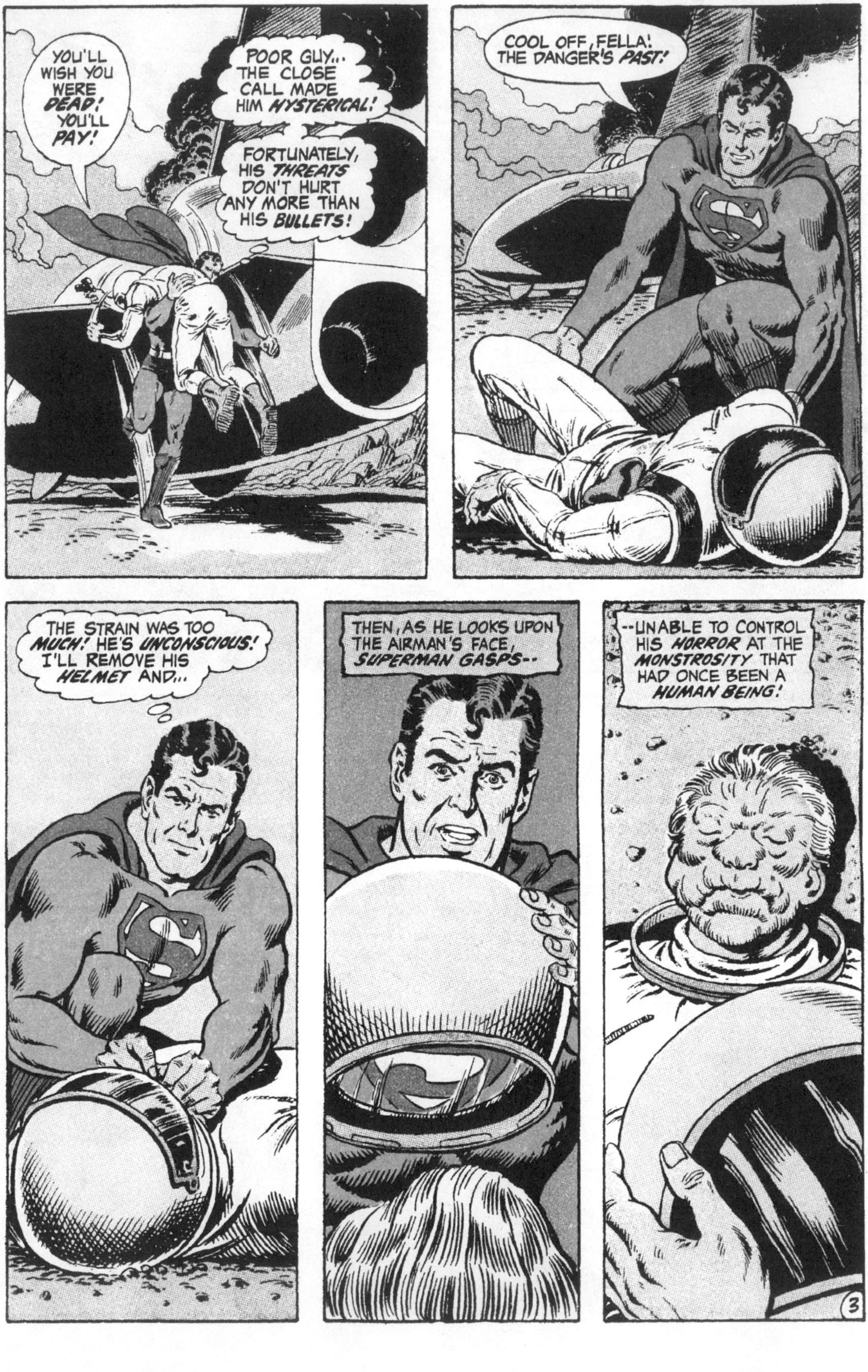
YOU'LL WISH YOU WERE DEAD! YOU'LL PAY!
POOR GUY... THE CLOSE CALL MADE HIM HYSTERICAL!
FORTUNATELY, HIS THREATS DON'T HURT ANY MORE THAN HIS BULLETS!
COOL OFF, FELLA! THE DANGER'S PAST!
THE STRAIN WAS TOO MUCH! HE'S UNCONSCIOUS! I'LL REMOVE HIS HELMET AND...
THEN, AS HE LOOKS UPON THE AIRMAN'S FACE, SUPERMAN GASPS--
--UNABLE TO CONTROL HIS HORROR AT THE MONSTROSITY THAT HAD ONCE BEEN A HUMAN BEING!
3

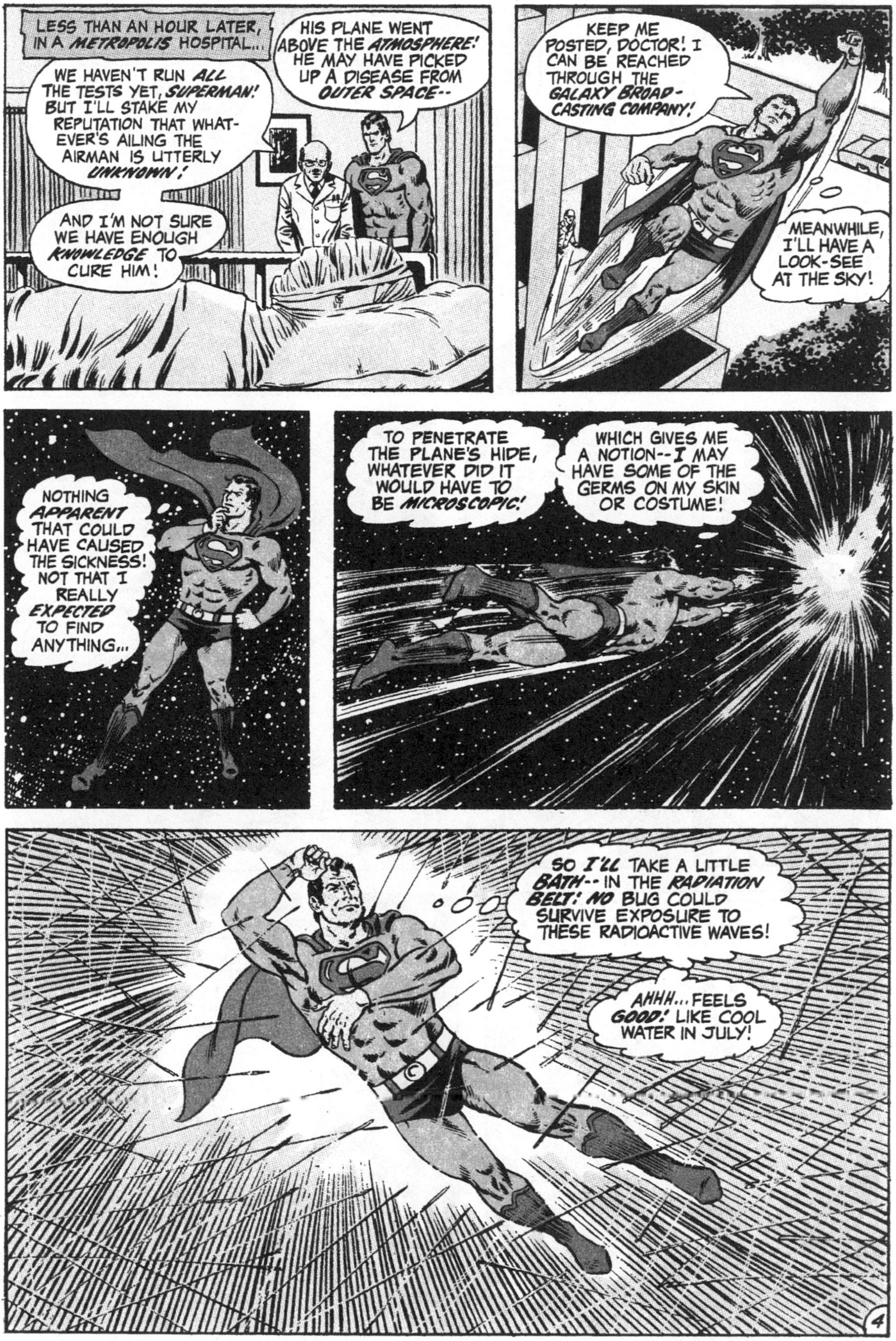
LESS THAN AN HOUR LATER, IN A METROPOLIS HOSPITAL...
HIS PLANE WENT ABOVE THE ATMOSPHERE! HE MAY HAVE PICKED UP A DISEASE FROM OUTER SPACE--
WE HAVEN'T RUN ALL THE TESTS YET, SUPERMAN! BUT I'LL STAKE MY REPUTATION THAT WHATEVER'S AILING THE AIRMAN IS UTTERLY UNKNOWN!
AND I'M NOT SURE WE HAVE ENOUGH KNOWLEDGE TO CURE HIM!
KEEP ME POSTED, DOCTOR! I CAN BE REACHED THROUGH THE GALAXY BROADCASTING COMPANY!
MEANWHILE, I'LL HAVE A LOOK-SEE AT THE SKY!
NOTHING APPARENT THAT COULD HAVE CAUSED THE SICKNESS! NOT THAT I REALLY EXPECTED TO FIND ANYTHING...
TO PENETRATE THE PLANE'S HIDE, WHATEVER DID IT WOULD HAVE TO BE MICROSCOPIC!
WHICH GIVES ME A NOTION--I MAY HAVE SOME OF THE GERMS ON MY SKIN OR COSTUME!
SO I'LL TAKE A LITTLE BATH--IN THE RADIATION BELT! NO BUG COULD SURVIVE EXPOSURE TO THESE RADIOACTIVE WAVES!
AHHH... FEELS GOOD! LIKE COOL WATER IN JULY!
4

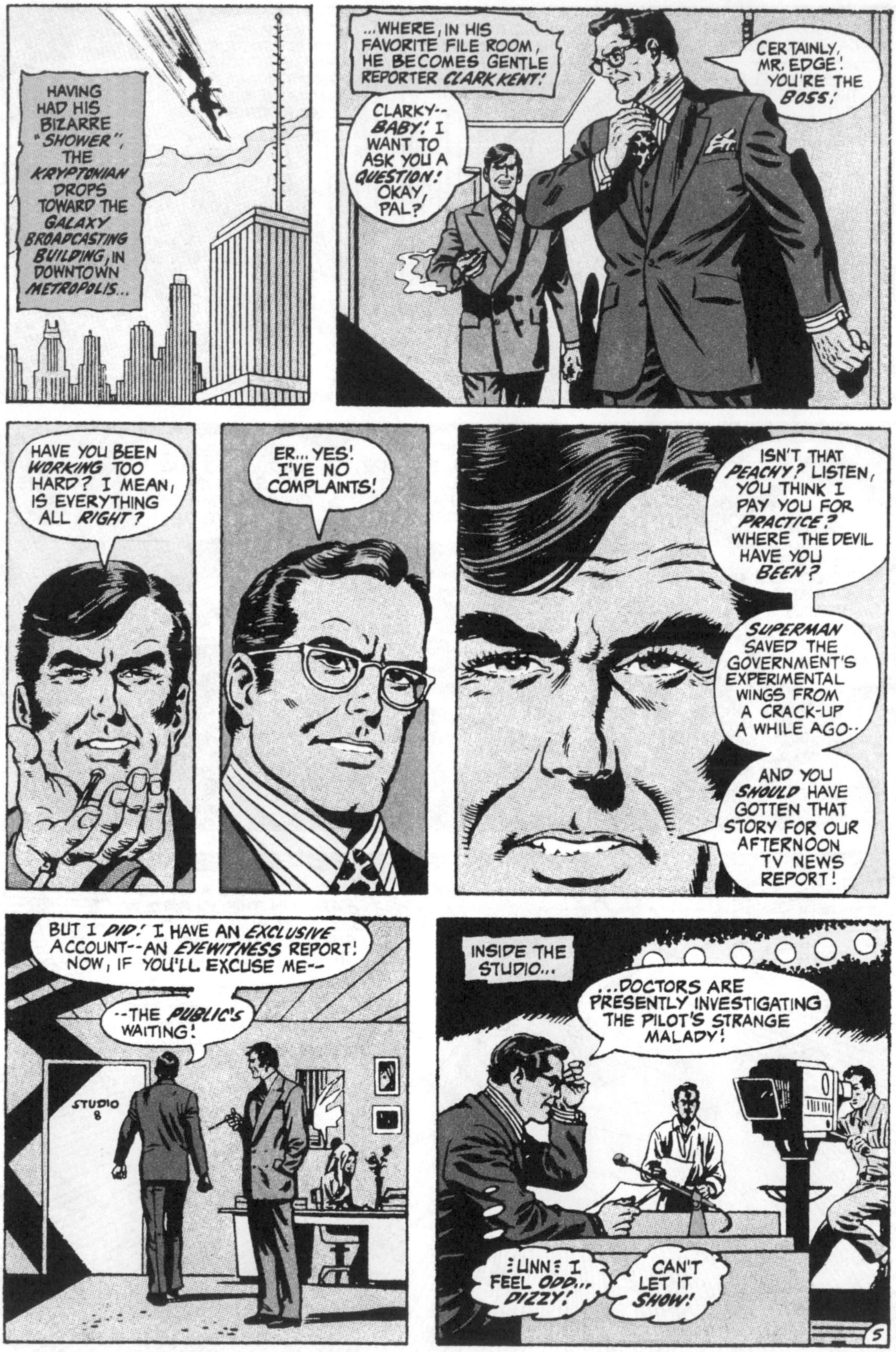
HAVING HAD HIS BIZARRE "SHOWER", THE KRYPTONIAN DROPS TOWARD THE GALAXY BROADCASTING BUILDING, IN DOWNTOWN METROPOLIS...
...WHERE, IN HIS FAVORITE FILE ROOM, HE BECOMES GENTLE REPORTER CLARK KENT!
CLARKY--BABY! I WANT TO ASK YOU A QUESTION! OKAY, PAL?
CERTAINLY, MR. EDGE! YOU'RE THE BOSS!
HAVE YOU BEEN WORKING TOO HARD? I MEAN, IS EVERYTHING ALL RIGHT?
ER... YES! I'VE NO COMPLAINTS!
ISN'T THAT PEACHY? LISTEN, YOU THINK I PAY YOU FOR PRACTICE? WHERE THE DEVIL HAVE YOU BEEN?
SUPERMAN SAVED THE GOVERNMENT'S EXPERIMENTAL WINGS FROM A CRACK-UP A WHILE AGO--
AND YOU SHOULD HAVE GOTTEN THAT STORY FOR OUR AFTERNOON TV NEWS REPORT!
BUT I DID! I HAVE AN EXCLUSIVE ACCOUNT--AN EYEWITNESS REPORT! NOW, IF YOU'LL EXCUSE ME--
--THE PUBLIC'S WAITING!
STUDIO 8
INSIDE THE STUDIO...
...DOCTORS ARE PRESENTLY INVESTIGATING THE PILOT'S STRANGE MALADY!
UNN! I FEEL ODD... DIZZY!
CAN'T LET IT SHOW!
5

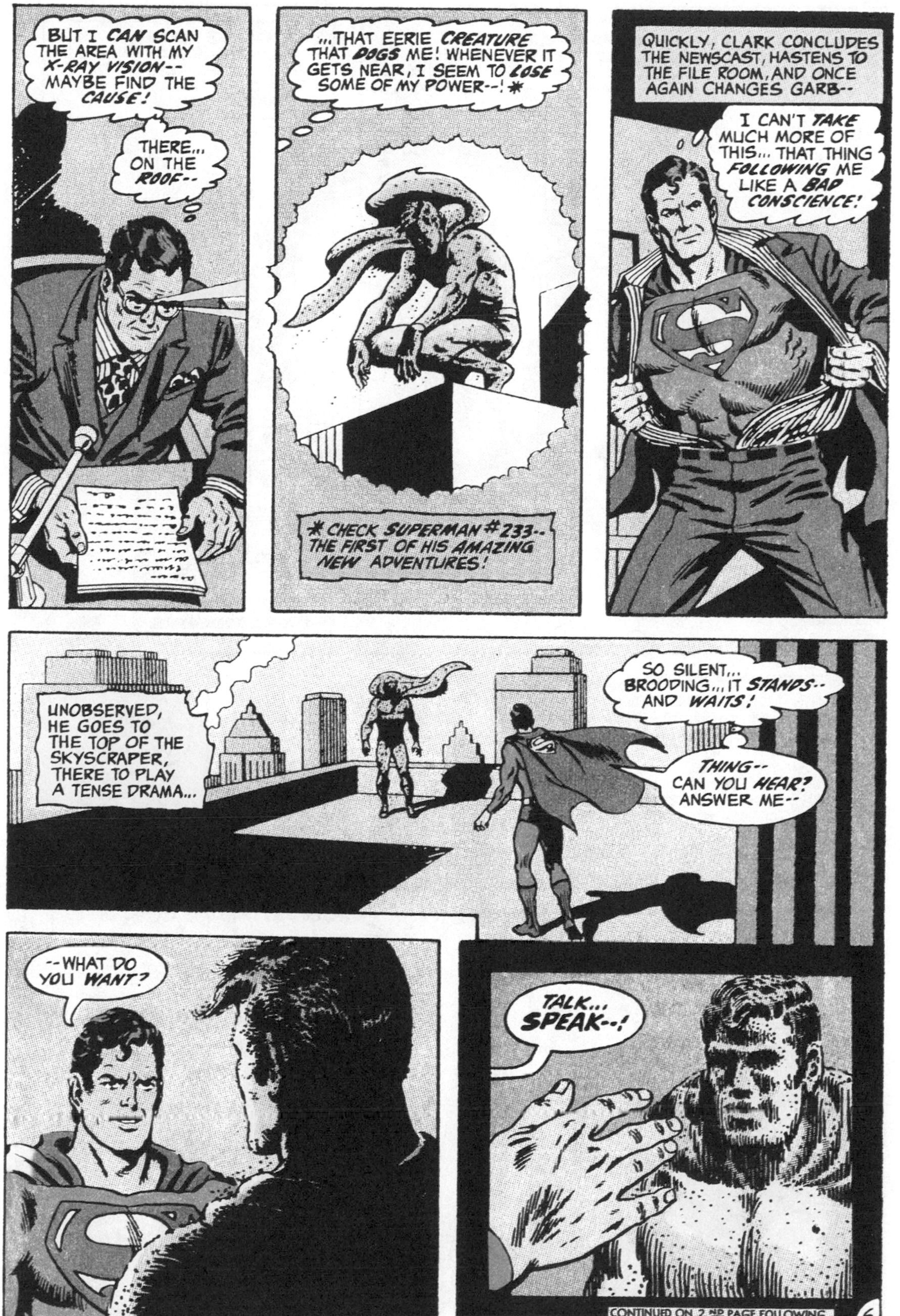

BUT I CAN SCAN THE AREA WITH MY X-RAY VISION-- MAYBE FIND THE CAUSE!
THERE... ON THE ROOF--
...THAT EERIE CREATURE THAT DOGS ME! WHENEVER IT GETS NEAR, I SEEM TO LOSE SOME OF MY POWER--! *
* CHECK SUPERMAN #233-- THE FIRST OF HIS AMAZING NEW ADVENTURES!
QUICKLY, CLARK CONCLUDES THE NEWSCAST, HASTENS TO THE FILE ROOM, AND ONCE AGAIN CHANGES GARB--
I CAN'T TAKE MUCH MORE OF THIS... THAT THING FOLLOWING ME LIKE A BAD CONSCIENCE!
UNOBSERVED, HE GOES TO THE TOP OF THE SKYSCRAPER, THERE TO PLAY A TENSE DRAMA...
SO SILENT... BROODING... IT STANDS-- AND WAITS!
THING-- CAN YOU HEAR? ANSWER ME--
--WHAT DO YOU WANT?
TALK... SPEAK--!
CONTINUED ON 2ND PAGE FOLLOWING.
6

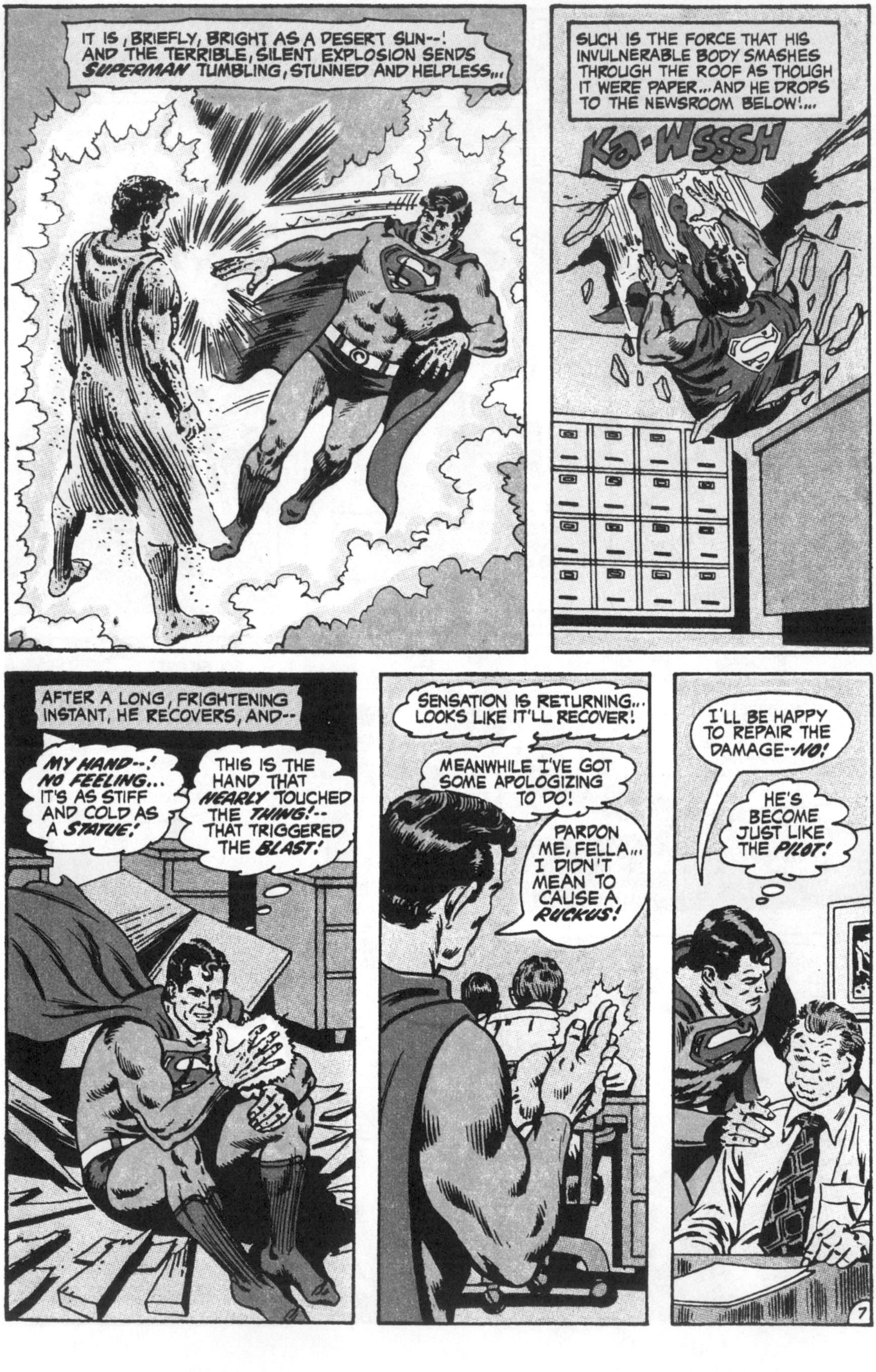
IT IS, BRIEFLY, BRIGHT AS A DESERT SUN--! AND THE TERRIBLE, SILENT EXPLOSION SENDS SUPERMAN TUMBLING, STUNNED AND HELPLESS,..
SUCH IS THE FORCE THAT HIS INVULNERABLE BODY SMASHES THROUGH THE ROOF AS THOUGH IT WERE PAPER...AND HE DROPS TO THE NEWSROOM BELOW!...
KA-WSSSH
AFTER A LONG, FRIGHTENING INSTANT, HE RECOVERS, AND--
MY HAND--! NO FEELING... IT'S AS STIFF AND COLD AS A STATUE!
THIS IS THE HAND THAT NEARLY TOUCHED THE THING!--THAT TRIGGERED THE BLAST!
SENSATION IS RETURNING... LOOKS LIKE IT'LL RECOVER!
MEANWHILE I'VE GOT SOME APOLOGIZING TO DO!
PARDON ME, FELLA... I DIDN'T MEAN TO CAUSE A RUCKUS!
I'LL BE HAPPY TO REPAIR THE DAMAGE--NO!
HE'S BECOME JUST LIKE THE PILOT!
7

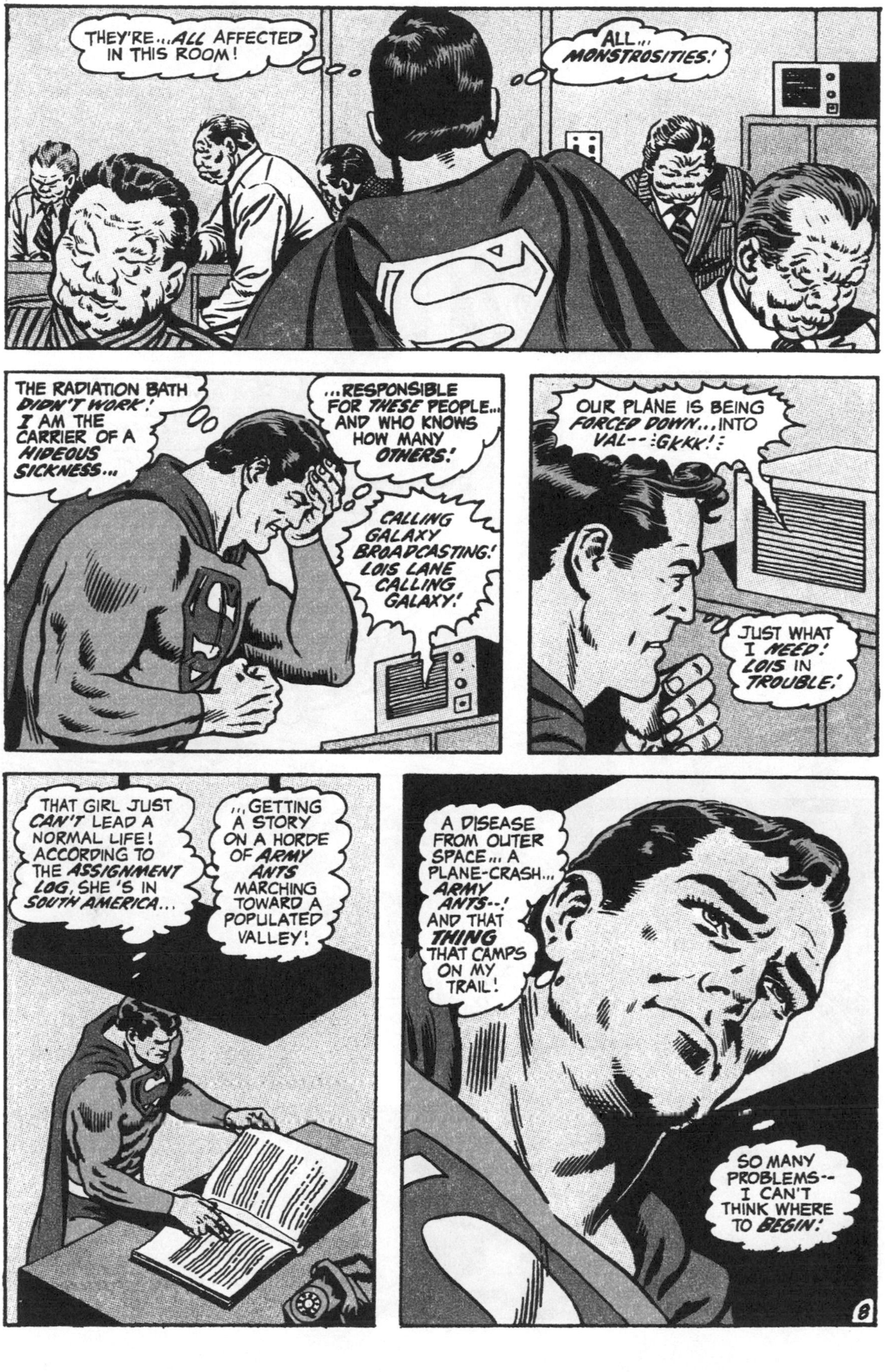
THEY'RE... ALL AFFECTED IN THIS ROOM!
ALL... MONSTROSITIES!
THE RADIATION BATH DIDN'T WORK! I AM THE CARRIER OF A HIDEOUS SICKNESS...
...RESPONSIBLE FOR THESE PEOPLE... AND WHO KNOWS HOW MANY OTHERS!
CALLING GALAXY BROADCASTING! LOIS LANE CALLING GALAXY!
OUR PLANE IS BEING FORCED DOWN... INTO VAL-- GKKK!
JUST WHAT I NEED! LOIS IN TROUBLE!
THAT GIRL JUST CAN'T LEAD A NORMAL LIFE! ACCORDING TO THE ASSIGNMENT LOG, SHE'S IN SOUTH AMERICA...
...GETTING A STORY ON A HORDE OF ARMY ANTS MARCHING TOWARD A POPULATED VALLEY!
A DISEASE FROM OUTER SPACE... A PLANE-CRASH... ARMY ANTS--! AND THAT THING THAT CAMPS ON MY TRAIL!
SO MANY PROBLEMS-- I CAN'T THINK WHERE TO BEGIN!
8

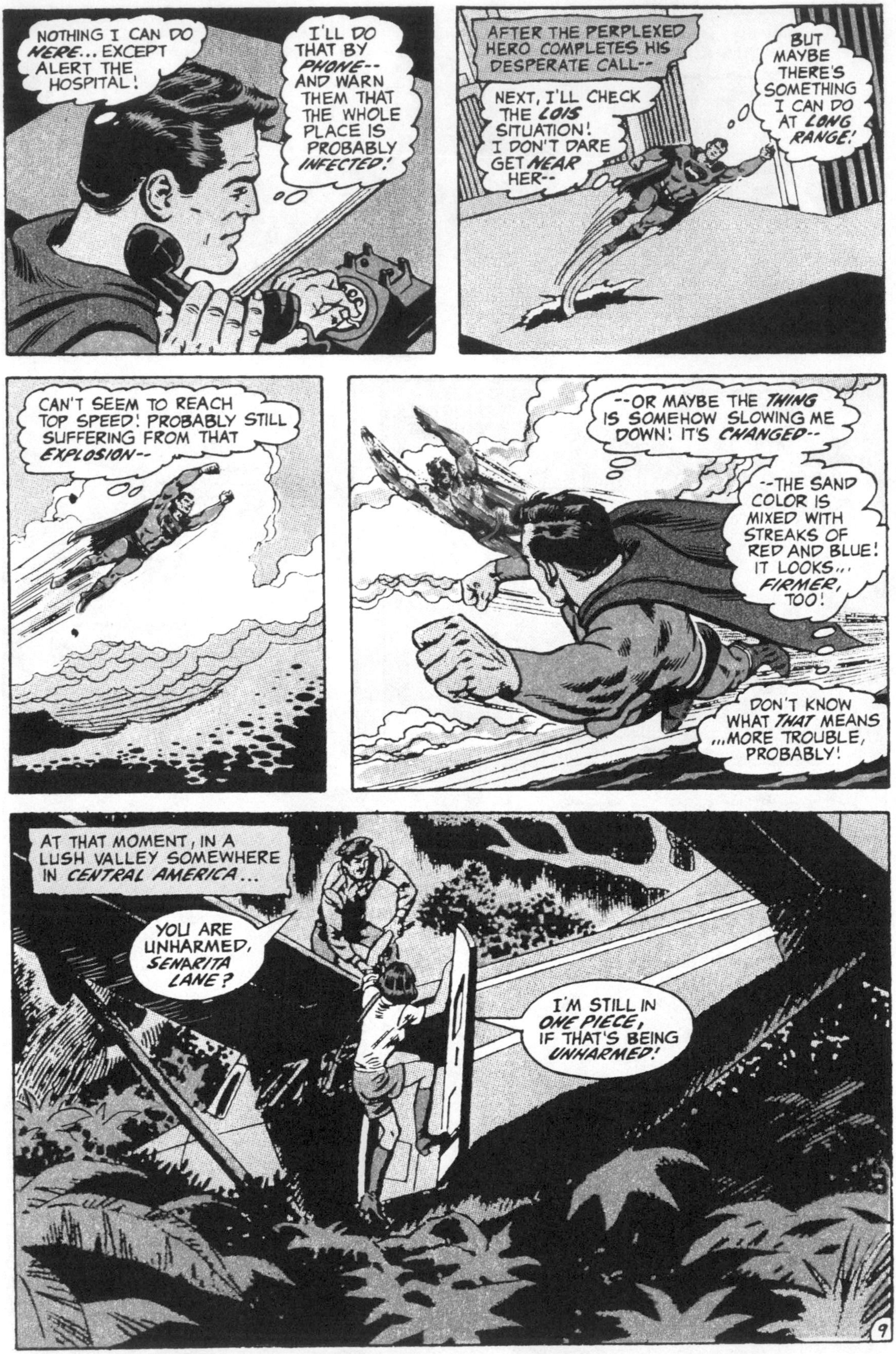
NOTHING I CAN DO HERE... EXCEPT ALERT THE HOSPITAL!
I'LL DO THAT BY PHONE-- AND WARN THEM THAT THE WHOLE PLACE IS PROBABLY INFECTED!
AFTER THE PERPLEXED HERO COMPLETES HIS DESPERATE CALL--
NEXT, I'LL CHECK THE LOIS SITUATION! I DON'T DARE GET NEAR HER--
BUT MAYBE THERE'S SOMETHING I CAN DO AT LONG RANGE!
CAN'T SEEM TO REACH TOP SPEED! PROBABLY STILL SUFFERING FROM THAT EXPLOSION--
--OR MAYBE THE THING IS SOMEHOW SLOWING ME DOWN! IT'S CHANGED--
--THE SAND COLOR IS MIXED WITH STREAKS OF RED AND BLUE! IT LOOKS... FIRMER, TOO!
DON'T KNOW WHAT THAT MEANS ...MORE TROUBLE, PROBABLY!
AT THAT MOMENT, IN A LUSH VALLEY SOMEWHERE IN CENTRAL AMERICA...
YOU ARE UNHARMED, SENARITA LANE?
I'M STILL IN ONE PIECE, IF THAT'S BEING UNHARMED!
9

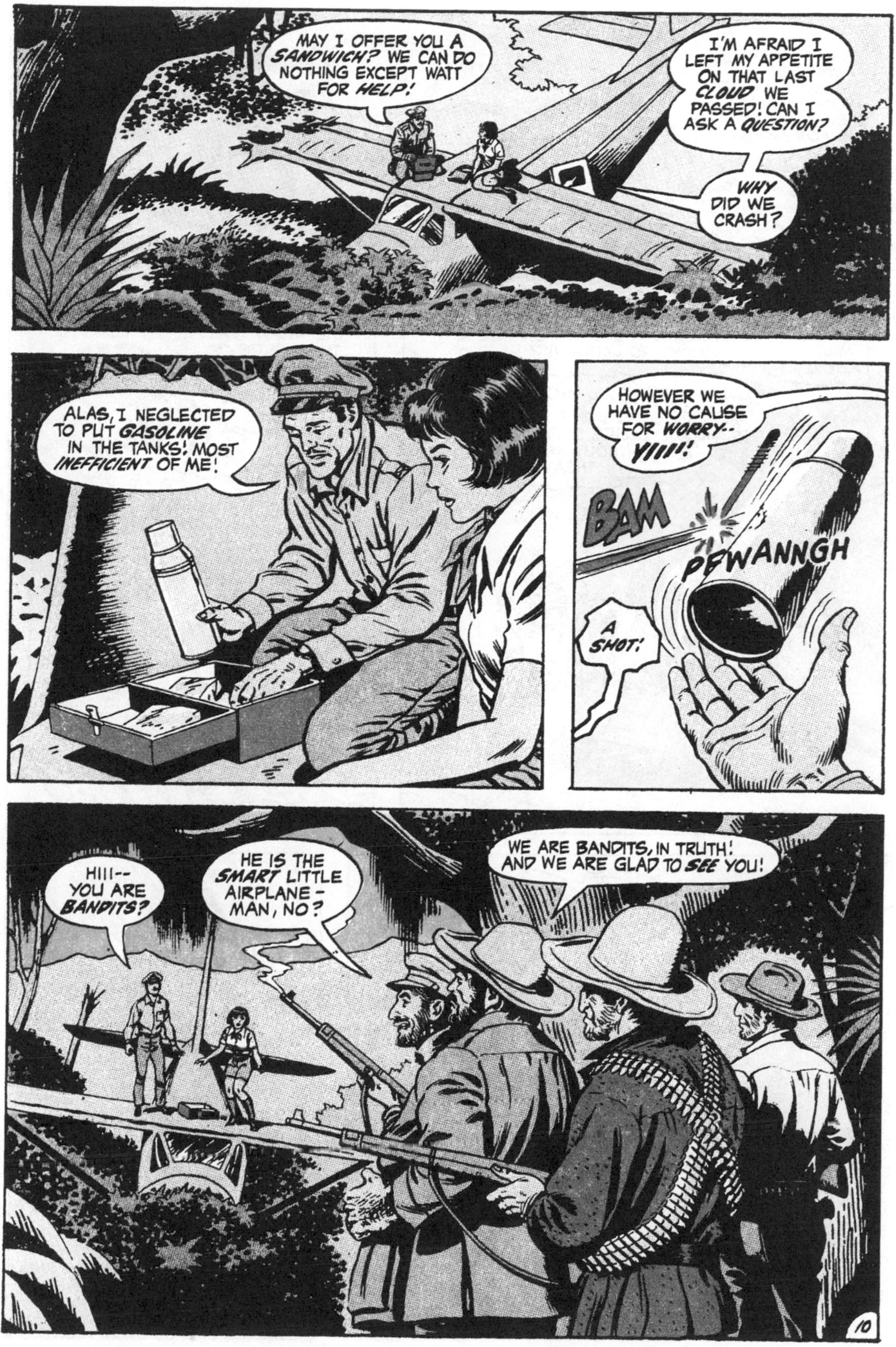

MAY I OFFER YOU A SANDWICH? WE CAN DO NOTHING EXCEPT WAIT FOR HELP!
I'M AFRAID I LEFT MY APPETITE ON THAT LAST CLOUD WE PASSED! CAN I ASK A QUESTION?
WHY DID WE CRASH?
ALAS, I NEGLECTED TO PUT GASOLINE IN THE TANKS! MOST INEFFICIENT OF ME!
HOWEVER WE HAVE NO CAUSE FOR WORRY-- YIIII!
BAM
PFWANNGH
A SHOT!
HIII-- YOU ARE BANDITS?
HE IS THE SMART LITTLE AIRPLANE-MAN, NO?
WE ARE BANDITS, IN TRUTH! AND WE ARE GLAD TO SEE YOU!
10

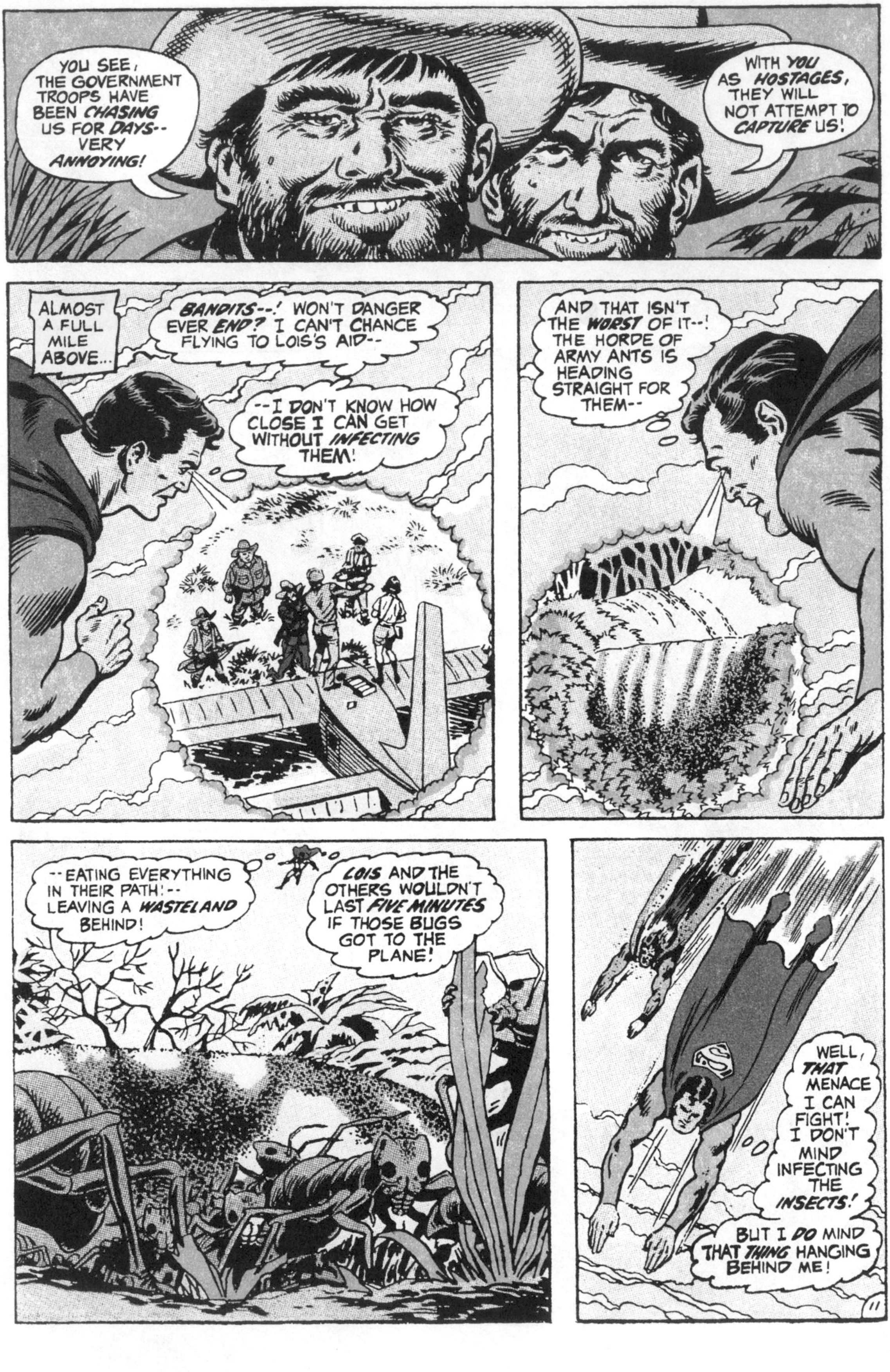
YOU SEE, THE GOVERNMENT TROOPS HAVE BEEN CHASING US FOR DAYS-- VERY ANNOYING!
WITH YOU AS HOSTAGES, THEY WILL NOT ATTEMPT TO CAPTURE US!
ALMOST A FULL MILE ABOVE...
BANDITS--! WON'T DANGER EVER END? I CAN'T CHANCE FLYING TO LOIS'S AID--
--I DON'T KNOW HOW CLOSE I CAN GET WITHOUT INFECTING THEM!
AND THAT ISN'T THE WORST OF IT--! THE HORDE OF ARMY ANTS IS HEADING STRAIGHT FOR THEM--
--EATING EVERYTHING IN THEIR PATH!-- LEAVING A WASTELAND BEHIND!
LOIS AND THE OTHERS WOULDN'T LAST FIVE MINUTES IF THOSE BUGS GOT TO THE PLANE!
WELL, THAT MENACE I CAN FIGHT! I DON'T MIND INFECTING THE INSECTS!
BUT I DO MIND THAT THING HANGING BEHIND ME!
11

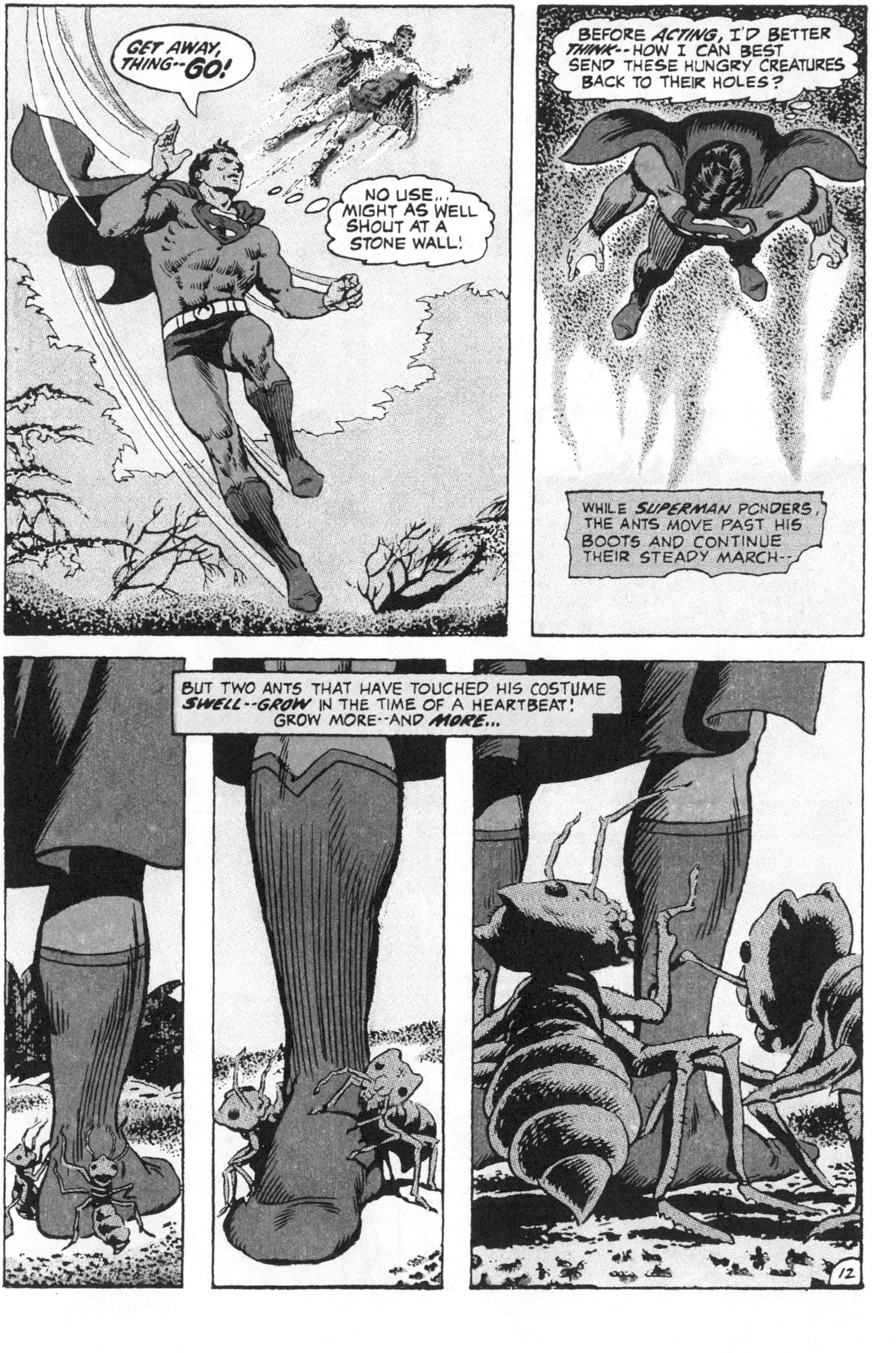

GET AWAY, THING--GO!
NO USE... MIGHT AS WELL SHOUT AT A STONE WALL!
BEFORE ACTING, I'D BETTER THINK--HOW I CAN BEST SEND THESE HUNGRY CREATURES BACK TO THEIR HOLES?
WHILE SUPERMAN PONDERS, THE ANTS MOVE PAST HIS BOOTS AND CONTINUE THEIR STEADY MARCH--
BUT TWO ANTS THAT HAVE TOUCHED HIS COSTUME SWELL--GROW IN THE TIME OF A HEARTBEAT! GROW MORE--AND MORE...
12

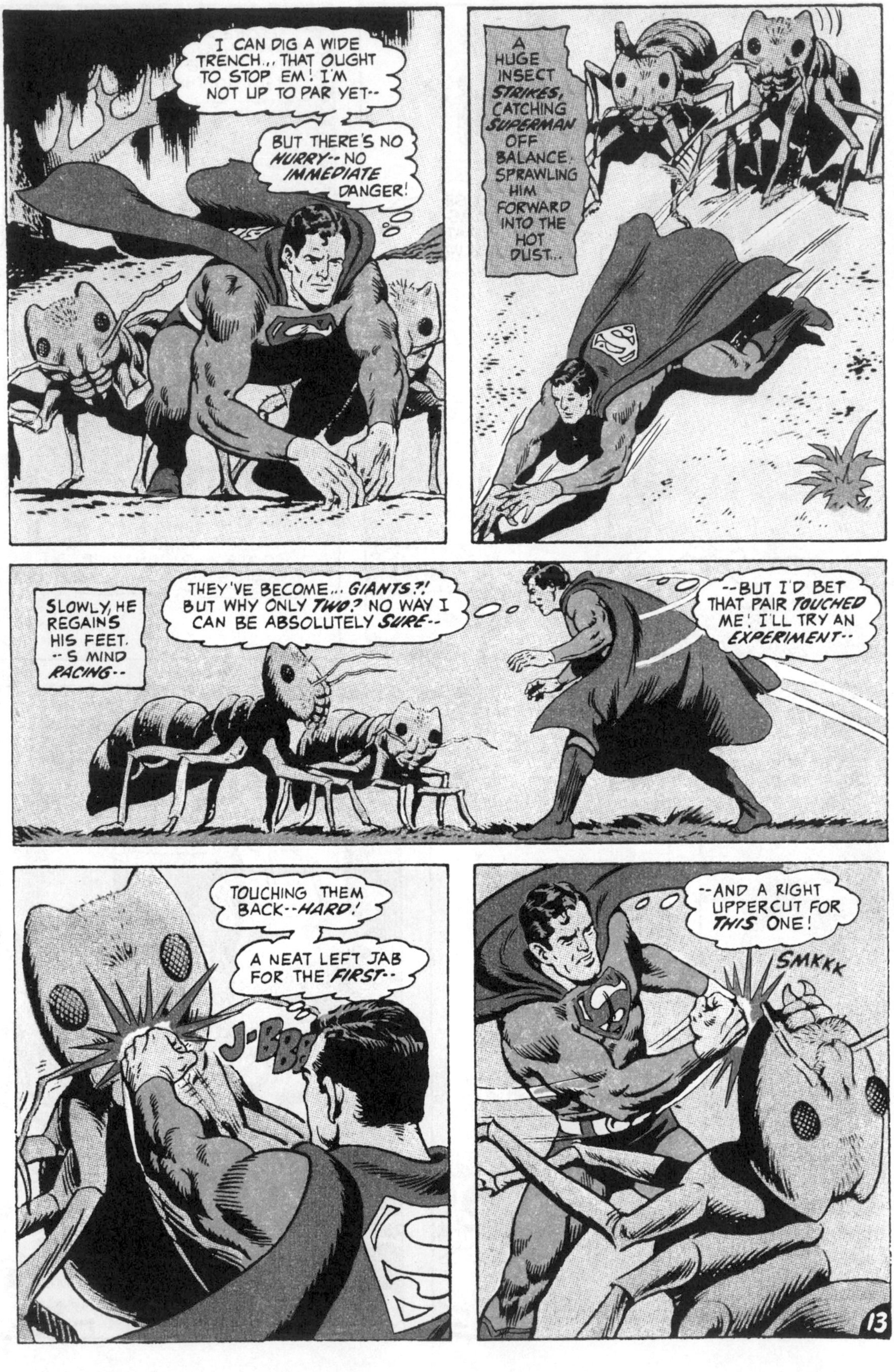
I CAN DIG A WIDE TRENCH... THAT OUGHT TO STOP EM! I'M NOT UP TO PAR YET--
BUT THERE'S NO HURRY-- NO IMMEDIATE DANGER!
A HUGE INSECT STRIKES, CATCHING SUPERMAN OFF BALANCE, SPRAWLING HIM FORWARD INTO THE HOT DUST...
SLOWLY, HE REGAINS HIS FEET. --S MIND RACING--
THEY'VE BECOME... GIANTS?! BUT WHY ONLY TWO? NO WAY I CAN BE ABSOLUTELY SURE--
--BUT I'D BET THAT PAIR TOUCHED ME! I'LL TRY AN EXPERIMENT--
TOUCHING THEM BACK--HARD!
A NEAT LEFT JAB FOR THE FIRST--
J-BBB
--AND A RIGHT UPPERCUT FOR THIS ONE!
SMKKK
13

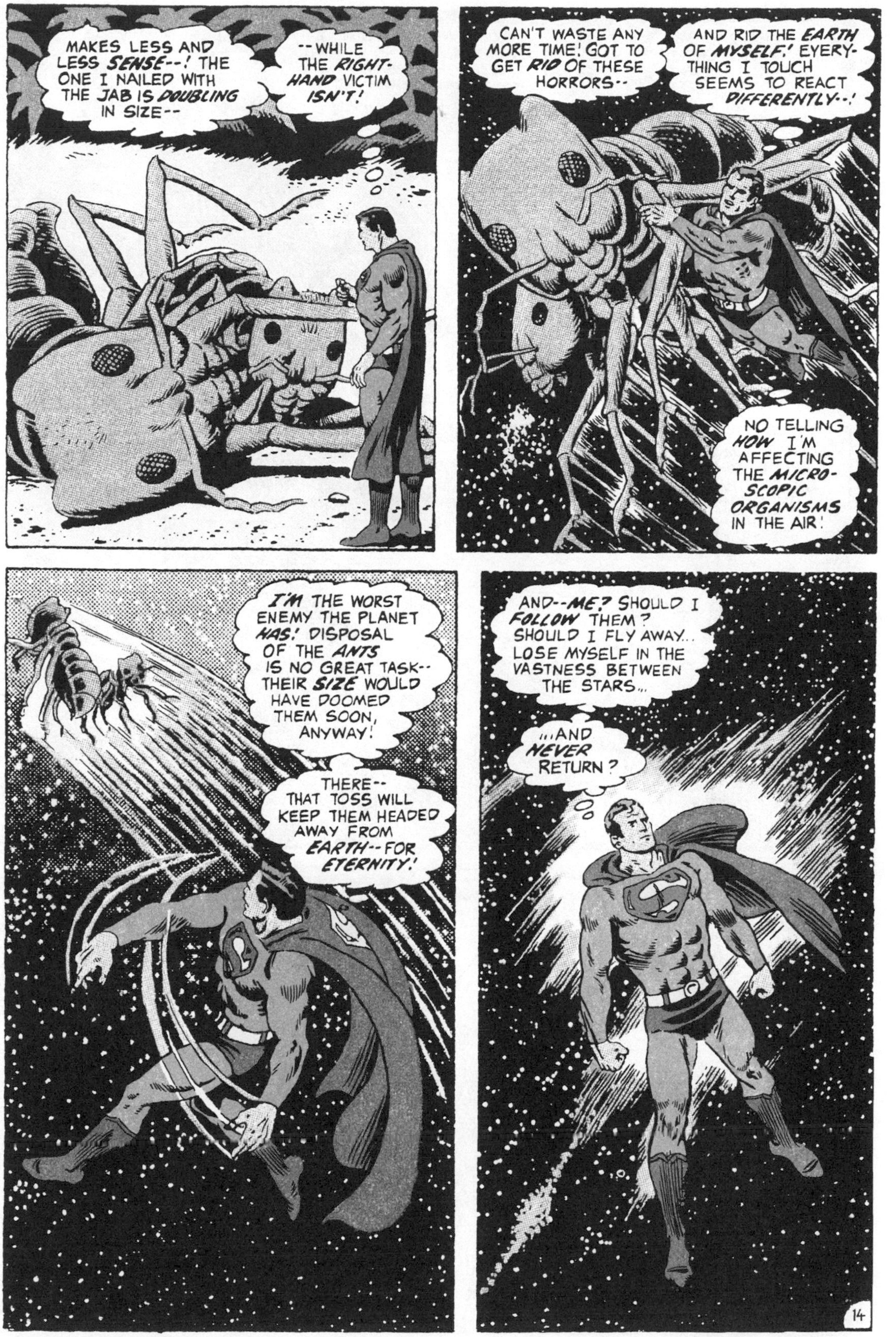
MAKES LESS AND LESS SENSE--! THE ONE I NAILED WITH THE JAB IS DOUBLING IN SIZE--
--WHILE THE RIGHT-HAND VICTIM ISN'T!
CAN'T WASTE ANY MORE TIME! GOT TO GET RID OF THESE HORRORS--
AND RID THE EARTH OF MYSELF! EVERYTHING I TOUCH SEEMS TO REACT DIFFERENTLY--!
NO TELLING HOW I'M AFFECTING THE MICRO-SCOPIC ORGANISMS IN THE AIR!
I'M THE WORST ENEMY THE PLANET HAS! DISPOSAL OF THE ANTS IS NO GREAT TASK--THEIR SIZE WOULD HAVE DOOMED THEM SOON, ANYWAY!
THERE--THAT TOSS WILL KEEP THEM HEADED AWAY FROM EARTH--FOR ETERNITY!
AND--ME? SHOULD I FOLLOW THEM? SHOULD I FLY AWAY... LOSE MYSELF IN THE VASTNESS BETWEEN THE STARS...
...AND NEVER RETURN?
14

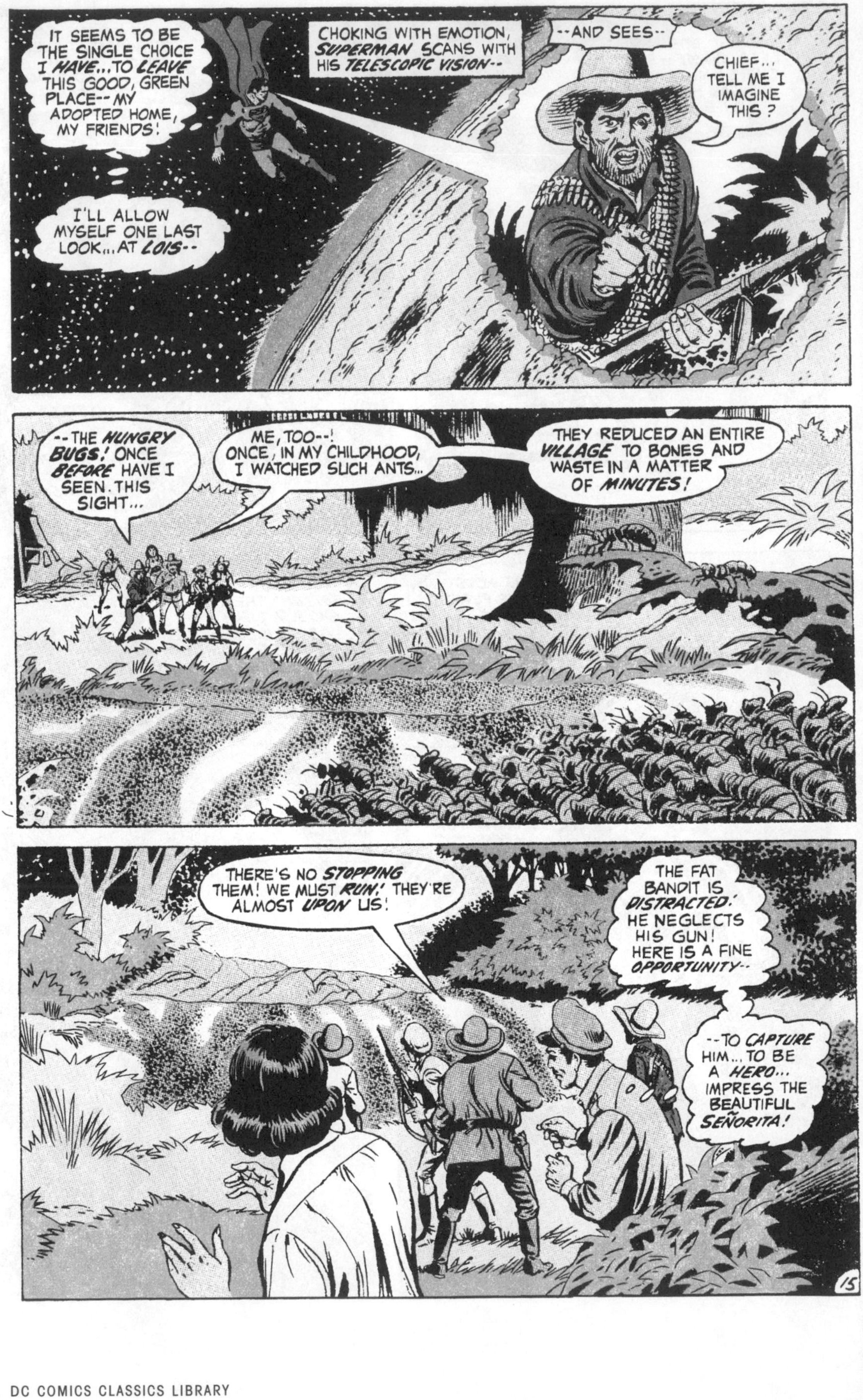
IT SEEMS TO BE THE SINGLE CHOICE I HAVE...TO LEAVE THIS GOOD, GREEN PLACE-- MY ADOPTED HOME, MY FRIENDS!
I'LL ALLOW MYSELF ONE LAST LOOK...AT LOIS--
CHOKING WITH EMOTION, SUPERMAN SCANS WITH HIS TELESCOPIC VISION--
--AND SEES--
CHIEF... TELL ME I IMAGINE THIS ?
--THE HUNGRY BUGS! ONCE BEFORE HAVE I SEEN THIS SIGHT...
ME, TOO--! ONCE, IN MY CHILDHOOD, I WATCHED SUCH ANTS...
THEY REDUCED AN ENTIRE VILLAGE TO BONES AND WASTE IN A MATTER OF MINUTES!
THERE'S NO STOPPING THEM! WE MUST RUN! THEY'RE ALMOST UPON US!
THE FAT BANDIT IS DISTRACTED! HE NEGLECTS HIS GUN! HERE IS A FINE OPPORTUNITY--
--TO CAPTURE HIM... TO BE A HERO... IMPRESS THE BEAUTIFUL SEÑORITA!
15

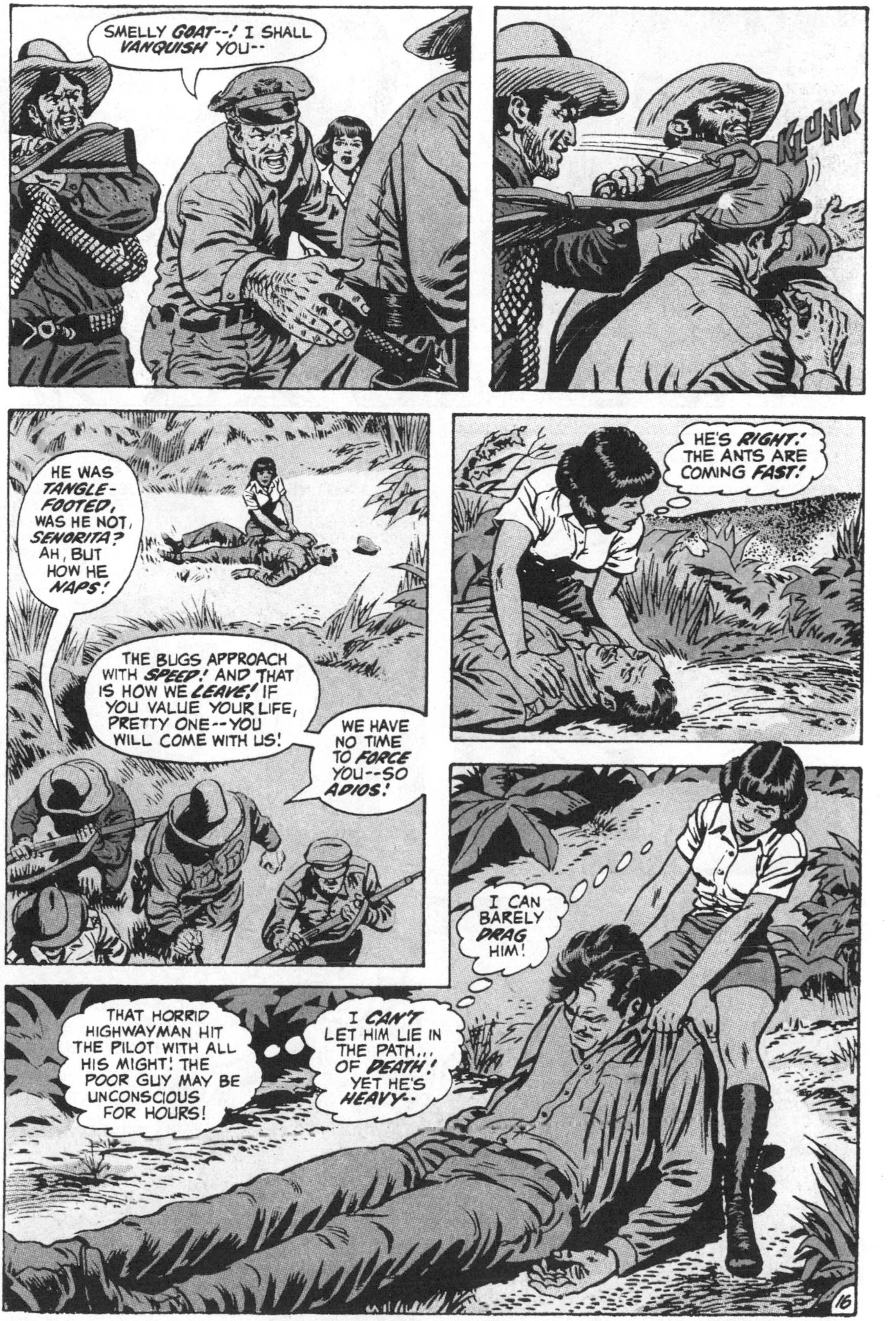
SMELLY GOAT--! I SHALL VANQUISH YOU--
KLUNK
HE WAS TANGLE-FOOTED, WAS HE NOT, SENORITA? AH, BUT HOW HE NAPS!
THE BUGS APPROACH WITH SPEED! AND THAT IS HOW WE LEAVE! IF YOU VALUE YOUR LIFE, PRETTY ONE--YOU WILL COME WITH US!
WE HAVE NO TIME TO FORCE YOU--SO ADIOS!
HE'S RIGHT! THE ANTS ARE COMING FAST!
I CAN BARELY DRAG HIM!
THAT HORRID HIGHWAYMAN HIT THE PILOT WITH ALL HIS MIGHT! THE POOR GUY MAY BE UNCONSCIOUS FOR HOURS!
I CAN'T LET HIM LIE IN THE PATH... OF DEATH! YET HE'S HEAVY--
16

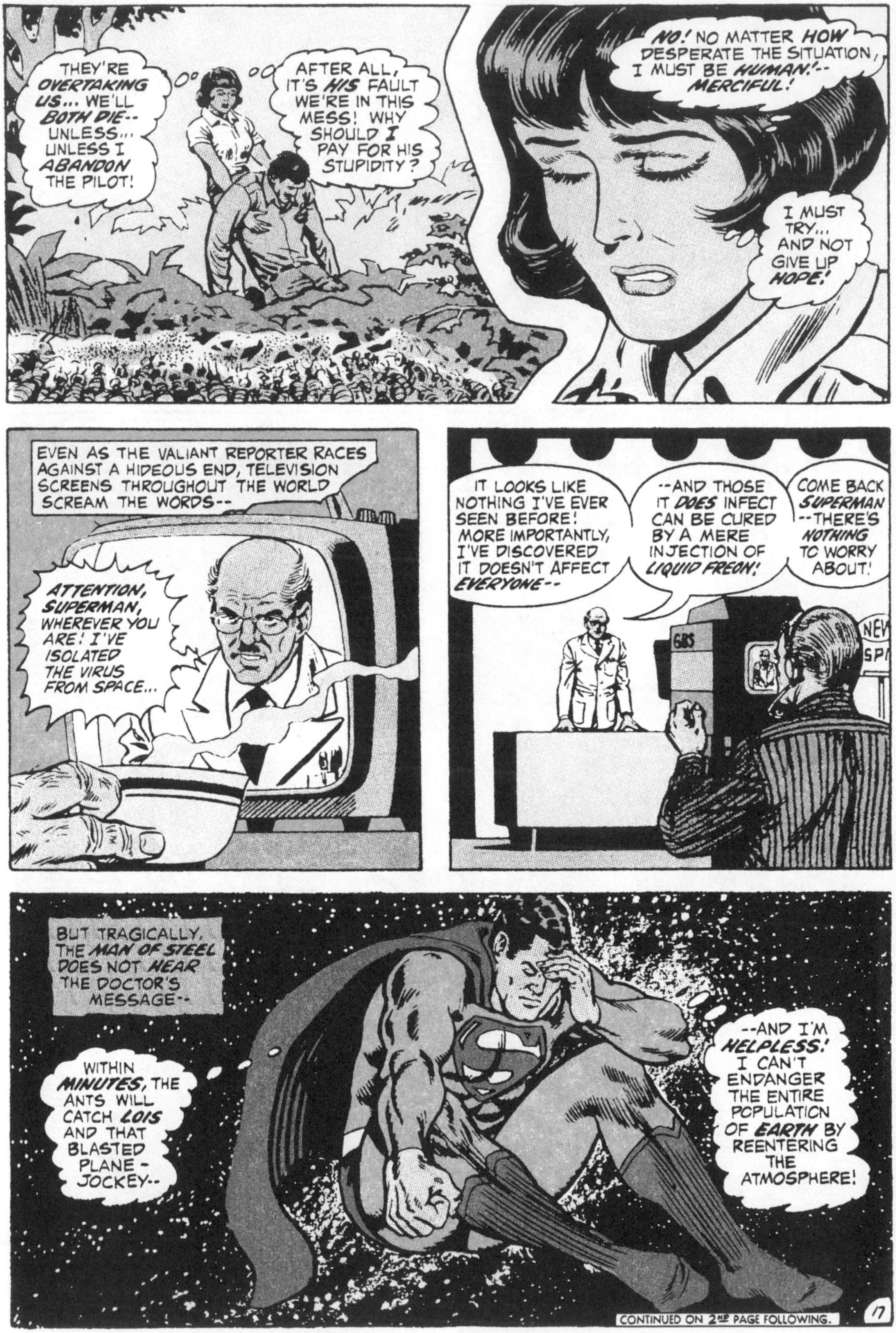
THEY'RE OVERTAKING US... WE'LL BOTH DIE-- UNLESS... UNLESS I ABANDON THE PILOT!
AFTER ALL, IT'S HIS FAULT WE'RE IN THIS MESS! WHY SHOULD I PAY FOR HIS STUPIDITY?
NO! NO MATTER HOW DESPERATE THE SITUATION, I MUST BE HUMAN!--MERCIFUL!
I MUST TRY... AND NOT GIVE UP HOPE!
EVEN AS THE VALIANT REPORTER RACES AGAINST A HIDEOUS END, TELEVISION SCREENS THROUGHOUT THE WORLD SCREAM THE WORDS--
ATTENTION, SUPERMAN, WHEREVER YOU ARE! I'VE ISOLATED THE VIRUS FROM SPACE...
IT LOOKS LIKE NOTHING I'VE EVER SEEN BEFORE! MORE IMPORTANTLY, I'VE DISCOVERED IT DOESN'T AFFECT EVERYONE--
--AND THOSE IT DOES INFECT CAN BE CURED BY A MERE INJECTION OF LIQUID FREON!
COME BACK SUPERMAN --THERE'S NOTHING TO WORRY ABOUT!
GBS
BUT TRAGICALLY, THE MAN OF STEEL DOES NOT HEAR THE DOCTOR'S MESSAGE--
WITHIN MINUTES, THE ANTS WILL CATCH LOIS AND THAT BLASTED PLANE-JOCKEY--
--AND I'M HELPLESS! I CAN'T ENDANGER THE ENTIRE POPULATION OF EARTH BY REENTERING THE ATMOSPHERE!
CONTINUED ON 2ND PAGE FOLLOWING.
17

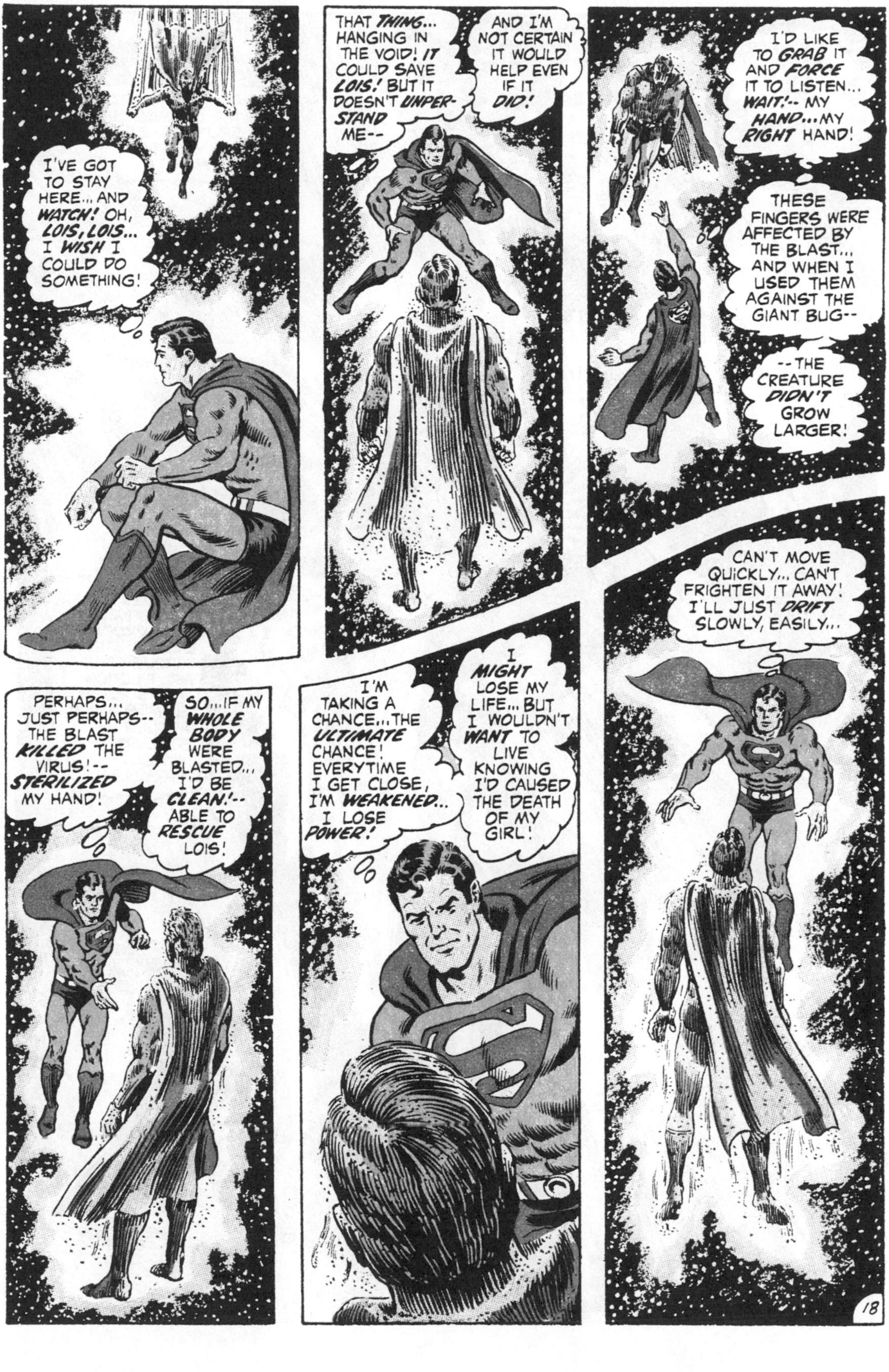

I'VE GOT TO STAY HERE... AND WATCH! OH, LOIS, LOIS... I WISH I COULD DO SOMETHING!
THAT THING... HANGING IN THE VOID! IT COULD SAVE LOIS! BUT IT DOESN'T UNDERSTAND ME--
AND I'M NOT CERTAIN IT WOULD HELP EVEN IF IT DID!
I'D LIKE TO GRAB IT AND FORCE IT TO LISTEN... WAIT!-- MY HAND... MY RIGHT HAND!
THESE FINGERS WERE AFFECTED BY THE BLAST... AND WHEN I USED THEM AGAINST THE GIANT BUG--
--THE CREATURE DIDN'T GROW LARGER!
PERHAPS... JUST PERHAPS-- THE BLAST KILLED THE VIRUS!-- STERILIZED MY HAND!
SO... IF MY WHOLE BODY WERE BLASTED... I'D BE CLEAN!-- ABLE TO RESCUE LOIS!
I'M TAKING A CHANCE... THE ULTIMATE CHANCE! EVERYTIME I GET CLOSE, I'M WEAKENED... I LOSE POWER!
I MIGHT LOSE MY LIFE... BUT I WOULDN'T WANT TO LIVE KNOWING I'D CAUSED THE DEATH OF MY GIRL!
CAN'T MOVE QUICKLY... CAN'T FRIGHTEN IT AWAY! I'LL JUST DRIFT SLOWLY, EASILY...
18

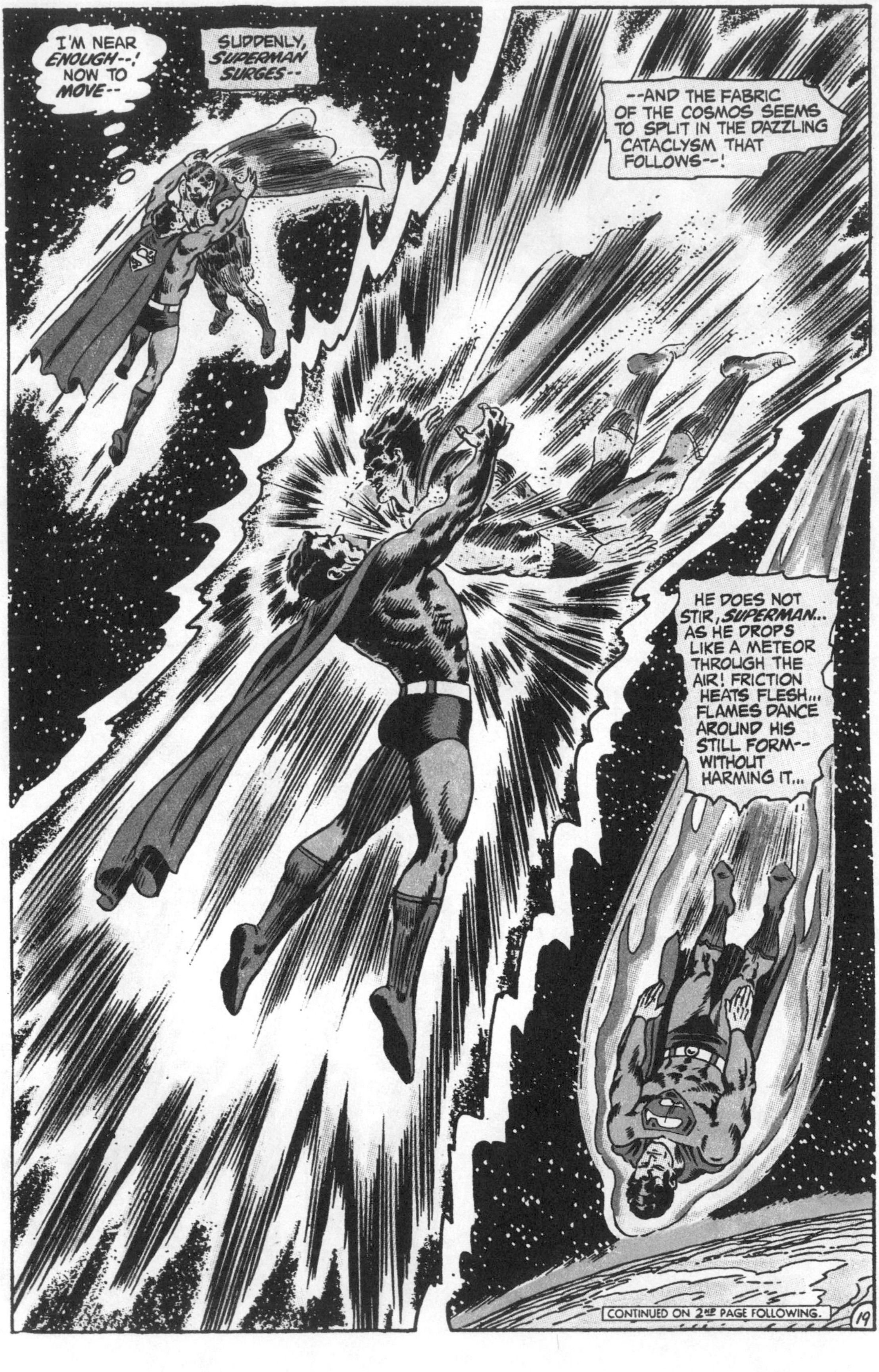
I'M NEAR ENOUGH--! NOW TO MOVE--
SUDDENLY, SUPERMAN SURGES--
--AND THE FABRIC OF THE COSMOS SEEMS TO SPLIT IN THE DAZZLING CATACLYSM THAT FOLLOWS--!
HE DOES NOT STIR, SUPERMAN... AS HE DROPS LIKE A METEOR THROUGH THE AIR! FRICTION HEATS FLESH... FLAMES DANCE AROUND HIS STILL FORM--WITHOUT HARMING IT...
CONTINUED ON 2ND PAGE FOLLOWING.
19

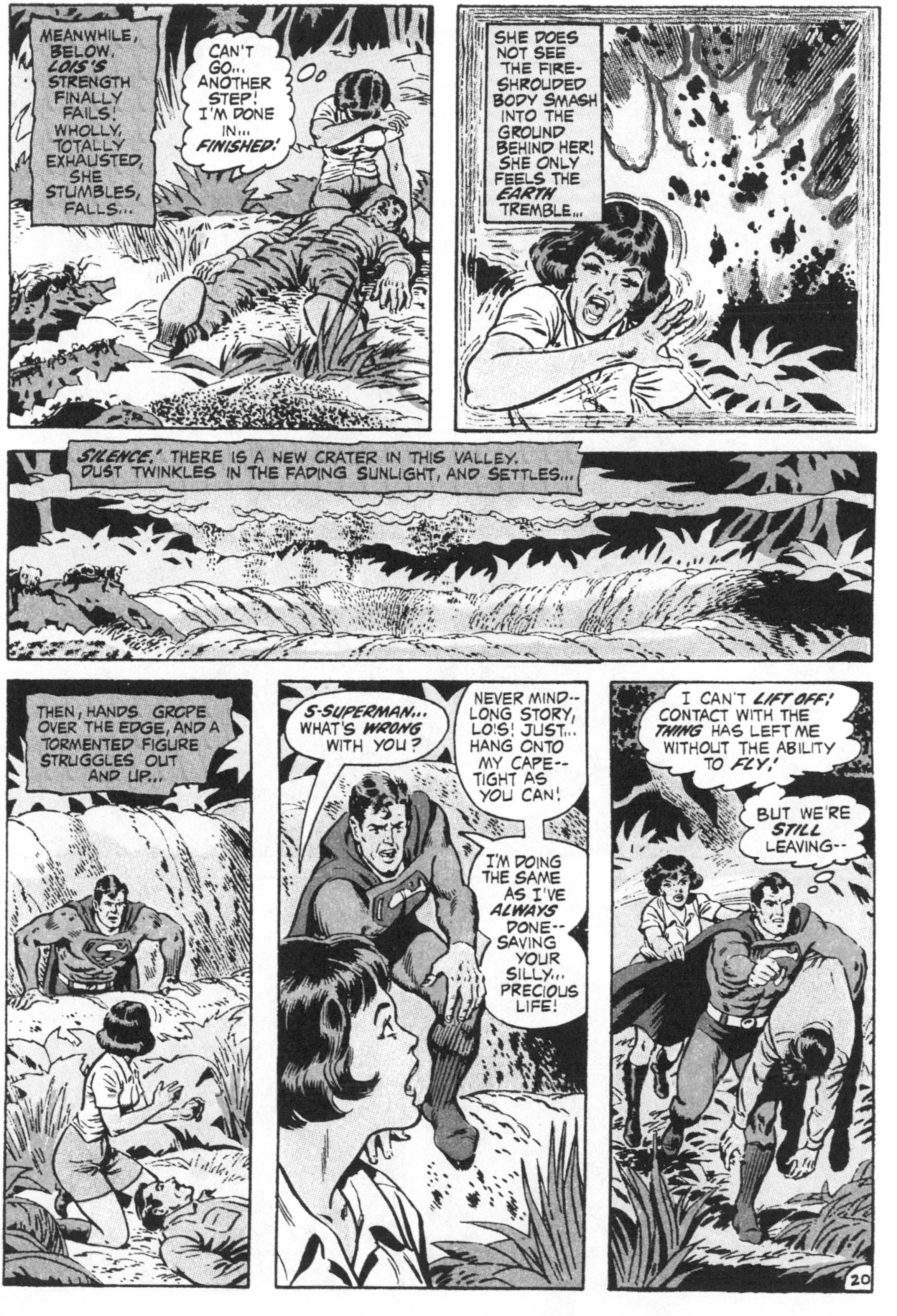
MEANWHILE, BELOW, LOIS'S STRENGTH FINALLY FAILS! WHOLLY, TOTALLY EXHAUSTED, SHE STUMBLES, FALLS...
CAN'T GO... ANOTHER STEP! I'M DONE IN... FINISHED!
SHE DOES NOT SEE THE FIRE-SHROUDED BODY SMASH INTO THE GROUND BEHIND HER! SHE ONLY FEELS THE EARTH TREMBLE...
SILENCE! THERE IS A NEW CRATER IN THIS VALLEY. DUST TWINKLES IN THE FADING SUNLIGHT, AND SETTLES...
THEN, HANDS GROPE OVER THE EDGE, AND A TORMENTED FIGURE STRUGGLES OUT AND UP...
S-SUPERMAN... WHAT'S WRONG WITH YOU?
NEVER MIND-- LONG STORY, LOIS! JUST... HANG ONTO MY CAPE-- TIGHT AS YOU CAN!
I'M DOING THE SAME AS I'VE ALWAYS DONE-- SAVING YOUR SILLY... PRECIOUS LIFE!
I CAN'T LIFT OFF! CONTACT WITH THE THING HAS LEFT ME WITHOUT THE ABILITY TO FLY!
BUT WE'RE STILL LEAVING--
20

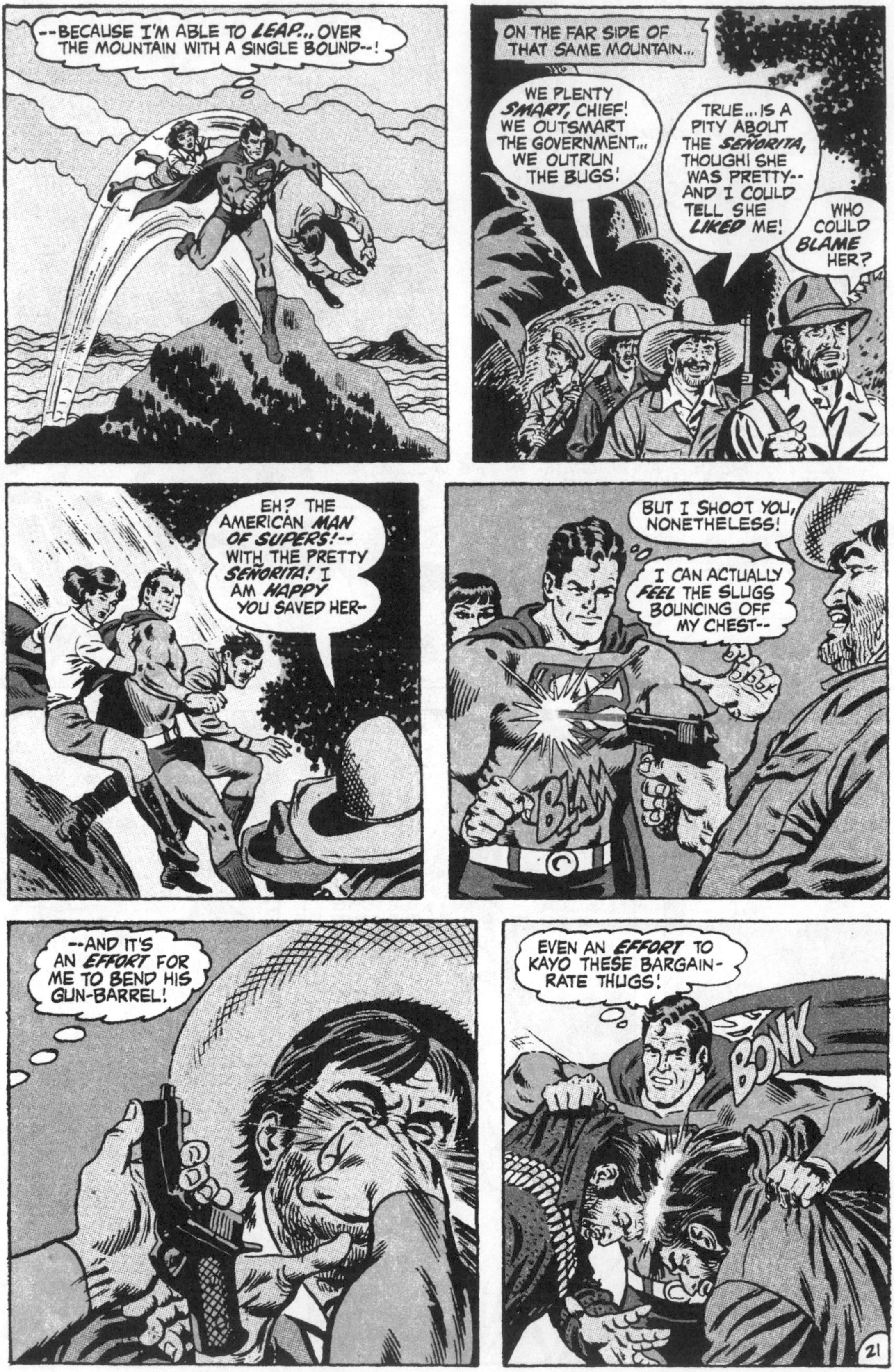
--BECAUSE I'M ABLE TO LEAP... OVER THE MOUNTAIN WITH A SINGLE BOUND--!
ON THE FAR SIDE OF THAT SAME MOUNTAIN...
WE PLENTY SMART, CHIEF! WE OUTSMART THE GOVERNMENT... WE OUTRUN THE BUGS!
TRUE... IS A PITY ABOUT THE SEÑORITA, THOUGH! SHE WAS PRETTY-- AND I COULD TELL SHE LIKED ME!
WHO COULD BLAME HER?
EH? THE AMERICAN MAN OF SUPERS!-- WITH THE PRETTY SEÑORITA! I AM HAPPY YOU SAVED HER--
BUT I SHOOT YOU, NONETHELESS!
I CAN ACTUALLY FEEL THE SLUGS BOUNCING OFF MY CHEST--
BLAM
--AND IT'S AN EFFORT FOR ME TO BEND HIS GUN-BARREL!
EVEN AN EFFORT TO KAYO THESE BARGAIN-RATE THUGS!
BONK
21

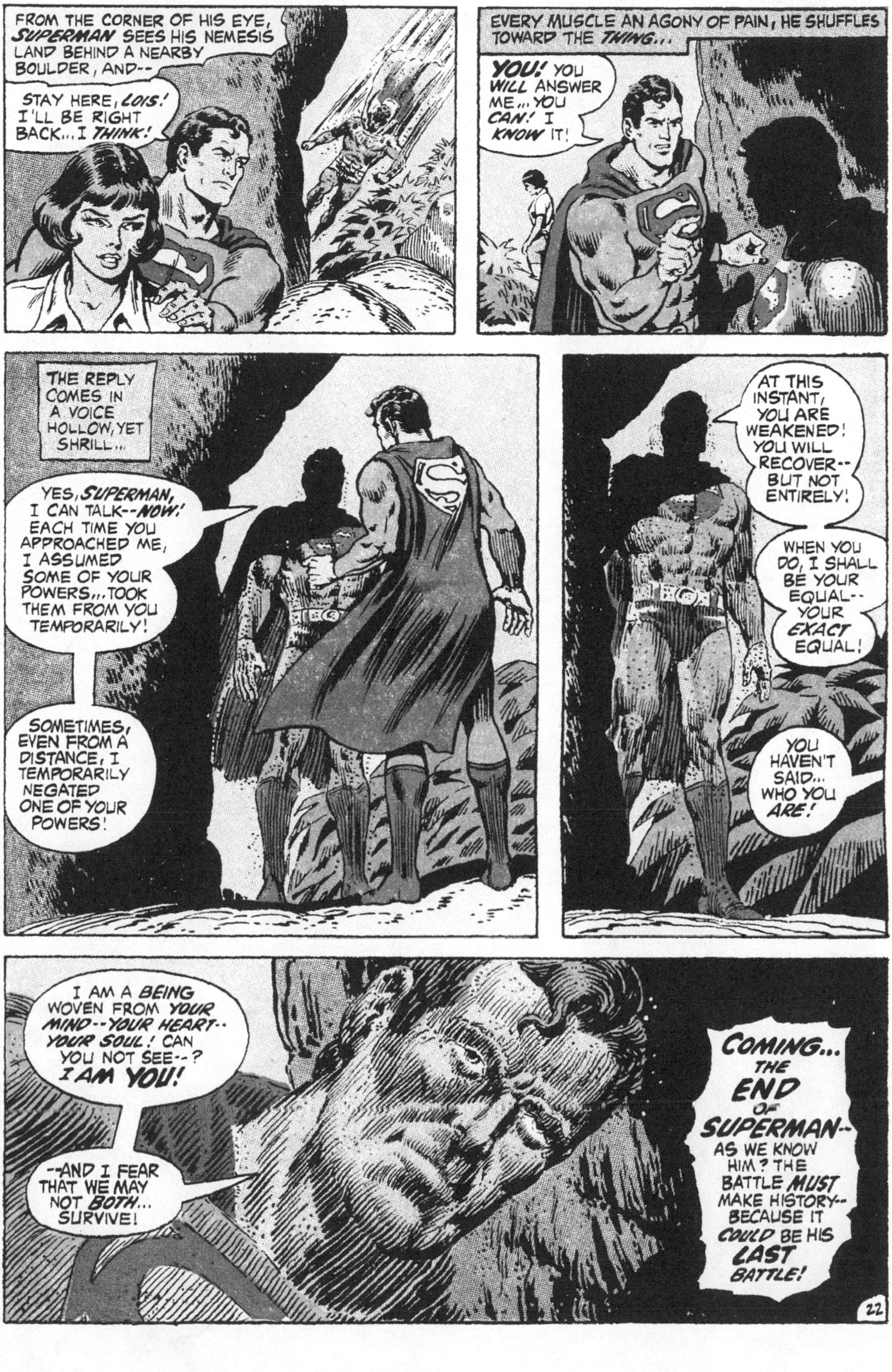
FROM THE CORNER OF HIS EYE, SUPERMAN SEES HIS NEMESIS LAND BEHIND A NEARBY BOULDER, AND--
STAY HERE, LOIS! I'LL BE RIGHT BACK... I THINK!
EVERY MUSCLE AN AGONY OF PAIN, HE SHUFFLES TOWARD THE THING...
YOU! YOU WILL ANSWER ME... YOU CAN! I KNOW IT!
THE REPLY COMES IN A VOICE HOLLOW, YET SHRILL...
YES, SUPERMAN, I CAN TALK--NOW! EACH TIME YOU APPROACHED ME, I ASSUMED SOME OF YOUR POWERS... TOOK THEM FROM YOU TEMPORARILY!
SOMETIMES, EVEN FROM A DISTANCE, I TEMPORARILY NEGATED ONE OF YOUR POWERS!
AT THIS INSTANT, YOU ARE WEAKENED! YOU WILL RECOVER-- BUT NOT ENTIRELY!
WHEN YOU DO, I SHALL BE YOUR EQUAL-- YOUR EXACT EQUAL!
YOU HAVEN'T SAID... WHO YOU ARE!
I AM A BEING WOVEN FROM YOUR MIND--YOUR HEART-- YOUR SOUL! CAN YOU NOT SEE--? I AM YOU!
--AND I FEAR THAT WE MAY NOT BOTH... SURVIVE!
COMING... THE END OF SUPERMAN-- AS WE KNOW HIM? THE BATTLE MUST MAKE HISTORY-- BECAUSE IT COULD BE HIS LAST BATTLE!
22

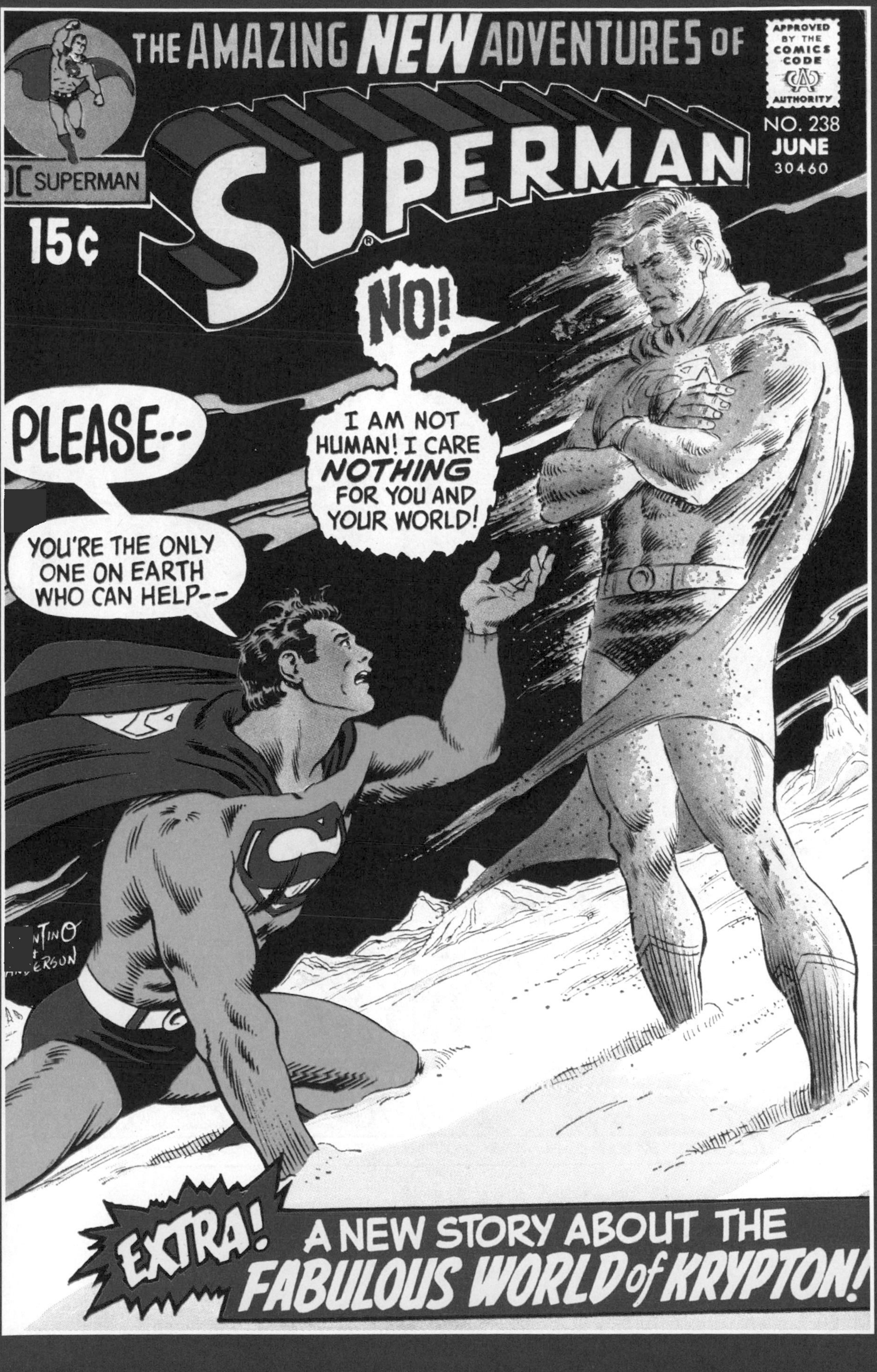

THE AMAZING NEW ADVENTURES OF
SUPERMAN
DC SUPERMAN
15¢
APPROVED BY THE COMICS CODE AUTHORITY
NO. 238
JUNE
30460
NO!
I AM NOT HUMAN! I CARE NOTHING FOR YOU AND YOUR WORLD!
PLEASE--
YOU'RE THE ONLY ONE ON EARTH WHO CAN HELP--
EXTRA!
A NEW STORY ABOUT THE FABULOUS WORLD of KRYPTON!

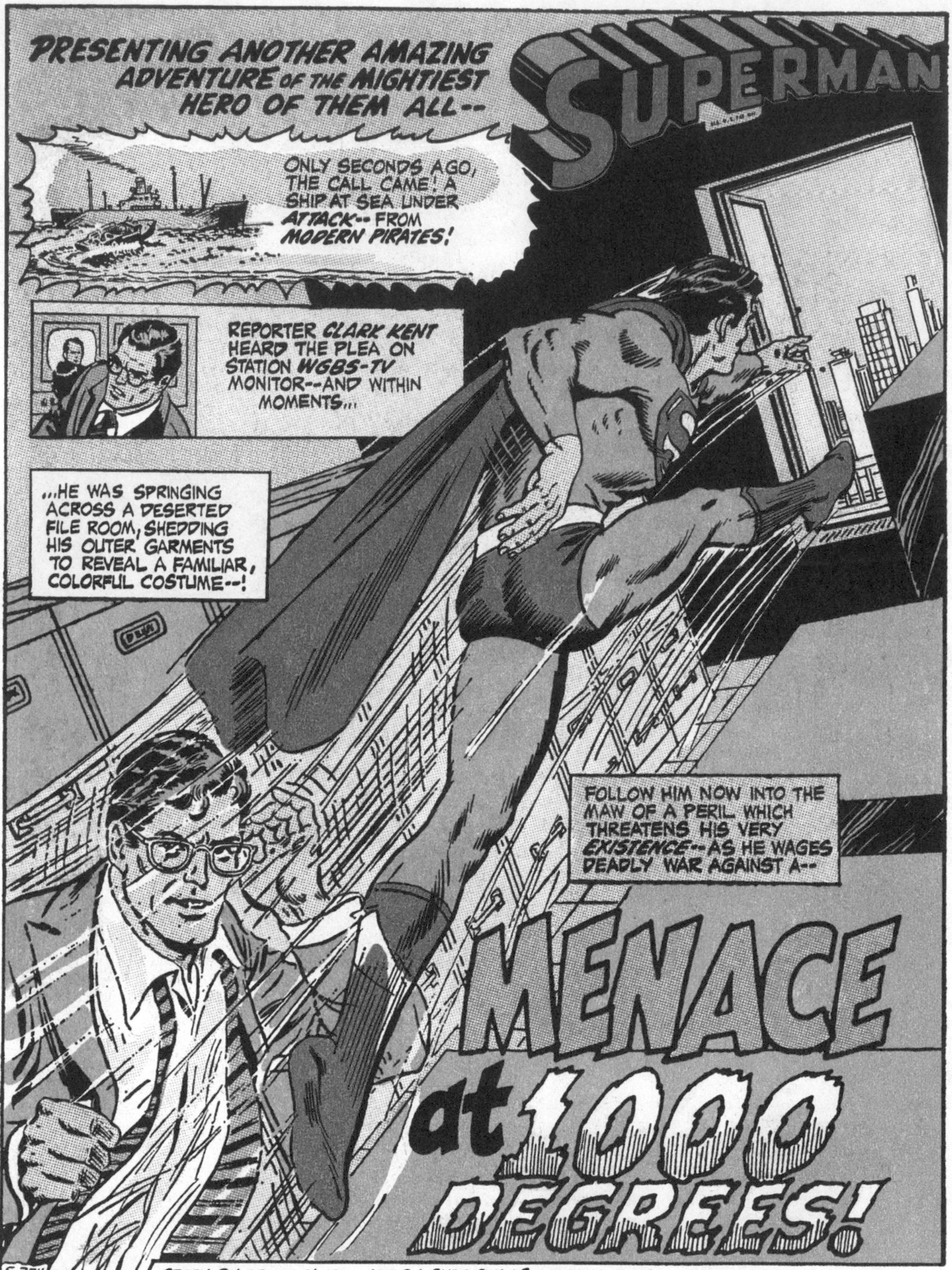
PRESENTING ANOTHER AMAZING ADVENTURE OF THE MIGHTIEST HERO OF THEM ALL--
SUPERMAN
ONLY SECONDS AGO, THE CALL CAME! A SHIP AT SEA UNDER ATTACK-- FROM MODERN PIRATES!
REPORTER CLARK KENT HEARD THE PLEA ON STATION WGBS-TV MONITOR--AND WITHIN MOMENTS...
...HE WAS SPRINGING ACROSS A DESERTED FILE ROOM, SHEDDING HIS OUTER GARMENTS TO REVEAL A FAMILIAR, COLORFUL COSTUME--!
FOLLOW HIM NOW INTO THE MAW OF A PERIL WHICH THREATENS HIS VERY EXISTENCE--AS HE WAGES DEADLY WAR AGAINST A--
MENACE at 1000 DEGREES!
S-774
STORY BY DENNY O'NEIL-ART BY CURT SWAN & MURPHY ANDERSON-EDITED BY JULIUS SCHWARTZ

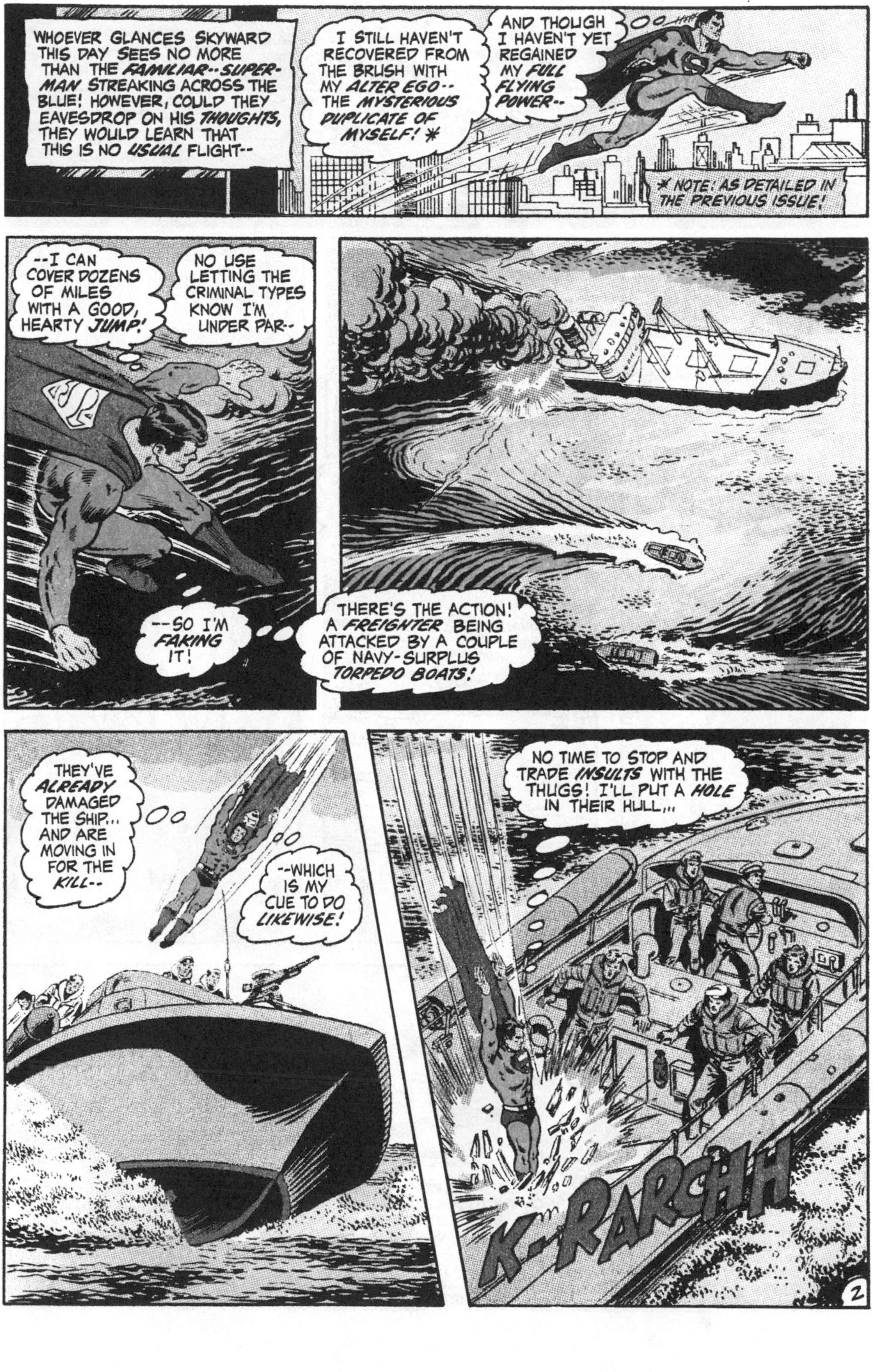
WHOEVER GLANCES SKYWARD THIS DAY SEES NO MORE THAN THE FAMILIAR--SUPERMAN STREAKING ACROSS THE BLUE! HOWEVER, COULD THEY EAVESDROP ON HIS THOUGHTS, THEY WOULD LEARN THAT THIS IS NO USUAL FLIGHT--
I STILL HAVEN'T RECOVERED FROM THE BRUSH WITH MY ALTER EGO--THE MYSTERIOUS DUPLICATE OF MYSELF! *
AND THOUGH I HAVEN'T YET REGAINED MY FULL FLYING POWER--
* NOTE: AS DETAILED IN THE PREVIOUS ISSUE!
--I CAN COVER DOZENS OF MILES WITH A GOOD, HEARTY JUMP!
NO USE LETTING THE CRIMINAL TYPES KNOW I'M UNDER PAR--
--SO I'M FAKING IT!
THERE'S THE ACTION! A FREIGHTER BEING ATTACKED BY A COUPLE OF NAVY-SURPLUS TORPEDO BOATS!
THEY'VE ALREADY DAMAGED THE SHIP... AND ARE MOVING IN FOR THE KILL--
--WHICH IS MY CUE TO DO LIKEWISE!
NO TIME TO STOP AND TRADE INSULTS WITH THE THUGS! I'LL PUT A HOLE IN THEIR HULL...
K-RARCHH
2

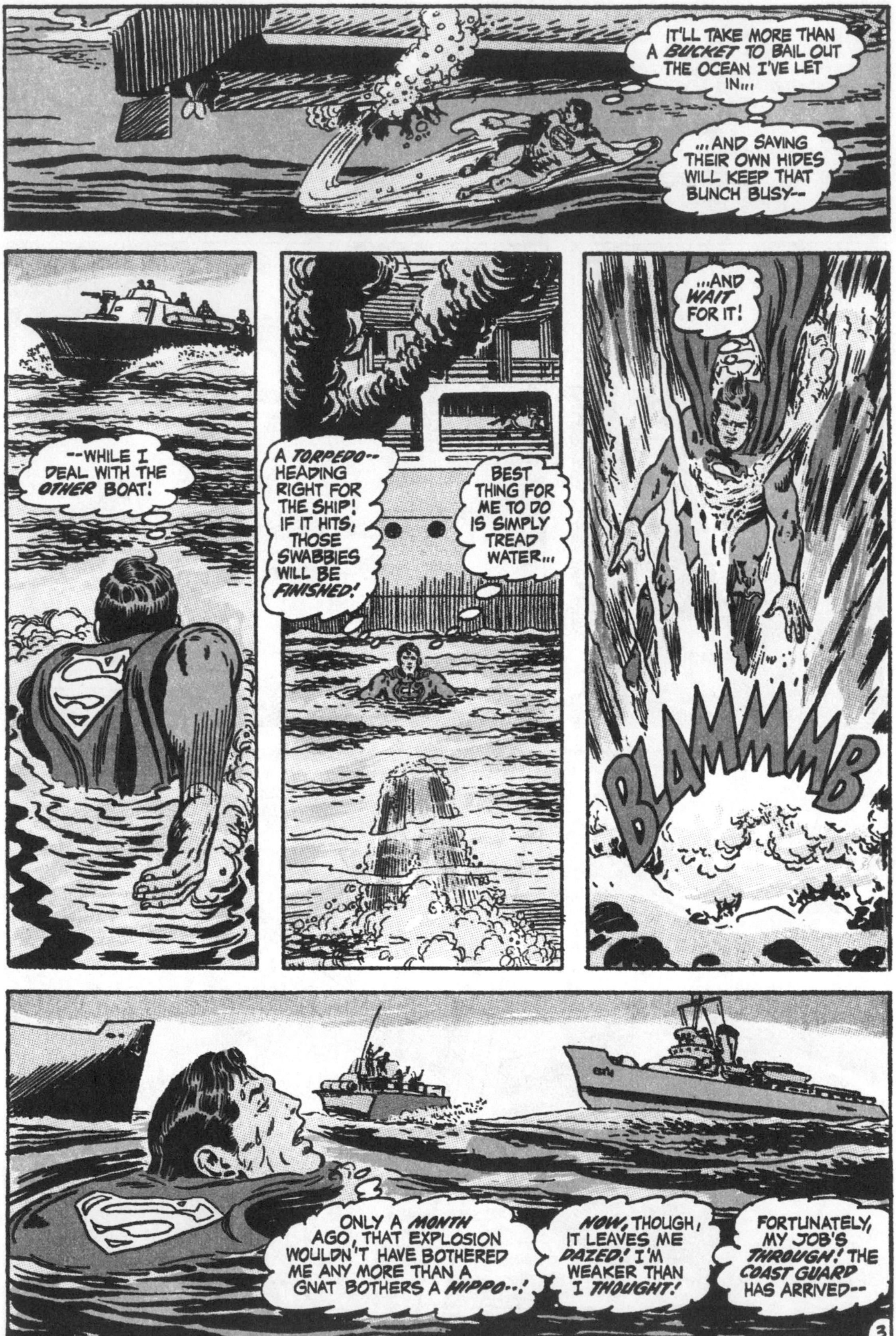
IT'LL TAKE MORE THAN A BUCKET TO BAIL OUT THE OCEAN I'VE LET IN...
...AND SAVING THEIR OWN HIDES WILL KEEP THAT BUNCH BUSY--
--WHILE I DEAL WITH THE OTHER BOAT!
A TORPEDO-- HEADING RIGHT FOR THE SHIP! IF IT HITS, THOSE SWABBIES WILL BE FINISHED!
BEST THING FOR ME TO DO IS SIMPLY TREAD WATER...
...AND WAIT FOR IT!
BLAMMMB
ONLY A MONTH AGO, THAT EXPLOSION WOULDN'T HAVE BOTHERED ME ANY MORE THAN A GNAT BOTHERS A HIPPO..!
NOW, THOUGH, IT LEAVES ME DAZED! I'M WEAKER THAN I THOUGHT!
FORTUNATELY, MY JOB'S THROUGH! THE COAST GUARD HAS ARRIVED--
3

THEN, ABOARD THE GOVERNMENT VESSEL--

WE ROUNDED THEM UP, *SUPERMAN!* NO SWEAT... YOU TOOK THE WIND OUT OF THEIR SAILS!

ANY IDEAS *WHY* THEY PULLED THIS STUNT, CAPTAIN?

THE LEADER SAID HE WAS TOLD THAT SUPPLY SHIP WAS FULL OF *GOLD*--WHICH IS *HOGWASH!* NOTHING ON IT EXCEPT FOOD AND--

CAPTAIN! A RADIOGRAM FOR YOU... *URGENT!*

BAD... *REAL BAD! PROJECT MAGMA* HAS BEEN *CAPTURED!*

COME INTO MY CABIN... I'LL FILL YOU IN!

YOU SEE, *SUPERMAN,* THE PLANET *EARTH* IS FAST RUNNING OUT OF *ENERGY-SOURCES-- FUEL!* WITHIN A FEW GENERATIONS, IT'LL BE *EXHAUSTED--*

OIL, COAL, GAS, EVEN *URANIUM--* EVERYTHING WILL BE *GONE!*

OBVIOUSLY, WE NEED TO DEVELOP *SUBSTITUTES!*

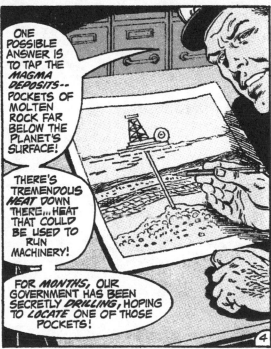

ONE POSSIBLE ANSWER IS TO TAP THE *MAGMA DEPOSITS--* POCKETS OF MOLTEN ROCK FAR BELOW THE PLANET'S SURFACE!

THERE'S TREMENDOUS *HEAT* DOWN THERE... HEAT THAT COULD BE USED TO RUN MACHINERY!

FOR *MONTHS,* OUR GOVERNMENT HAS BEEN SECRETLY *DRILLING,* HOPING TO *LOCATE* ONE OF THOSE POCKETS!

4

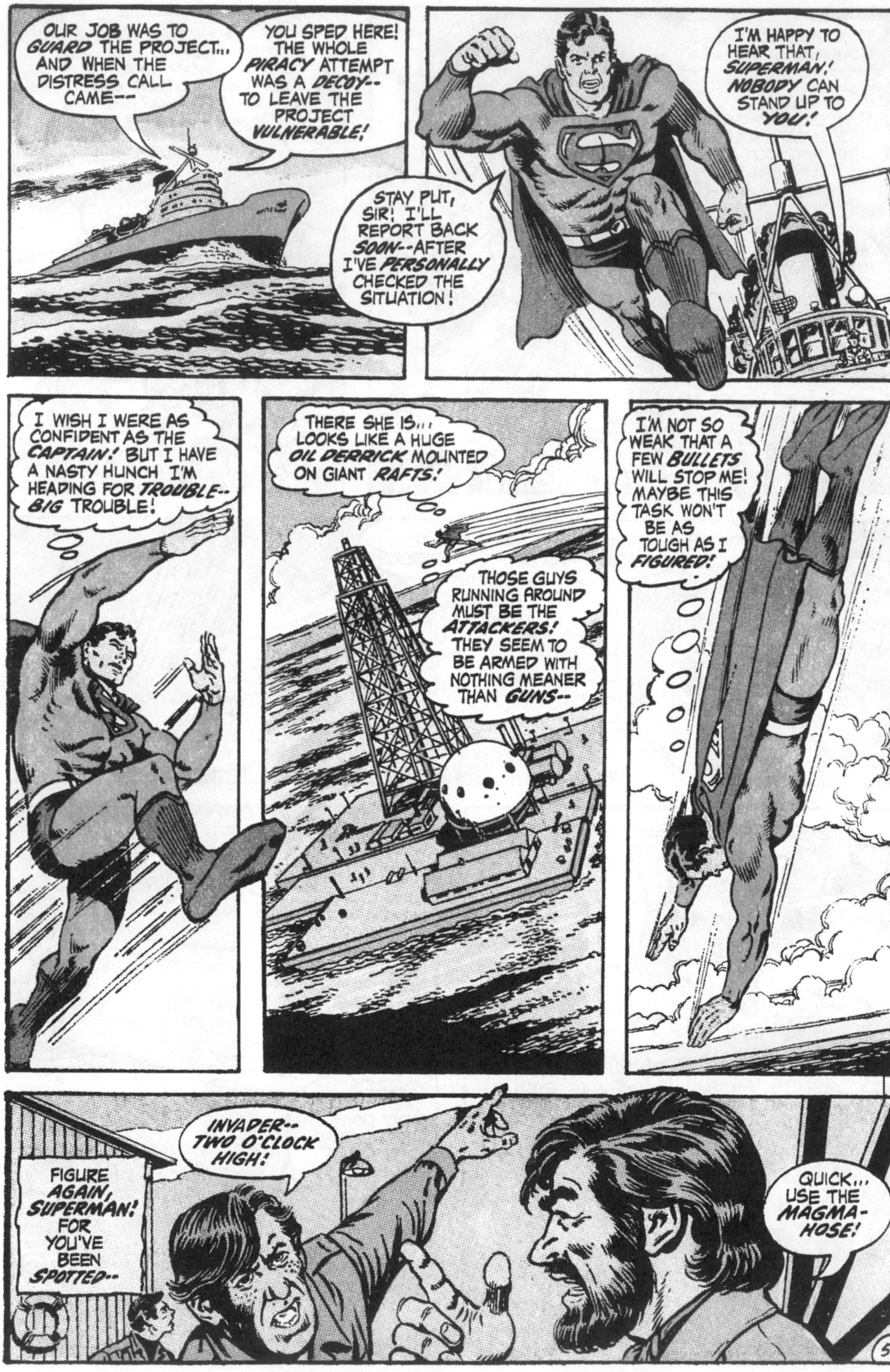

OUR JOB WAS TO GUARD THE PROJECT... AND WHEN THE DISTRESS CALL CAME--
YOU SPED HERE! THE WHOLE PIRACY ATTEMPT WAS A DECOY-- TO LEAVE THE PROJECT VULNERABLE!
I'M HAPPY TO HEAR THAT, SUPERMAN! NOBODY CAN STAND UP TO YOU!
STAY PUT, SIR! I'LL REPORT BACK SOON--AFTER I'VE PERSONALLY CHECKED THE SITUATION!
I WISH I WERE AS CONFIDENT AS THE CAPTAIN! BUT I HAVE A NASTY HUNCH I'M HEADING FOR TROUBLE-- BIG TROUBLE!
THERE SHE IS... LOOKS LIKE A HUGE OIL DERRICK MOUNTED ON GIANT RAFTS!
THOSE GUYS RUNNING AROUND MUST BE THE ATTACKERS! THEY SEEM TO BE ARMED WITH NOTHING MEANER THAN GUNS--
I'M NOT SO WEAK THAT A FEW BULLETS WILL STOP ME! MAYBE THIS TASK WON'T BE AS TOUGH AS I FIGURED!
FIGURE AGAIN, SUPERMAN! FOR YOU'VE BEEN SPOTTED--
INVADER-- TWO O'CLOCK HIGH!
QUICK... USE THE MAGMA-HOSE!
5

MAGMA-- IGNEOUS ROCK HEATED TO A TEMPERATURE OF 1,000 DEGREES BY THE ENORMOUS PRESSURES IN THE HEART OF THE PLANET! SUCH IS THE STUFF THAT SPURTS FROM A SPECIALLY TEMPERED NOZZLE AIMED BY THESE LEADEN-EYED CRIMINALS...

SUCH IS THE STUFF THAT SLAMS INTO *SUPERMAN,* INSTANTLY COVERING HIM, INSTANTLY IMPRISONING HIM IN A SHROUD OF HOT STONE...

CAN'T MANEUVER... CAN'T *DODGE!* NOTHING TO DO EXCEPT--*TAKE IT!*

MY FORWARD LEAP WAS *STOPPED-- DEAD!* TO MAKE MATTERS WORSE, THE WATER IS COOLING THE MAGMA...

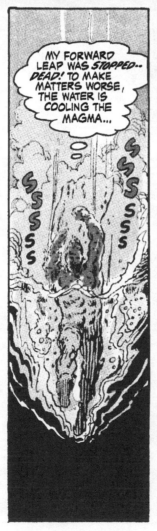

...CAUSING IT TO STICK TO ME LIKE A *SECOND SKIN!*-- IT MUST WEIGH A *TON!*

I'LL BE STUCK HERE *FOREVER*--A PART OF THE UNDERSEA *SCENERY*--

--UNLESS I SUMMON UP ENOUGH STRENGTH TO BREAK...*OUT!*

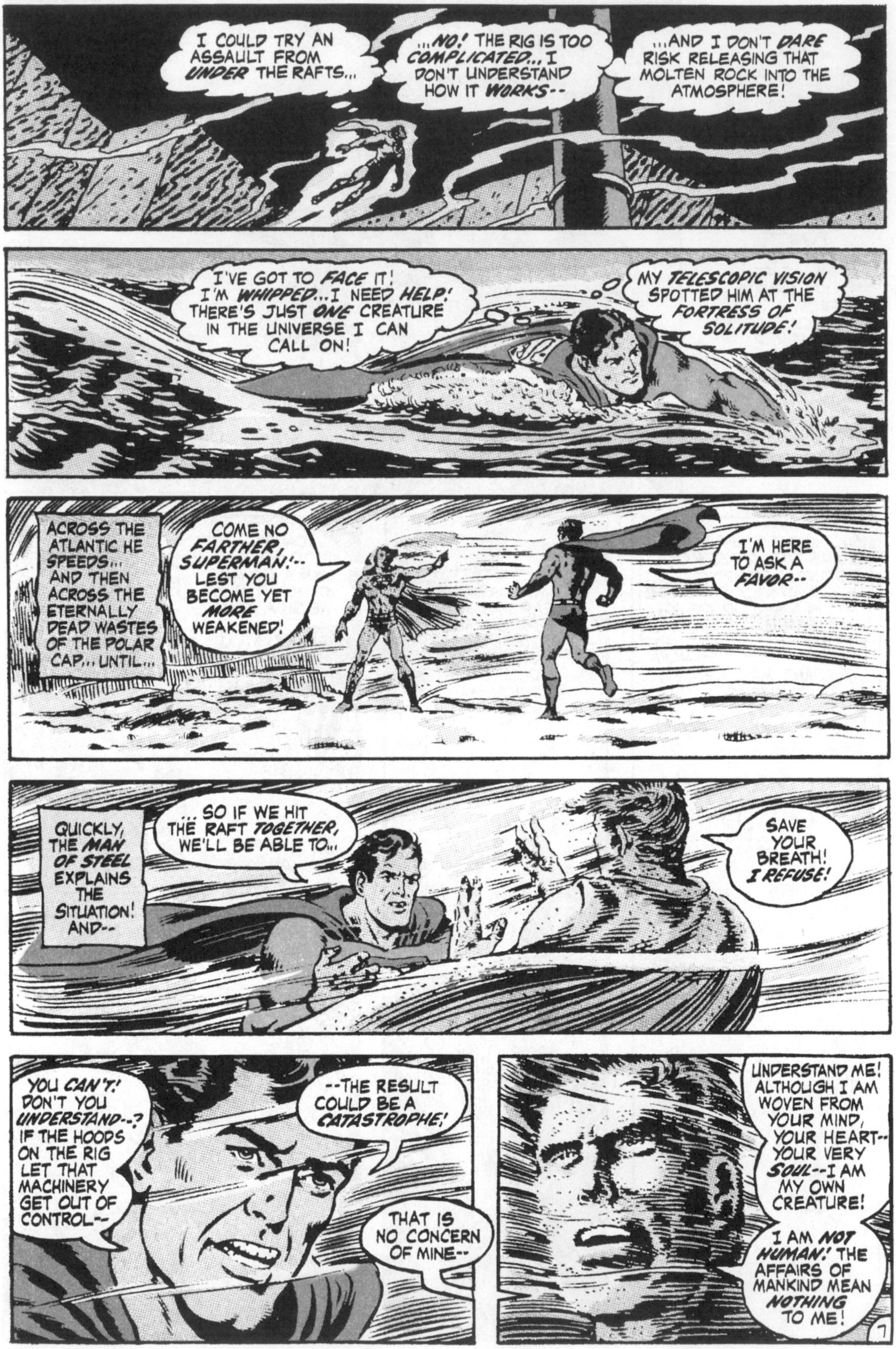
I COULD TRY AN ASSAULT FROM UNDER THE RAFTS...
...NO! THE RIG IS TOO COMPLICATED... I DON'T UNDERSTAND HOW IT WORKS--
...AND I DON'T DARE RISK RELEASING THAT MOLTEN ROCK INTO THE ATMOSPHERE!
I'VE GOT TO FACE IT! I'M WHIPPED...I NEED HELP! THERE'S JUST ONE CREATURE IN THE UNIVERSE I CAN CALL ON!
MY TELESCOPIC VISION SPOTTED HIM AT THE FORTRESS OF SOLITUDE!
ACROSS THE ATLANTIC HE SPEEDS... AND THEN ACROSS THE ETERNALLY DEAD WASTES OF THE POLAR CAP... UNTIL...
COME NO FARTHER, SUPERMAN!-- LEST YOU BECOME YET MORE WEAKENED!
I'M HERE TO ASK A FAVOR--
QUICKLY, THE MAN OF STEEL EXPLAINS THE SITUATION! AND--
... SO IF WE HIT THE RAFT TOGETHER, WE'LL BE ABLE TO...
SAVE YOUR BREATH! I REFUSE!
YOU CAN'T! DON'T YOU UNDERSTAND--? IF THE HOODS ON THE RIG LET THAT MACHINERY GET OUT OF CONTROL--
--THE RESULT COULD BE A CATASTROPHE!
THAT IS NO CONCERN OF MINE--
UNDERSTAND ME! ALTHOUGH I AM WOVEN FROM YOUR MIND, YOUR HEART-- YOUR VERY SOUL--I AM MY OWN CREATURE!
I AM NOT HUMAN! THE AFFAIRS OF MANKIND MEAN NOTHING TO ME!
7

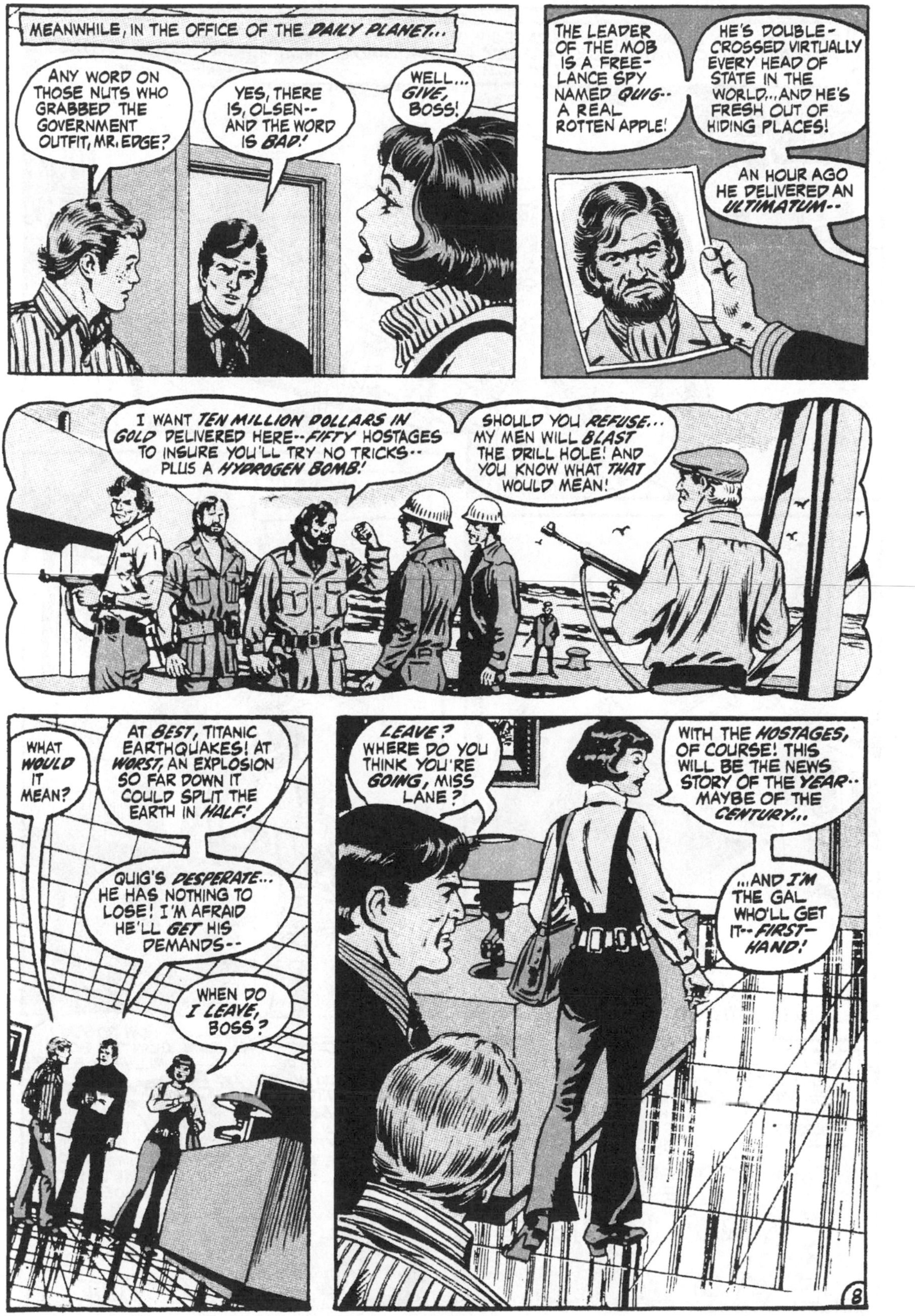
MEANWHILE, IN THE OFFICE OF THE DAILY PLANET...
ANY WORD ON THOSE NUTS WHO GRABBED THE GOVERNMENT OUTFIT, MR. EDGE?
YES, THERE IS, OLSEN-- AND THE WORD IS BAD!
WELL... GIVE, BOSS!
THE LEADER OF THE MOB IS A FREE-LANCE SPY NAMED QUIG-- A REAL ROTTEN APPLE!
HE'S DOUBLE-CROSSED VIRTUALLY EVERY HEAD OF STATE IN THE WORLD...AND HE'S FRESH OUT OF HIDING PLACES!
AN HOUR AGO HE DELIVERED AN ULTIMATUM--
I WANT TEN MILLION DOLLARS IN GOLD DELIVERED HERE--FIFTY HOSTAGES TO INSURE YOU'LL TRY NO TRICKS-- PLUS A HYDROGEN BOMB!
SHOULD YOU REFUSE... MY MEN WILL BLAST THE DRILL HOLE! AND YOU KNOW WHAT THAT WOULD MEAN!
WHAT WOULD IT MEAN?
AT BEST, TITANIC EARTHQUAKES! AT WORST, AN EXPLOSION SO FAR DOWN IT COULD SPLIT THE EARTH IN HALF!
QUIG'S DESPERATE... HE HAS NOTHING TO LOSE! I'M AFRAID HE'LL GET HIS DEMANDS--
WHEN DO I LEAVE, BOSS?
LEAVE? WHERE DO YOU THINK YOU'RE GOING, MISS LANE?
WITH THE HOSTAGES, OF COURSE! THIS WILL BE THE NEWS STORY OF THE YEAR-- MAYBE OF THE CENTURY...
...AND I'M THE GAL WHO'LL GET IT--FIRST-HAND!
8

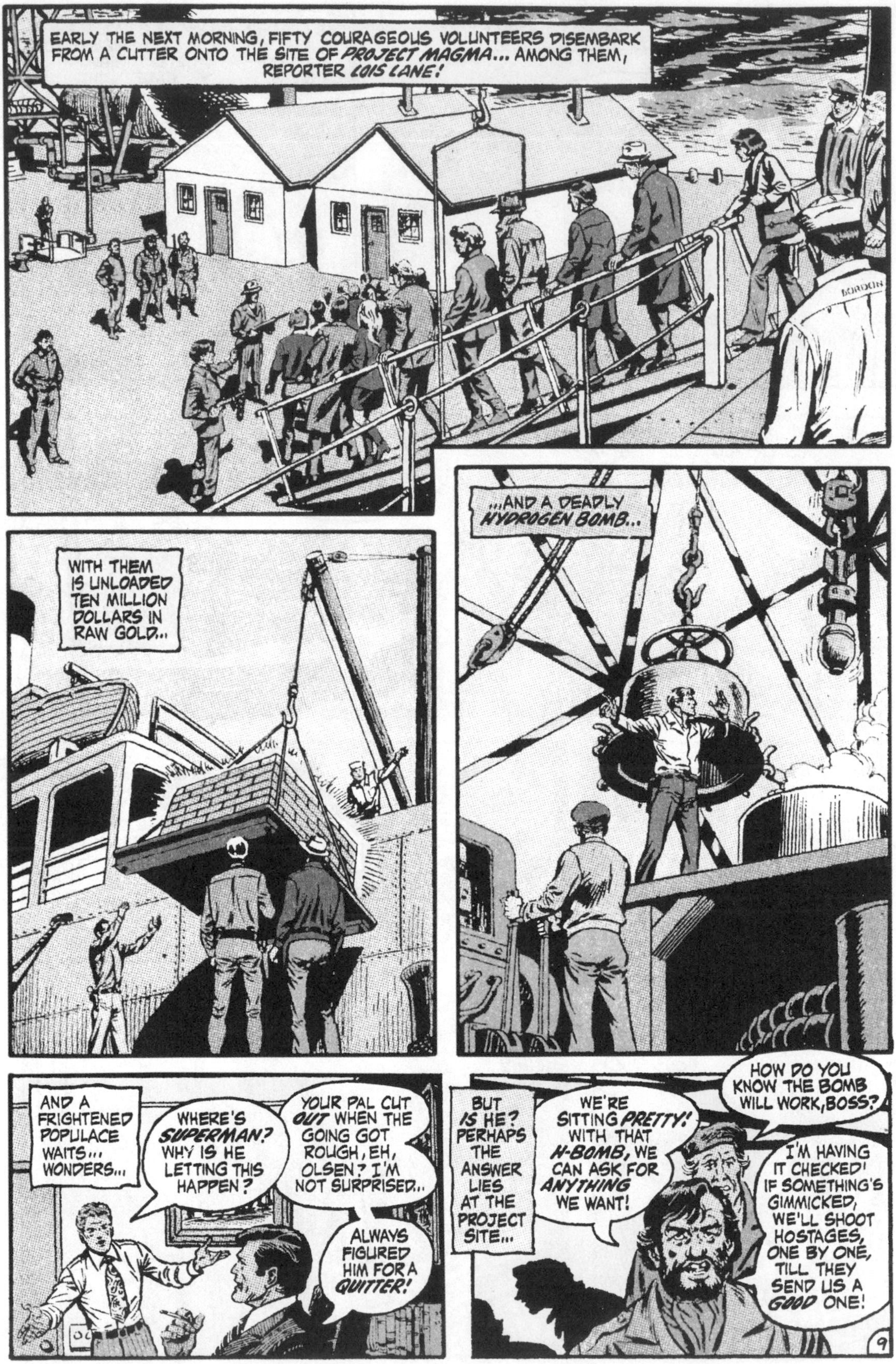
EARLY THE NEXT MORNING, FIFTY COURAGEOUS VOLUNTEERS DISEMBARK FROM A CUTTER ONTO THE SITE OF PROJECT MAGMA... AMONG THEM, REPORTER LOIS LANE!
WITH THEM IS UNLOADED TEN MILLION DOLLARS IN RAW GOLD...
...AND A DEADLY HYDROGEN BOMB...
AND A FRIGHTENED POPULACE WAITS... WONDERS...
WHERE'S SUPERMAN? WHY IS HE LETTING THIS HAPPEN?
YOUR PAL CUT OUT WHEN THE GOING GOT ROUGH, EH, OLSEN? I'M NOT SURPRISED...
ALWAYS FIGURED HIM FOR A QUITTER!
BUT IS HE? PERHAPS THE ANSWER LIES AT THE PROJECT SITE...
WE'RE SITTING PRETTY! WITH THAT H-BOMB, WE CAN ASK FOR ANYTHING WE WANT!
HOW DO YOU KNOW THE BOMB WILL WORK, BOSS?
I'M HAVING IT CHECKED! IF SOMETHING'S GIMMICKED, WE'LL SHOOT HOSTAGES, ONE BY ONE, TILL THEY SEND US A GOOD ONE!
9

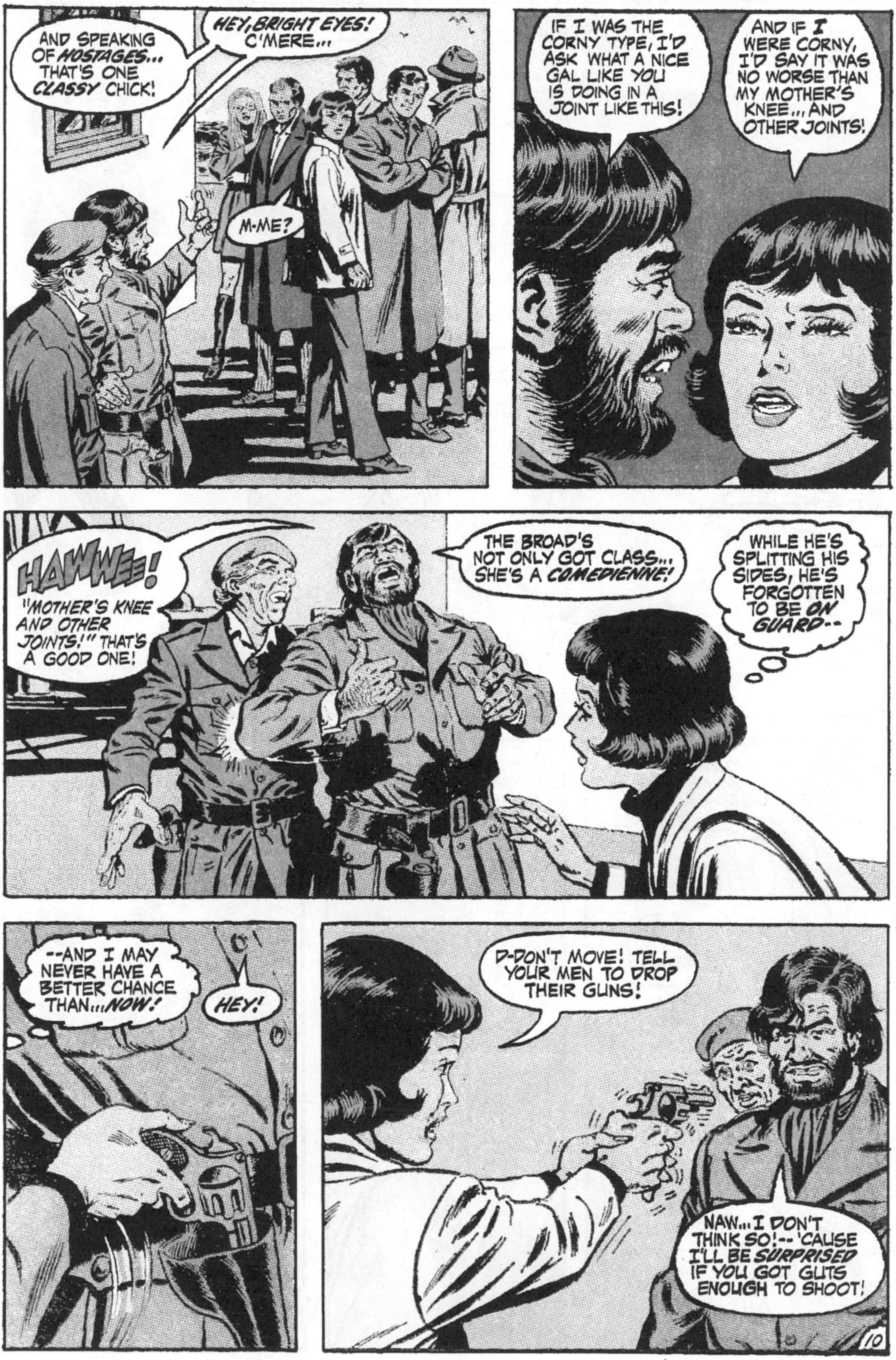
AND SPEAKING OF HOSTAGES... THAT'S ONE CLASSY CHICK!
HEY, BRIGHT EYES! C'MERE...
M-ME?
IF I WAS THE CORNY TYPE, I'D ASK WHAT A NICE GAL LIKE YOU IS DOING IN A JOINT LIKE THIS!
AND IF I WERE CORNY, I'D SAY IT WAS NO WORSE THAN MY MOTHER'S KNEE... AND OTHER JOINTS!
HAWWEE!
"MOTHER'S KNEE AND OTHER JOINTS!" THAT'S A GOOD ONE!
THE BROAD'S NOT ONLY GOT CLASS... SHE'S A COMEDIENNE!
WHILE HE'S SPLITTING HIS SIDES, HE'S FORGOTTEN TO BE ON GUARD--
--AND I MAY NEVER HAVE A BETTER CHANCE THAN... NOW!
HEY!
D-DON'T MOVE! TELL YOUR MEN TO DROP THEIR GUNS!
NAW... I DON'T THINK SO!-- 'CAUSE I'LL BE SURPRISED IF YOU GOT GUTS ENOUGH TO SHOOT!
10

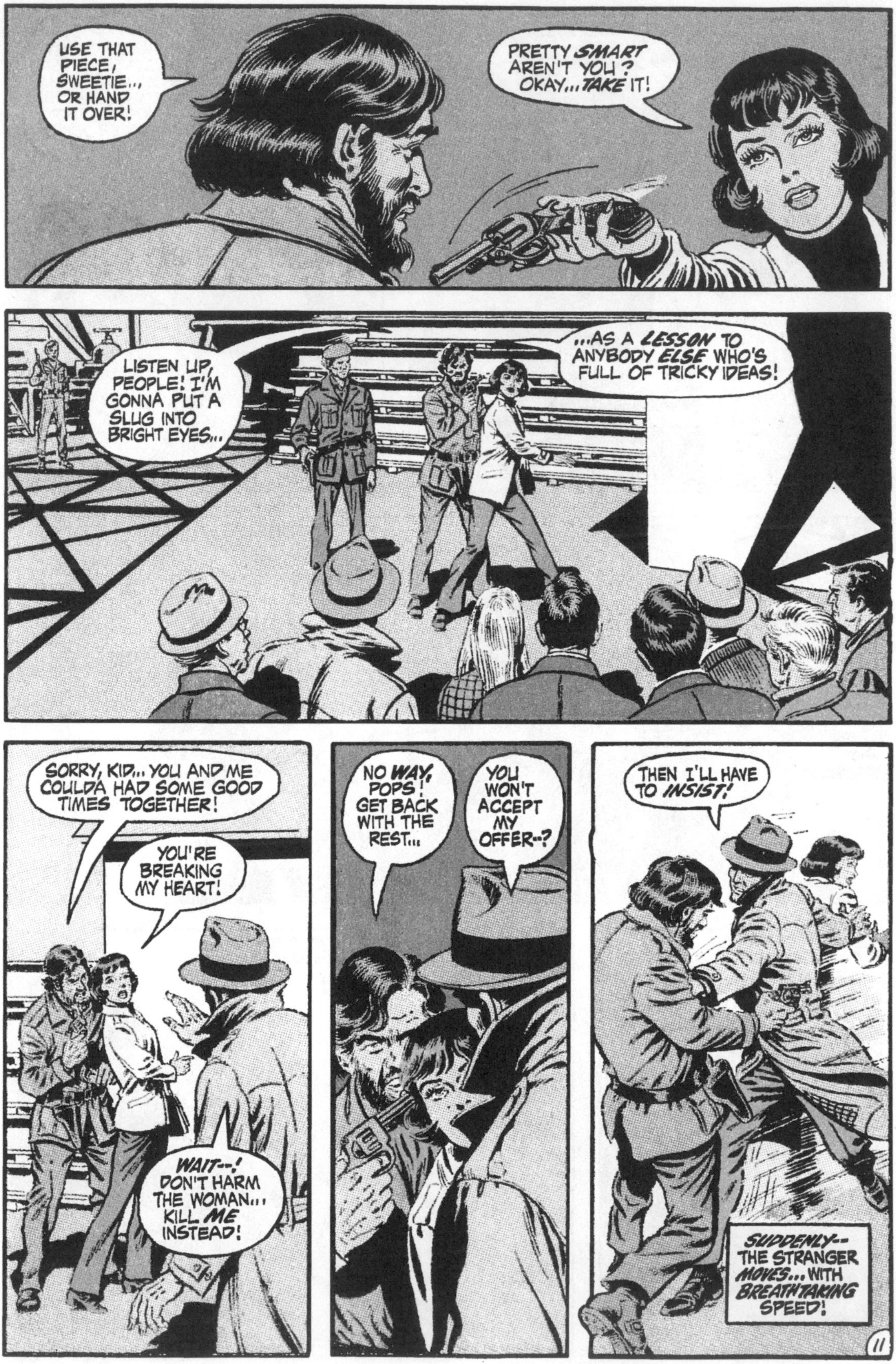
USE THAT PIECE, SWEETIE..., OR HAND IT OVER!
PRETTY SMART AREN'T YOU? OKAY...TAKE IT!
LISTEN UP, PEOPLE! I'M GONNA PUT A SLUG INTO BRIGHT EYES...
...AS A LESSON TO ANYBODY ELSE WHO'S FULL OF TRICKY IDEAS!
SORRY, KID... YOU AND ME COULDA HAD SOME GOOD TIMES TOGETHER!
YOU'RE BREAKING MY HEART!
WAIT--! DON'T HARM THE WOMAN... KILL ME INSTEAD!
NO WAY, POPS! GET BACK WITH THE REST...
YOU WON'T ACCEPT MY OFFER--?
THEN I'LL HAVE TO INSIST!
SUDDENLY-- THE STRANGER MOVES... WITH BREATHTAKING SPEED!
11

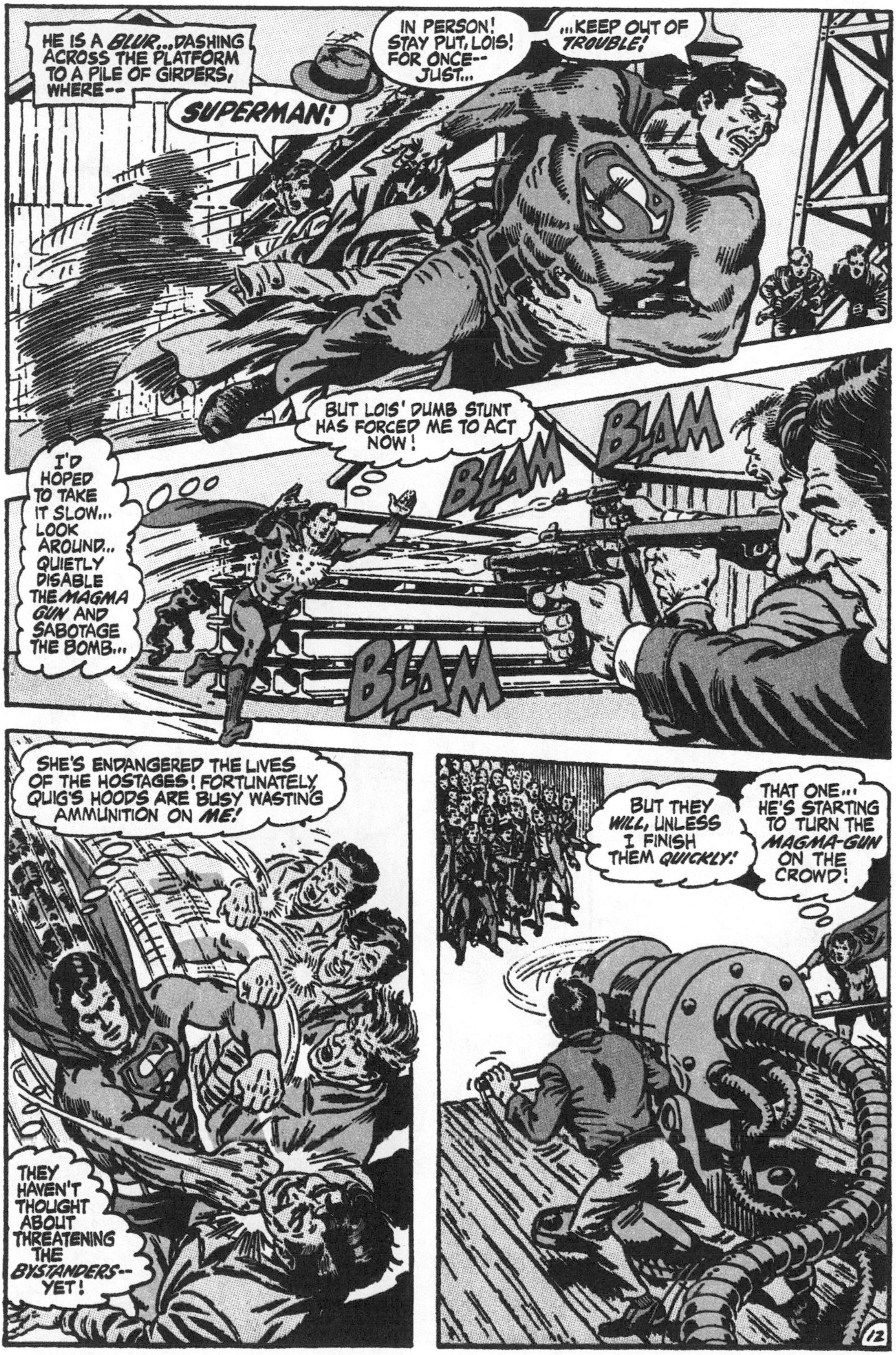
HE IS A BLUR...DASHING ACROSS THE PLATFORM TO A PILE OF GIRDERS, WHERE--
SUPERMAN!
IN PERSON! STAY PUT, LOIS! FOR ONCE-- JUST...
...KEEP OUT OF TROUBLE!
I'D HOPED TO TAKE IT SLOW... LOOK AROUND... QUIETLY DISABLE THE MAGMA GUN AND SABOTAGE THE BOMB...
BUT LOIS' DUMB STUNT HAS FORCED ME TO ACT NOW!
BLAM
BLAM
BLAM
SHE'S ENDANGERED THE LIVES OF THE HOSTAGES! FORTUNATELY, QUIG'S HOODS ARE BUSY WASTING AMMUNITION ON ME!
THEY HAVEN'T THOUGHT ABOUT THREATENING THE BYSTANDERS-- YET!
BUT THEY WILL, UNLESS I FINISH THEM QUICKLY!
THAT ONE... HE'S STARTING TO TURN THE MAGMA-GUN ON THE CROWD!
12

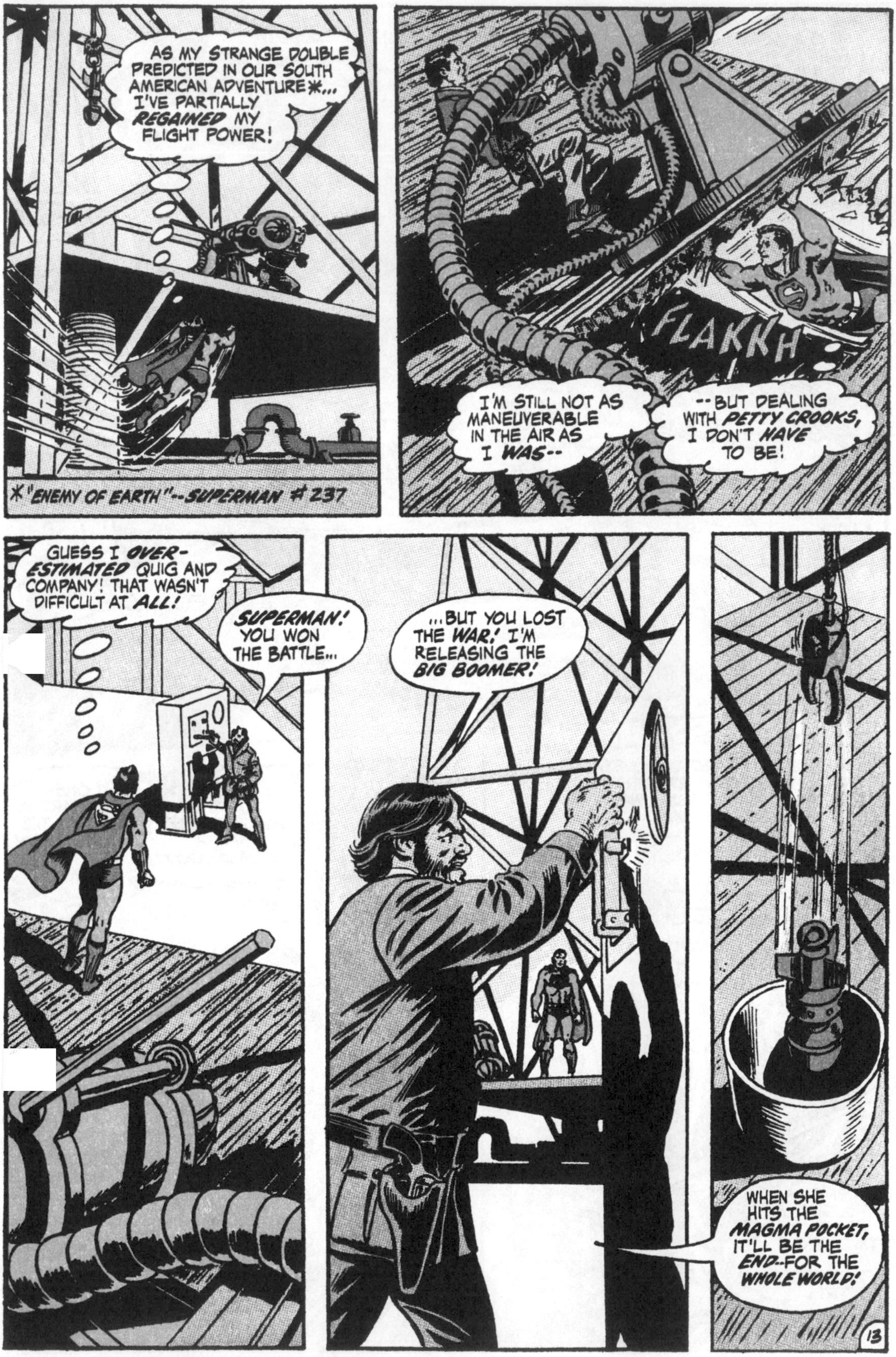
AS MY STRANGE DOUBLE PREDICTED IN OUR SOUTH AMERICAN ADVENTURE*... I'VE PARTIALLY REGAINED MY FLIGHT POWER!
*"ENEMY OF EARTH"--SUPERMAN #237
FLAKKH
I'M STILL NOT AS MANEUVERABLE IN THE AIR AS I WAS--
--BUT DEALING WITH PETTY CROOKS, I DON'T HAVE TO BE!
GUESS I OVER-ESTIMATED QUIG AND COMPANY! THAT WASN'T DIFFICULT AT ALL!
SUPERMAN! YOU WON THE BATTLE...
...BUT YOU LOST THE WAR! I'M RELEASING THE BIG BOOMER!
WHEN SHE HITS THE MAGMA POCKET, IT'LL BE THE END--FOR THE WHOLE WORLD!
13

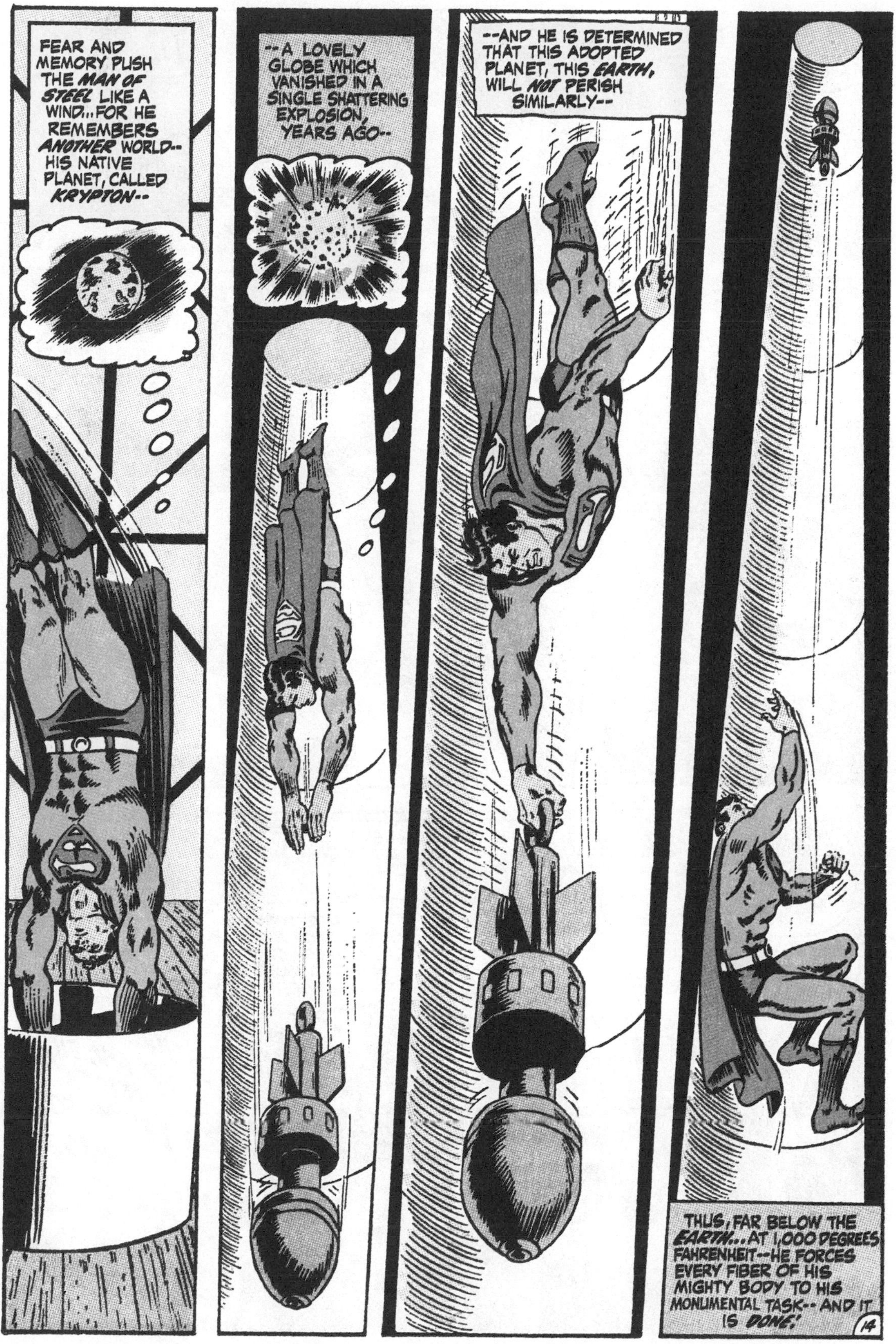
FEAR AND MEMORY PUSH THE MAN OF STEEL LIKE A WIND...FOR HE REMEMBERS ANOTHER WORLD-- HIS NATIVE PLANET, CALLED KRYPTON--
--A LOVELY GLOBE WHICH VANISHED IN A SINGLE SHATTERING EXPLOSION, YEARS AGO--
--AND HE IS DETERMINED THAT THIS ADOPTED PLANET, THIS EARTH, WILL NOT PERISH SIMILARLY--
THUS, FAR BELOW THE EARTH...AT 1,000 DEGREES FAHRENHEIT--HE FORCES EVERY FIBER OF HIS MIGHTY BODY TO HIS MONUMENTAL TASK-- AND IT IS DONE!
14

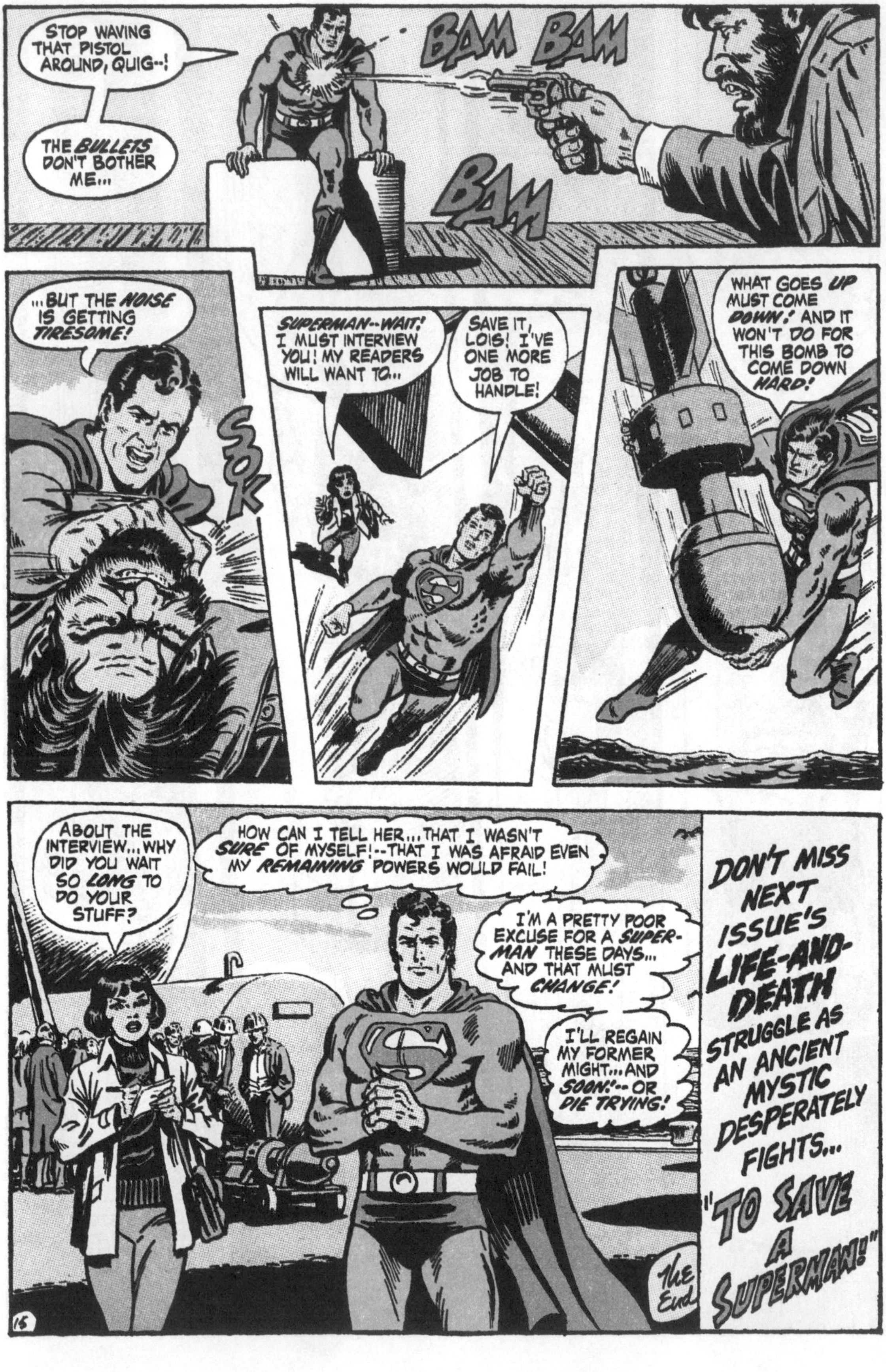
STOP WAVING THAT PISTOL AROUND, QUIG--!
THE BULLETS DON'T BOTHER ME...
BAM BAM
BAM
...BUT THE NOISE IS GETTING TIRESOME!
SOK
SUPERMAN--WAIT! I MUST INTERVIEW YOU! MY READERS WILL WANT TO...
SAVE IT, LOIS! I'VE ONE MORE JOB TO HANDLE!
WHAT GOES UP MUST COME DOWN! AND IT WON'T DO FOR THIS BOMB TO COME DOWN HARD!
ABOUT THE INTERVIEW... WHY DID YOU WAIT SO LONG TO DO YOUR STUFF?
HOW CAN I TELL HER... THAT I WASN'T SURE OF MYSELF!--THAT I WAS AFRAID EVEN MY REMAINING POWERS WOULD FAIL!
I'M A PRETTY POOR EXCUSE FOR A SUPER-MAN THESE DAYS... AND THAT MUST CHANGE!
I'LL REGAIN MY FORMER MIGHT... AND SOON!--OR DIE TRYING!
DON'T MISS NEXT ISSUE'S LIFE-AND-DEATH STRUGGLE AS AN ANCIENT MYSTIC DESPERATELY FIGHTS... "TO SAVE A SUPERMAN!"
The End
15

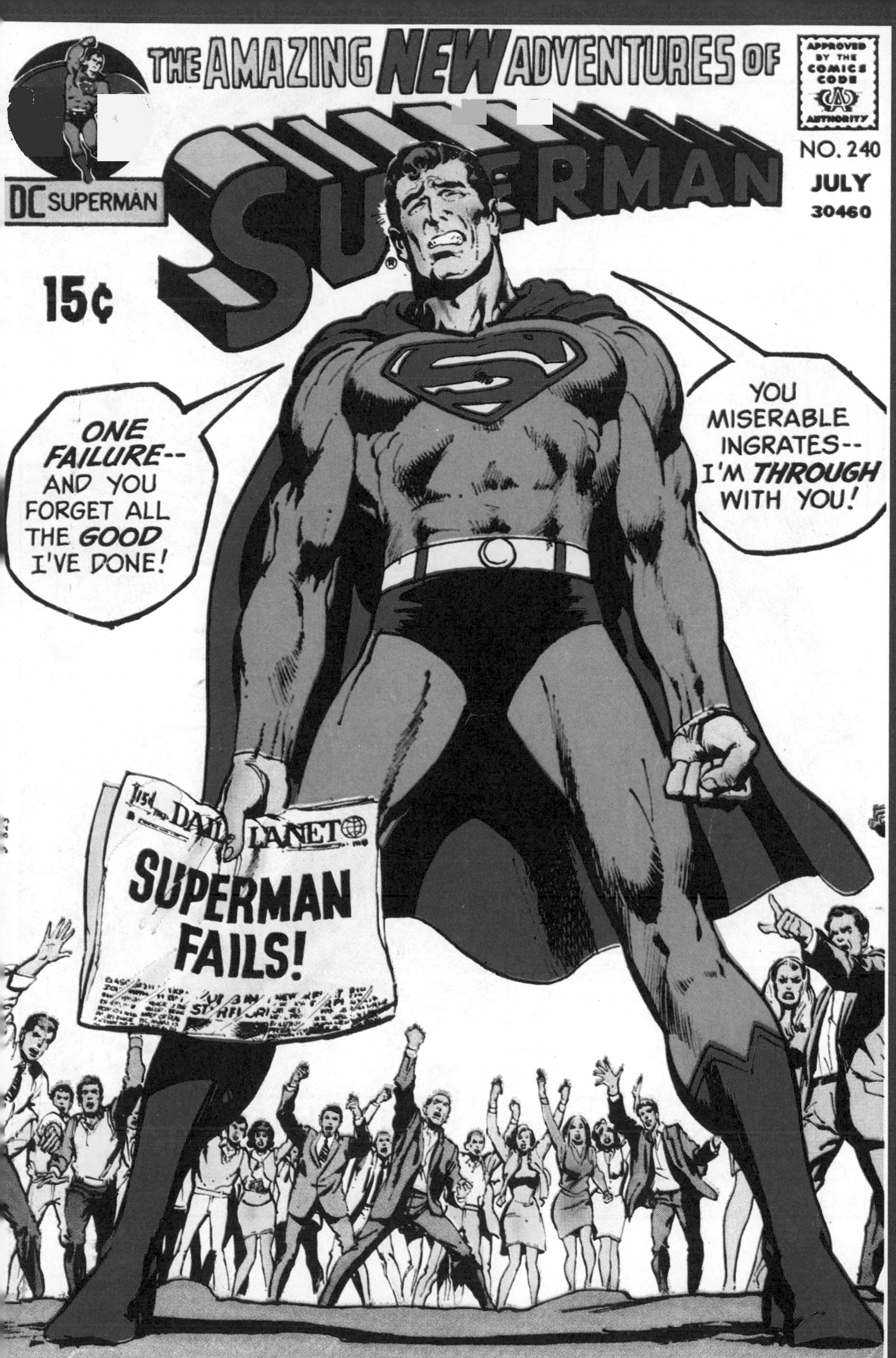
THE AMAZING NEW ADVENTURES OF
SUPERMAN
DC SUPERMAN
APPROVED BY THE COMICS CODE AUTHORITY
NO. 240
JULY
30460
15¢
ONE FAILURE-- AND YOU FORGET ALL THE GOOD I'VE DONE!
YOU MISERABLE INGRATES-- I'M THROUGH WITH YOU!
DAILY PLANET
SUPERMAN FAILS!

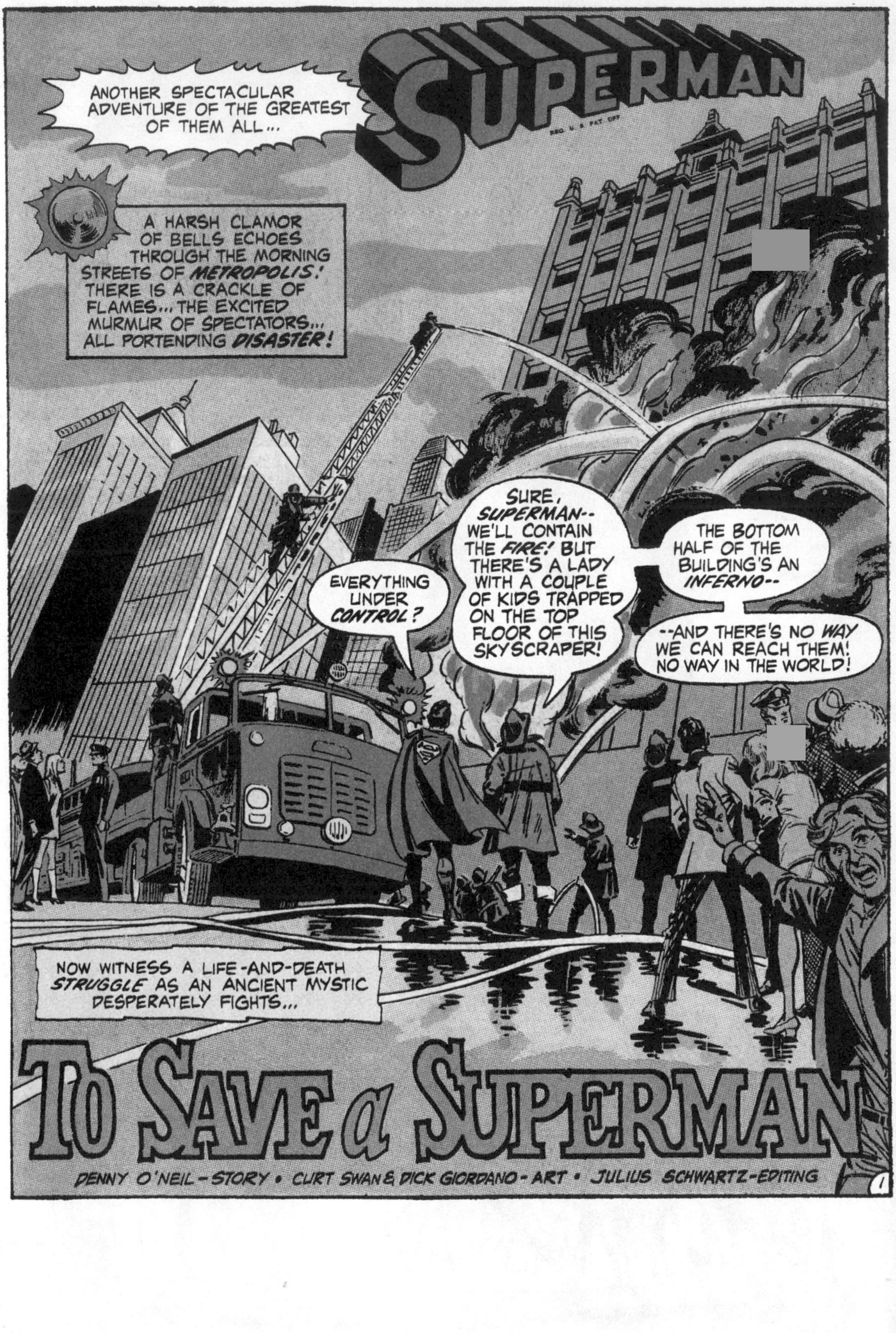
SUPERMAN
ANOTHER SPECTACULAR ADVENTURE OF THE GREATEST OF THEM ALL...
A HARSH CLAMOR OF BELLS ECHOES THROUGH THE MORNING STREETS OF METROPOLIS! THERE IS A CRACKLE OF FLAMES... THE EXCITED MURMUR OF SPECTATORS... ALL PORTENDING DISASTER!
EVERYTHING UNDER CONTROL?
SURE, SUPERMAN-- WE'LL CONTAIN THE FIRE! BUT THERE'S A LADY WITH A COUPLE OF KIDS TRAPPED ON THE TOP FLOOR OF THIS SKYSCRAPER!
THE BOTTOM HALF OF THE BUILDING'S AN INFERNO--
--AND THERE'S NO WAY WE CAN REACH THEM! NO WAY IN THE WORLD!
NOW WITNESS A LIFE-AND-DEATH STRUGGLE AS AN ANCIENT MYSTIC DESPERATELY FIGHTS...
TO SAVE A SUPERMAN
DENNY O'NEIL-STORY • CURT SWAN & DICK GIORDANO-ART • JULIUS SCHWARTZ-EDITING
1

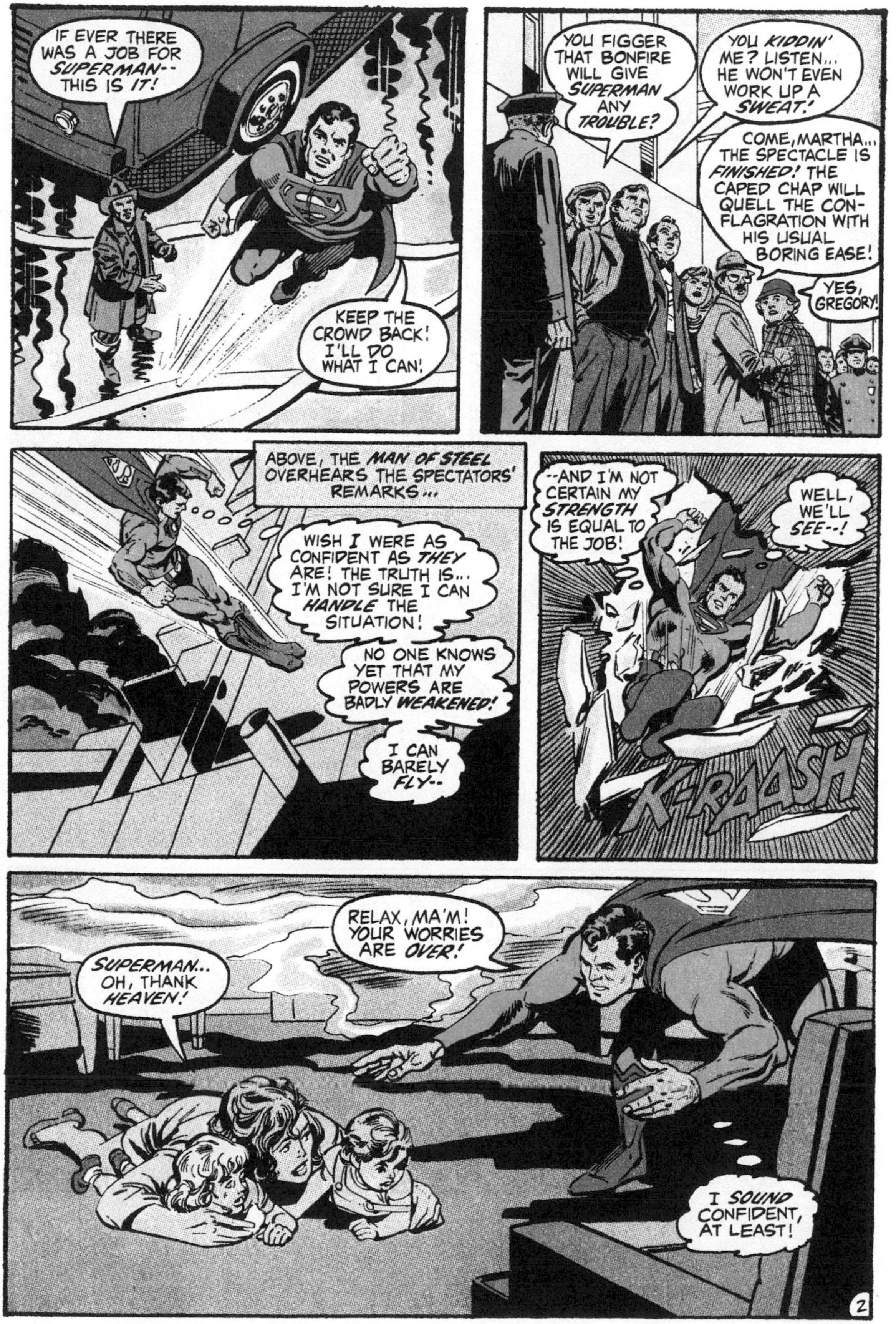
IF EVER THERE WAS A JOB FOR SUPERMAN-- THIS IS IT!
KEEP THE CROWD BACK! I'LL DO WHAT I CAN!
YOU FIGGER THAT BONFIRE WILL GIVE SUPERMAN ANY TROUBLE?
YOU KIDDIN' ME? LISTEN... HE WON'T EVEN WORK UP A SWEAT!
COME, MARTHA... THE SPECTACLE IS FINISHED! THE CAPED CHAP WILL QUELL THE CON-FLAGRATION WITH HIS USUAL BORING EASE!
YES, GREGORY!
ABOVE, THE MAN OF STEEL OVERHEARS THE SPECTATORS' REMARKS...
WISH I WERE AS CONFIDENT AS THEY ARE! THE TRUTH IS... I'M NOT SURE I CAN HANDLE THE SITUATION!
NO ONE KNOWS YET THAT MY POWERS ARE BADLY WEAKENED!
I CAN BARELY FLY--
--AND I'M NOT CERTAIN MY STRENGTH IS EQUAL TO THE JOB!
WELL, WE'LL SEE--!
K-RAASH
SUPERMAN... OH, THANK HEAVEN!
RELAX, MA'M! YOUR WORRIES ARE OVER!
I SOUND CONFIDENT, AT LEAST!
2

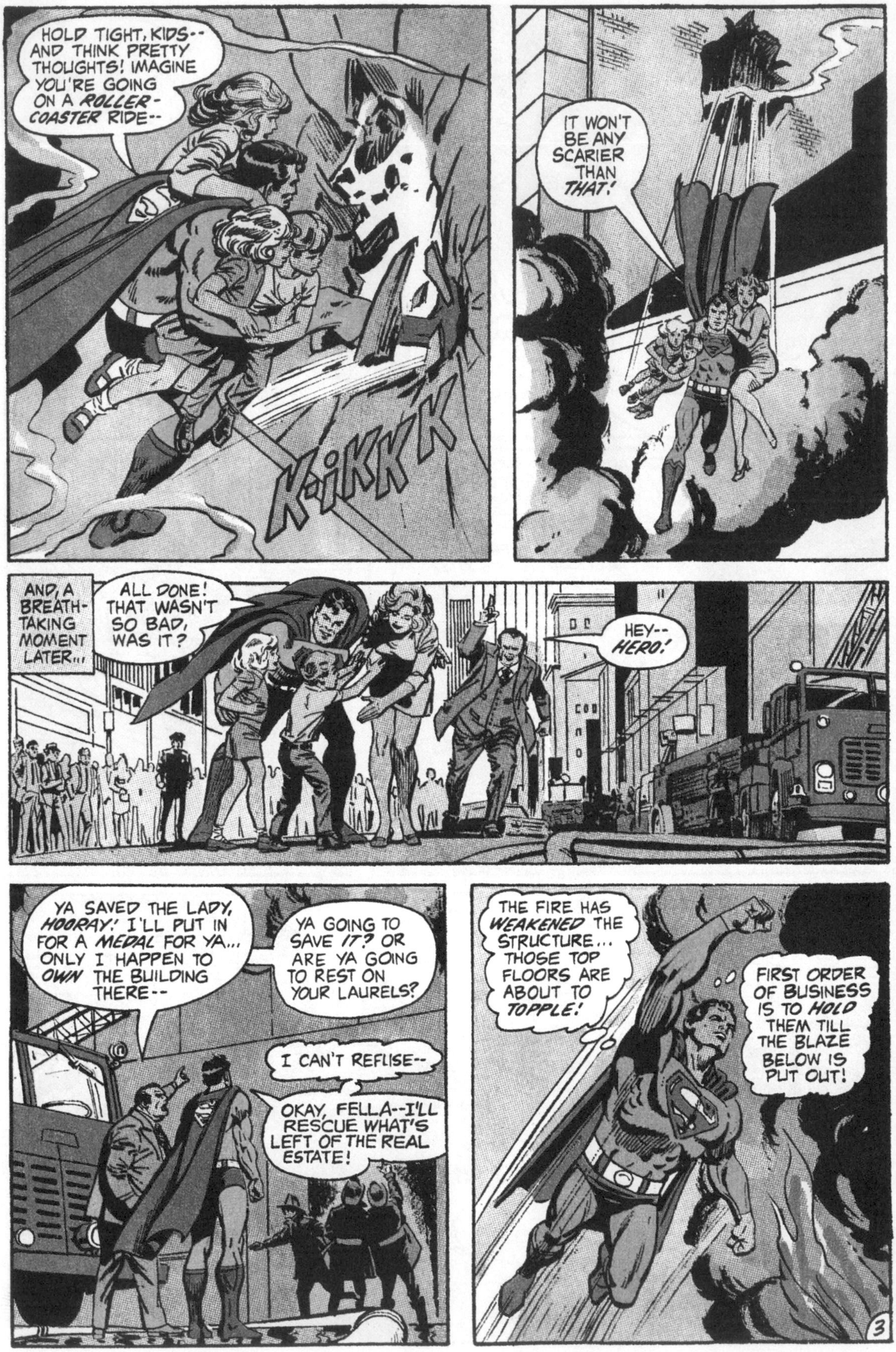
HOLD TIGHT, KIDS-- AND THINK PRETTY THOUGHTS! IMAGINE YOU'RE GOING ON A *ROLLER-COASTER* RIDE--
K-iKKK
IT WON'T BE ANY SCARIER THAN *THAT!*
AND, A BREATH-TAKING MOMENT LATER...
ALL DONE! THAT WASN'T SO BAD, WAS IT?
HEY-- *HERO!*
YA SAVED THE LADY, *HOORAY!* I'LL PUT IN FOR A *MEDAL* FOR YA... ONLY I HAPPEN TO *OWN* THE BUILDING THERE--
YA GOING TO SAVE *IT?* OR ARE YA GOING TO REST ON YOUR LAURELS?
I CAN'T REFUSE--
OKAY, FELLA--I'LL RESCUE WHAT'S LEFT OF THE REAL ESTATE!
THE FIRE HAS *WEAKENED* THE STRUCTURE... THOSE TOP FLOORS ARE ABOUT TO *TOPPLE!*
FIRST ORDER OF BUSINESS IS TO *HOLD* THEM TILL THE BLAZE BELOW IS PUT OUT!
3

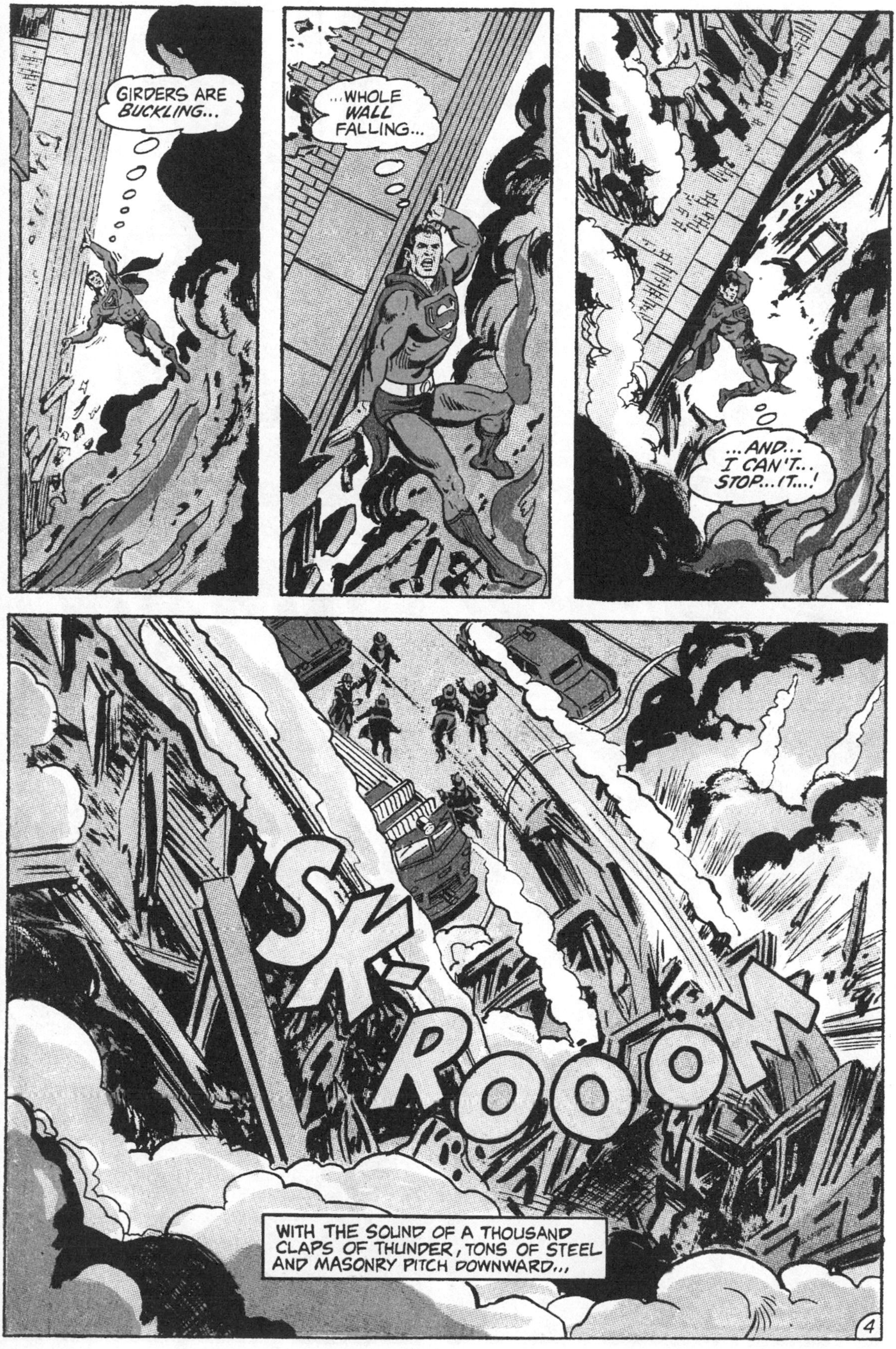
GIRDERS ARE BUCKLING...
...WHOLE WALL FALLING...
...AND... I CAN'T... STOP...IT...!
SK-ROOOM
WITH THE SOUND OF A THOUSAND CLAPS OF THUNDER, TONS OF STEEL AND MASONRY PITCH DOWNWARD...
4

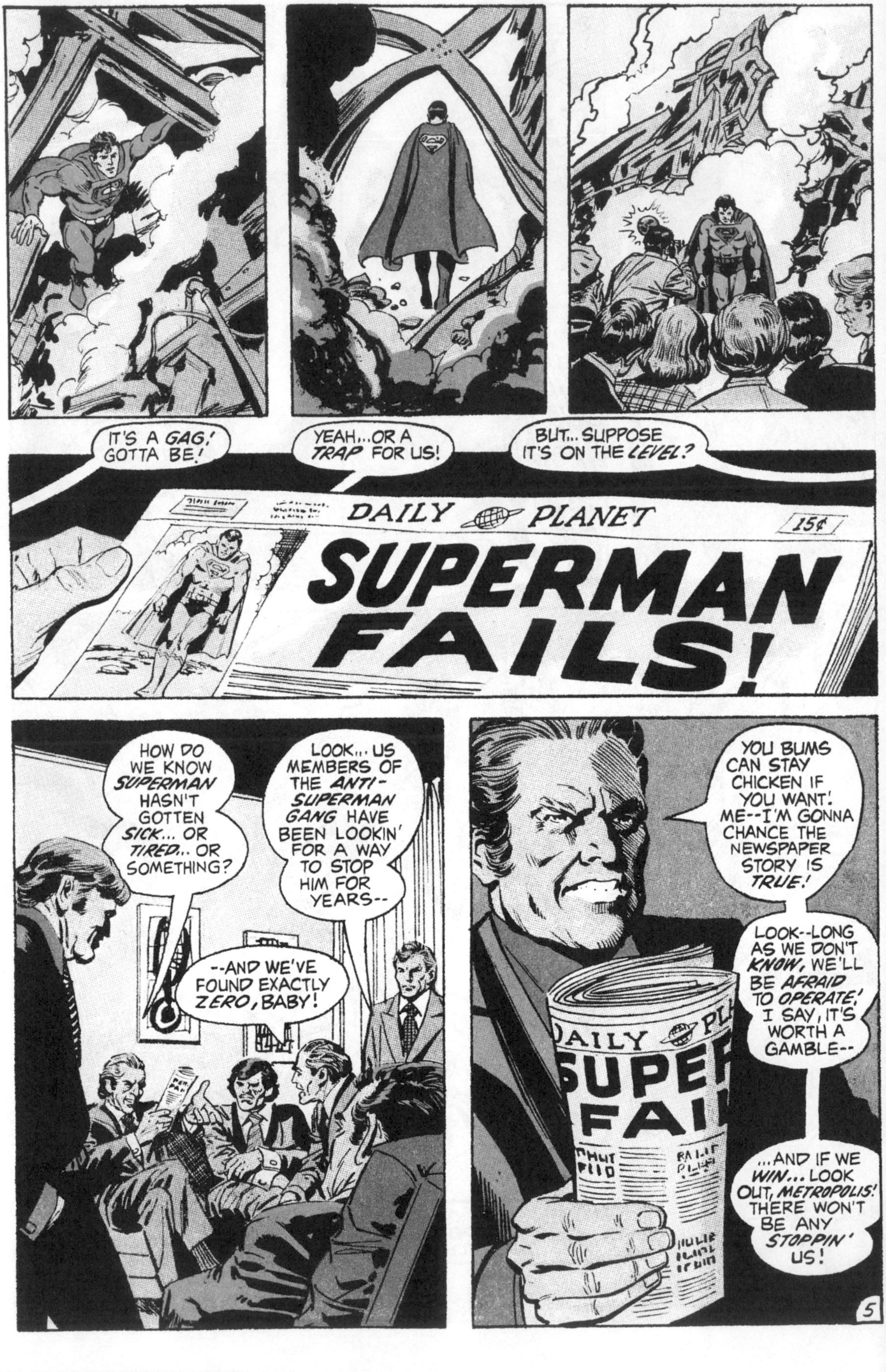

IT'S A GAG! GOTTA BE!
YEAH...OR A TRAP FOR US!
BUT... SUPPOSE IT'S ON THE LEVEL?
DAILY PLANET
15¢
SUPERMAN FAILS!
HOW DO WE KNOW SUPERMAN HASN'T GOTTEN SICK... OR TIRED... OR SOMETHING?
LOOK... US MEMBERS OF THE ANTI-SUPERMAN GANG HAVE BEEN LOOKIN' FOR A WAY TO STOP HIM FOR YEARS--
--AND WE'VE FOUND EXACTLY ZERO, BABY!
YOU BUMS CAN STAY CHICKEN IF YOU WANT! ME--I'M GONNA CHANCE THE NEWSPAPER STORY IS TRUE!
LOOK--LONG AS WE DON'T KNOW, WE'LL BE AFRAID TO OPERATE! I SAY, IT'S WORTH A GAMBLE--
...AND IF WE WIN... LOOK OUT, METROPOLIS! THERE WON'T BE ANY STOPPIN' US!
5

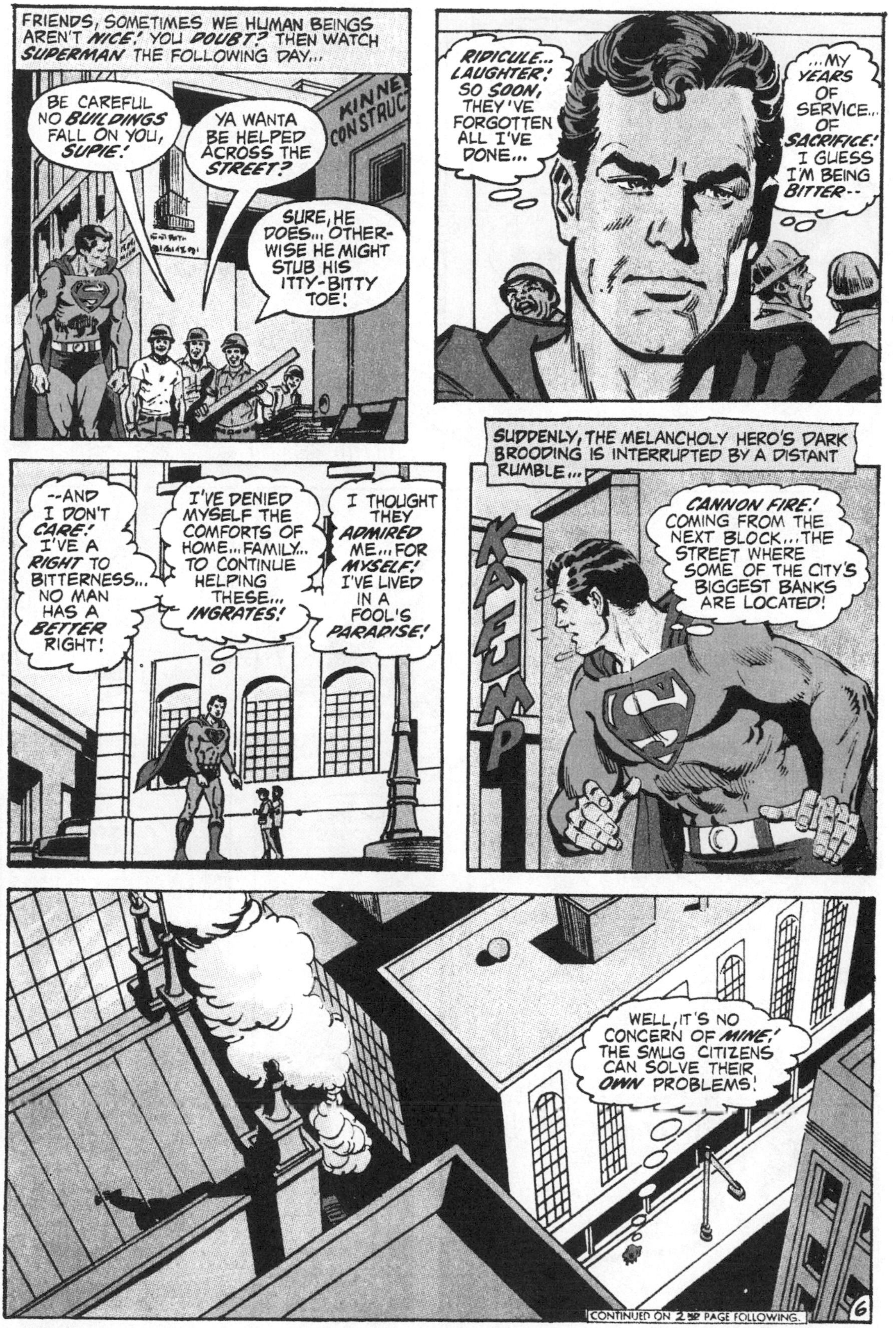
FRIENDS, SOMETIMES WE HUMAN BEINGS AREN'T NICE! YOU DOUBT? THEN WATCH SUPERMAN THE FOLLOWING DAY...
BE CAREFUL NO BUILDINGS FALL ON YOU, SUPIE!
YA WANTA BE HELPED ACROSS THE STREET?
SURE, HE DOES... OTHER-WISE HE MIGHT STUB HIS ITTY-BITTY TOE!
RIDICULE... LAUGHTER! SO SOON, THEY'VE FORGOTTEN ALL I'VE DONE...
...MY YEARS OF SERVICE... OF SACRIFICE! I GUESS I'M BEING BITTER--
--AND I DON'T CARE! I'VE A RIGHT TO BITTERNESS... NO MAN HAS A BETTER RIGHT!
I'VE DENIED MYSELF THE COMFORTS OF HOME... FAMILY... TO CONTINUE HELPING THESE... INGRATES!
I THOUGHT THEY ADMIRED ME... FOR MYSELF! I'VE LIVED IN A FOOL'S PARADISE!
SUDDENLY, THE MELANCHOLY HERO'S DARK BROODING IS INTERRUPTED BY A DISTANT RUMBLE...
KA-FUMP
CANNON FIRE! COMING FROM THE NEXT BLOCK... THE STREET WHERE SOME OF THE CITY'S BIGGEST BANKS ARE LOCATED!
WELL, IT'S NO CONCERN OF MINE! THE SMUG CITIZENS CAN SOLVE THEIR OWN PROBLEMS!
CONTINUED ON 2ND PAGE FOLLOWING.
6

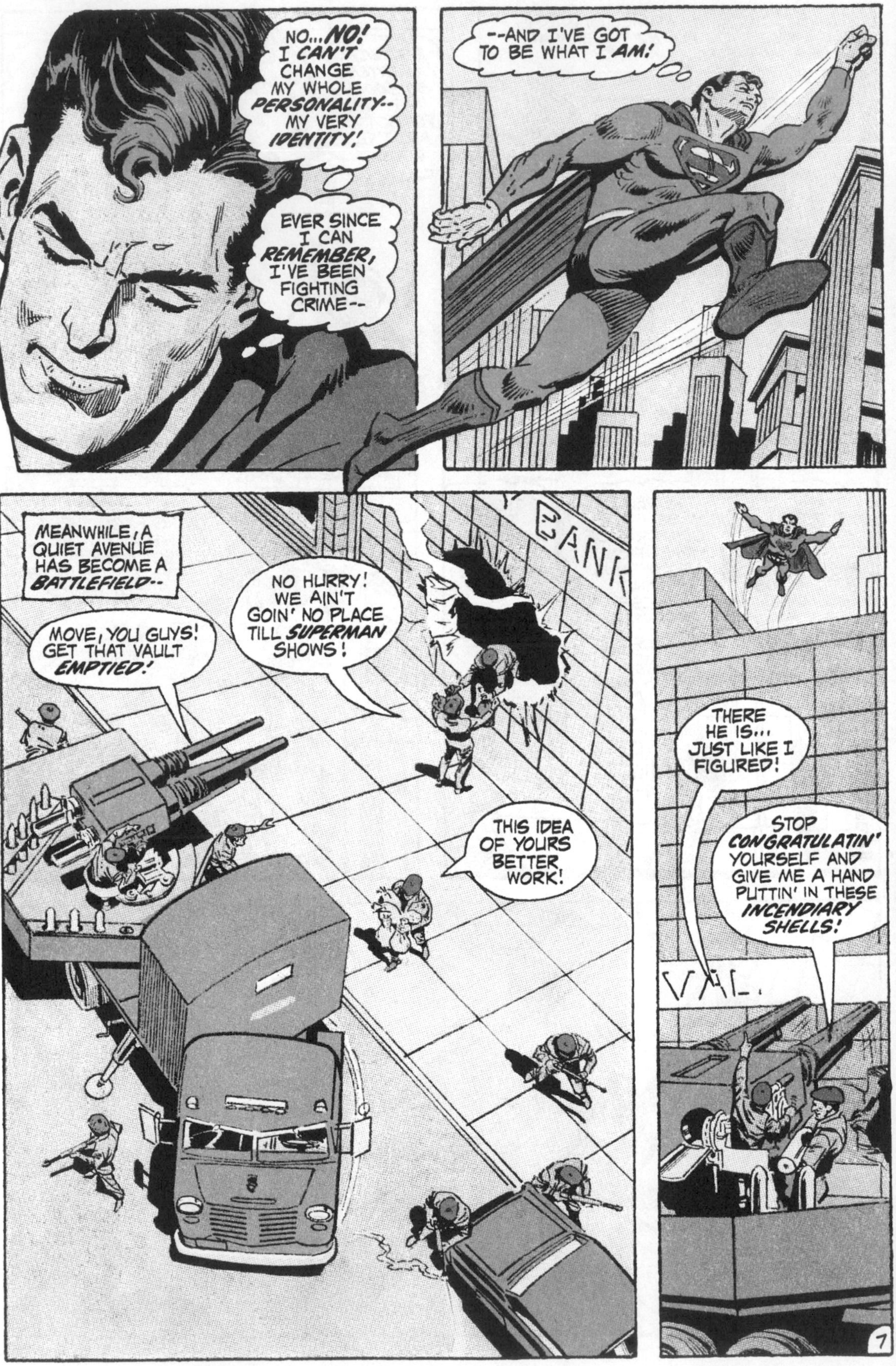
NO... NO! I CAN'T CHANGE MY WHOLE PERSONALITY-- MY VERY IDENTITY!
EVER SINCE I CAN REMEMBER, I'VE BEEN FIGHTING CRIME--
--AND I'VE GOT TO BE WHAT I AM!
MEANWHILE, A QUIET AVENUE HAS BECOME A BATTLEFIELD--
BANK
MOVE, YOU GUYS! GET THAT VAULT EMPTIED!
NO HURRY! WE AIN'T GOIN' NO PLACE TILL SUPERMAN SHOWS!
THIS IDEA OF YOURS BETTER WORK!
THERE HE IS... JUST LIKE I FIGURED!
STOP CONGRATULATIN' YOURSELF AND GIVE ME A HAND PUTTIN' IN THESE INCENDIARY SHELLS!
7

MAYBE HE *HAS* LOST HIS POWERS! HE'S MOVING SLOW ENOUGH FOR ME TO DRAW A *BEAD*--

AND *THAT'S* NEVER HAPPENED BEFORE!

KRUMP

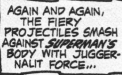

AGAIN AND AGAIN, THE FIERY PROJECTILES SMASH AGAINST *SUPERMAN'S* BODY WITH JUGGER-NALIT FORCE...

VAOOOM

...UNTIL HE WEAKENS...

VAOOOM

...AND *DROPS!*

KAHFLAMBE

WE *DID* IT! WE *GUNNED* HIM!

8

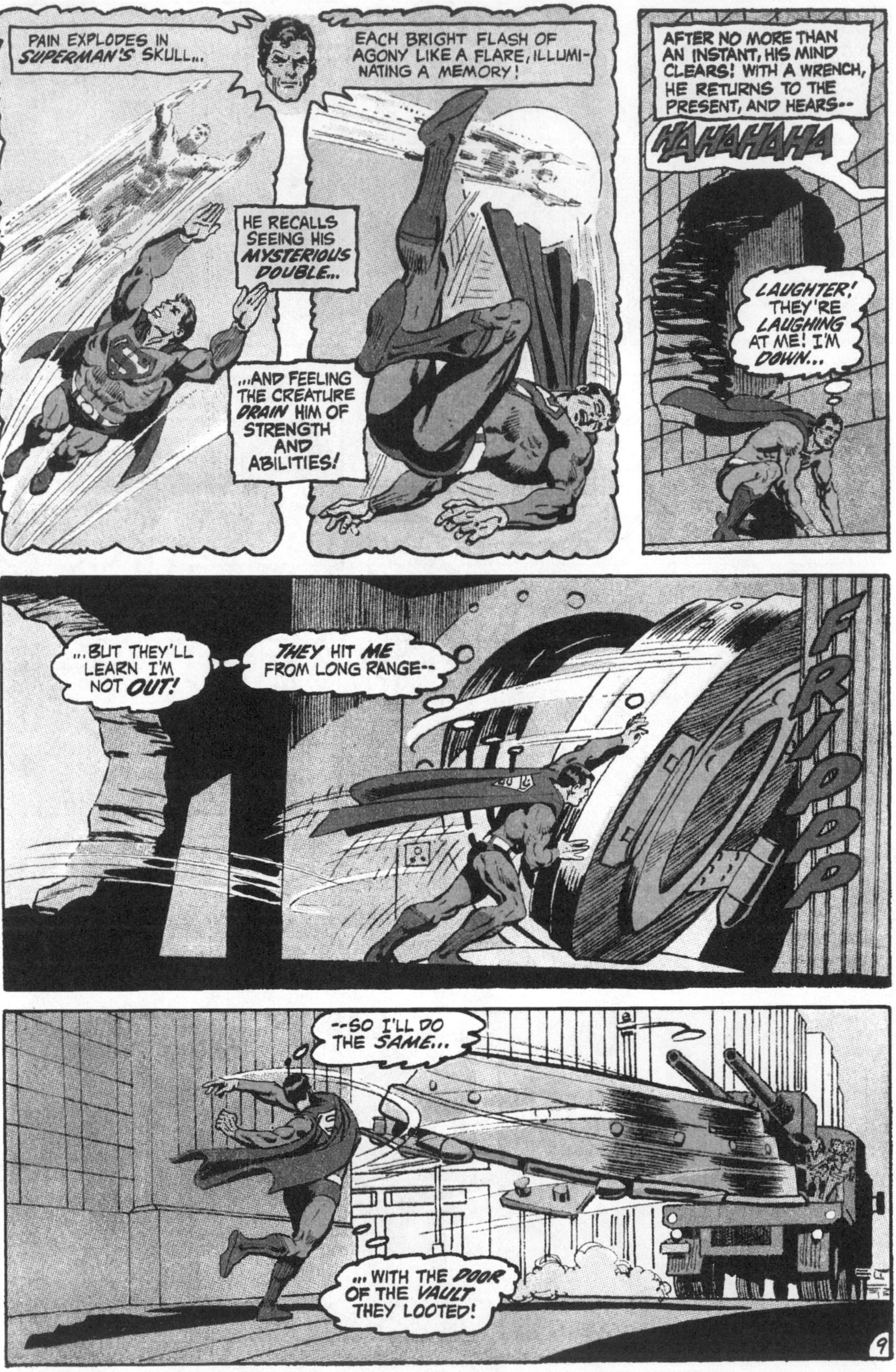
PAIN EXPLODES IN SUPERMAN'S SKULL...
EACH BRIGHT FLASH OF AGONY LIKE A FLARE, ILLUMINATING A MEMORY!
HE RECALLS SEEING HIS MYSTERIOUS DOUBLE...
...AND FEELING THE CREATURE DRAIN HIM OF STRENGTH AND ABILITIES!
AFTER NO MORE THAN AN INSTANT, HIS MIND CLEARS! WITH A WRENCH, HE RETURNS TO THE PRESENT, AND HEARS--
HAHAHAHA
LAUGHTER! THEY'RE LAUGHING AT ME! I'M DOWN...
...BUT THEY'LL LEARN I'M NOT OUT!
THEY HIT ME FROM LONG RANGE--
FRIPPP
--SO I'LL DO THE SAME...
...WITH THE DOOR OF THE VAULT THEY LOOTED!
9

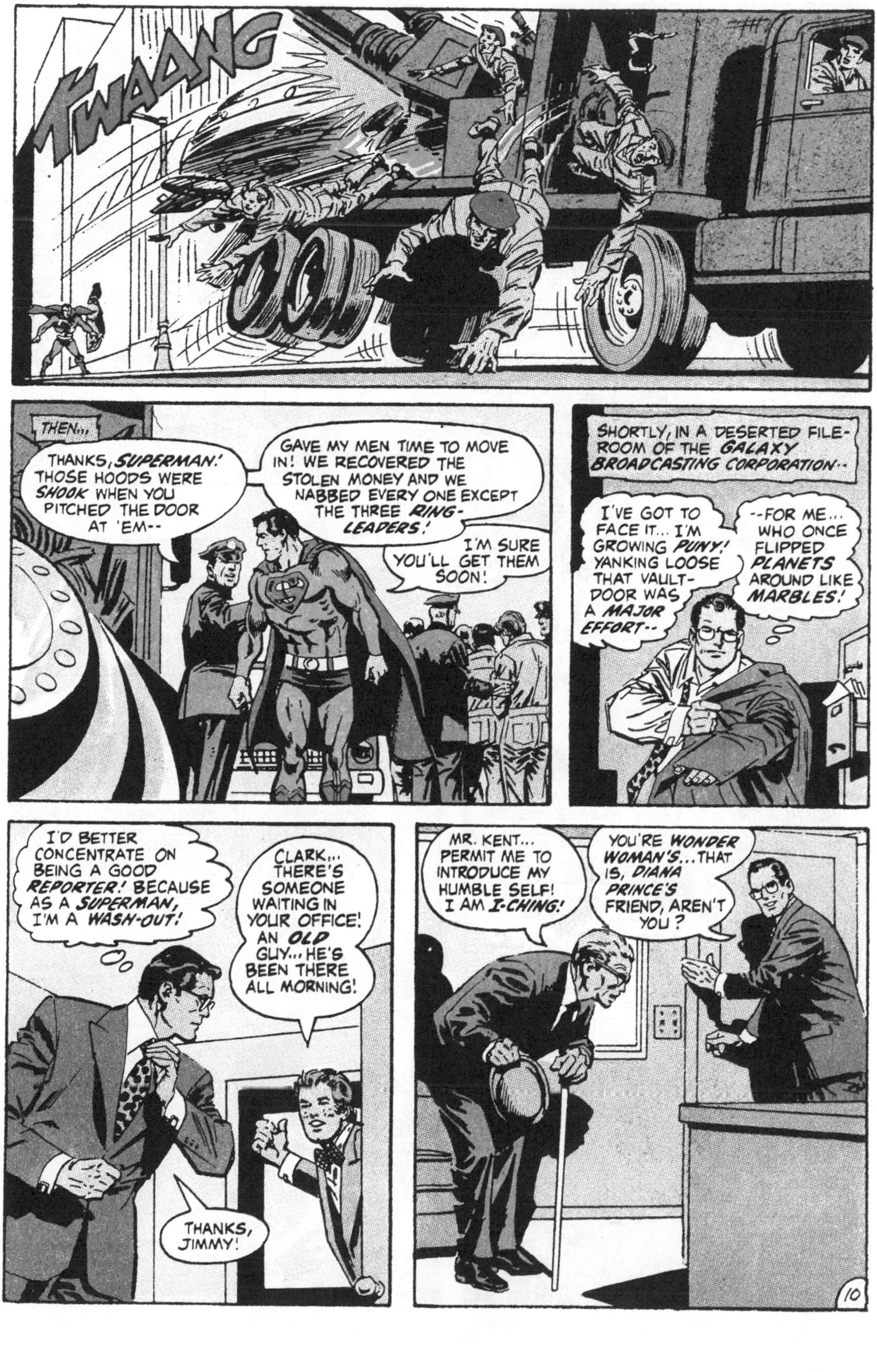
KWAANG
THEN...
THANKS, SUPERMAN! THOSE HOODS WERE SHOOK WHEN YOU PITCHED THE DOOR AT 'EM--
GAVE MY MEN TIME TO MOVE IN! WE RECOVERED THE STOLEN MONEY AND WE NABBED EVERY ONE EXCEPT THE THREE RING-LEADERS!
I'M SURE YOU'LL GET THEM SOON!
SHORTLY, IN A DESERTED FILE-ROOM OF THE GALAXY BROADCASTING CORPORATION--
I'VE GOT TO FACE IT... I'M GROWING PUNY! YANKING LOOSE THAT VAULT-DOOR WAS A MAJOR EFFORT--
--FOR ME... WHO ONCE FLIPPED PLANETS AROUND LIKE MARBLES!
I'D BETTER CONCENTRATE ON BEING A GOOD REPORTER! BECAUSE AS A SUPERMAN, I'M A WASH-OUT!
CLARK... THERE'S SOMEONE WAITING IN YOUR OFFICE! AN OLD GUY... HE'S BEEN THERE ALL MORNING!
THANKS, JIMMY!
MR. KENT... PERMIT ME TO INTRODUCE MY HUMBLE SELF! I AM I-CHING!
YOU'RE WONDER WOMAN'S... THAT IS, DIANA PRINCE'S FRIEND, AREN'T YOU?
10

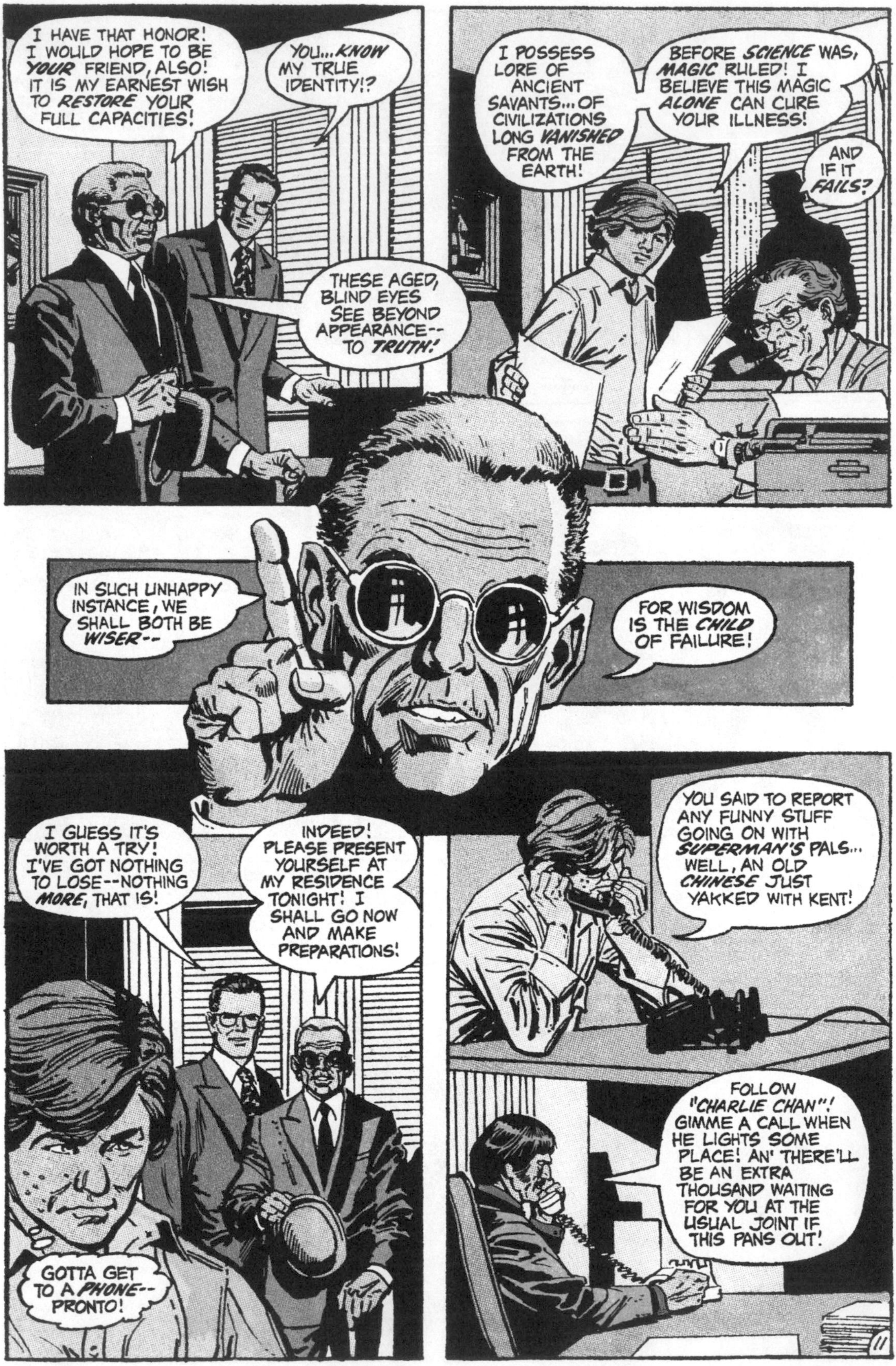

I HAVE THAT HONOR! I WOULD HOPE TO BE YOUR FRIEND, ALSO! IT IS MY EARNEST WISH TO RESTORE YOUR FULL CAPACITIES!
YOU...KNOW MY TRUE IDENTITY!?
THESE AGED, BLIND EYES SEE BEYOND APPEARANCE-- TO TRUTH!
I POSSESS LORE OF ANCIENT SAVANTS...OF CIVILIZATIONS LONG VANISHED FROM THE EARTH!
BEFORE SCIENCE WAS, MAGIC RULED! I BELIEVE THIS MAGIC ALONE CAN CURE YOUR ILLNESS!
AND IF IT FAILS?
IN SUCH UNHAPPY INSTANCE, WE SHALL BOTH BE WISER--
FOR WISDOM IS THE CHILD OF FAILURE!
I GUESS IT'S WORTH A TRY! I'VE GOT NOTHING TO LOSE--NOTHING MORE, THAT IS!
INDEED! PLEASE PRESENT YOURSELF AT MY RESIDENCE TONIGHT! I SHALL GO NOW AND MAKE PREPARATIONS!
GOTTA GET TO A PHONE-- PRONTO!
YOU SAID TO REPORT ANY FUNNY STUFF GOING ON WITH SUPERMAN'S PALS... WELL, AN OLD CHINESE JUST YAKKED WITH KENT!
FOLLOW "CHARLIE CHAN"! GIMME A CALL WHEN HE LIGHTS SOME PLACE! AN' THERE'LL BE AN EXTRA THOUSAND WAITING FOR YOU AT THE USUAL JOINT IF THIS PANS OUT!
11

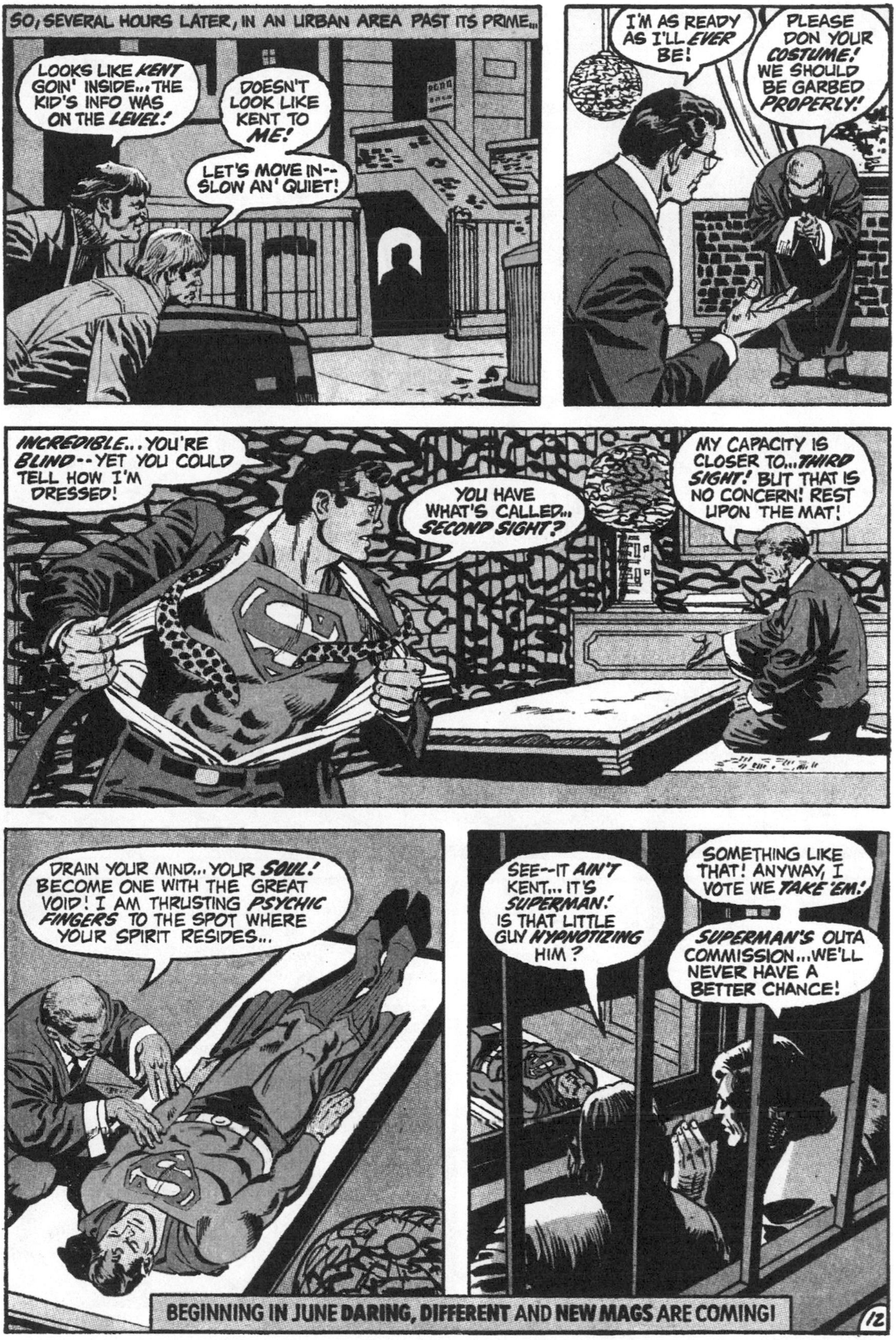
SO, SEVERAL HOURS LATER, IN AN URBAN AREA PAST ITS PRIME...
LOOKS LIKE KENT GOIN' INSIDE... THE KID'S INFO WAS ON THE LEVEL!
DOESN'T LOOK LIKE KENT TO ME!
LET'S MOVE IN-- SLOW AN' QUIET!
I'M AS READY AS I'LL EVER BE!
PLEASE DON YOUR COSTUME! WE SHOULD BE GARBED PROPERLY!
INCREDIBLE.. YOU'RE BLIND--YET YOU COULD TELL HOW I'M DRESSED!
YOU HAVE WHAT'S CALLED... SECOND SIGHT?
MY CAPACITY IS CLOSER TO... THIRD SIGHT! BUT THAT IS NO CONCERN! REST UPON THE MAT!
DRAIN YOUR MIND... YOUR SOUL! BECOME ONE WITH THE GREAT VOID! I AM THRUSTING PSYCHIC FINGERS TO THE SPOT WHERE YOUR SPIRIT RESIDES...
SEE--IT AIN'T KENT... IT'S SUPERMAN! IS THAT LITTLE GUY HYPNOTIZING HIM?
SOMETHING LIKE THAT! ANYWAY, I VOTE WE TAKE 'EM!
SUPERMAN'S OUTA COMMISSION... WE'LL NEVER HAVE A BETTER CHANCE!
BEGINNING IN JUNE DARING, DIFFERENT AND NEW MAGS ARE COMING!
12

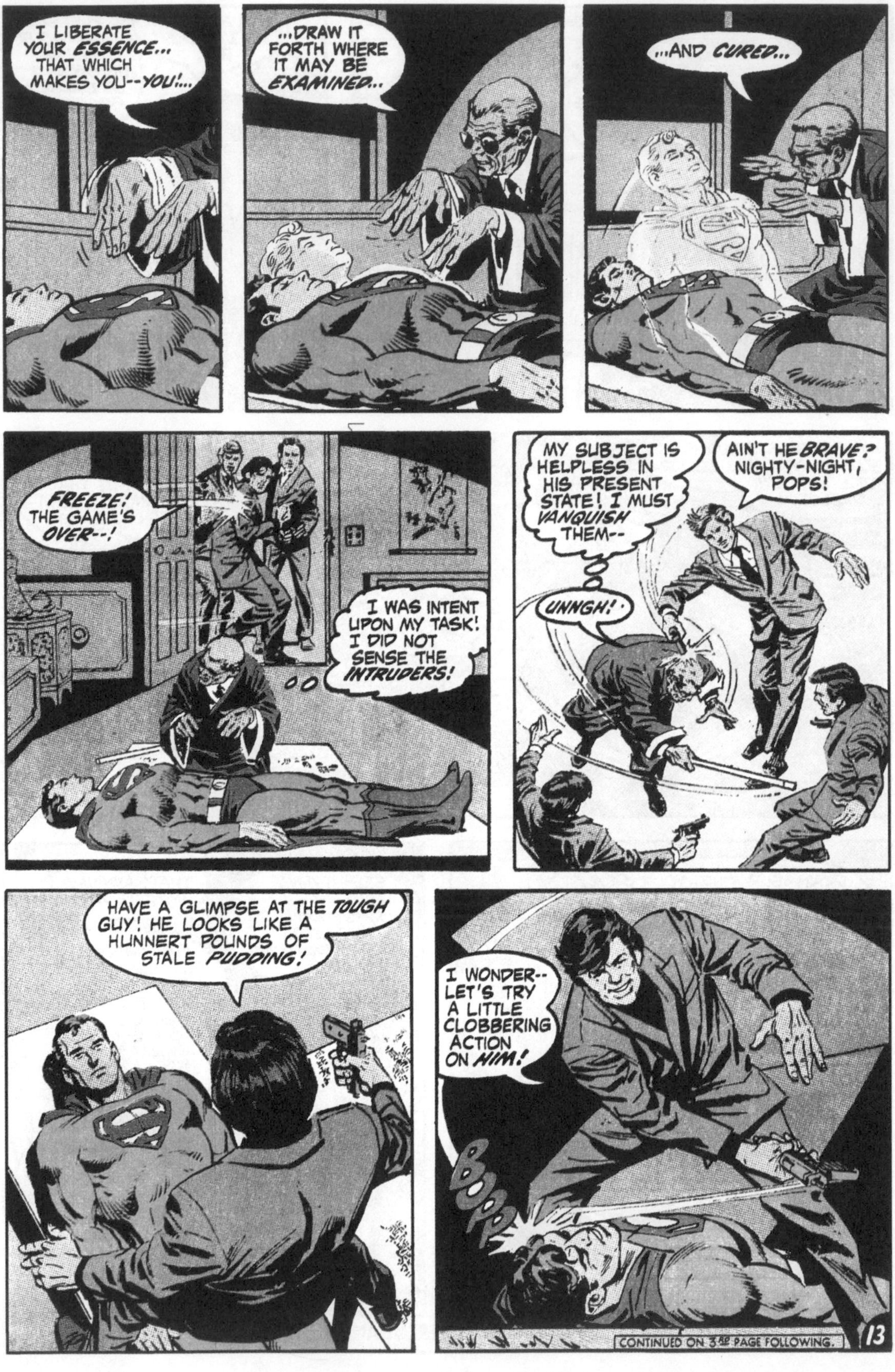
I LIBERATE YOUR ESSENCE... THAT WHICH MAKES YOU--YOU!...
...DRAW IT FORTH WHERE IT MAY BE EXAMINED...
...AND CURED...
FREEZE! THE GAME'S OVER--!
I WAS INTENT UPON MY TASK! I DID NOT SENSE THE INTRUDERS!
MY SUBJECT IS HELPLESS IN HIS PRESENT STATE! I MUST VANQUISH THEM--
AIN'T HE BRAVE? NIGHTY-NIGHT, POPS!
UNNGH!
HAVE A GLIMPSE AT THE TOUGH GUY! HE LOOKS LIKE A HUNNERT POUNDS OF STALE PUDDING!
I WONDER-- LET'S TRY A LITTLE CLOBBERING ACTION ON HIM!
BOOO
CONTINUED ON 3RD PAGE FOLLOWING.
13

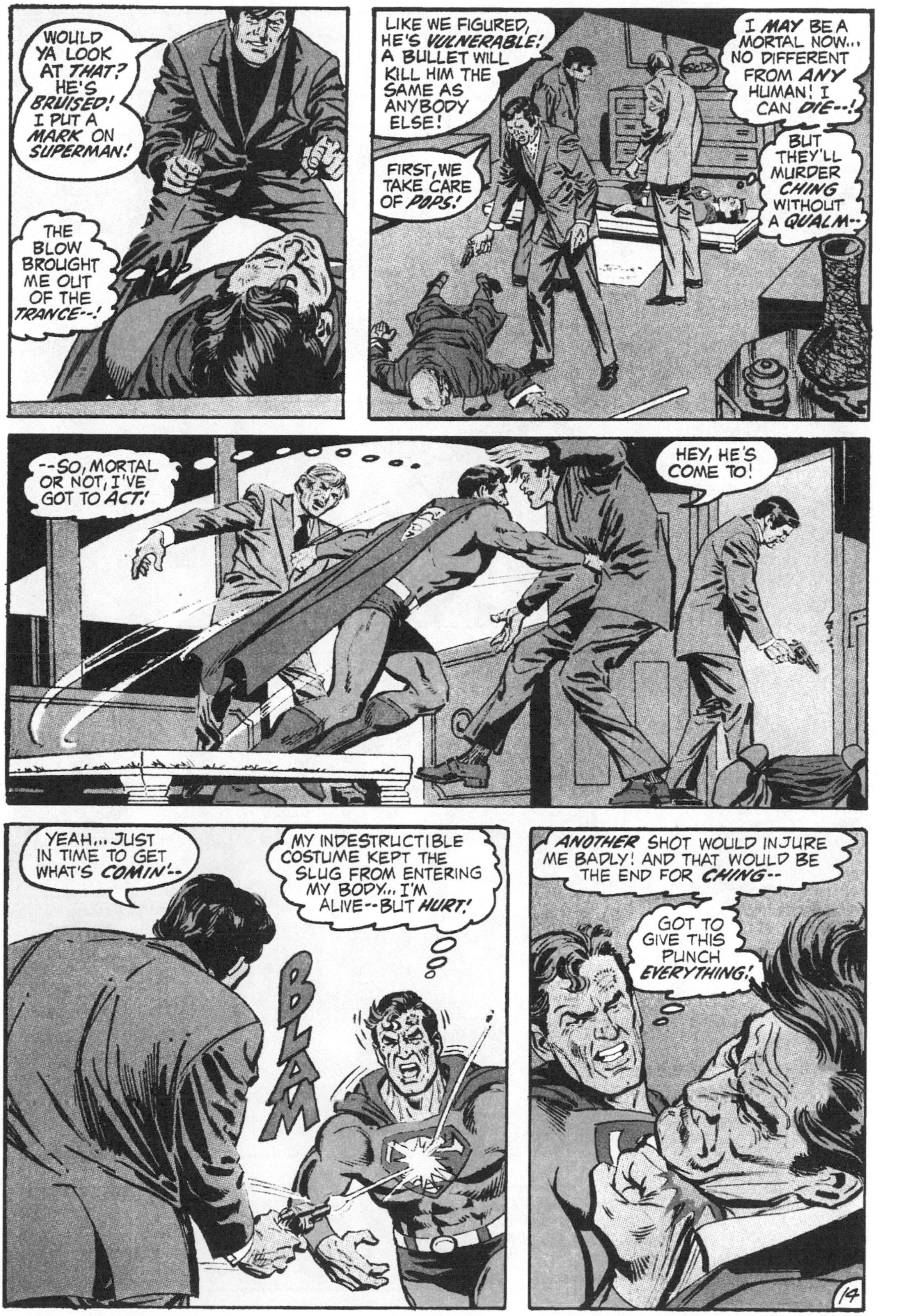
WOULD YA LOOK AT THAT? HE'S BRUISED! I PUT A MARK ON SUPERMAN!
THE BLOW BROUGHT ME OUT OF THE TRANCE--!
LIKE WE FIGURED, HE'S VULNERABLE! A BULLET WILL KILL HIM THE SAME AS ANYBODY ELSE!
FIRST, WE TAKE CARE OF POPS!
I MAY BE A MORTAL NOW... NO DIFFERENT FROM ANY HUMAN! I CAN DIE--!
BUT THEY'LL MURDER CHING WITHOUT A QUALM--
--SO, MORTAL OR NOT, I'VE GOT TO ACT!
HEY, HE'S COME TO!
YEAH... JUST IN TIME TO GET WHAT'S COMIN'--
MY INDESTRUCTIBLE COSTUME KEPT THE SLUG FROM ENTERING MY BODY... I'M ALIVE--BUT HURT!
BLAM
ANOTHER SHOT WOULD INJURE ME BADLY! AND THAT WOULD BE THE END FOR CHING--
GOT TO GIVE THIS PUNCH EVERYTHING!
14

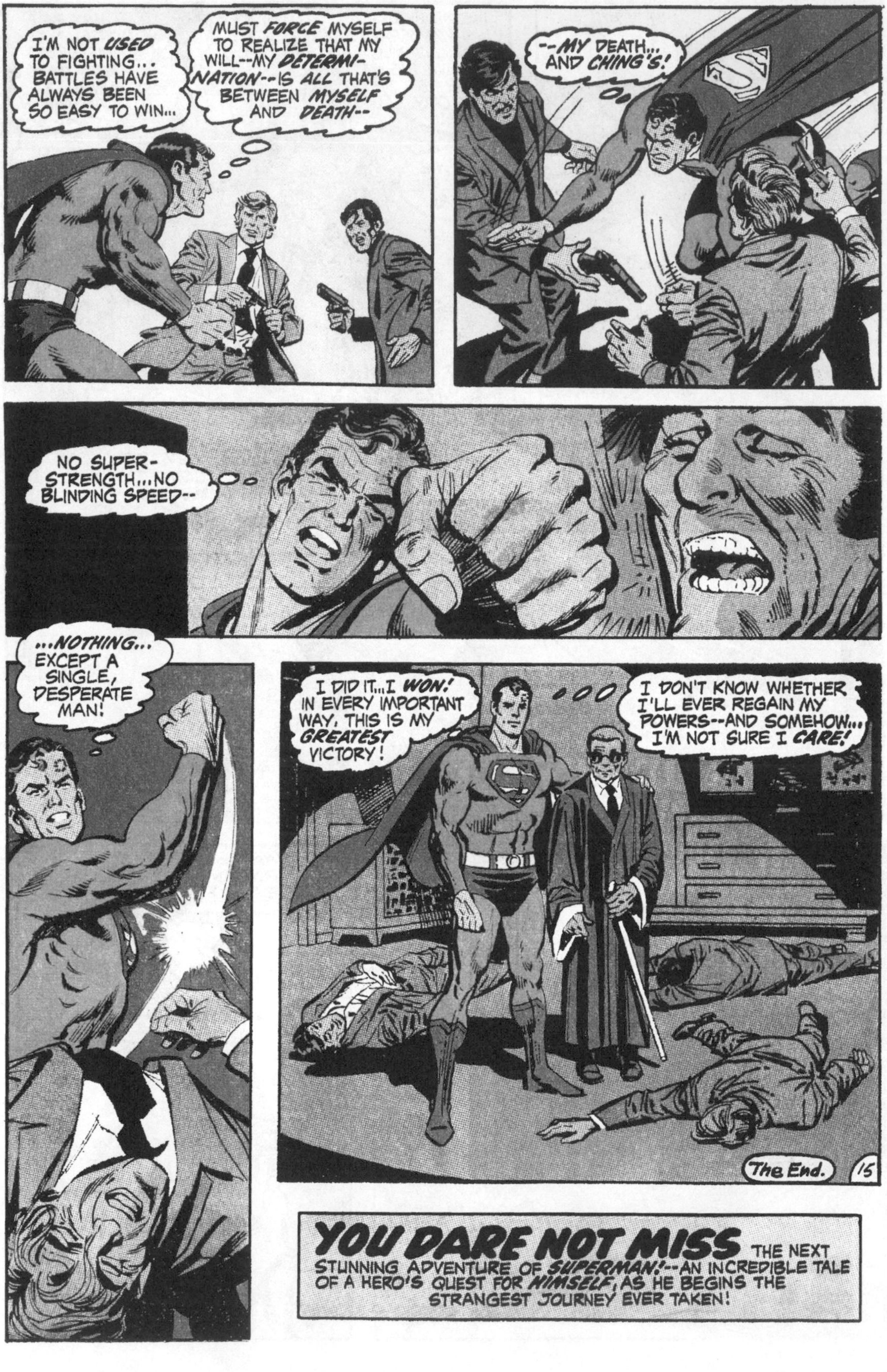
I'M NOT USED TO FIGHTING... BATTLES HAVE ALWAYS BEEN SO EASY TO WIN...
MUST FORCE MYSELF TO REALIZE THAT MY WILL--MY DETERMINATION--IS ALL THAT'S BETWEEN MYSELF AND DEATH--
--MY DEATH... AND CHING'S!
NO SUPER-STRENGTH...NO BLINDING SPEED--
...NOTHING... EXCEPT A SINGLE, DESPERATE MAN!
I DID IT...I WON! IN EVERY IMPORTANT WAY, THIS IS MY GREATEST VICTORY!
I DON'T KNOW WHETHER I'LL EVER REGAIN MY POWERS--AND SOMEHOW... I'M NOT SURE I CARE!
The End.
15
YOU DARE NOT MISS THE NEXT STUNNING ADVENTURE OF SUPERMAN!--AN INCREDIBLE TALE OF A HERO'S QUEST FOR HIMSELF, AS HE BEGINS THE STRANGEST JOURNEY EVER TAKEN!

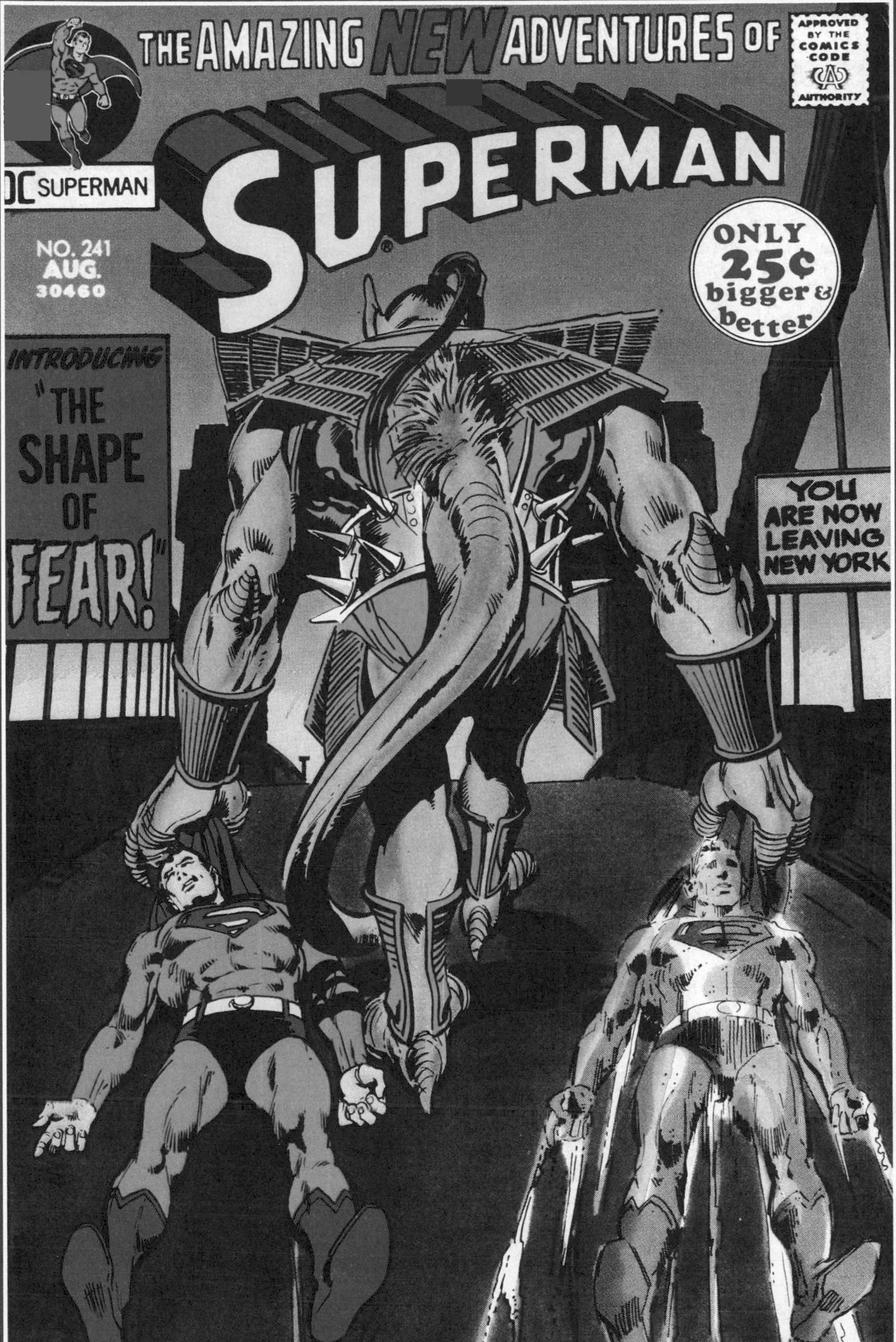
THE AMAZING NEW ADVENTURES OF
APPROVED BY THE COMICS CODE AUTHORITY
DC SUPERMAN
SUPERMAN
NO. 241
AUG.
30460
ONLY 25¢ bigger & better
INTRODUCING
"THE SHAPE OF FEAR!"
YOU ARE NOW LEAVING NEW YORK

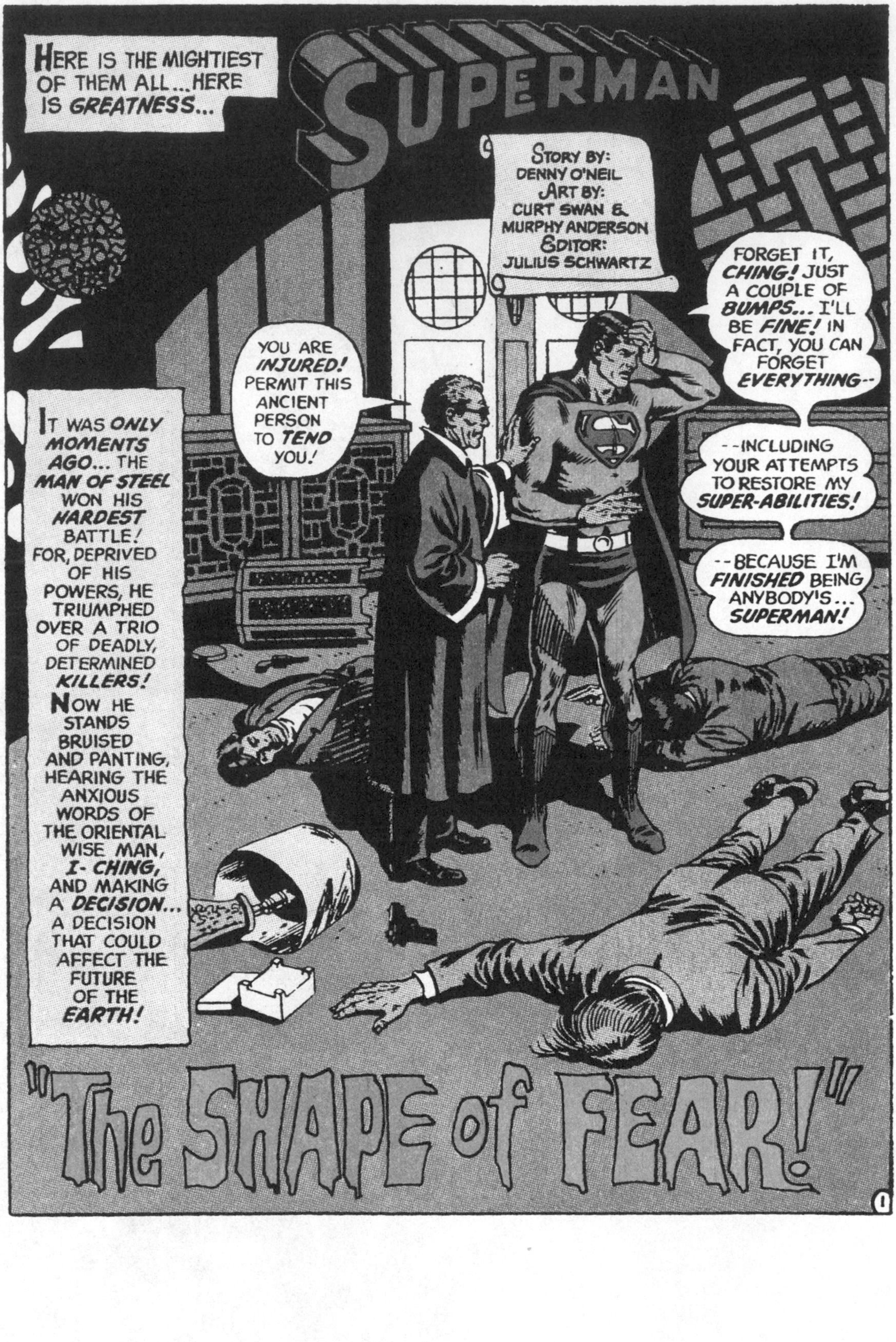
HERE IS THE MIGHTIEST OF THEM ALL... HERE IS GREATNESS...
SUPERMAN
STORY BY: DENNY O'NEIL ART BY: CURT SWAN & MURPHY ANDERSON EDITOR: JULIUS SCHWARTZ
IT WAS ONLY MOMENTS AGO... THE MAN OF STEEL WON HIS HARDEST BATTLE! FOR, DEPRIVED OF HIS POWERS, HE TRIUMPHED OVER A TRIO OF DEADLY, DETERMINED KILLERS! NOW HE STANDS BRUISED AND PANTING, HEARING THE ANXIOUS WORDS OF THE ORIENTAL WISE MAN, I-CHING, AND MAKING A DECISION... A DECISION THAT COULD AFFECT THE FUTURE OF THE EARTH!
YOU ARE INJURED! PERMIT THIS ANCIENT PERSON TO TEND YOU!
FORGET IT, CHING! JUST A COUPLE OF BUMPS... I'LL BE FINE! IN FACT, YOU CAN FORGET EVERYTHING--
--INCLUDING YOUR ATTEMPTS TO RESTORE MY SUPER-ABILITIES!
--BECAUSE I'M FINISHED BEING ANYBODY'S... SUPERMAN!
"The SHAPE of FEAR!"
1

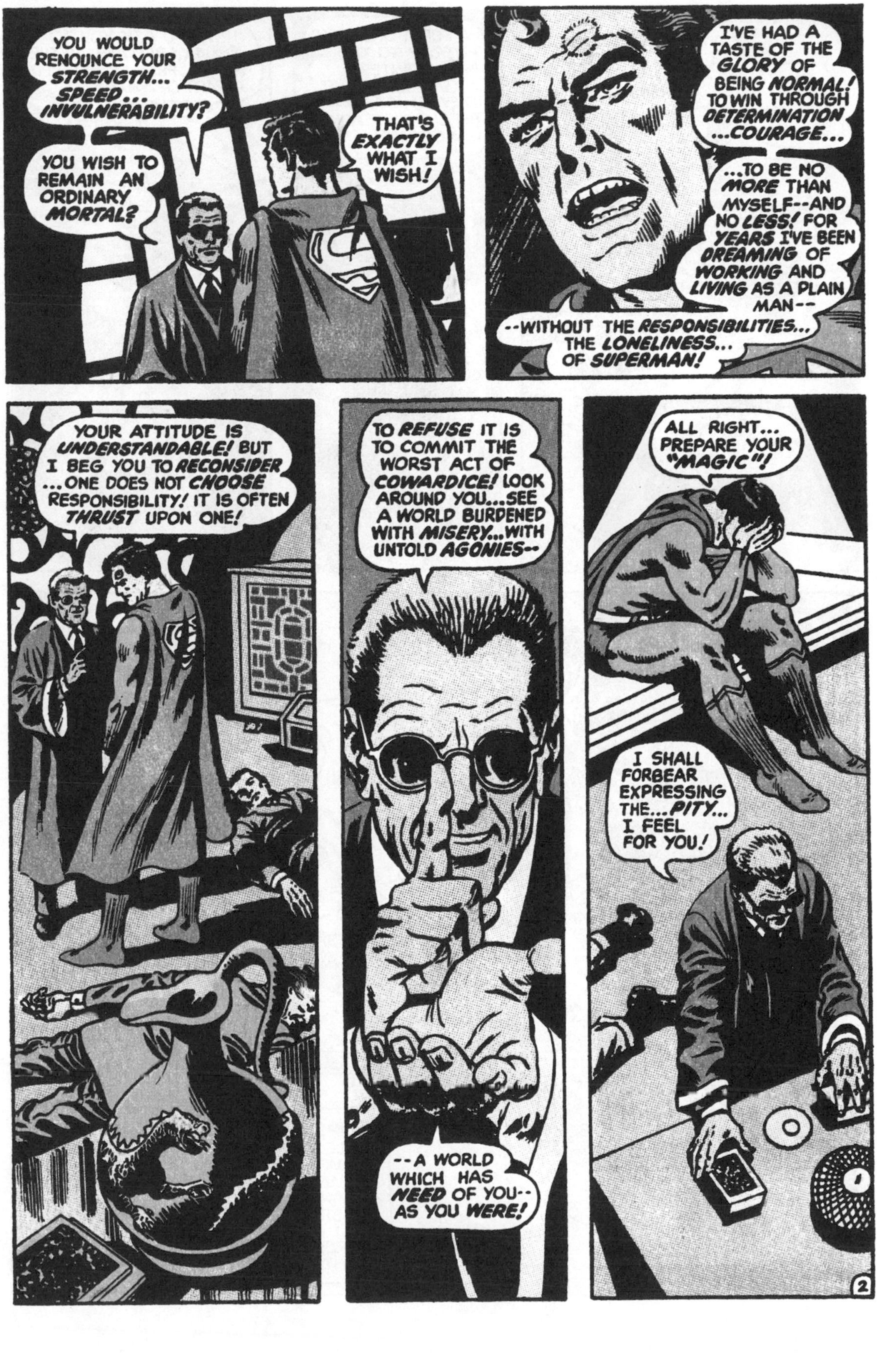
YOU WOULD RENOUNCE YOUR STRENGTH... SPEED... INVULNERABILITY?
YOU WISH TO REMAIN AN ORDINARY MORTAL?
THAT'S EXACTLY WHAT I WISH!
I'VE HAD A TASTE OF THE GLORY OF BEING NORMAL! TO WIN THROUGH DETERMINATION ...COURAGE...
...TO BE NO MORE THAN MYSELF--AND NO LESS! FOR YEARS I'VE BEEN DREAMING OF WORKING AND LIVING AS A PLAIN MAN--
--WITHOUT THE RESPONSIBILITIES... THE LONELINESS... OF SUPERMAN!
YOUR ATTITUDE IS UNDERSTANDABLE! BUT I BEG YOU TO RECONSIDER ...ONE DOES NOT CHOOSE RESPONSIBILITY! IT IS OFTEN THRUST UPON ONE!
TO REFUSE IT IS TO COMMIT THE WORST ACT OF COWARDICE! LOOK AROUND YOU...SEE A WORLD BURDENED WITH MISERY...WITH UNTOLD AGONIES--
--A WORLD WHICH HAS NEED OF YOU-- AS YOU WERE!
ALL RIGHT... PREPARE YOUR "MAGIC"!
I SHALL FORBEAR EXPRESSING THE... PITY... I FEEL FOR YOU!
2

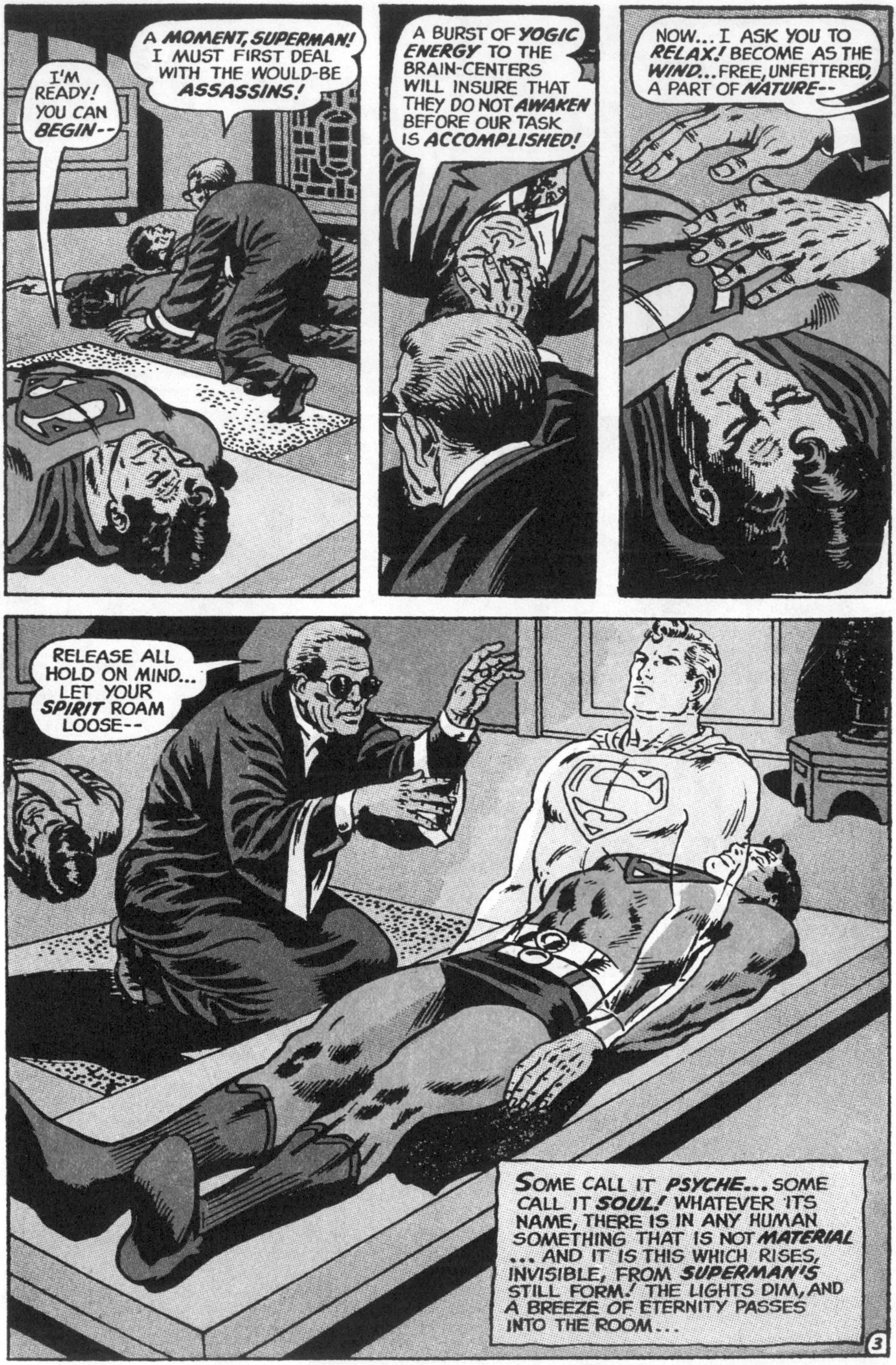
I'M READY! YOU CAN BEGIN--
A MOMENT, SUPERMAN! I MUST FIRST DEAL WITH THE WOULD-BE ASSASSINS!
A BURST OF YOGIC ENERGY TO THE BRAIN-CENTERS WILL INSURE THAT THEY DO NOT AWAKEN BEFORE OUR TASK IS ACCOMPLISHED!
NOW... I ASK YOU TO RELAX! BECOME AS THE WIND... FREE, UNFETTERED, A PART OF NATURE--
RELEASE ALL HOLD ON MIND... LET YOUR SPIRIT ROAM LOOSE--
SOME CALL IT PSYCHE... SOME CALL IT SOUL! WHATEVER ITS NAME, THERE IS IN ANY HUMAN SOMETHING THAT IS NOT MATERIAL ... AND IT IS THIS WHICH RISES, INVISIBLE, FROM SUPERMAN'S STILL FORM! THE LIGHTS DIM, AND A BREEZE OF ETERNITY PASSES INTO THE ROOM...
3

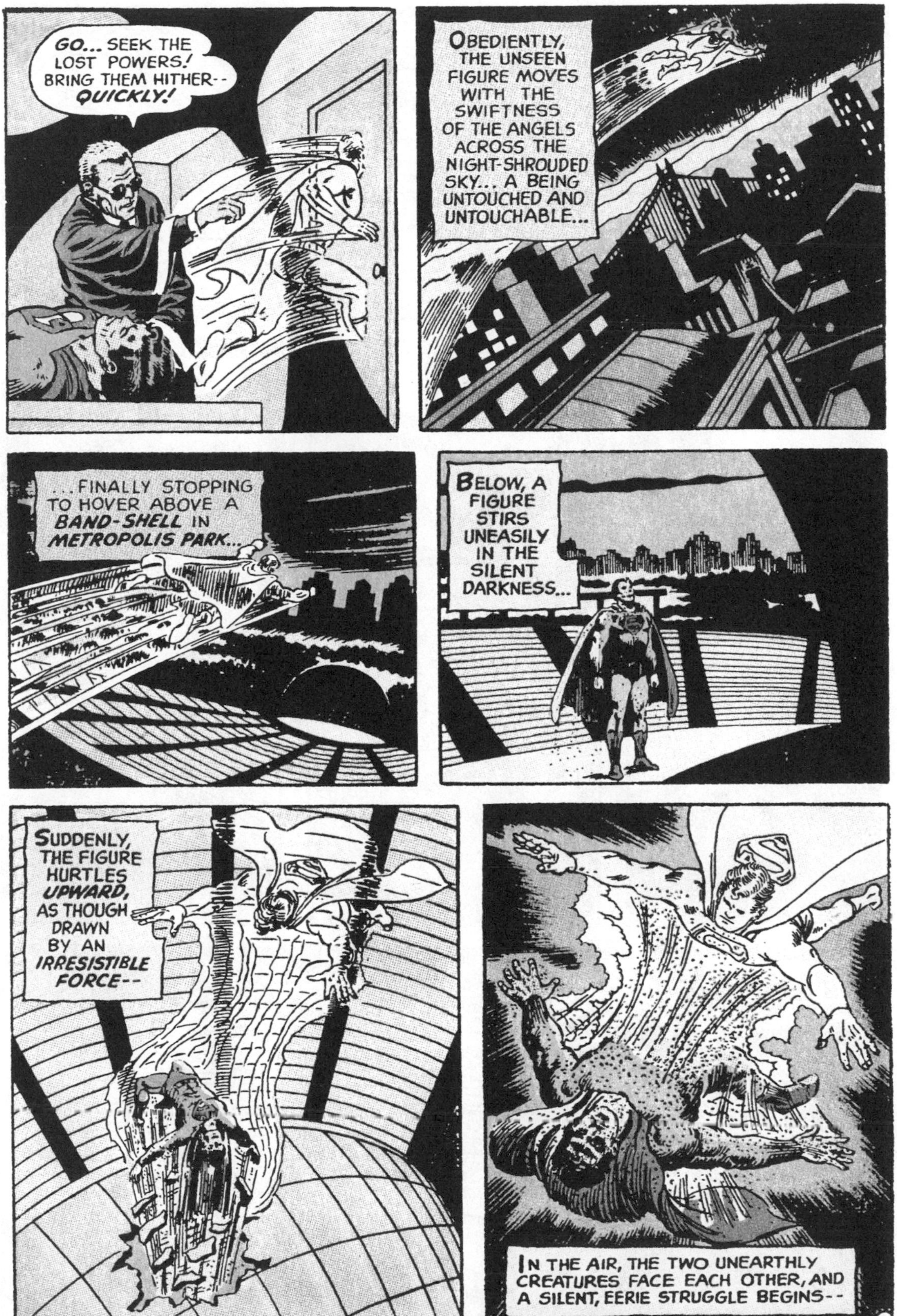
GO... SEEK THE LOST POWERS! BRING THEM HITHER-- QUICKLY!
OBEDIENTLY, THE UNSEEN FIGURE MOVES WITH THE SWIFTNESS OF THE ANGELS ACROSS THE NIGHT-SHROUDED SKY... A BEING UNTOUCHED AND UNTOUCHABLE...
...FINALLY STOPPING TO HOVER ABOVE A BAND-SHELL IN METROPOLIS PARK...
BELOW, A FIGURE STIRS UNEASILY IN THE SILENT DARKNESS...
SUDDENLY, THE FIGURE HURTLES UPWARD, AS THOUGH DRAWN BY AN IRRESISTIBLE FORCE--
IN THE AIR, THE TWO UNEARTHLY CREATURES FACE EACH OTHER, AND A SILENT, EERIE STRUGGLE BEGINS--
4

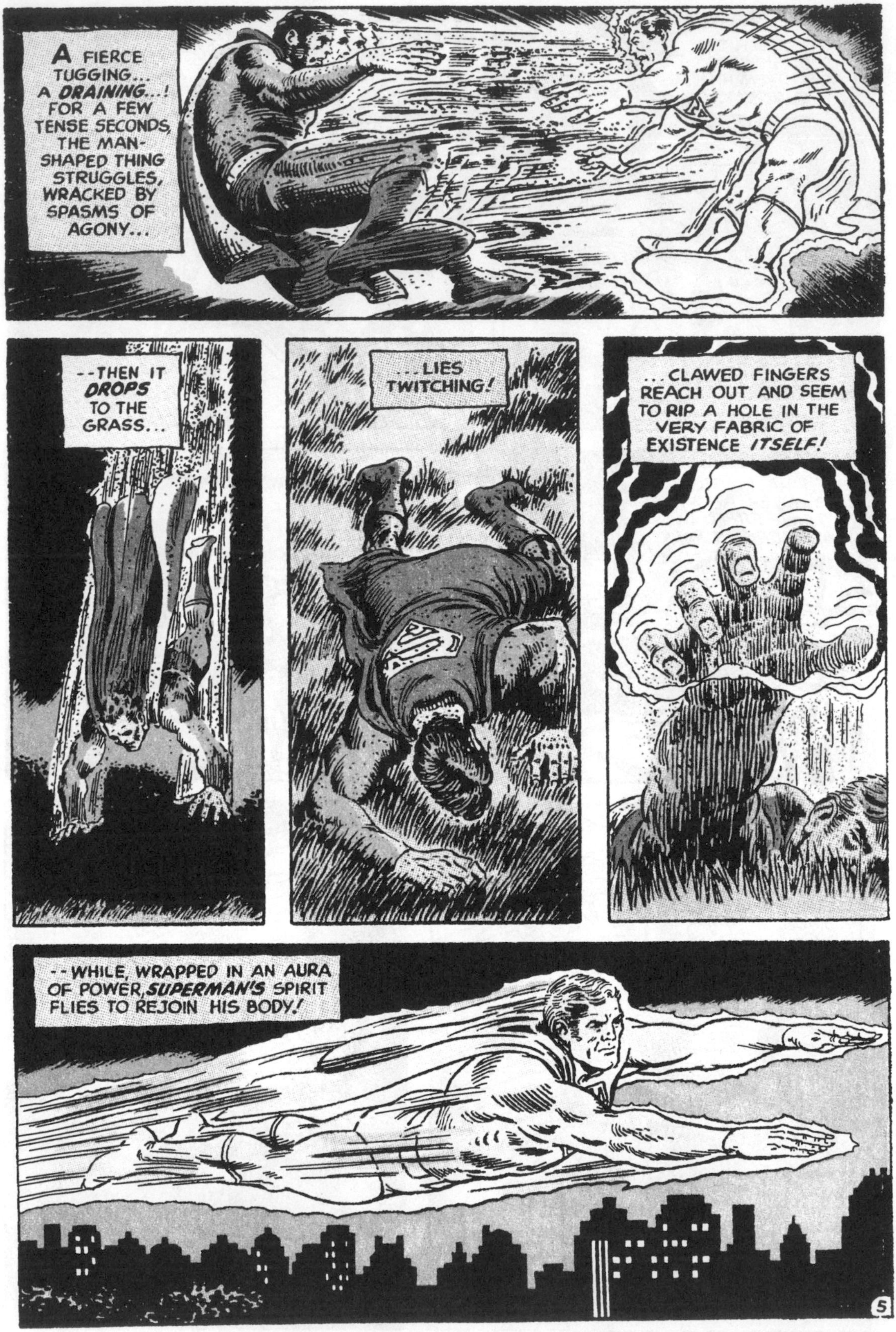
A FIERCE TUGGING... A DRAINING...! FOR A FEW TENSE SECONDS, THE MAN-SHAPED THING STRUGGLES, WRACKED BY SPASMS OF AGONY...
--THEN IT DROPS TO THE GRASS...
...LIES TWITCHING!
...CLAWED FINGERS REACH OUT AND SEEM TO RIP A HOLE IN THE VERY FABRIC OF EXISTENCE ITSELF!
--WHILE, WRAPPED IN AN AURA OF POWER, SUPERMAN'S SPIRIT FLIES TO REJOIN HIS BODY!
5

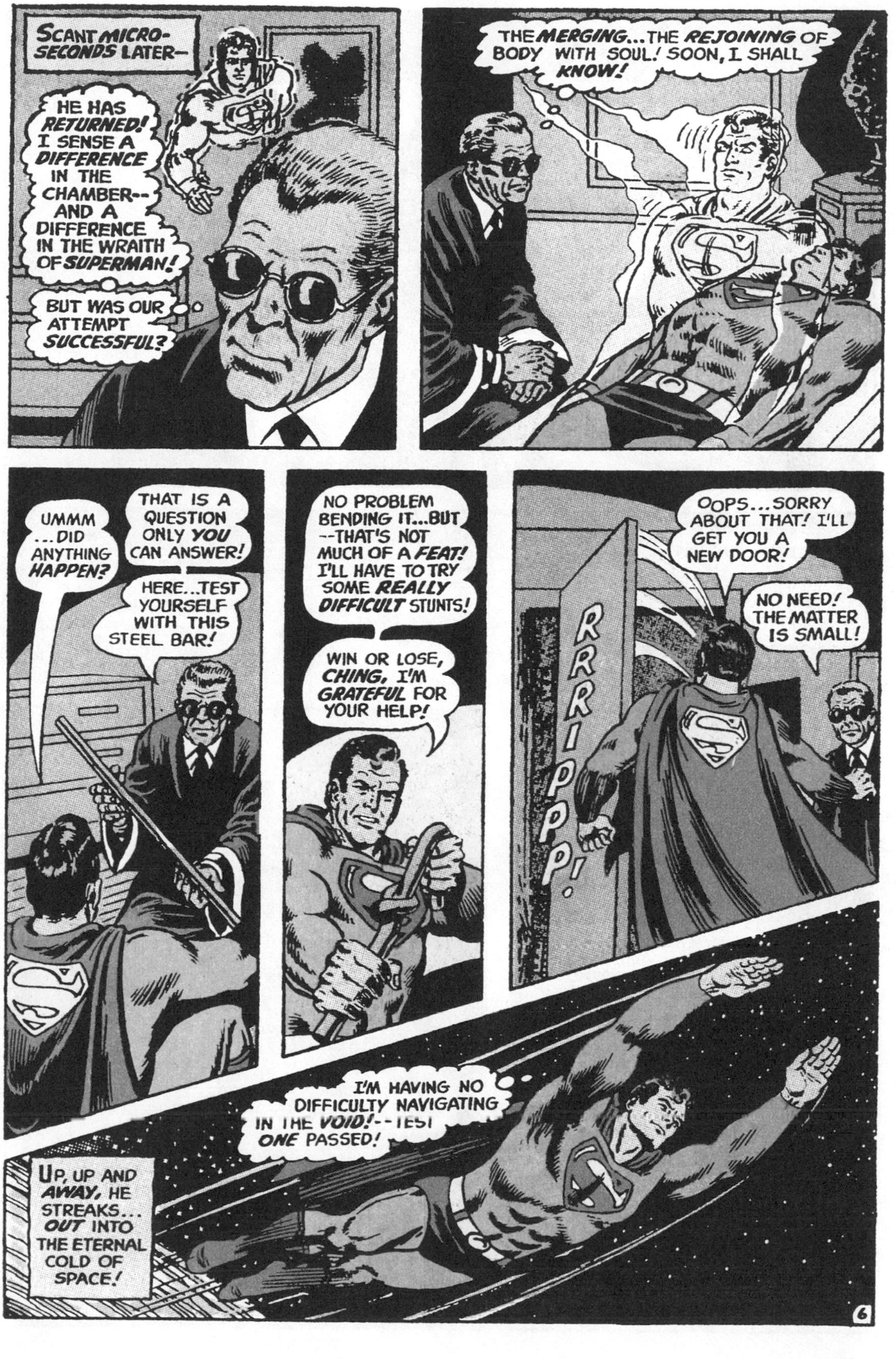
SCANT MICRO-SECONDS LATER--
HE HAS RETURNED! I SENSE A DIFFERENCE IN THE CHAMBER-- AND A DIFFERENCE IN THE WRAITH OF SUPERMAN!
BUT WAS OUR ATTEMPT SUCCESSFUL?
THE MERGING...THE REJOINING OF BODY WITH SOUL! SOON, I SHALL KNOW!
UMMM ...DID ANYTHING HAPPEN?
THAT IS A QUESTION ONLY YOU CAN ANSWER!
HERE...TEST YOURSELF WITH THIS STEEL BAR!
NO PROBLEM BENDING IT...BUT --THAT'S NOT MUCH OF A FEAT! I'LL HAVE TO TRY SOME REALLY DIFFICULT STUNTS!
WIN OR LOSE, CHING, I'M GRATEFUL FOR YOUR HELP!
OOPS...SORRY ABOUT THAT! I'LL GET YOU A NEW DOOR!
NO NEED! THE MATTER IS SMALL!
RRRIPPP!
I'M HAVING NO DIFFICULTY NAVIGATING IN THE VOID!--TEST ONE PASSED!
UP, UP AND AWAY, HE STREAKS... OUT INTO THE ETERNAL COLD OF SPACE!
6

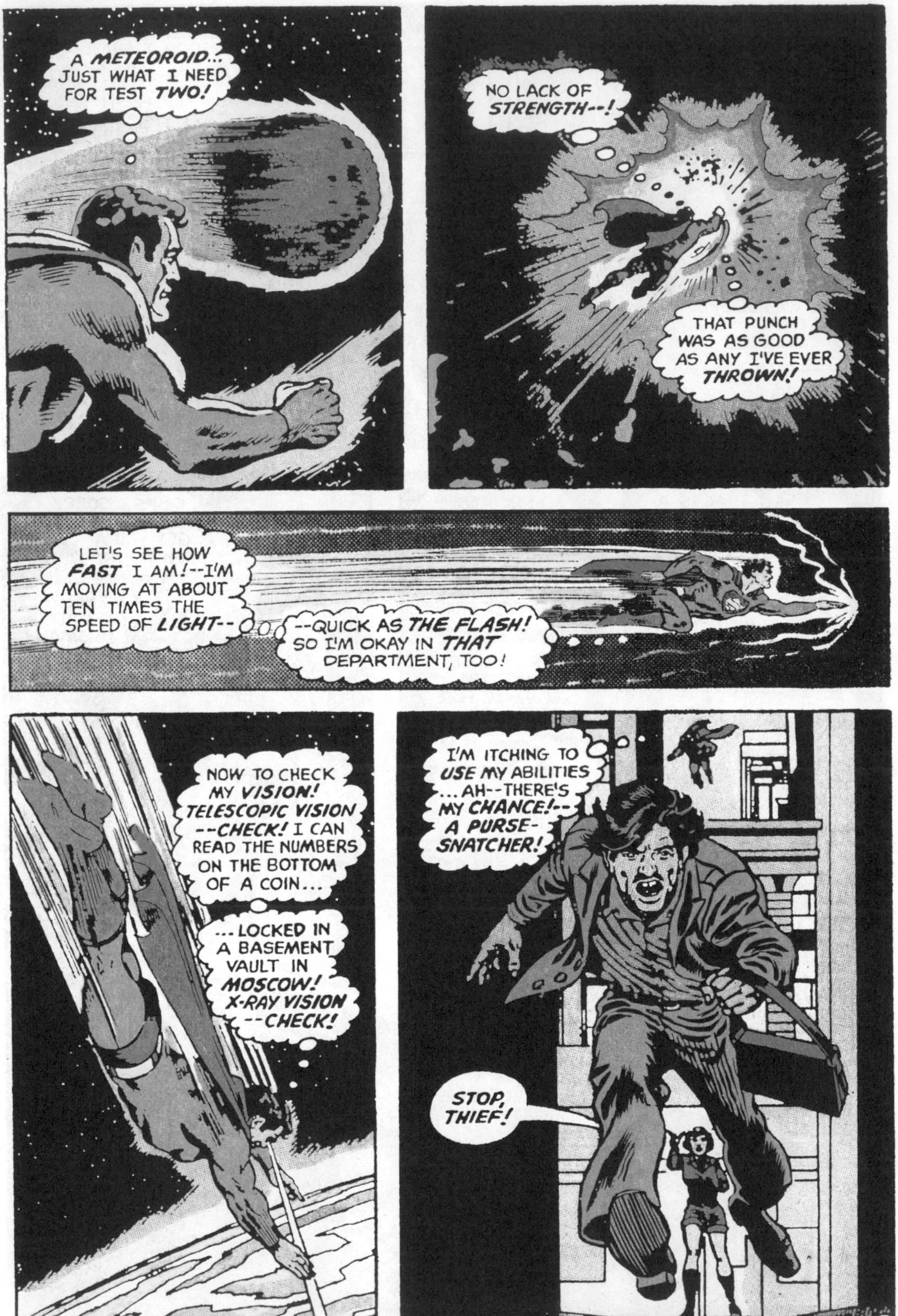
A METEOROID... JUST WHAT I NEED FOR TEST TWO!
NO LACK OF STRENGTH--!
THAT PUNCH WAS AS GOOD AS ANY I'VE EVER THROWN!
LET'S SEE HOW FAST I AM!--I'M MOVING AT ABOUT TEN TIMES THE SPEED OF LIGHT--
--QUICK AS THE FLASH! SO I'M OKAY IN THAT DEPARTMENT, TOO!
NOW TO CHECK MY VISION! TELESCOPIC VISION --CHECK! I CAN READ THE NUMBERS ON THE BOTTOM OF A COIN...
...LOCKED IN A BASEMENT VAULT IN MOSCOW! X-RAY VISION --CHECK!
I'M ITCHING TO USE MY ABILITIES ...AH--THERE'S MY CHANCE!--A PURSE-SNATCHER!
STOP, THIEF!
7

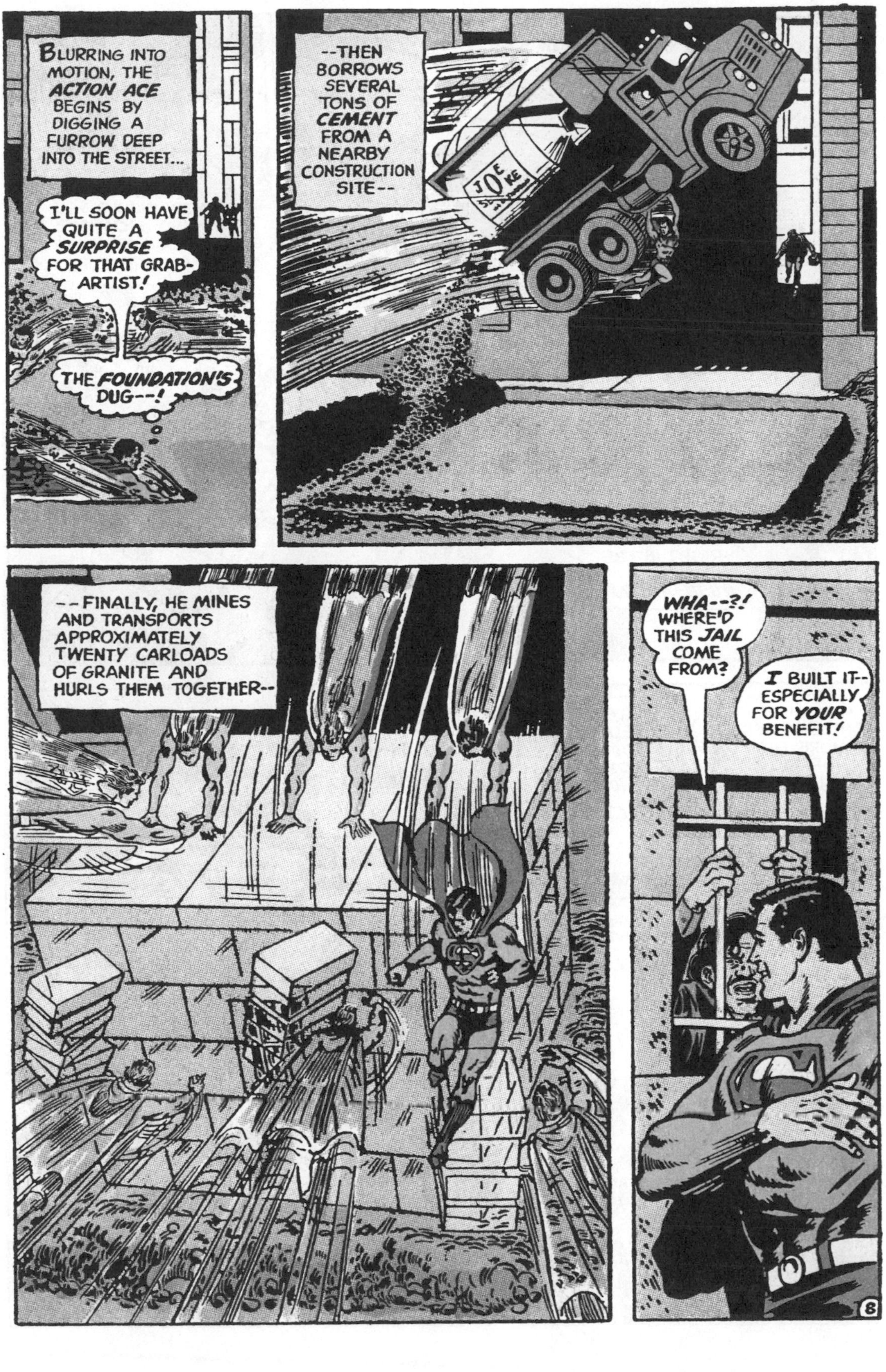

BLURRING INTO MOTION, THE ACTION ACE BEGINS BY DIGGING A FURROW DEEP INTO THE STREET...
I'LL SOON HAVE QUITE A SURPRISE FOR THAT GRAB-ARTIST!
THE FOUNDATION'S DUG--!
--THEN BORROWS SEVERAL TONS OF CEMENT FROM A NEARBY CONSTRUCTION SITE--
--FINALLY, HE MINES AND TRANSPORTS APPROXIMATELY TWENTY CARLOADS OF GRANITE AND HURLS THEM TOGETHER--
WHA--?! WHERE'D THIS JAIL COME FROM?
I BUILT IT--ESPECIALLY FOR YOUR BENEFIT!
8

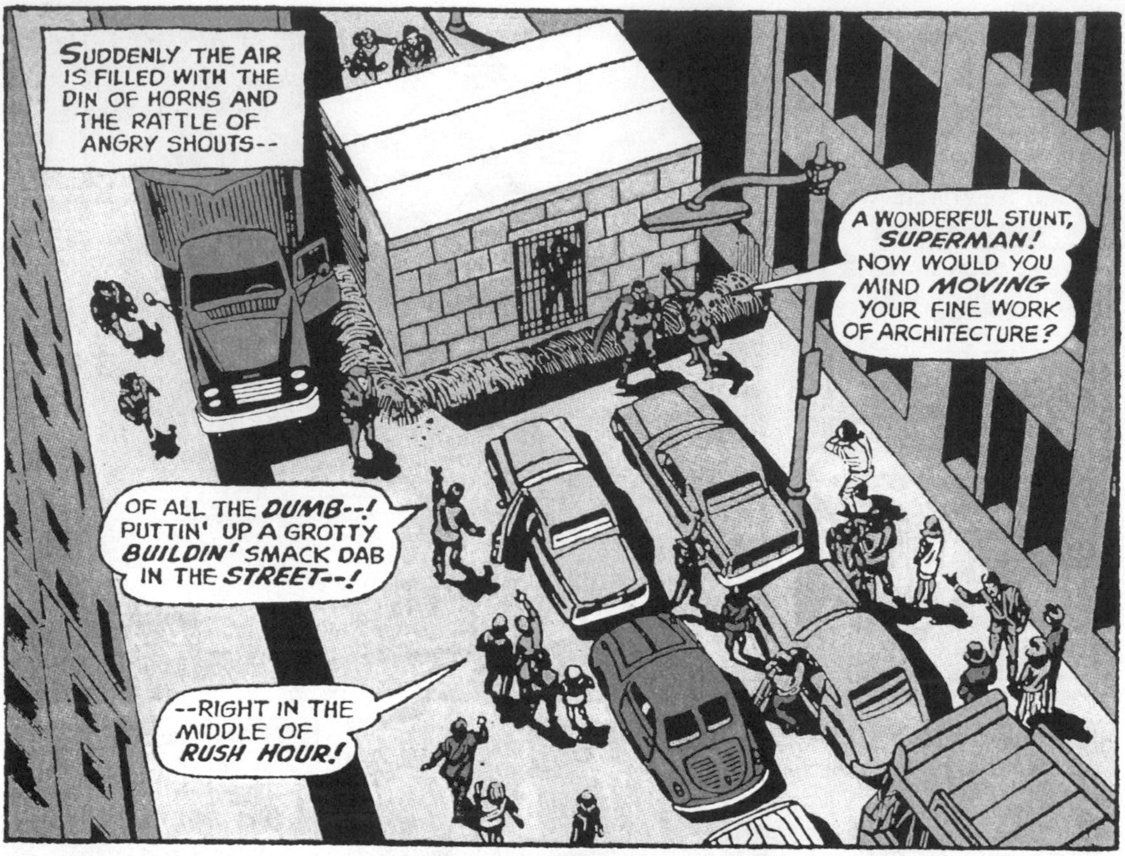

SUDDENLY THE AIR IS FILLED WITH THE DIN OF HORNS AND THE RATTLE OF ANGRY SHOUTS--
A WONDERFUL STUNT, SUPERMAN! NOW WOULD YOU MIND MOVING YOUR FINE WORK OF ARCHITECTURE?
OF ALL THE DUMB--! PUTTIN' UP A GROTTY BUILDIN' SMACK DAB IN THE STREET--!
--RIGHT IN THE MIDDLE OF RUSH HOUR!

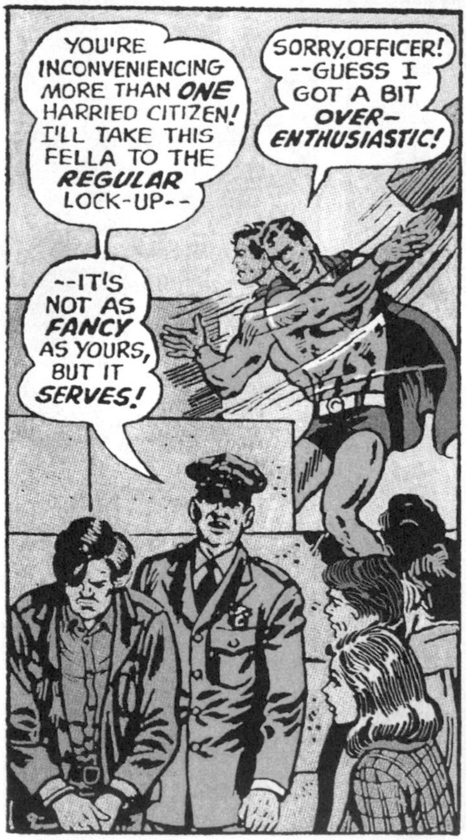

YOU'RE INCONVENIENCING MORE THAN ONE HARRIED CITIZEN! I'LL TAKE THIS FELLA TO THE REGULAR LOCK-UP--
SORRY, OFFICER! --GUESS I GOT A BIT OVER-ENTHUSIASTIC!
--IT'S NOT AS FANCY AS YOURS, BUT IT SERVES!

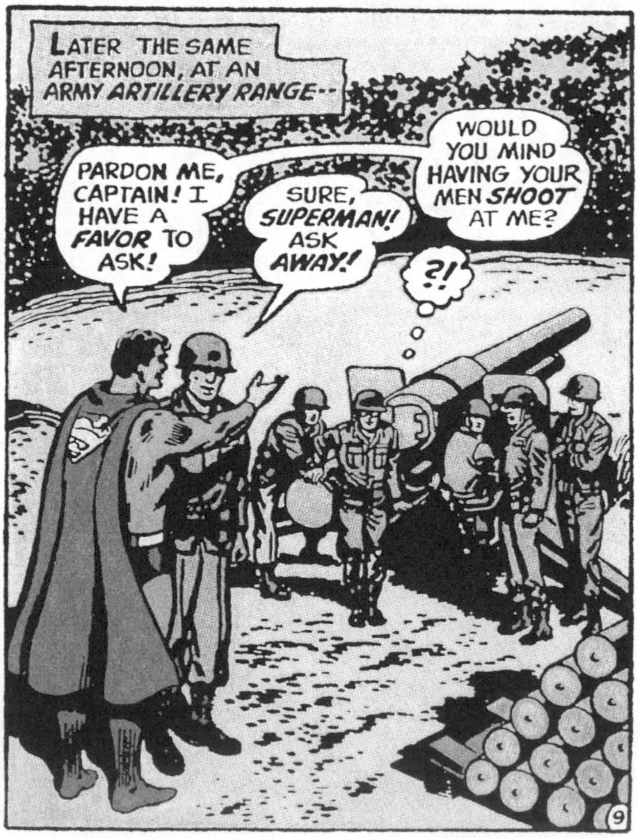

LATER THE SAME AFTERNOON, AT AN ARMY ARTILLERY RANGE--
PARDON ME, CAPTAIN! I HAVE A FAVOR TO ASK!
SURE, SUPERMAN! ASK AWAY!
WOULD YOU MIND HAVING YOUR MEN SHOOT AT ME?
?!
9

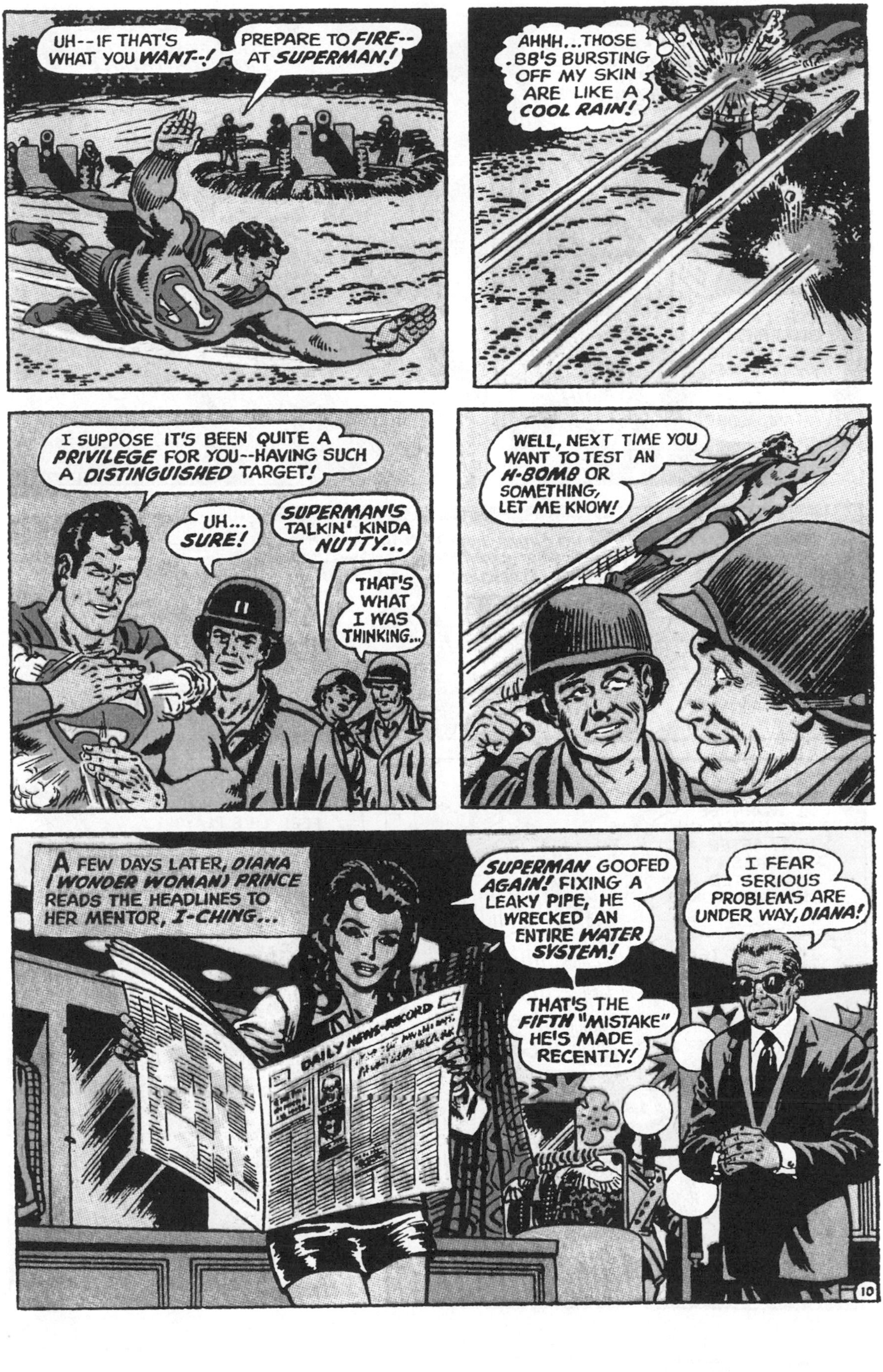

UH--IF THAT'S WHAT YOU WANT--!
PREPARE TO FIRE--AT SUPERMAN!
AHHH...THOSE BB'S BURSTING OFF MY SKIN ARE LIKE A COOL RAIN!
I SUPPOSE IT'S BEEN QUITE A PRIVILEGE FOR YOU--HAVING SUCH A DISTINGUISHED TARGET!
UH... SURE!
SUPERMAN'S TALKIN' KINDA NUTTY...
THAT'S WHAT I WAS THINKING...
WELL, NEXT TIME YOU WANT TO TEST AN H-BOMB OR SOMETHING, LET ME KNOW!
A FEW DAYS LATER, DIANA (WONDER WOMAN) PRINCE READS THE HEADLINES TO HER MENTOR, I-CHING...
SUPERMAN GOOFED AGAIN! FIXING A LEAKY PIPE, HE WRECKED AN ENTIRE WATER SYSTEM!
THAT'S THE FIFTH "MISTAKE" HE'S MADE RECENTLY!
I FEAR SERIOUS PROBLEMS ARE UNDER WAY, DIANA!
DAILY NEWS-RECORD
10

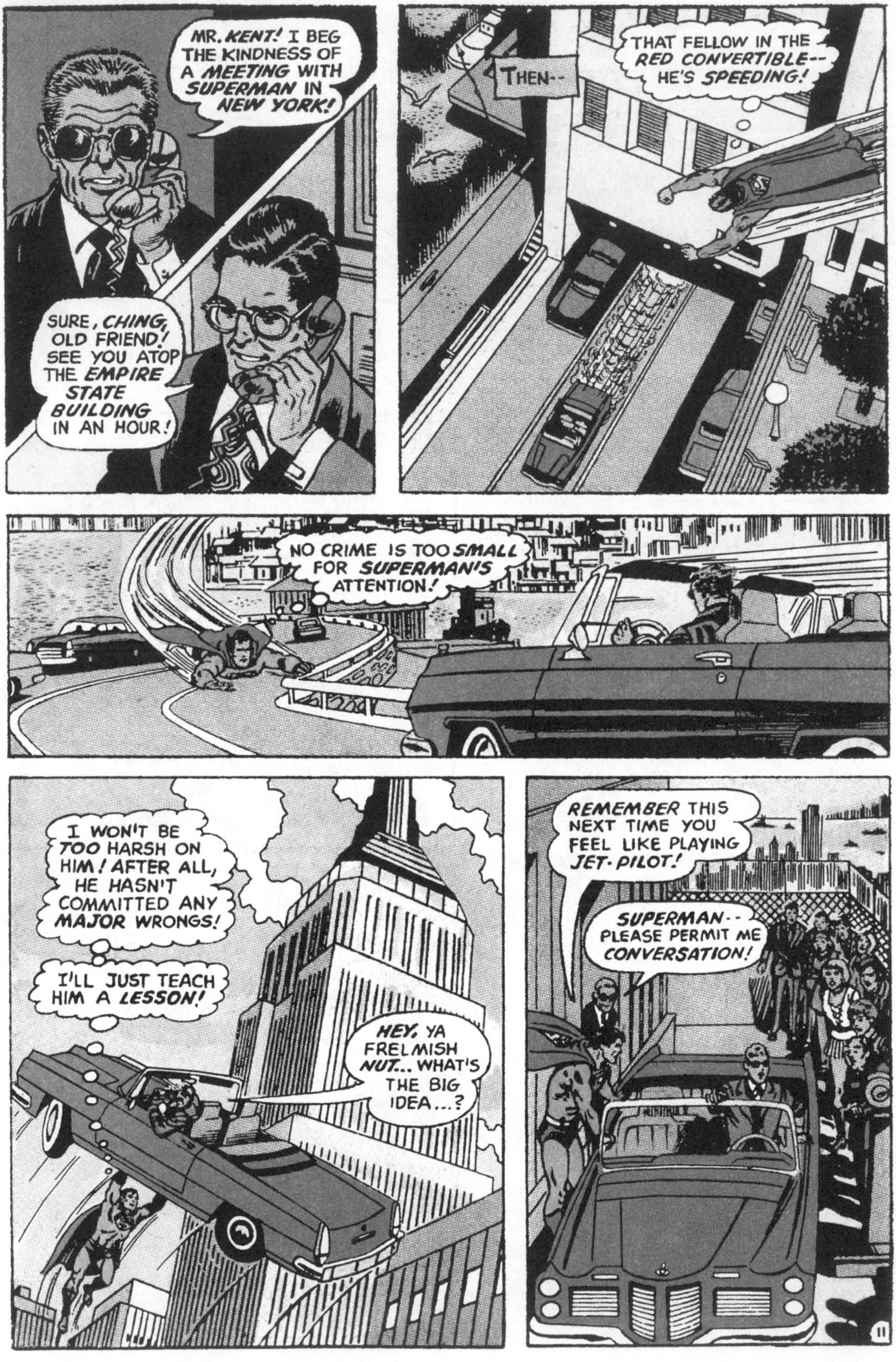
MR. KENT! I BEG THE KINDNESS OF A MEETING WITH SUPERMAN IN NEW YORK!
SURE, CHING, OLD FRIEND! SEE YOU ATOP THE EMPIRE STATE BUILDING IN AN HOUR!
THEN--
THAT FELLOW IN THE RED CONVERTIBLE-- HE'S SPEEDING!
NO CRIME IS TOO SMALL FOR SUPERMAN'S ATTENTION!
I WON'T BE TOO HARSH ON HIM! AFTER ALL, HE HASN'T COMMITTED ANY MAJOR WRONGS!
I'LL JUST TEACH HIM A LESSON!
HEY, YA FRELMISH NUT... WHAT'S THE BIG IDEA...?
REMEMBER THIS NEXT TIME YOU FEEL LIKE PLAYING JET-PILOT!
SUPERMAN-- PLEASE PERMIT ME CONVERSATION!
11

I WISH *SUPERMAN* WOULD *THINK* BEFORE HE ACTS! IT'LL COST A *FORTUNE* TO GET THE CAR DOWN!

YEAH! AND MEAN- WHILE OUR *TOURISTS* ARE BEING BUGGED--

--TO SAY NOTHING OF THE CAR INTERFERING WITH THE *TELEVISION TRANSMISSIONS* FROM UP HERE!

THIS AGED PERSON HAS BEEN *OBSERVING* YOUR DEEDS OF LATE, AND FEARS FOR YOUR *HEALTH!*

MY HEALTH? OLD GUY, YOU'RE TALKING TO *SUPERMAN!* NOBODY'S HEALTHIER THAN *ME!*

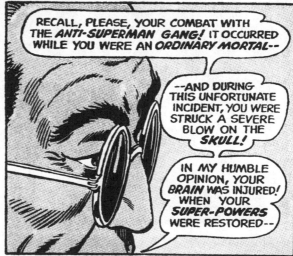

RECALL, PLEASE, YOUR COMBAT WITH THE *ANTI-SUPERMAN GANG!* IT OCCURRED WHILE YOU WERE AN *ORDINARY MORTAL--*

--AND DURING THIS UNFORTUNATE INCIDENT, YOU WERE STRUCK A SEVERE BLOW ON THE *SKULL!*

IN MY HUMBLE OPINION, YOUR *BRAIN* WAS INJURED! WHEN YOUR *SUPER-POWERS* WERE RESTORED--

-- THE INJURY WAS *FIXED-* MADE *PERMANENT!* YOU ARE SUFFERING FROM... *BRAIN DAMAGE!*

NONSENSE! THAT'S THE SILLIEST THING I'VE EVER *HEARD--!*

YOU'RE JUST *JEALOUS* BECAUSE YOU'RE *WEAK*... LIKE EVERYONE *ELSE!*

WHACCCK

12

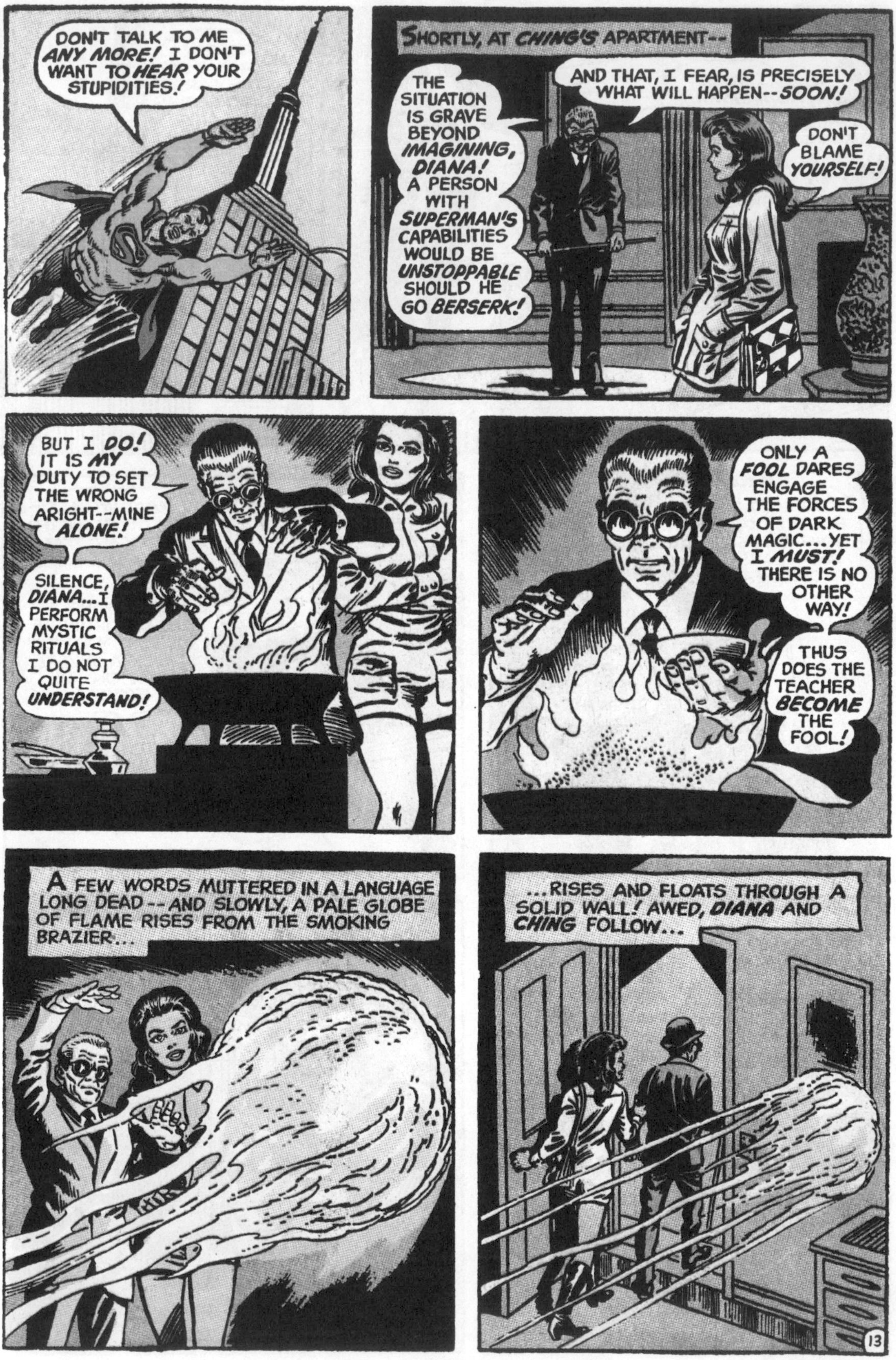
DON'T TALK TO ME ANY MORE! I DON'T WANT TO HEAR YOUR STUPIDITIES!
SHORTLY, AT CHING'S APARTMENT--
AND THAT, I FEAR, IS PRECISELY WHAT WILL HAPPEN--SOON!
THE SITUATION IS GRAVE BEYOND IMAGINING, DIANA! A PERSON WITH SUPERMAN'S CAPABILITIES WOULD BE UNSTOPPABLE SHOULD HE GO BERSERK!
DON'T BLAME YOURSELF!
BUT I DO! IT IS MY DUTY TO SET THE WRONG ARIGHT--MINE ALONE!
SILENCE, DIANA...I PERFORM MYSTIC RITUALS I DO NOT QUITE UNDERSTAND!
ONLY A FOOL DARES ENGAGE THE FORCES OF DARK MAGIC...YET I MUST! THERE IS NO OTHER WAY!
THUS DOES THE TEACHER BECOME THE FOOL!
A FEW WORDS MUTTERED IN A LANGUAGE LONG DEAD--AND SLOWLY, A PALE GLOBE OF FLAME RISES FROM THE SMOKING BRAZIER...
...RISES AND FLOATS THROUGH A SOLID WALL! AWED, DIANA AND CHING FOLLOW...
13

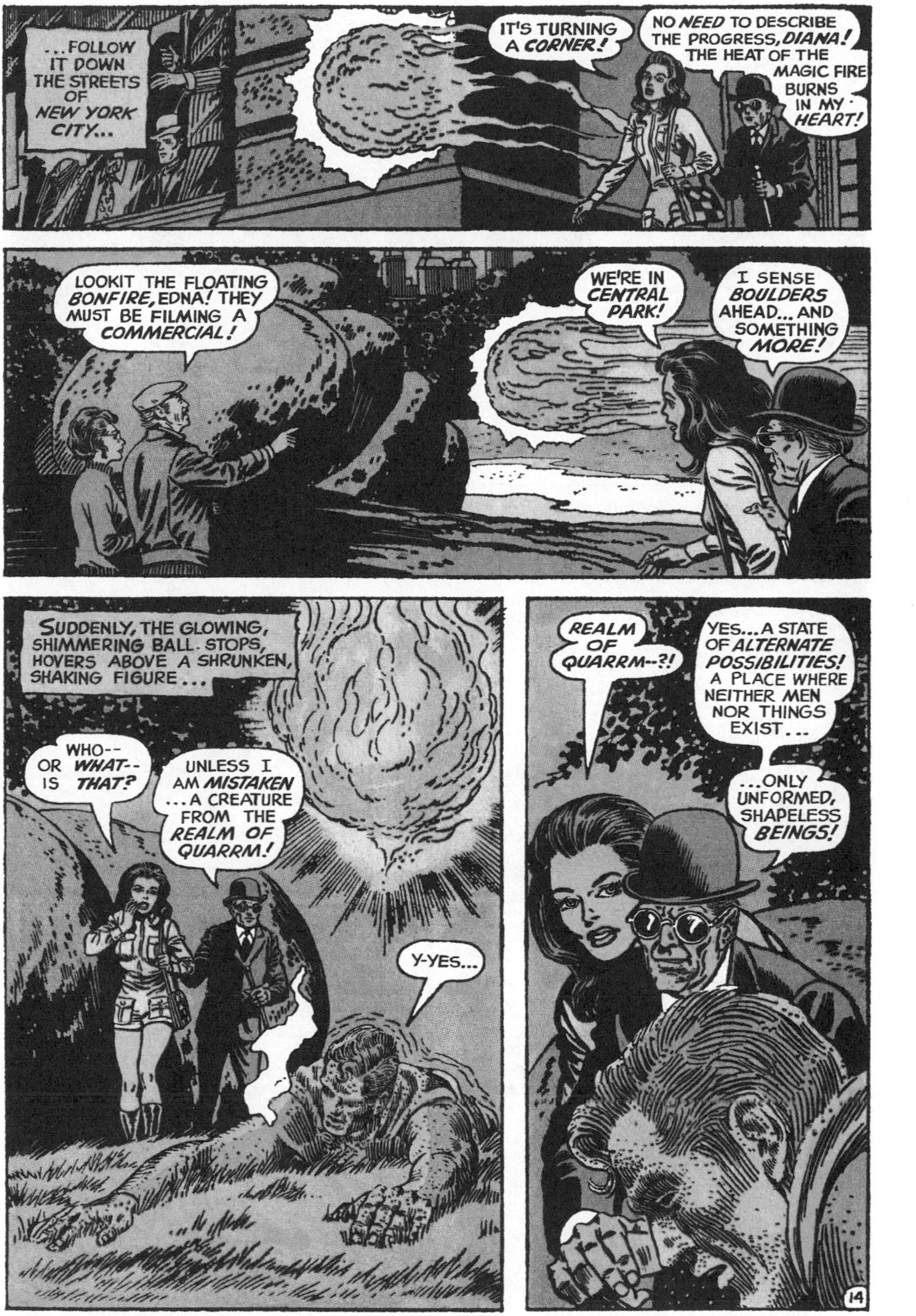
...FOLLOW IT DOWN THE STREETS OF NEW YORK CITY...
IT'S TURNING A CORNER!
NO NEED TO DESCRIBE THE PROGRESS, DIANA! THE HEAT OF THE MAGIC FIRE BURNS IN MY HEART!
LOOKIT THE FLOATING BONFIRE, EDNA! THEY MUST BE FILMING A COMMERCIAL!
WE'RE IN CENTRAL PARK!
I SENSE BOULDERS AHEAD... AND SOMETHING MORE!
SUDDENLY, THE GLOWING, SHIMMERING BALL STOPS, HOVERS ABOVE A SHRUNKEN, SHAKING FIGURE...
WHO-- OR WHAT-- IS THAT?
UNLESS I AM MISTAKEN ...A CREATURE FROM THE REALM OF QUARRM!
Y-YES...
REALM OF QUARRM--?!
YES...A STATE OF ALTERNATE POSSIBILITIES! A PLACE WHERE NEITHER MEN NOR THINGS EXIST...
...ONLY UNFORMED, SHAPELESS BEINGS!
14

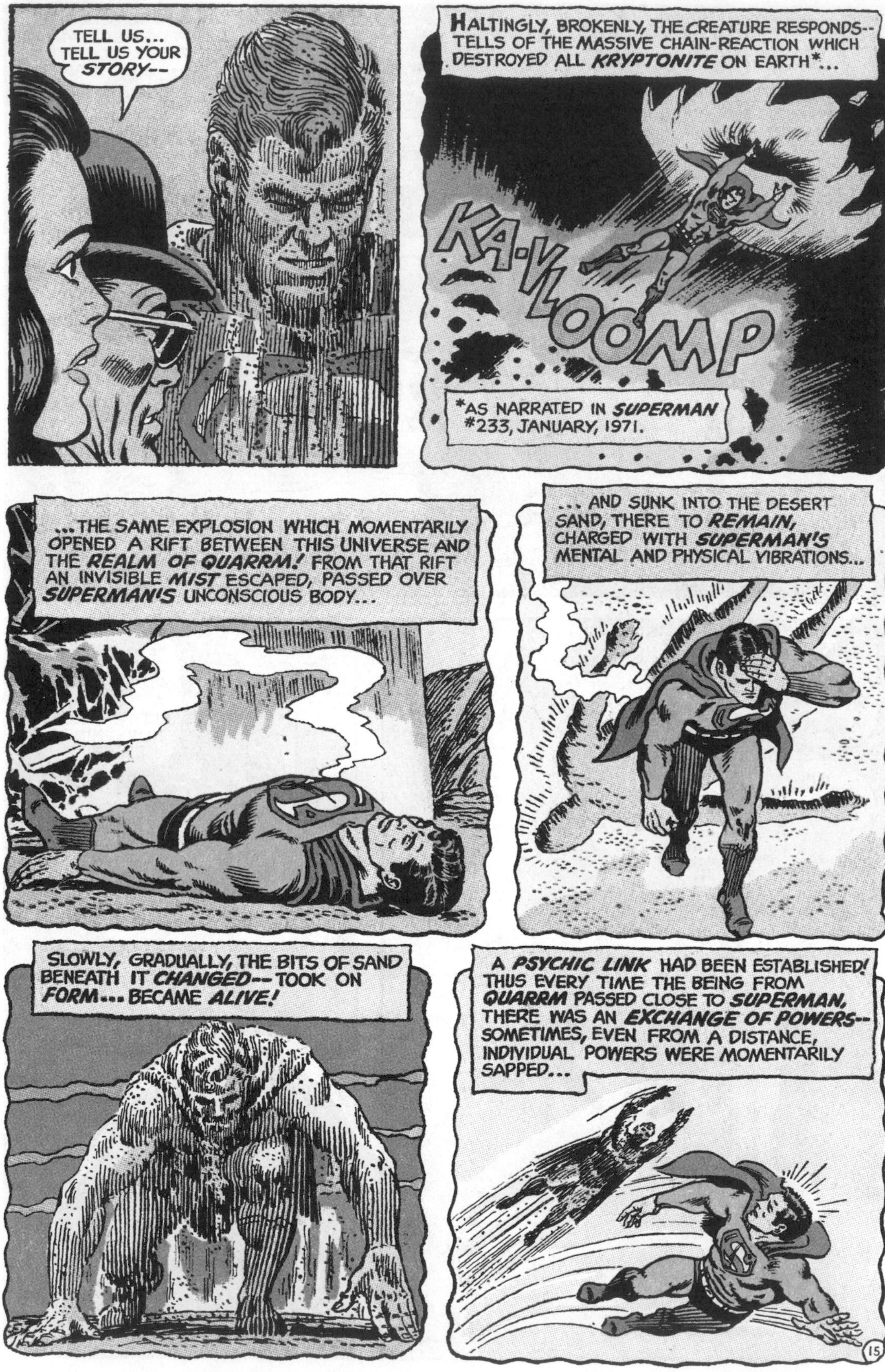
TELL US... TELL US YOUR STORY--
HALTINGLY, BROKENLY, THE CREATURE RESPONDS--TELLS OF THE MASSIVE CHAIN-REACTION WHICH DESTROYED ALL KRYPTONITE ON EARTH*...
KA-VLOOMP
*AS NARRATED IN SUPERMAN #233, JANUARY, 1971.
...THE SAME EXPLOSION WHICH MOMENTARILY OPENED A RIFT BETWEEN THIS UNIVERSE AND THE REALM OF QUARRM! FROM THAT RIFT AN INVISIBLE MIST ESCAPED, PASSED OVER SUPERMAN'S UNCONSCIOUS BODY...
...AND SUNK INTO THE DESERT SAND, THERE TO REMAIN, CHARGED WITH SUPERMAN'S MENTAL AND PHYSICAL VIBRATIONS...
SLOWLY, GRADUALLY, THE BITS OF SAND BENEATH IT CHANGED--TOOK ON FORM...BECAME ALIVE!
A PSYCHIC LINK HAD BEEN ESTABLISHED! THUS EVERY TIME THE BEING FROM QUARRM PASSED CLOSE TO SUPERMAN, THERE WAS AN EXCHANGE OF POWERS--SOMETIMES, EVEN FROM A DISTANCE, INDIVIDUAL POWERS WERE MOMENTARILY SAPPED...
15

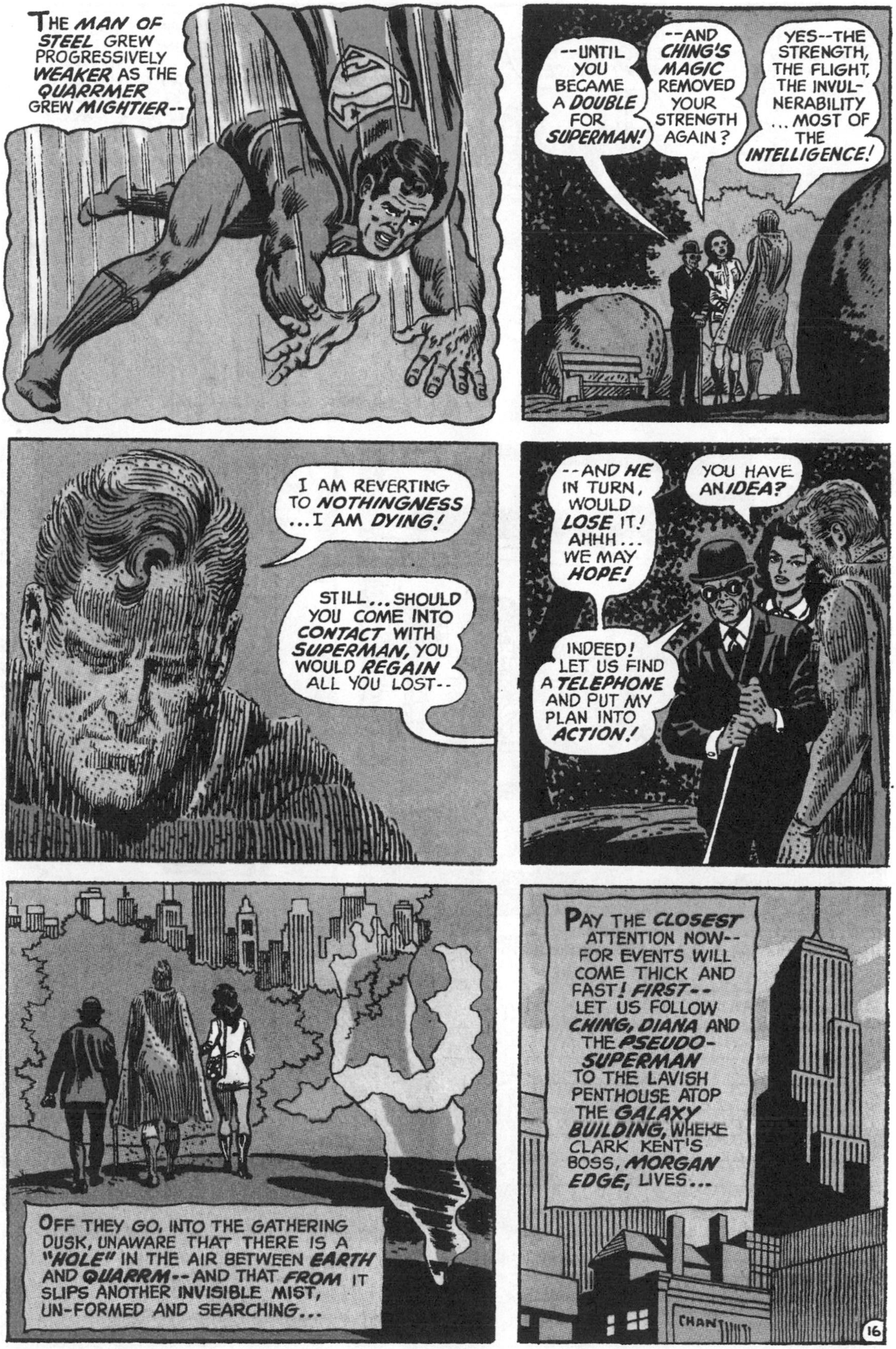
THE MAN OF STEEL GREW PROGRESSIVELY WEAKER AS THE QUARRMER GREW MIGHTIER--
--UNTIL YOU BECAME A DOUBLE FOR SUPERMAN!
--AND CHING'S MAGIC REMOVED YOUR STRENGTH AGAIN?
YES--THE STRENGTH, THE FLIGHT, THE INVUL-NERABILITY ...MOST OF THE INTELLIGENCE!
I AM REVERTING TO NOTHINGNESS ...I AM DYING!
STILL...SHOULD YOU COME INTO CONTACT WITH SUPERMAN, YOU WOULD REGAIN ALL YOU LOST--
--AND HE IN TURN, WOULD LOSE IT! AHHH... WE MAY HOPE!
YOU HAVE AN IDEA?
INDEED! LET US FIND A TELEPHONE AND PUT MY PLAN INTO ACTION!
OFF THEY GO, INTO THE GATHERING DUSK, UNAWARE THAT THERE IS A "HOLE" IN THE AIR BETWEEN EARTH AND QUARRM--AND THAT FROM IT SLIPS ANOTHER INVISIBLE MIST, UN-FORMED AND SEARCHING...
PAY THE CLOSEST ATTENTION NOW--FOR EVENTS WILL COME THICK AND FAST! FIRST--LET US FOLLOW CHING, DIANA AND THE PSEUDO-SUPERMAN TO THE LAVISH PENTHOUSE ATOP THE GALAXY BUILDING, WHERE CLARK KENT'S BOSS, MORGAN EDGE, LIVES...
CHAN
16

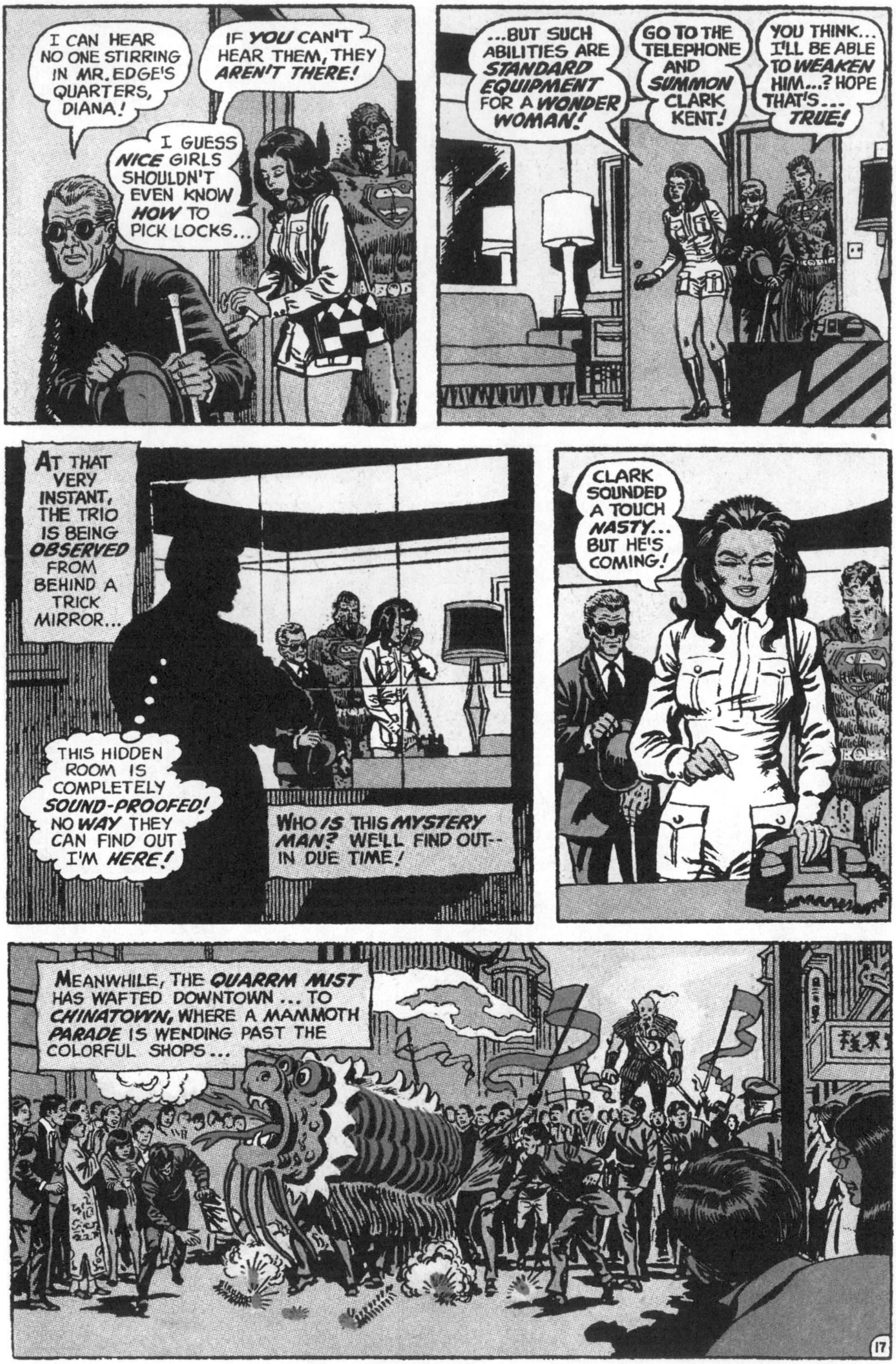
I CAN HEAR NO ONE STIRRING IN MR. EDGE'S QUARTERS, DIANA!
IF YOU CAN'T HEAR THEM, THEY AREN'T THERE!
I GUESS NICE GIRLS SHOULDN'T EVEN KNOW HOW TO PICK LOCKS...
...BUT SUCH ABILITIES ARE STANDARD EQUIPMENT FOR A WONDER WOMAN!
GO TO THE TELEPHONE AND SUMMON CLARK KENT!
YOU THINK... I'LL BE ABLE TO WEAKEN HIM...? HOPE THAT'S... TRUE!
AT THAT VERY INSTANT, THE TRIO IS BEING OBSERVED FROM BEHIND A TRICK MIRROR...
THIS HIDDEN ROOM IS COMPLETELY SOUND-PROOFED! NO WAY THEY CAN FIND OUT I'M HERE!
WHO IS THIS MYSTERY MAN? WE'LL FIND OUT-- IN DUE TIME!
CLARK SOUNDED A TOUCH NASTY... BUT HE'S COMING!
MEANWHILE, THE QUARRM MIST HAS WAFTED DOWNTOWN ... TO CHINATOWN, WHERE A MAMMOTH PARADE IS WENDING PAST THE COLORFUL SHOPS...
17

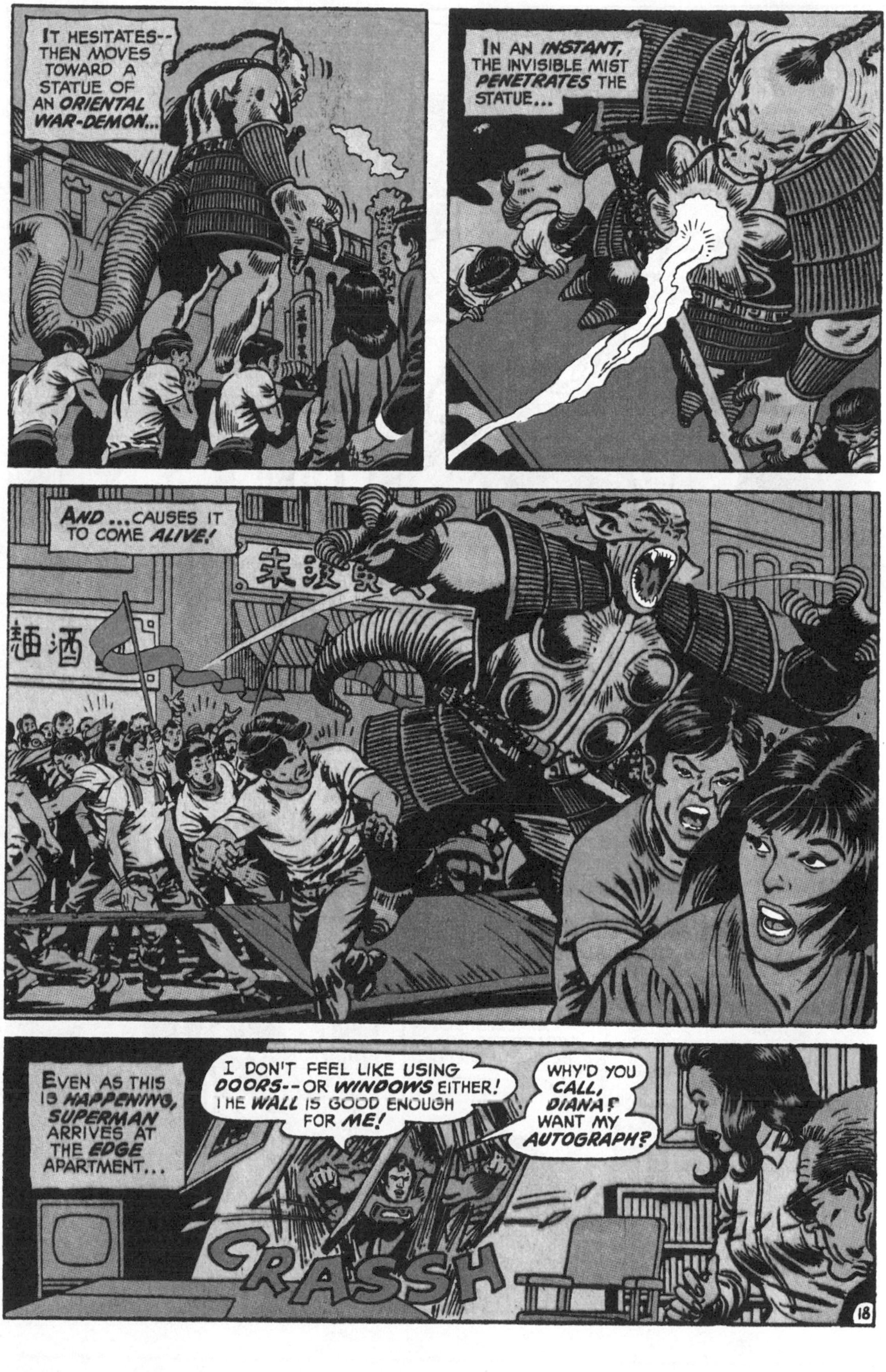
IT HESITATES-- THEN MOVES TOWARD A STATUE OF AN ORIENTAL WAR-DEMON...
IN AN INSTANT, THE INVISIBLE MIST PENETRATES THE STATUE...
AND ... CAUSES IT TO COME ALIVE!
麵 酒
EVEN AS THIS IS HAPPENING, SUPERMAN ARRIVES AT THE EDGE APARTMENT...
I DON'T FEEL LIKE USING DOORS--OR WINDOWS EITHER! THE WALL IS GOOD ENOUGH FOR ME!
WHY'D YOU CALL, DIANA? WANT MY AUTOGRAPH?
CRASSH
18

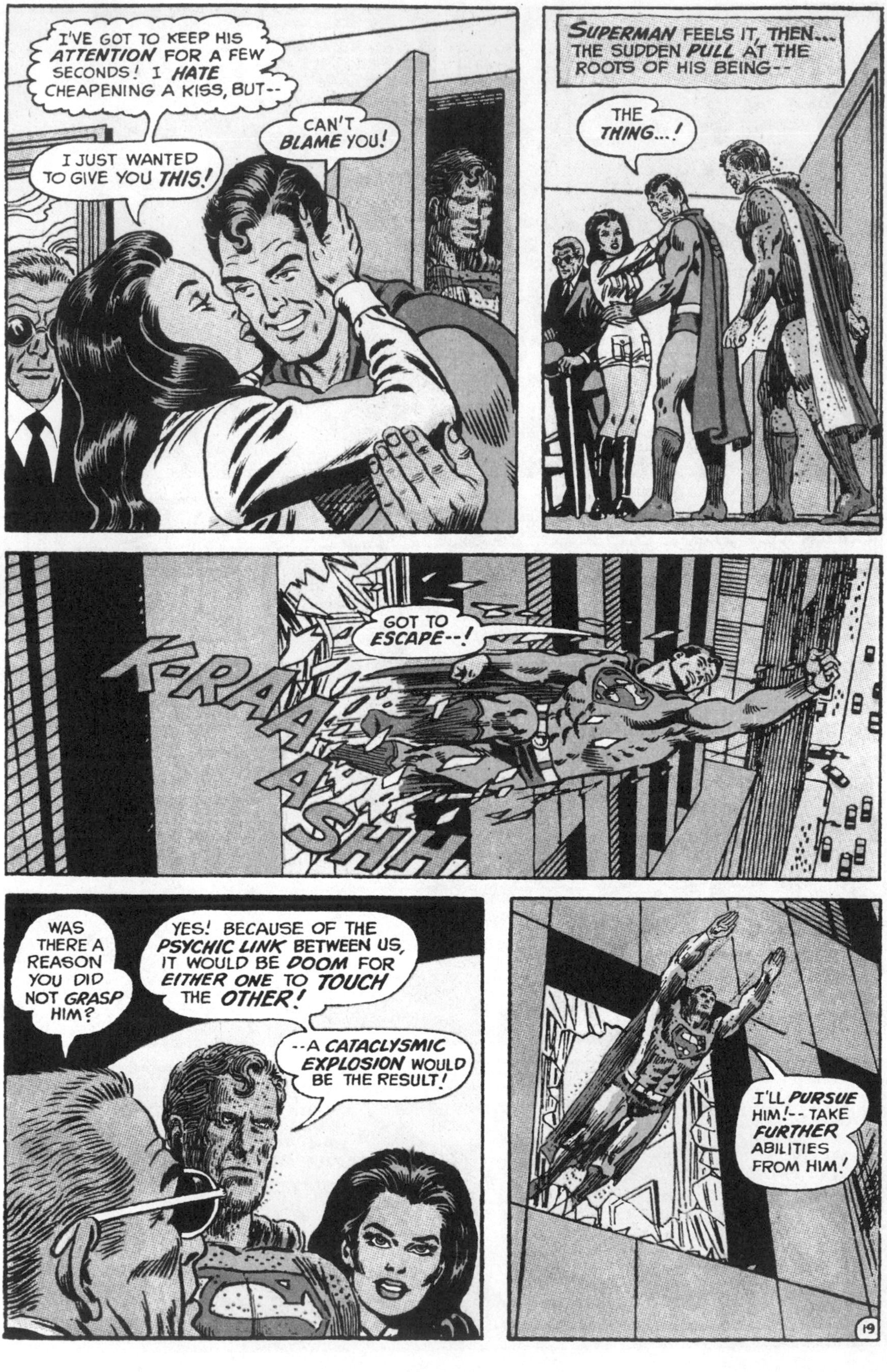
I'VE GOT TO KEEP HIS ATTENTION FOR A FEW SECONDS! I HATE CHEAPENING A KISS, BUT--
I JUST WANTED TO GIVE YOU THIS!
CAN'T BLAME YOU!
SUPERMAN FEELS IT, THEN... THE SUDDEN PULL AT THE ROOTS OF HIS BEING--
THE THING...!
GOT TO ESCAPE--!
K-RAAA-A-ASHH
WAS THERE A REASON YOU DID NOT GRASP HIM?
YES! BECAUSE OF THE PSYCHIC LINK BETWEEN US, IT WOULD BE DOOM FOR EITHER ONE TO TOUCH THE OTHER!
--A CATACLYSMIC EXPLOSION WOULD BE THE RESULT!
I'LL PURSUE HIM!-- TAKE FURTHER ABILITIES FROM HIM!
19

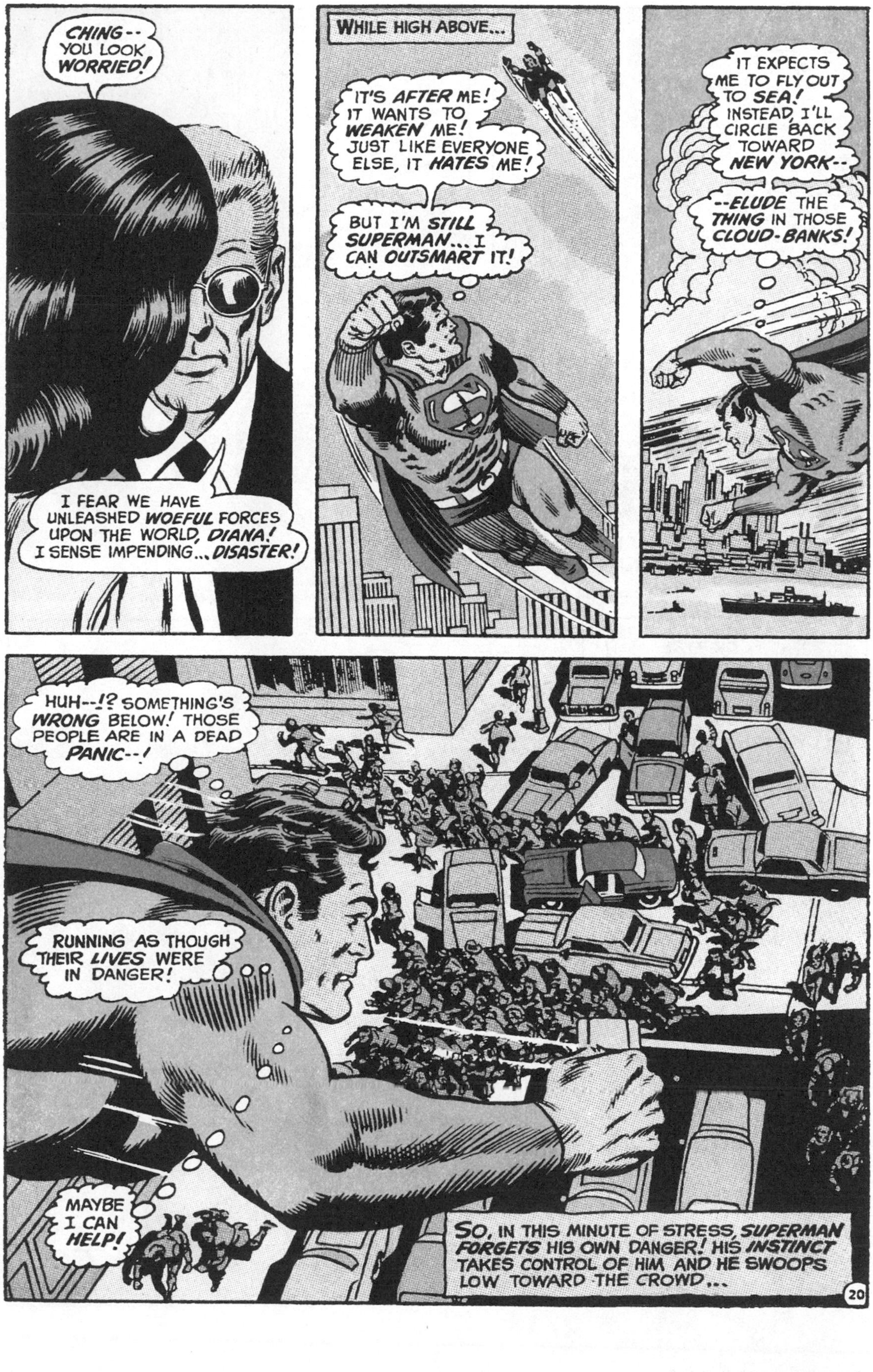
CHING-- YOU LOOK WORRIED!
I FEAR WE HAVE UNLEASHED WOEFUL FORCES UPON THE WORLD, DIANA! I SENSE IMPENDING... DISASTER!
WHILE HIGH ABOVE...
IT'S AFTER ME! IT WANTS TO WEAKEN ME! JUST LIKE EVERYONE ELSE, IT HATES ME!
BUT I'M STILL SUPERMAN... I CAN OUTSMART IT!
IT EXPECTS ME TO FLY OUT TO SEA! INSTEAD, I'LL CIRCLE BACK TOWARD NEW YORK--
--ELUDE THE THING IN THOSE CLOUD-BANKS!
HUH--!? SOMETHING'S WRONG BELOW! THOSE PEOPLE ARE IN A DEAD PANIC--!
RUNNING AS THOUGH THEIR LIVES WERE IN DANGER!
MAYBE I CAN HELP!
SO, IN THIS MINUTE OF STRESS, SUPERMAN FORGETS HIS OWN DANGER! HIS INSTINCT TAKES CONTROL OF HIM AND HE SWOOPS LOW TOWARD THE CROWD...
20

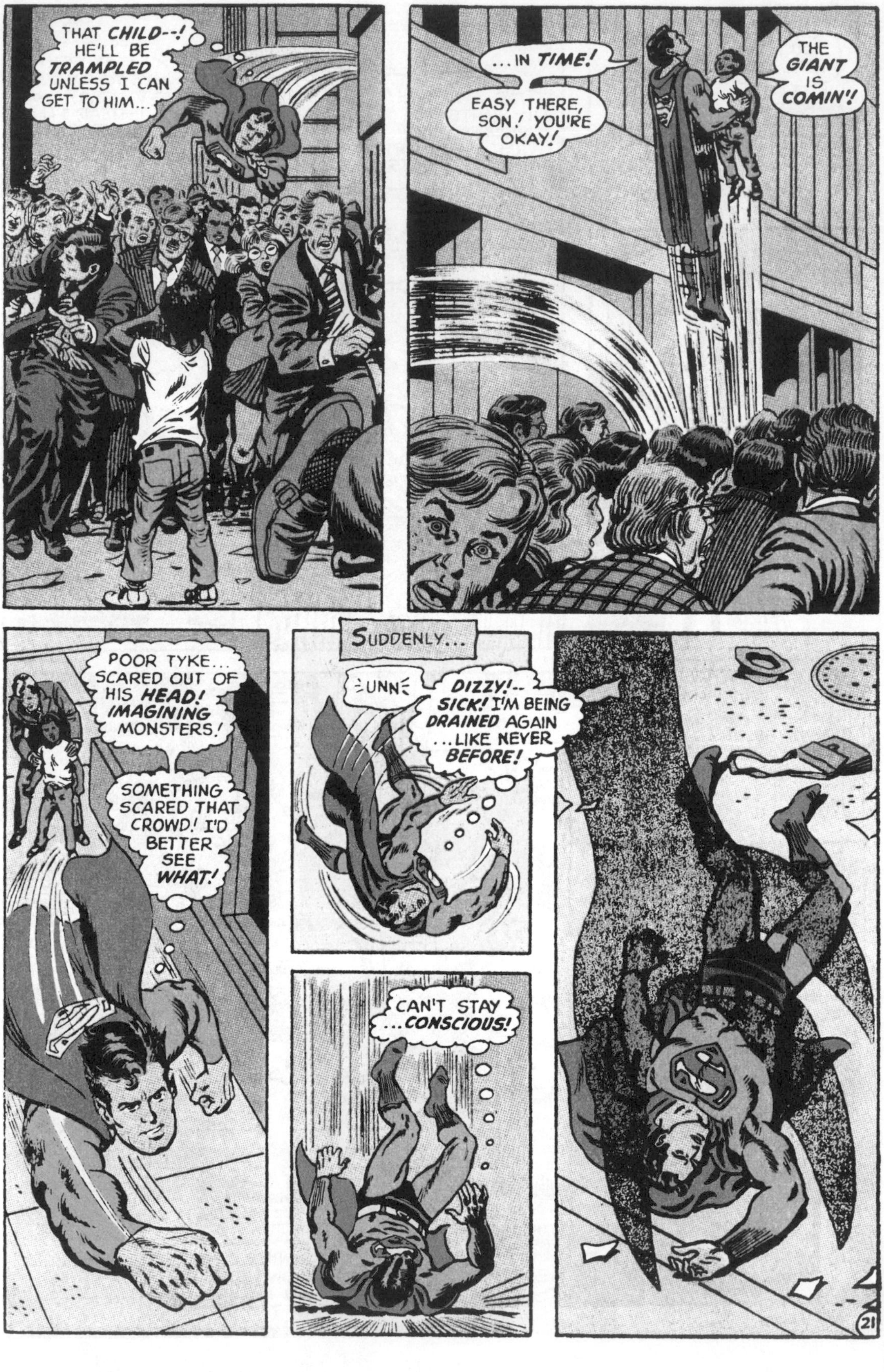

THAT CHILD--! HE'LL BE TRAMPLED UNLESS I CAN GET TO HIM...
...IN TIME!
EASY THERE, SON! YOU'RE OKAY!
THE GIANT IS COMIN'!
POOR TYKE... SCARED OUT OF HIS HEAD! IMAGINING MONSTERS!
SOMETHING SCARED THAT CROWD! I'D BETTER SEE WHAT!
SUDDENLY...
UNN
DIZZY!-- SICK! I'M BEING DRAINED AGAIN ...LIKE NEVER BEFORE!
CAN'T STAY ...CONSCIOUS!
21

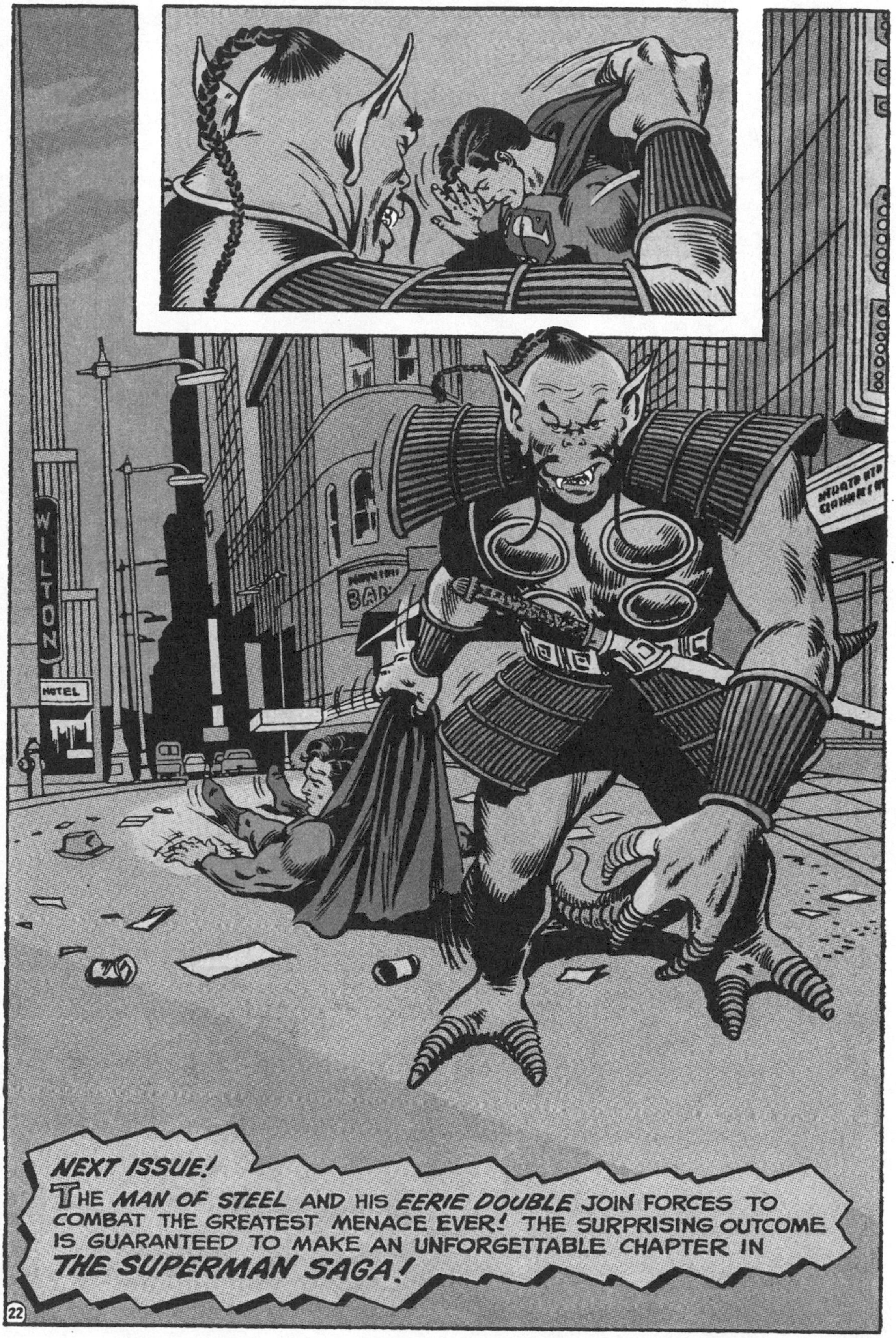
WILTON
HOTEL
BANK
NEXT ISSUE!
THE MAN OF STEEL AND HIS EERIE DOUBLE JOIN FORCES TO COMBAT THE GREATEST MENACE EVER! THE SURPRISING OUTCOME IS GUARANTEED TO MAKE AN UNFORGETTABLE CHAPTER IN THE SUPERMAN SAGA!
22

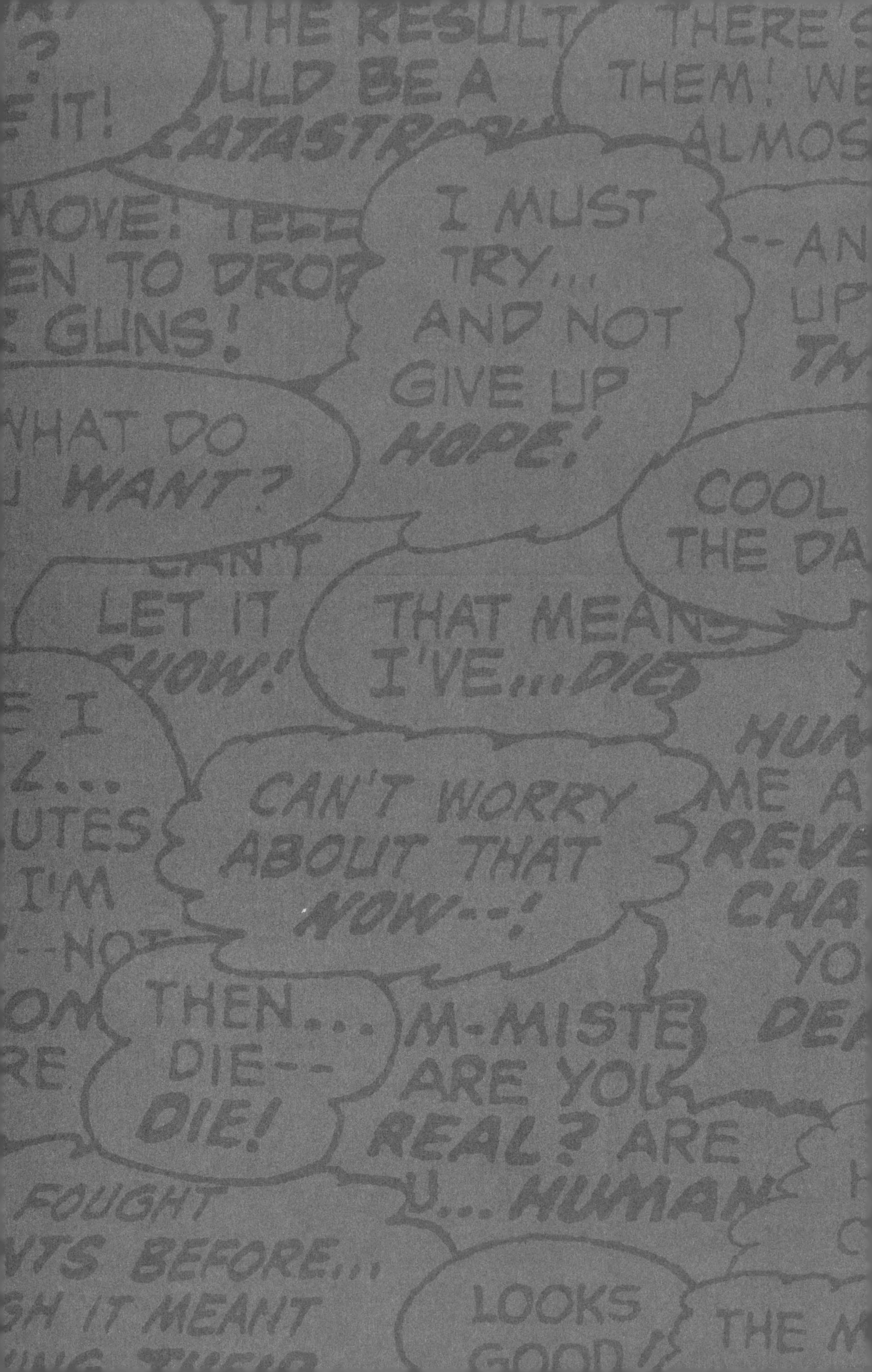
I MUST TRY... AND NOT GIVE UP HOPE!
LET IT SHOW!
THAT MEANS I'VE...DIED
CAN'T WORRY ABOUT THAT NOW--!
THEN... DIE-- DIE!
REAL? ARE
LOOKS GOOD!

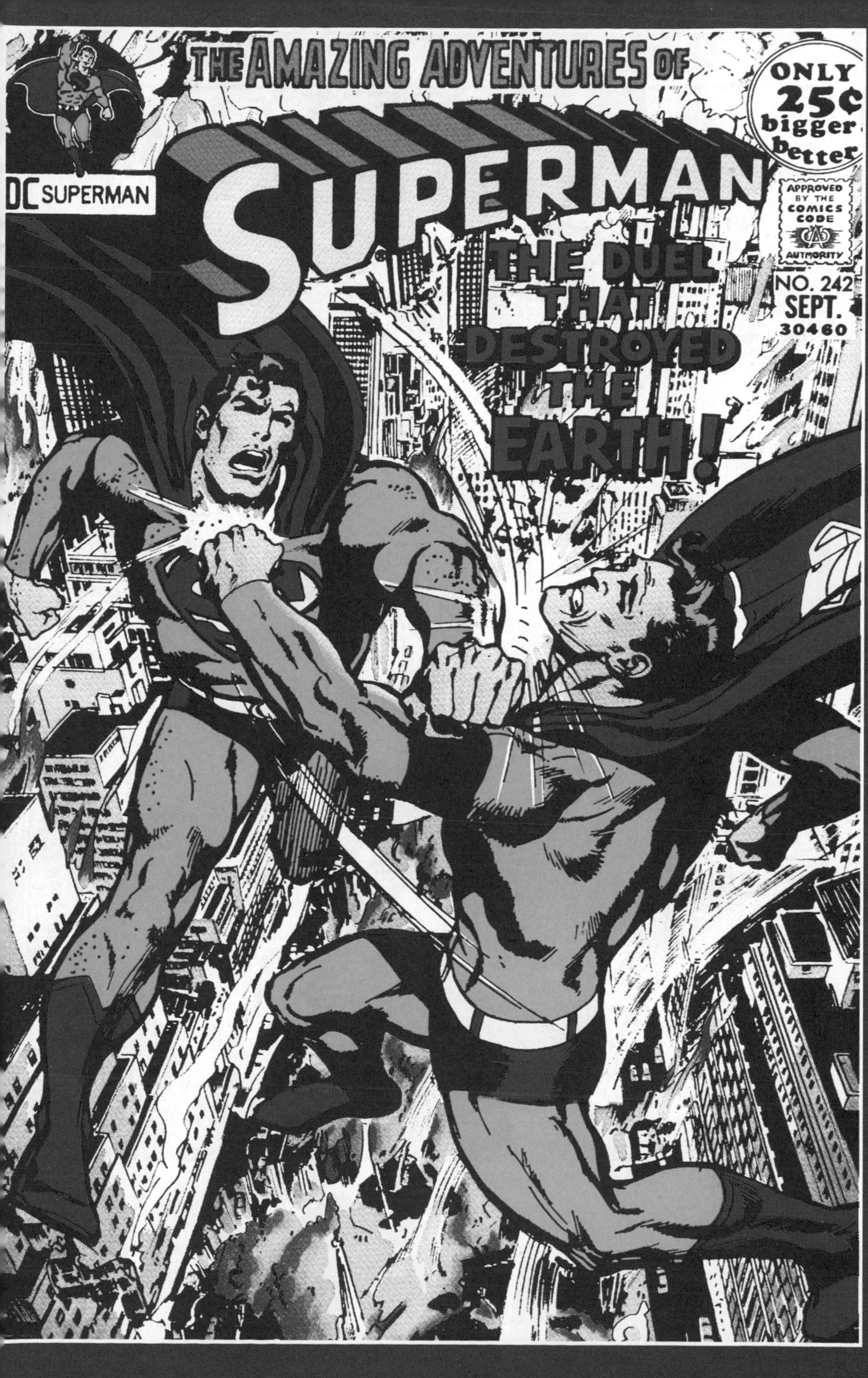
THE AMAZING ADVENTURES OF
SUPERMAN
DC SUPERMAN
ONLY 25¢ bigger better
APPROVED BY THE COMICS CODE AUTHORITY
NO. 242
SEPT.
30460
THE DUEL THAT DESTROYED THE EARTH!

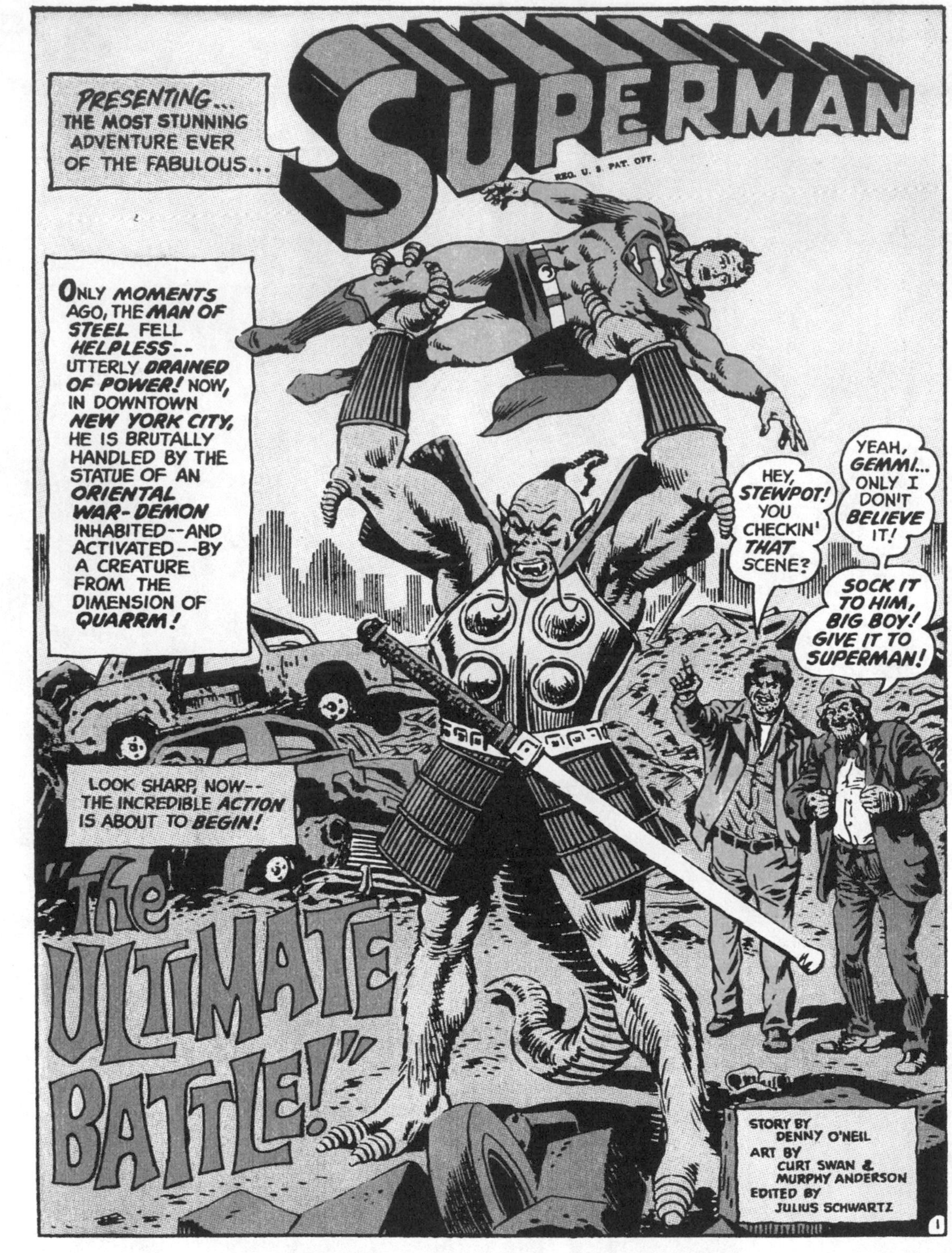
PRESENTING... THE MOST STUNNING ADVENTURE EVER OF THE FABULOUS...
SUPERMAN
REG. U.S. PAT. OFF.
ONLY MOMENTS AGO, THE MAN OF STEEL FELL HELPLESS-- UTTERLY DRAINED OF POWER! NOW, IN DOWNTOWN NEW YORK CITY, HE IS BRUTALLY HANDLED BY THE STATUE OF AN ORIENTAL WAR-DEMON INHABITED--AND ACTIVATED--BY A CREATURE FROM THE DIMENSION OF QUARRM!
HEY, STEWPOT! YOU CHECKIN' THAT SCENE?
YEAH, GEMMI... ONLY I DON'T BELIEVE IT!
SOCK IT TO HIM, BIG BOY! GIVE IT TO SUPERMAN!
LOOK SHARP, NOW-- THE INCREDIBLE ACTION IS ABOUT TO BEGIN!
"The ULTIMATE BATTLE!"
STORY BY DENNY O'NEIL
ART BY CURT SWAN & MURPHY ANDERSON
EDITED BY JULIUS SCHWARTZ
1

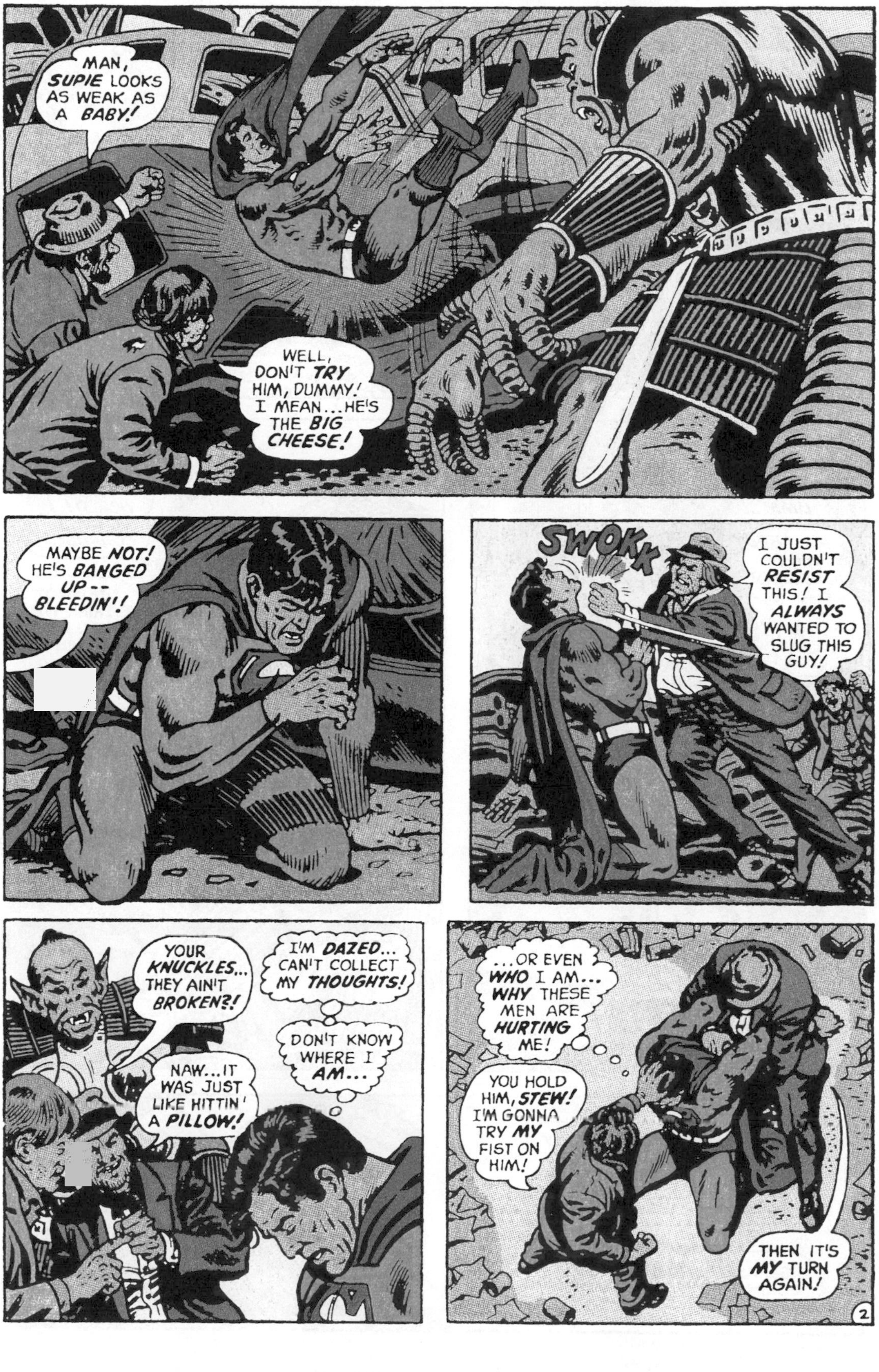
MAN, SUPIE LOOKS AS WEAK AS A BABY!
WELL, DON'T TRY HIM, DUMMY! I MEAN...HE'S THE BIG CHEESE!
MAYBE NOT! HE'S BANGED UP -- BLEEDIN'!
SWOKK
I JUST COULDN'T RESIST THIS! I ALWAYS WANTED TO SLUG THIS GUY!
YOUR KNUCKLES... THEY AIN'T BROKEN?!
NAW...IT WAS JUST LIKE HITTIN' A PILLOW!
I'M DAZED... CAN'T COLLECT MY THOUGHTS!
DON'T KNOW WHERE I AM...
...OR EVEN WHO I AM... WHY THESE MEN ARE HURTING ME!
YOU HOLD HIM, STEW! I'M GONNA TRY MY FIST ON HIM!
THEN IT'S MY TURN AGAIN!
2

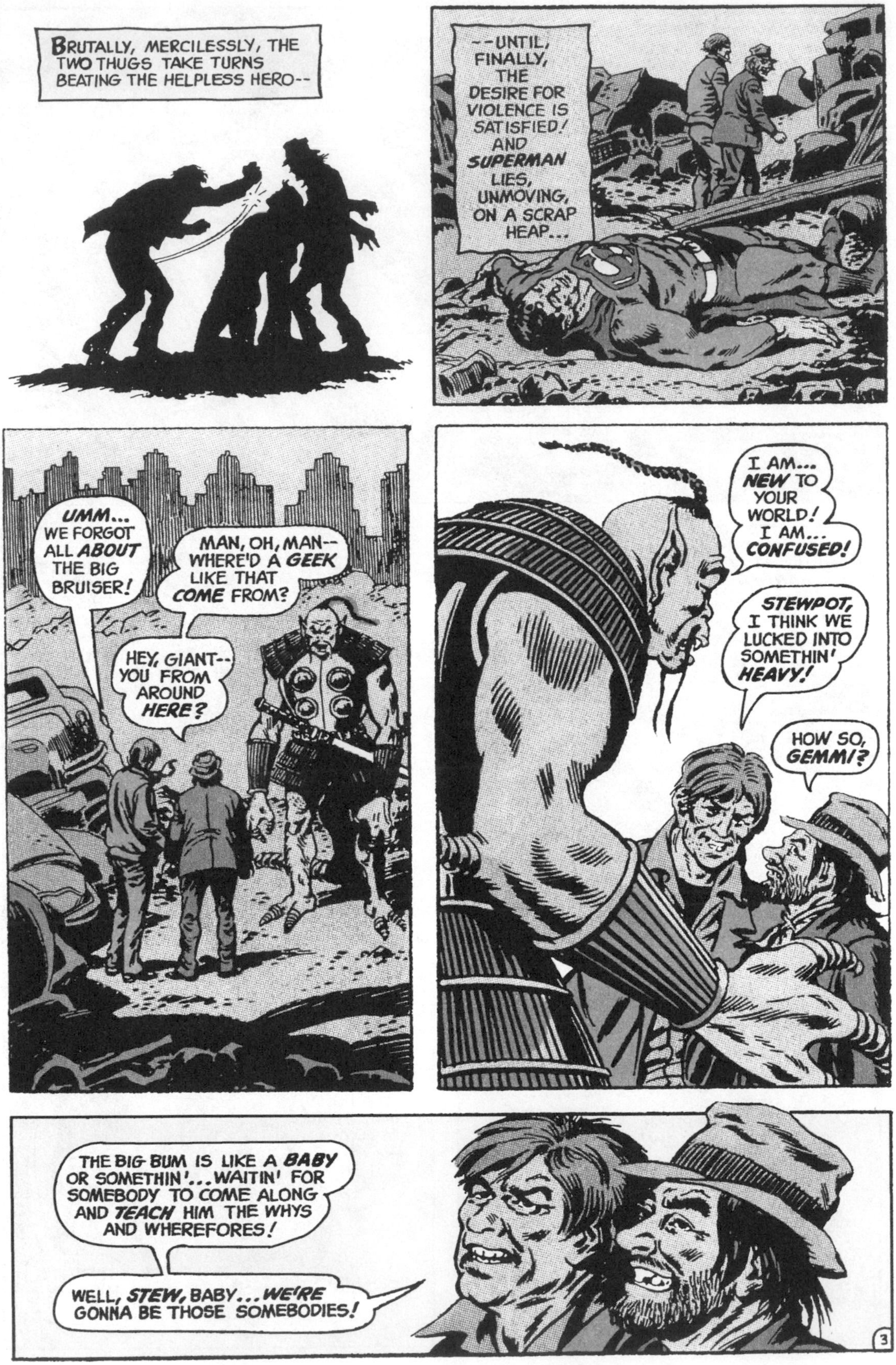
BRUTALLY, MERCILESSLY, THE TWO THUGS TAKE TURNS BEATING THE HELPLESS HERO--
--UNTIL, FINALLY, THE DESIRE FOR VIOLENCE IS SATISFIED! AND SUPERMAN LIES, UNMOVING, ON A SCRAP HEAP...
UMM... WE FORGOT ALL ABOUT THE BIG BRUISER!
MAN, OH, MAN-- WHERE'D A GEEK LIKE THAT COME FROM?
HEY, GIANT-- YOU FROM AROUND HERE?
I AM... NEW TO YOUR WORLD! I AM... CONFUSED!
STEWPOT, I THINK WE LUCKED INTO SOMETHIN' HEAVY!
HOW SO, GEMMI?
THE BIG BUM IS LIKE A BABY OR SOMETHIN'...WAITIN' FOR SOMEBODY TO COME ALONG AND TEACH HIM THE WHYS AND WHEREFORES!
WELL, STEW, BABY... WE'RE GONNA BE THOSE SOMEBODIES!
3

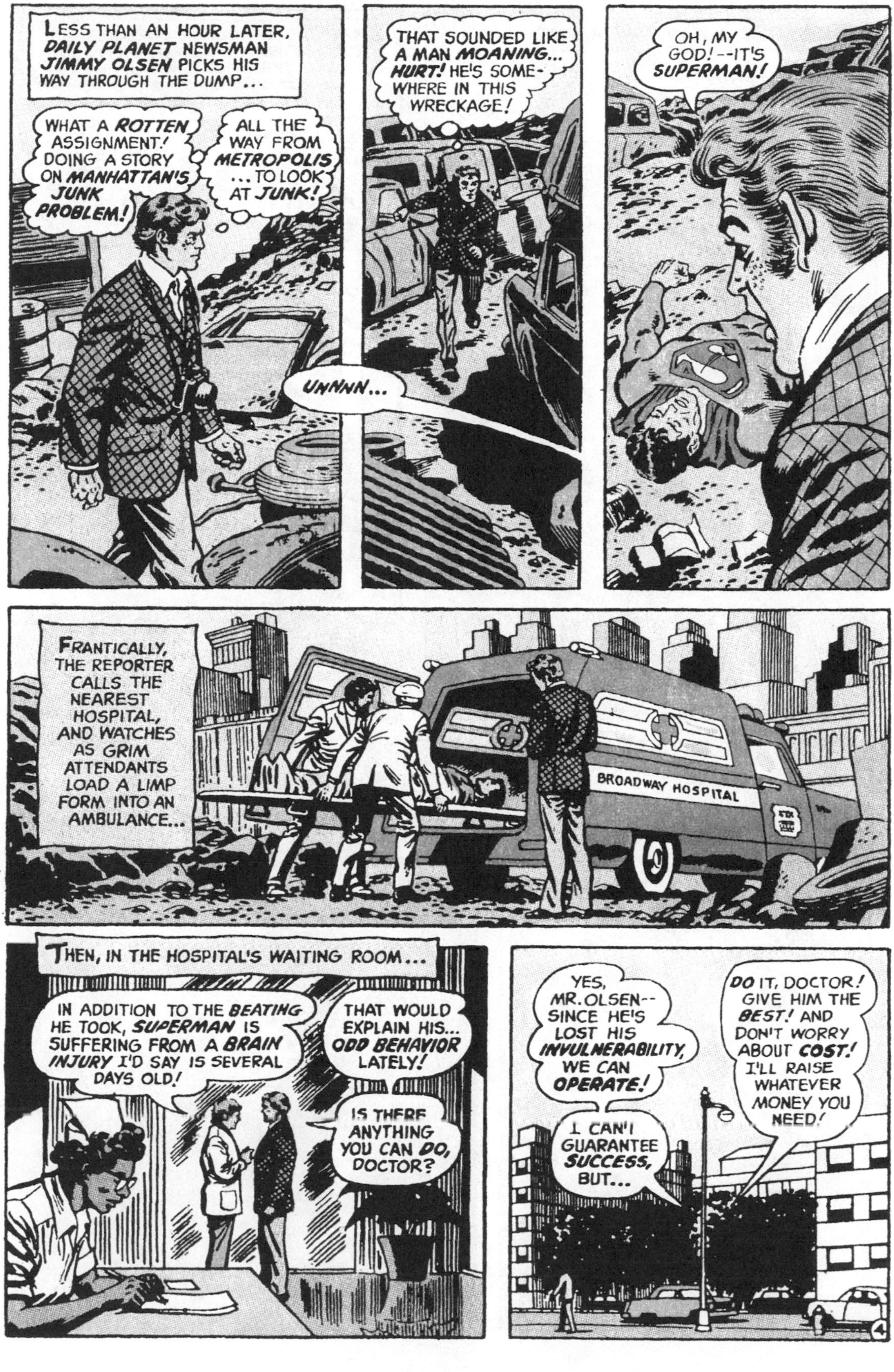
LESS THAN AN HOUR LATER, DAILY PLANET NEWSMAN JIMMY OLSEN PICKS HIS WAY THROUGH THE DUMP...
WHAT A ROTTEN ASSIGNMENT! DOING A STORY ON MANHATTAN'S JUNK PROBLEM!
ALL THE WAY FROM METROPOLIS ...TO LOOK AT JUNK!
THAT SOUNDED LIKE A MAN MOANING... HURT! HE'S SOMEWHERE IN THIS WRECKAGE!
UNNNN...
OH, MY GOD! --IT'S SUPERMAN!
FRANTICALLY, THE REPORTER CALLS THE NEAREST HOSPITAL, AND WATCHES AS GRIM ATTENDANTS LOAD A LIMP FORM INTO AN AMBULANCE...
BROADWAY HOSPITAL
THEN, IN THE HOSPITAL'S WAITING ROOM...
IN ADDITION TO THE BEATING HE TOOK, SUPERMAN IS SUFFERING FROM A BRAIN INJURY I'D SAY IS SEVERAL DAYS OLD!
THAT WOULD EXPLAIN HIS... ODD BEHAVIOR LATELY!
IS THERE ANYTHING YOU CAN DO, DOCTOR?
YES, MR. OLSEN-- SINCE HE'S LOST HIS INVULNERABILITY, WE CAN OPERATE!
I CAN'T GUARANTEE SUCCESS, BUT...
DO IT, DOCTOR! GIVE HIM THE BEST! AND DON'T WORRY ABOUT COST! I'LL RAISE WHATEVER MONEY YOU NEED!
4

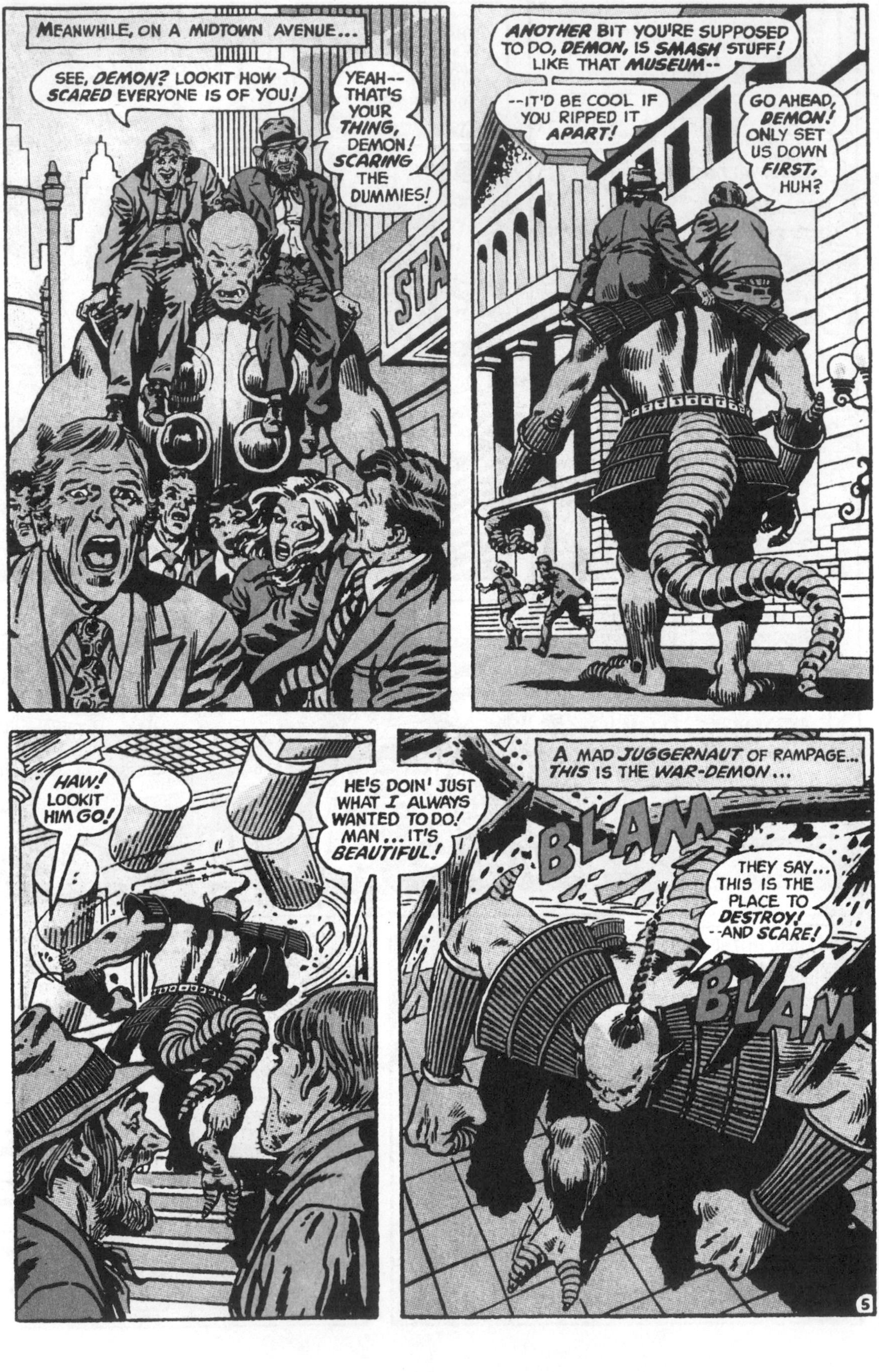

MEANWHILE, ON A MIDTOWN AVENUE...
SEE, DEMON? LOOKIT HOW SCARED EVERYONE IS OF YOU!
YEAH-- THAT'S YOUR THING, DEMON! SCARING THE DUMMIES!
ANOTHER BIT YOU'RE SUPPOSED TO DO, DEMON, IS SMASH STUFF! LIKE THAT MUSEUM--
--IT'D BE COOL IF YOU RIPPED IT APART!
GO AHEAD, DEMON! ONLY SET US DOWN FIRST, HUH?
HAW! LOOKIT HIM GO!
HE'S DOIN' JUST WHAT I ALWAYS WANTED TO DO! MAN... IT'S BEAUTIFUL!
A MAD JUGGERNAUT OF RAMPAGE... THIS IS THE WAR-DEMON...
BLAM
THEY SAY... THIS IS THE PLACE TO DESTROY! --AND SCARE!
BLAM
5

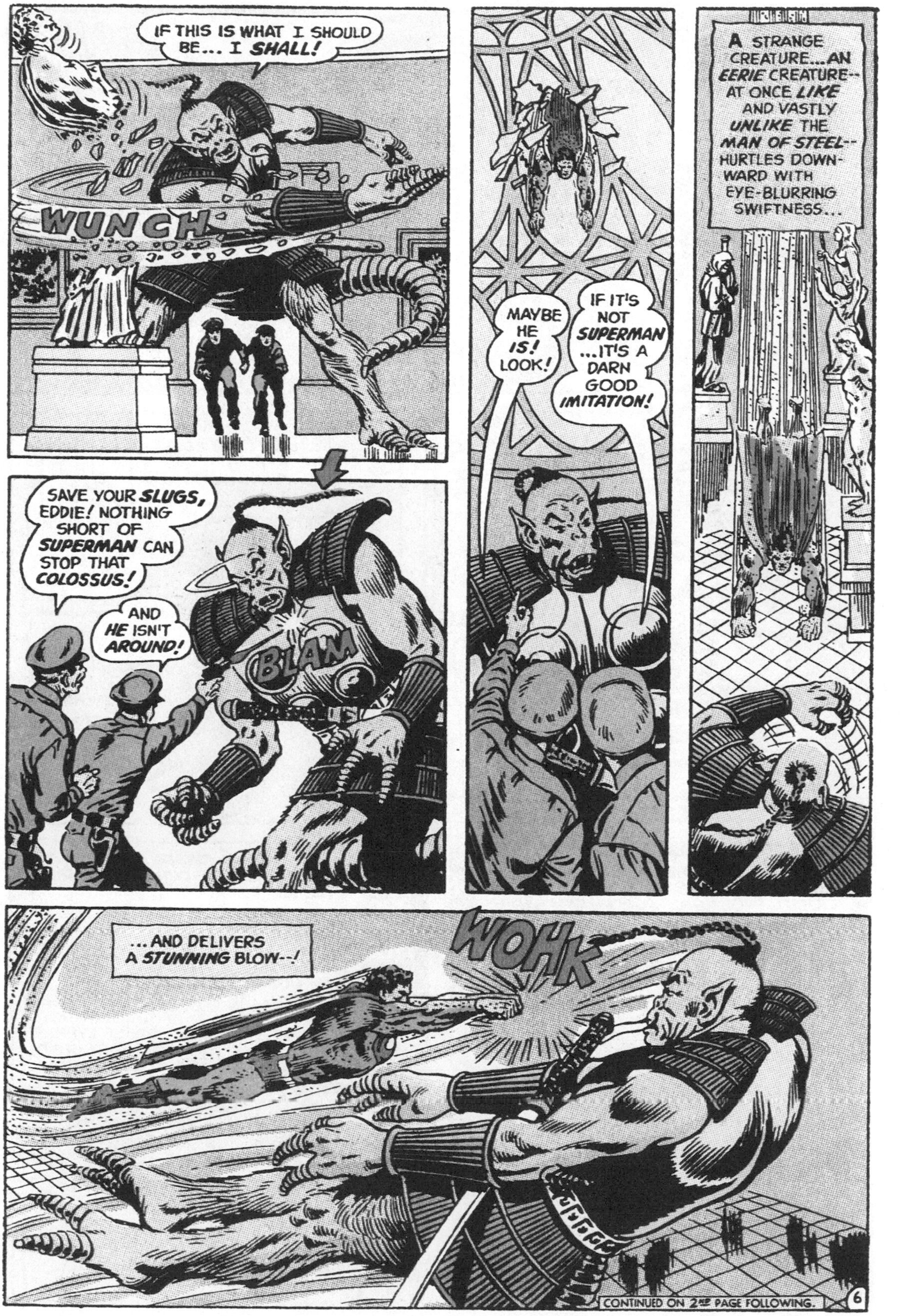
IF THIS IS WHAT I SHOULD BE... I SHALL!
WUNCH
A STRANGE CREATURE...AN EERIE CREATURE-- AT ONCE LIKE AND VASTLY UNLIKE THE MAN OF STEEL-- HURTLES DOWNWARD WITH EYE-BLURRING SWIFTNESS...
MAYBE HE IS! LOOK!
IF IT'S NOT SUPERMAN ...IT'S A DARN GOOD IMITATION!
SAVE YOUR SLUGS, EDDIE! NOTHING SHORT OF SUPERMAN CAN STOP THAT COLOSSUS!
AND HE ISN'T AROUND!
BLAM
...AND DELIVERS A STUNNING BLOW--!
WOHK
CONTINUED ON 2ND PAGE FOLLOWING.
6

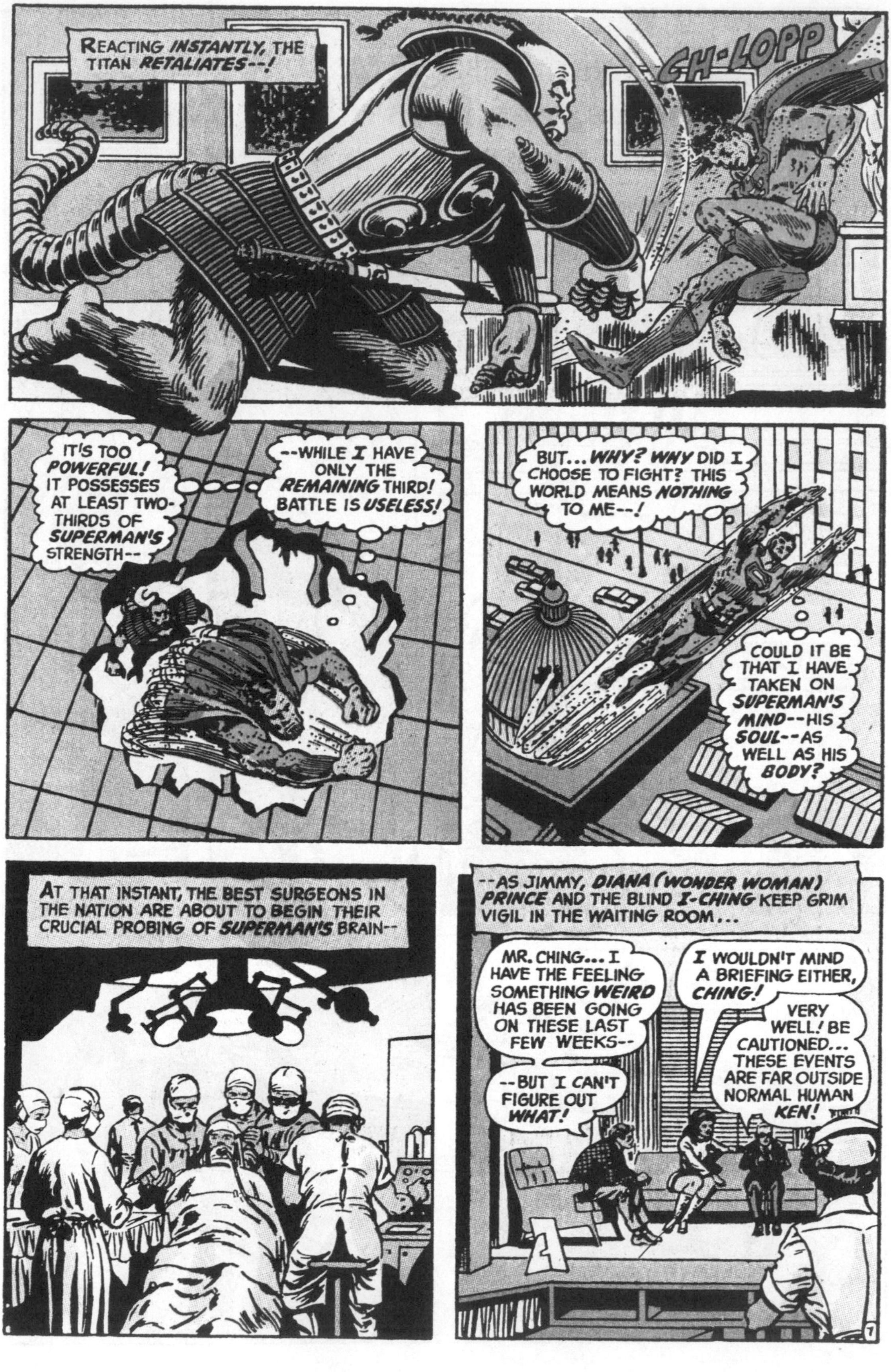
REACTING INSTANTLY, THE TITAN RETALIATES--!
CH-LOPP
IT'S TOO POWERFUL! IT POSSESSES AT LEAST TWO-THIRDS OF SUPERMAN'S STRENGTH--
--WHILE I HAVE ONLY THE REMAINING THIRD! BATTLE IS USELESS!
BUT... WHY? WHY DID I CHOOSE TO FIGHT? THIS WORLD MEANS NOTHING TO ME--!
COULD IT BE THAT I HAVE TAKEN ON SUPERMAN'S MIND--HIS SOUL--AS WELL AS HIS BODY?
AT THAT INSTANT, THE BEST SURGEONS IN THE NATION ARE ABOUT TO BEGIN THEIR CRUCIAL PROBING OF SUPERMAN'S BRAIN--
--AS JIMMY, DIANA (WONDER WOMAN) PRINCE AND THE BLIND I-CHING KEEP GRIM VIGIL IN THE WAITING ROOM...
MR. CHING... I HAVE THE FEELING SOMETHING WEIRD HAS BEEN GOING ON THESE LAST FEW WEEKS--
--BUT I CAN'T FIGURE OUT WHAT!
I WOULDN'T MIND A BRIEFING EITHER, CHING!
VERY WELL! BE CAUTIONED... THESE EVENTS ARE FAR OUTSIDE NORMAL HUMAN KEN!
7

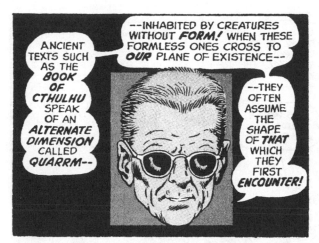

ANCIENT TEXTS SUCH AS THE *BOOK OF CTHULHU* SPEAK OF AN *ALTERNATE DIMENSION* CALLED *QUARRM*--

--INHABITED BY CREATURES WITHOUT *FORM!* WHEN THESE FORMLESS ONES CROSS TO *OUR* PLANE OF EXISTENCE--

--THEY OFTEN ASSUME THE SHAPE OF *THAT* WHICH THEY FIRST *ENCOUNTER!*

THEY *ALSO* DRAIN ANY EXTRAORDINARY *POWERS* FROM THOSE THEY MEET!

SO--*SUPERMAN'S DOUBLE IS FROM QUARRM!*

BUT HOW ABOUT THE GIANT THAT TORE UP THE *MUSEUM?*

THAT, TOO, IS A *QUARRM* ENTITY...

PARDON ME, FOLKS! I THOUGHT YOU'D LIKE TO KNOW...THE OPERATION IS *COMPLETE!*

H-HOW DID IT GO, DOC?

IT'S TOO EARLY TO TELL! THE PATIENT IS *WEAK!* HOWEVER, BARRING *COMPLICATIONS* OR FURTHER *SHOCK*--

--WE FEEL HE SHOULD RECOVER SATISFACTORILY!

ELSEWHERE, THE RAMPAGE *CONTINUES*...

GO, *DEMON!* GIVE 'EM A *SMASH!*

HEY, *DEMON*... GET ME A *NEWSPAPER!*

8

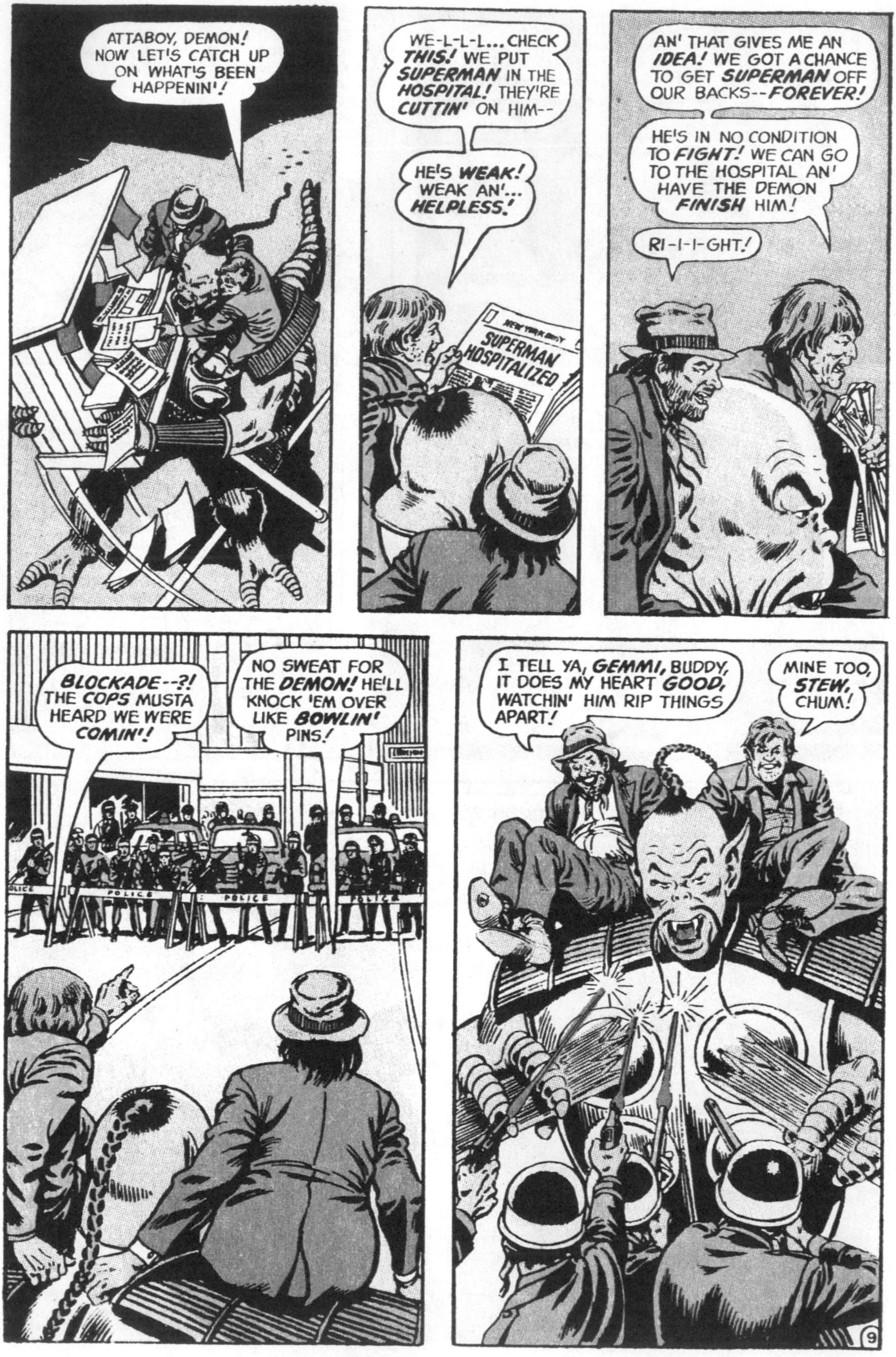
ATTABOY, DEMON! NOW LET'S CATCH UP ON WHAT'S BEEN HAPPENIN'!
WE-L-L-L... CHECK THIS! WE PUT SUPERMAN IN THE HOSPITAL! THEY'RE CUTTIN' ON HIM--
HE'S WEAK! WEAK AN'... HELPLESS!
NEW YORK DAILY
SUPERMAN HOSPITALIZED
AN' THAT GIVES ME AN IDEA! WE GOT A CHANCE TO GET SUPERMAN OFF OUR BACKS--FOREVER!
HE'S IN NO CONDITION TO FIGHT! WE CAN GO TO THE HOSPITAL AN' HAVE THE DEMON FINISH HIM!
RI-I-I-GHT!
BLOCKADE--?! THE COPS MUSTA HEARD WE WERE COMIN'!
NO SWEAT FOR THE DEMON! HE'LL KNOCK 'EM OVER LIKE BOWLIN' PINS!
POLICE
POLICE
POLICE
POLICE
I TELL YA, GEMMI, BUDDY, IT DOES MY HEART GOOD, WATCHIN' HIM RIP THINGS APART!
MINE TOO, STEW, CHUM!
9

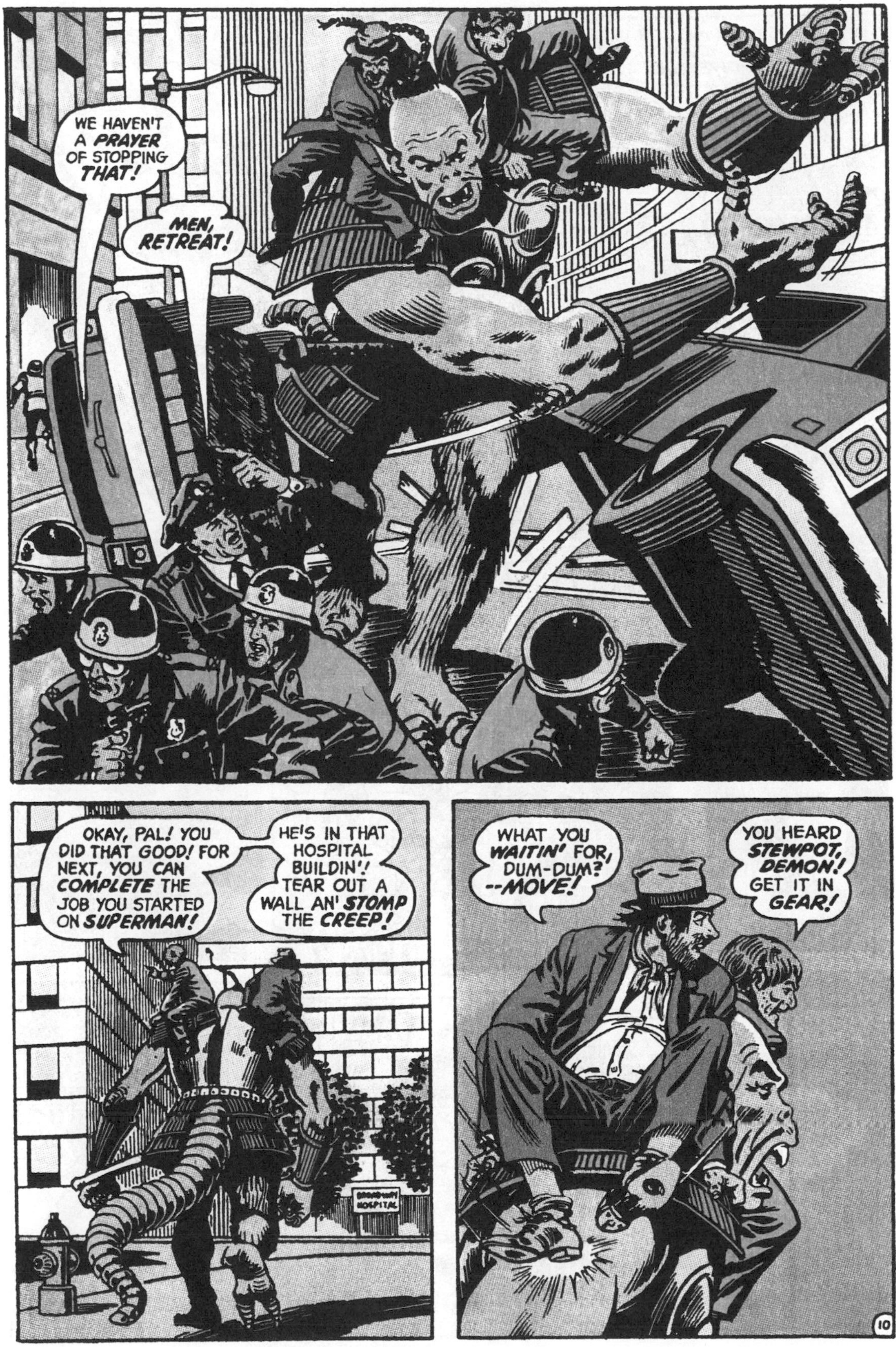
WE HAVEN'T A *PRAYER* OF STOPPING *THAT!*
MEN, RETREAT!
OKAY, PAL! YOU DID THAT *GOOD!* FOR NEXT, YOU CAN *COMPLETE* THE JOB YOU STARTED ON *SUPERMAN!*
HE'S IN THAT HOSPITAL BUILDIN'! TEAR OUT A WALL AN' *STOMP* THE *CREEP!*
WHAT YOU *WAITIN'* FOR, DUM-DUM? --*MOVE!*
YOU HEARD *STEWPOT, DEMON!* GET IT IN *GEAR!*
10

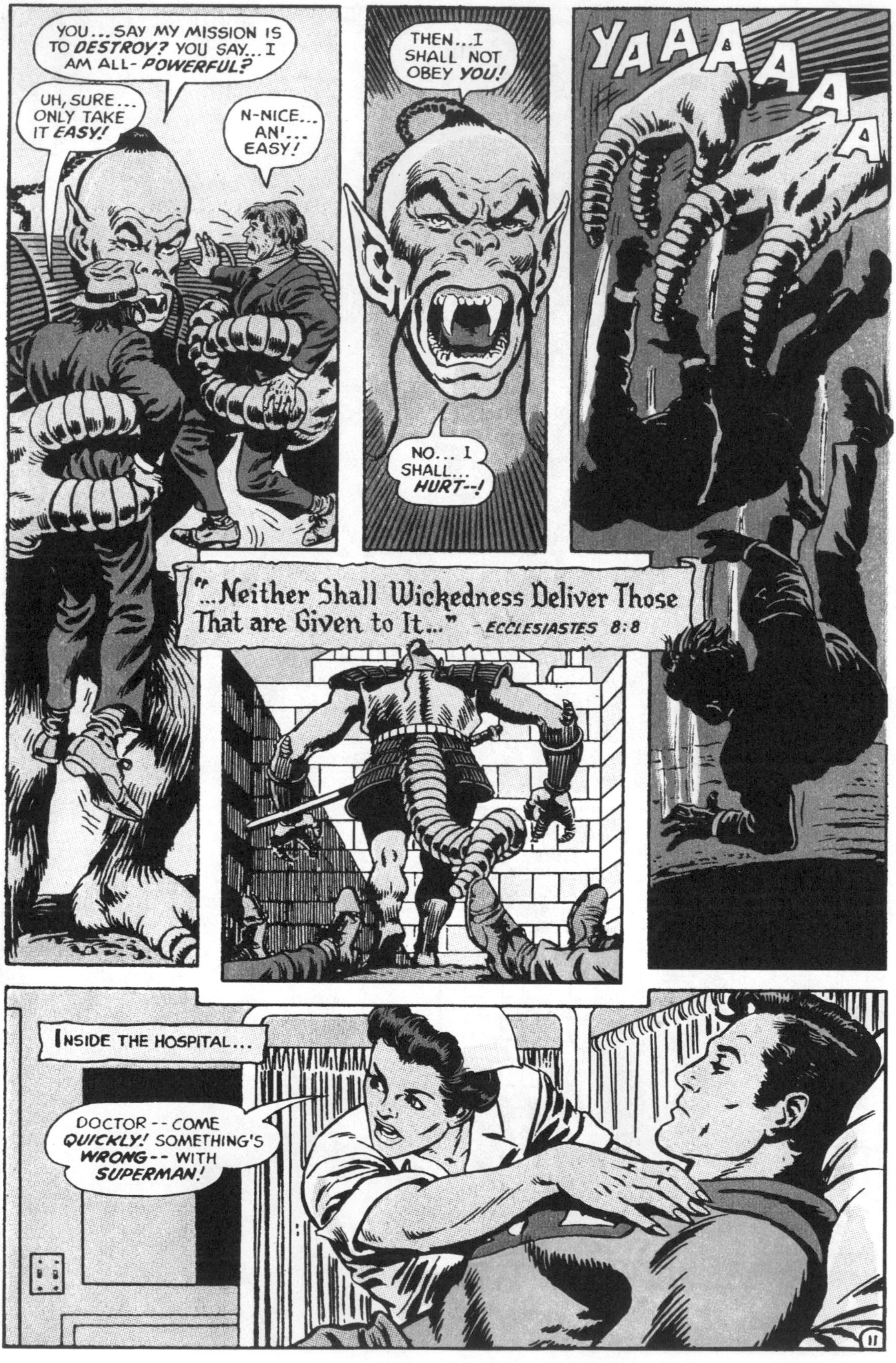
YOU... SAY MY MISSION IS TO DESTROY? YOU SAY... I AM ALL-POWERFUL?
UH, SURE... ONLY TAKE IT EASY!
N-NICE... AN'... EASY!
THEN... I SHALL NOT OBEY YOU!
NO... I SHALL... HURT--!
YAAAAAAA
"...Neither Shall Wickedness Deliver Those That are Given to It..." -ECCLESIASTES 8:8
INSIDE THE HOSPITAL...
DOCTOR -- COME QUICKLY! SOMETHING'S WRONG -- WITH SUPERMAN!
11

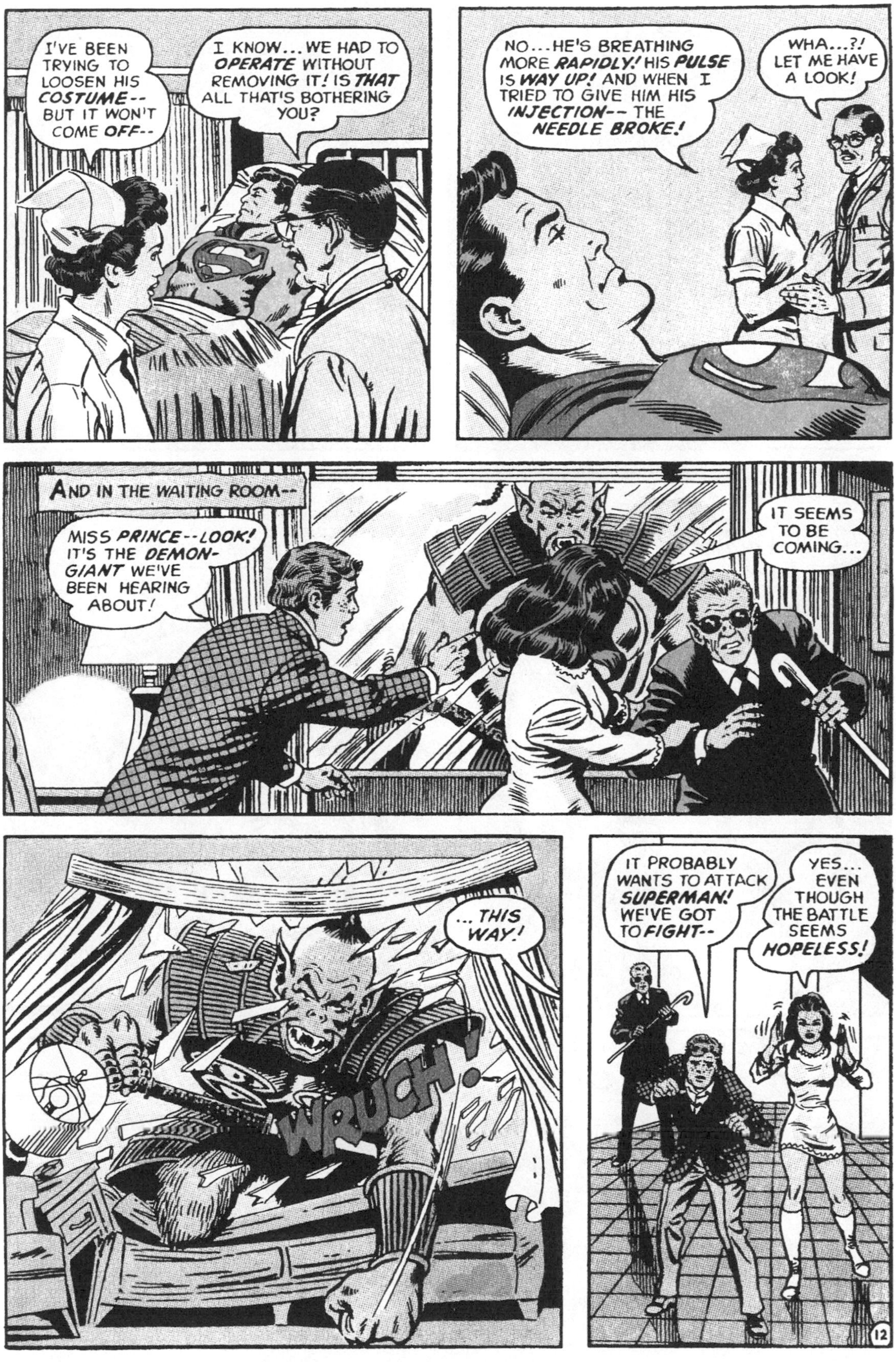
I'VE BEEN TRYING TO LOOSEN HIS COSTUME-- BUT IT WON'T COME OFF--
I KNOW... WE HAD TO OPERATE WITHOUT REMOVING IT! IS THAT ALL THAT'S BOTHERING YOU?
NO...HE'S BREATHING MORE RAPIDLY! HIS PULSE IS WAY UP! AND WHEN I TRIED TO GIVE HIM HIS INJECTION-- THE NEEDLE BROKE!
WHA...?! LET ME HAVE A LOOK!
AND IN THE WAITING ROOM--
MISS PRINCE--LOOK! IT'S THE DEMON-GIANT WE'VE BEEN HEARING ABOUT!
IT SEEMS TO BE COMING...
...THIS WAY!
WRUCH!
IT PROBABLY WANTS TO ATTACK SUPERMAN! WE'VE GOT TO FIGHT--
YES... EVEN THOUGH THE BATTLE SEEMS HOPELESS!
12

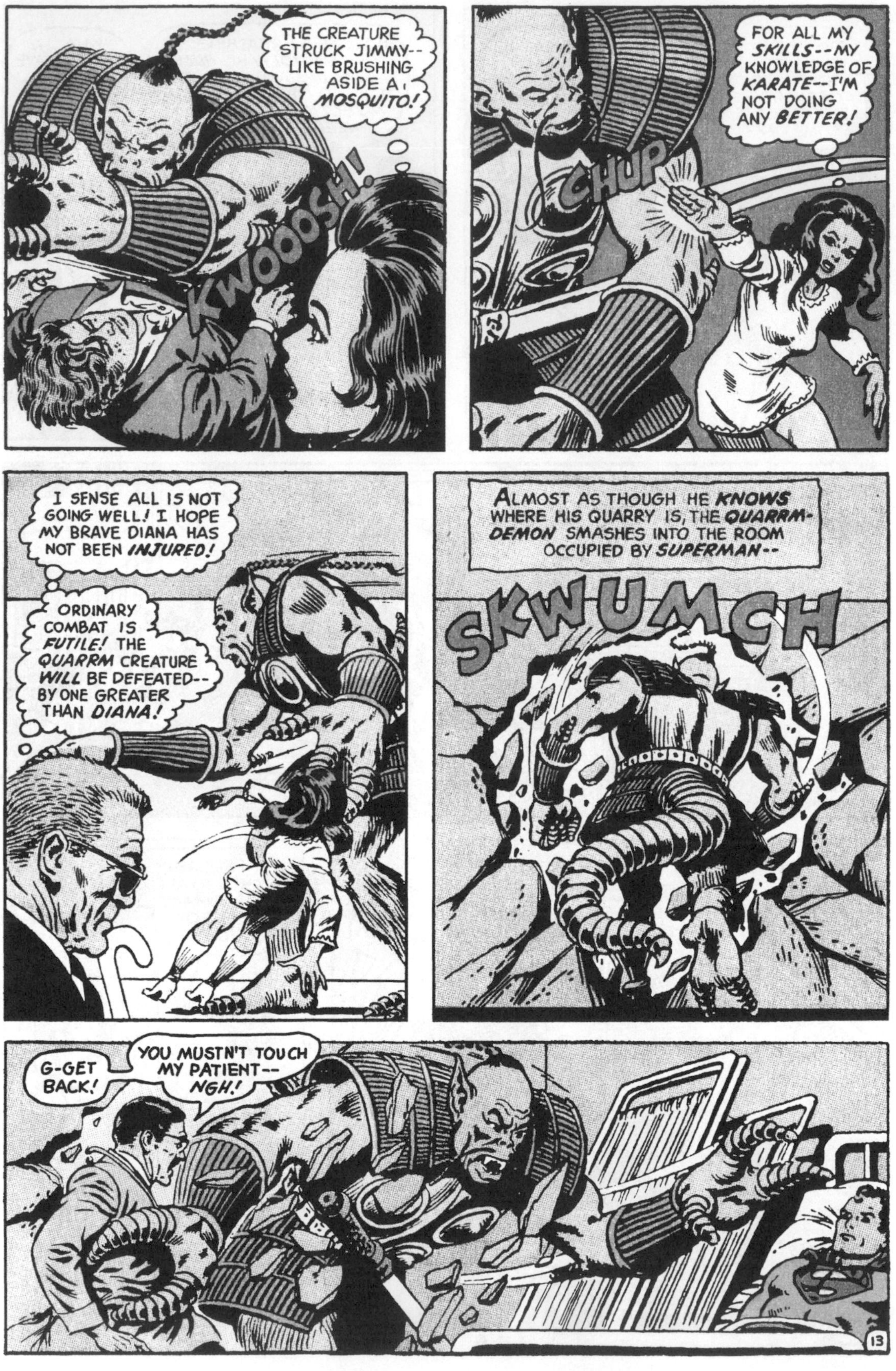
THE CREATURE STRUCK JIMMY-- LIKE BRUSHING ASIDE A MOSQUITO!
KWOOOSH!
FOR ALL MY SKILLS--MY KNOWLEDGE OF KARATE--I'M NOT DOING ANY BETTER!
CHUP
I SENSE ALL IS NOT GOING WELL! I HOPE MY BRAVE DIANA HAS NOT BEEN INJURED!
ORDINARY COMBAT IS FUTILE! THE QUARRM CREATURE WILL BE DEFEATED-- BY ONE GREATER THAN DIANA!
ALMOST AS THOUGH HE KNOWS WHERE HIS QUARRY IS, THE QUARRM-DEMON SMASHES INTO THE ROOM OCCUPIED BY SUPERMAN--
SKWUMCH
G-GET BACK!
YOU MUSTN'T TOUCH MY PATIENT-- NGH!
13

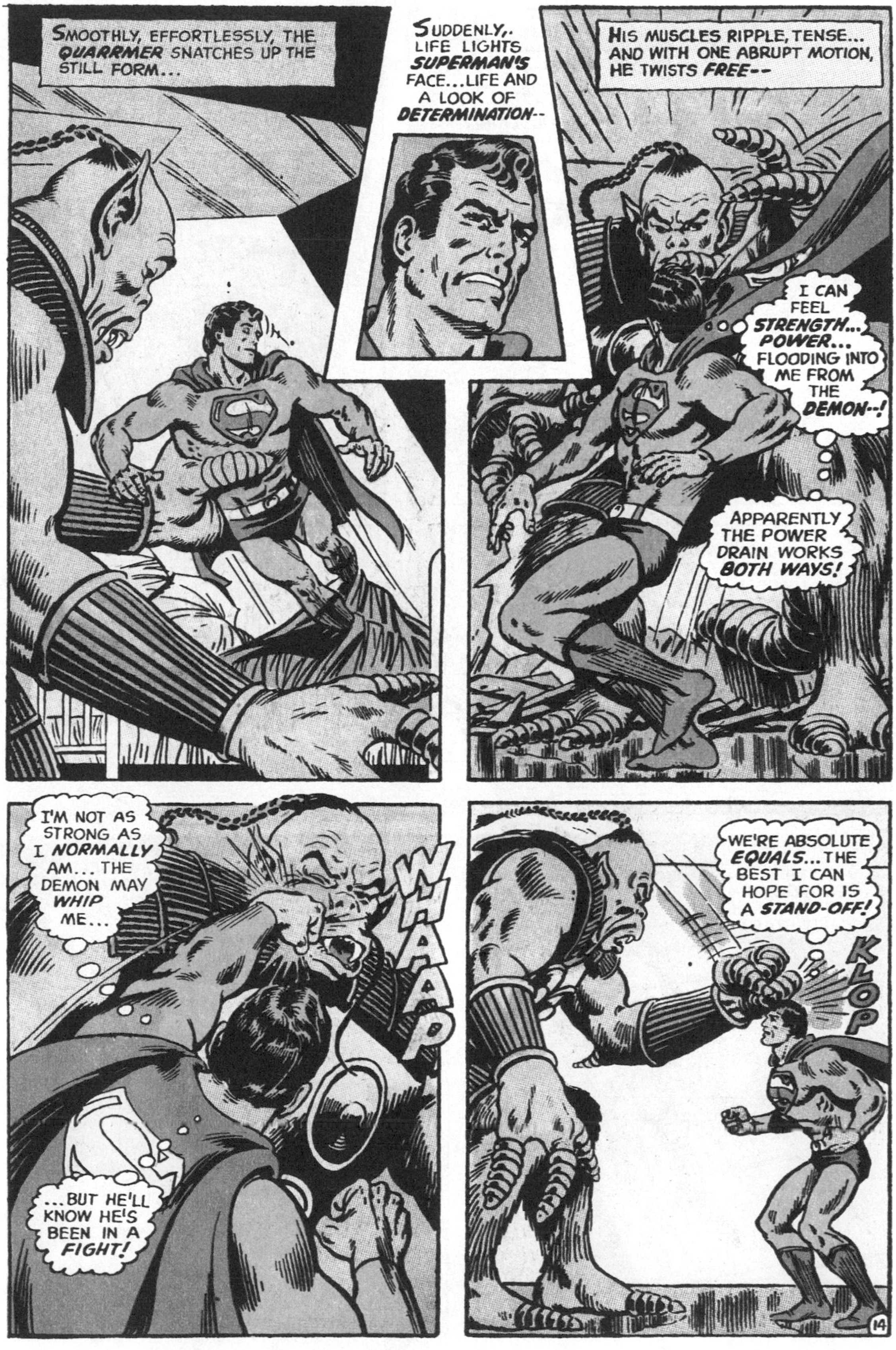

SMOOTHLY, EFFORTLESSLY, THE QUARRMER SNATCHES UP THE STILL FORM...
SUDDENLY, LIFE LIGHTS SUPERMAN'S FACE...LIFE AND A LOOK OF DETERMINATION--
HIS MUSCLES RIPPLE, TENSE... AND WITH ONE ABRUPT MOTION, HE TWISTS FREE--
I CAN FEEL STRENGTH... POWER... FLOODING INTO ME FROM THE DEMON--!
APPARENTLY THE POWER DRAIN WORKS BOTH WAYS!
I'M NOT AS STRONG AS I NORMALLY AM... THE DEMON MAY WHIP ME...
WHAAAP
...BUT HE'LL KNOW HE'S BEEN IN A FIGHT!
WE'RE ABSOLUTE EQUALS... THE BEST I CAN HOPE FOR IS A STAND-OFF!
KLOP
14

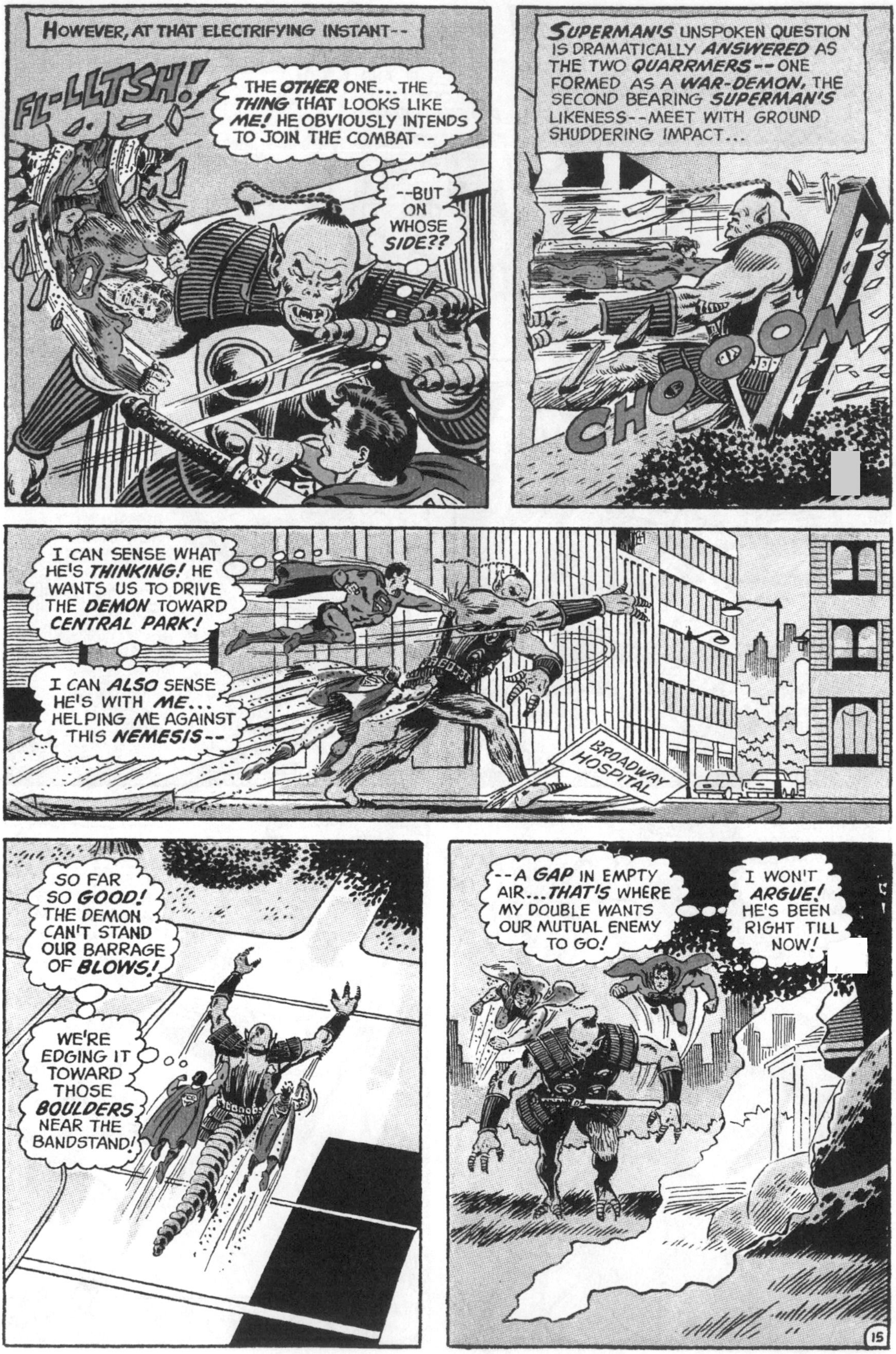
HOWEVER, AT THAT ELECTRIFYING INSTANT--
FL-LLTSH!
THE OTHER ONE...THE THING THAT LOOKS LIKE ME! HE OBVIOUSLY INTENDS TO JOIN THE COMBAT--
--BUT ON WHOSE SIDE??
SUPERMAN'S UNSPOKEN QUESTION IS DRAMATICALLY ANSWERED AS THE TWO QUARRMERS--ONE FORMED AS A WAR-DEMON, THE SECOND BEARING SUPERMAN'S LIKENESS--MEET WITH GROUND SHUDDERING IMPACT...
CHOOOOM
I CAN SENSE WHAT HE'S THINKING! HE WANTS US TO DRIVE THE DEMON TOWARD CENTRAL PARK!
I CAN ALSO SENSE HE'S WITH ME... HELPING ME AGAINST THIS NEMESIS--
BROADWAY HOSPITAL
SO FAR SO GOOD! THE DEMON CAN'T STAND OUR BARRAGE OF BLOWS!
WE'RE EDGING IT TOWARD THOSE BOULDERS NEAR THE BANDSTAND!
--A GAP IN EMPTY AIR...THAT'S WHERE MY DOUBLE WANTS OUR MUTUAL ENEMY TO GO!
I WON'T ARGUE! HE'S BEEN RIGHT TILL NOW!
15

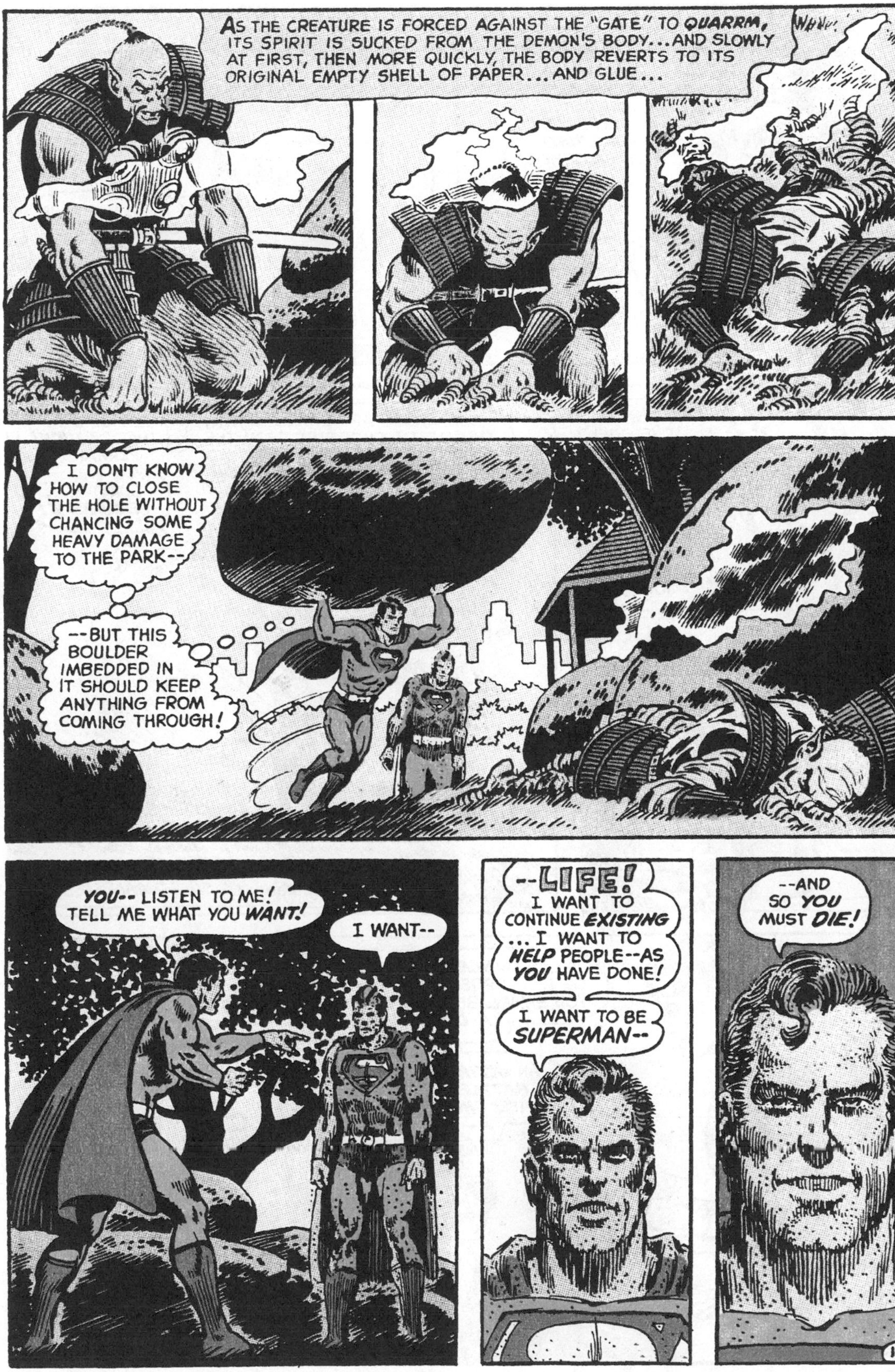
AS THE CREATURE IS FORCED AGAINST THE "GATE" TO QUARRM, ITS SPIRIT IS SUCKED FROM THE DEMON'S BODY... AND SLOWLY AT FIRST, THEN MORE QUICKLY, THE BODY REVERTS TO ITS ORIGINAL EMPTY SHELL OF PAPER... AND GLUE...
I DON'T KNOW HOW TO CLOSE THE HOLE WITHOUT CHANCING SOME HEAVY DAMAGE TO THE PARK--
--BUT THIS BOULDER IMBEDDED IN IT SHOULD KEEP ANYTHING FROM COMING THROUGH!
YOU-- LISTEN TO ME! TELL ME WHAT YOU WANT!
I WANT--
--LIFE! I WANT TO CONTINUE EXISTING ... I WANT TO HELP PEOPLE--AS YOU HAVE DONE!
I WANT TO BE SUPERMAN--
--AND SO YOU MUST DIE!
16

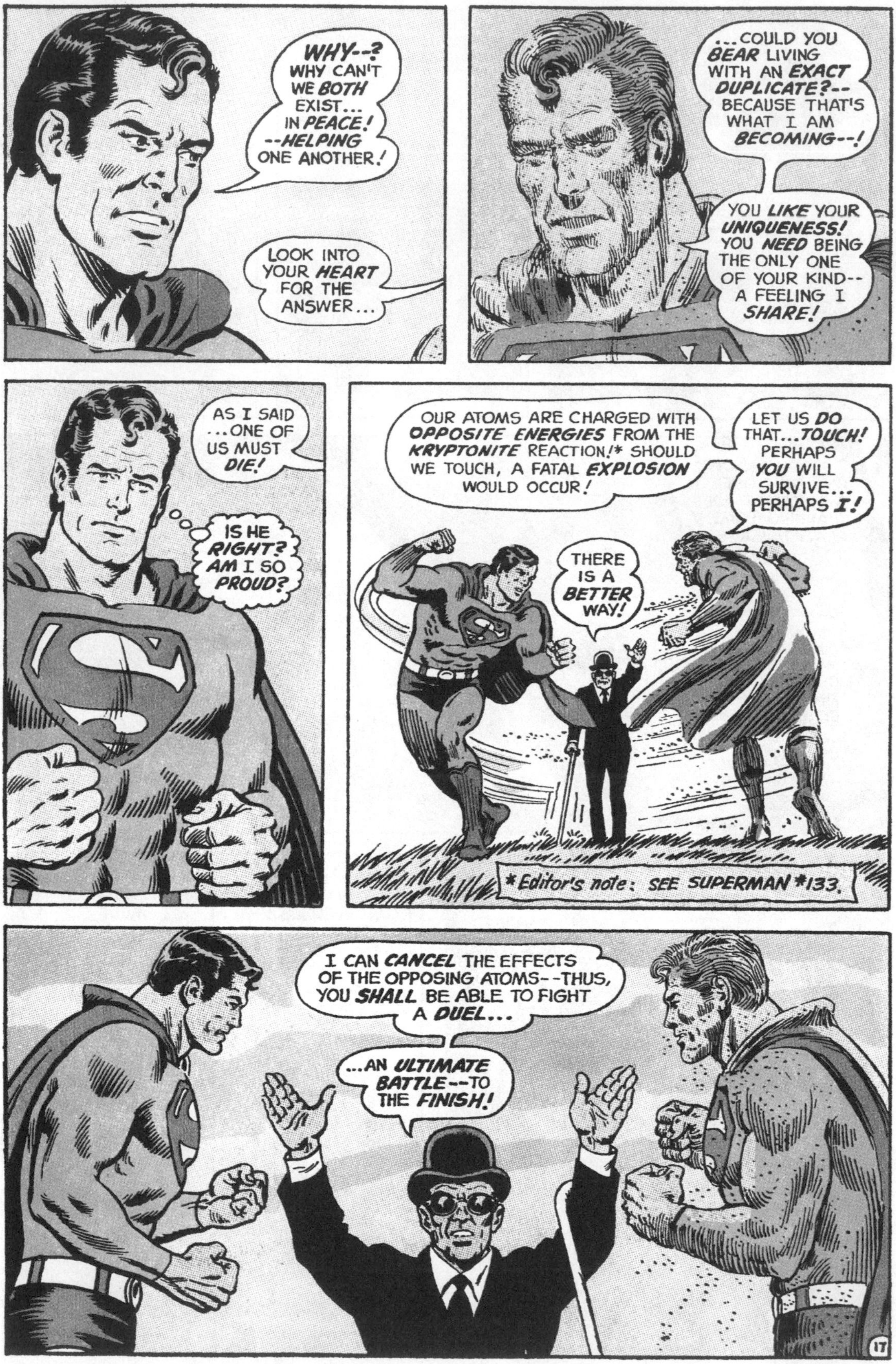
WHY--? WHY CAN'T WE BOTH EXIST... IN PEACE! --HELPING ONE ANOTHER!
LOOK INTO YOUR HEART FOR THE ANSWER...
...COULD YOU BEAR LIVING WITH AN EXACT DUPLICATE?-- BECAUSE THAT'S WHAT I AM BECOMING--!
YOU LIKE YOUR UNIQUENESS! YOU NEED BEING THE ONLY ONE OF YOUR KIND-- A FEELING I SHARE!
AS I SAID ...ONE OF US MUST DIE!
IS HE RIGHT? AM I SO PROUD?
OUR ATOMS ARE CHARGED WITH OPPOSITE ENERGIES FROM THE KRYPTONITE REACTION!* SHOULD WE TOUCH, A FATAL EXPLOSION WOULD OCCUR!
LET US DO THAT...TOUCH! PERHAPS YOU WILL SURVIVE... PERHAPS I!
THERE IS A BETTER WAY!
*Editor's note: SEE SUPERMAN #133.
I CAN CANCEL THE EFFECTS OF THE OPPOSING ATOMS--THUS, YOU SHALL BE ABLE TO FIGHT A DUEL...
...AN ULTIMATE BATTLE--TO THE FINISH!
17

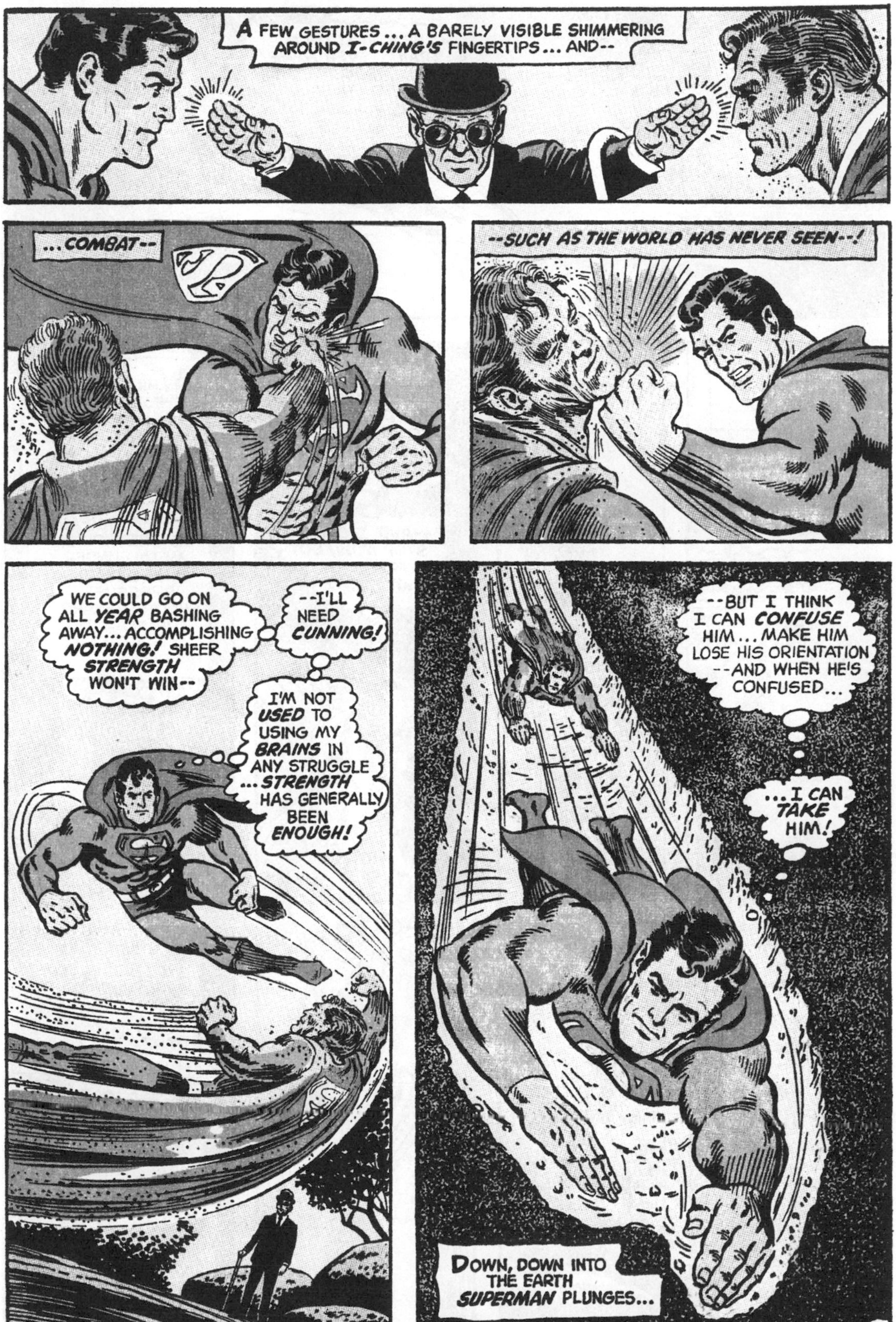
A FEW GESTURES ... A BARELY VISIBLE SHIMMERING AROUND I-CHING'S FINGERTIPS ... AND--
...COMBAT--
--SUCH AS THE WORLD HAS NEVER SEEN--!
WE COULD GO ON ALL YEAR BASHING AWAY... ACCOMPLISHING NOTHING! SHEER STRENGTH WON'T WIN--
--I'LL NEED CUNNING!
I'M NOT USED TO USING MY BRAINS IN ANY STRUGGLE ...STRENGTH HAS GENERALLY BEEN ENOUGH!
--BUT I THINK I CAN CONFUSE HIM ... MAKE HIM LOSE HIS ORIENTATION --AND WHEN HE'S CONFUSED...
...I CAN TAKE HIM!
DOWN, DOWN INTO THE EARTH SUPERMAN PLUNGES...
18

...DOWN TO THE VERY CORE OF THE PLANET... A BALL OF MOLTEN METAL...

HE'S STILL ON MY TRAIL... EVEN *HERE!* WELL, *GOOD!* LET HIM *STAY* THERE--

QUICKLY, HE SURGES OUT THE FAR SIDE...

IN ABOUT A *SECOND,* MY FOE WILL EMERGE...

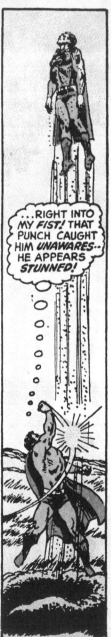

...RIGHT INTO MY *FIST!* THAT PUNCH CAUGHT HIM *UNAWARES*-- HE APPEARS *STUNNED!*

I'VE NEVER HIT ANYONE *HARD ENOUGH* TO KNOCK HIM CLEAR OUT OF THE ATMOSPHERE--

--AND I CAN'T STOP *NOW!* GOT TO PRESS THE *ATTACK!*

WHILE THE OPPONENTS RAGE IN SPACE, A *TRAGEDY* IS IN THE MAKING BELOW! FOR THEIR PASSAGE THROUGH THE EARTH'S CORE LEFT *TUNNELS*-- AND THE MOLTEN METAL, UNDER UNBELIEVABLE PRESSURE, SHOOTS TOWARD THE PLANET'S SURFACE !...

19

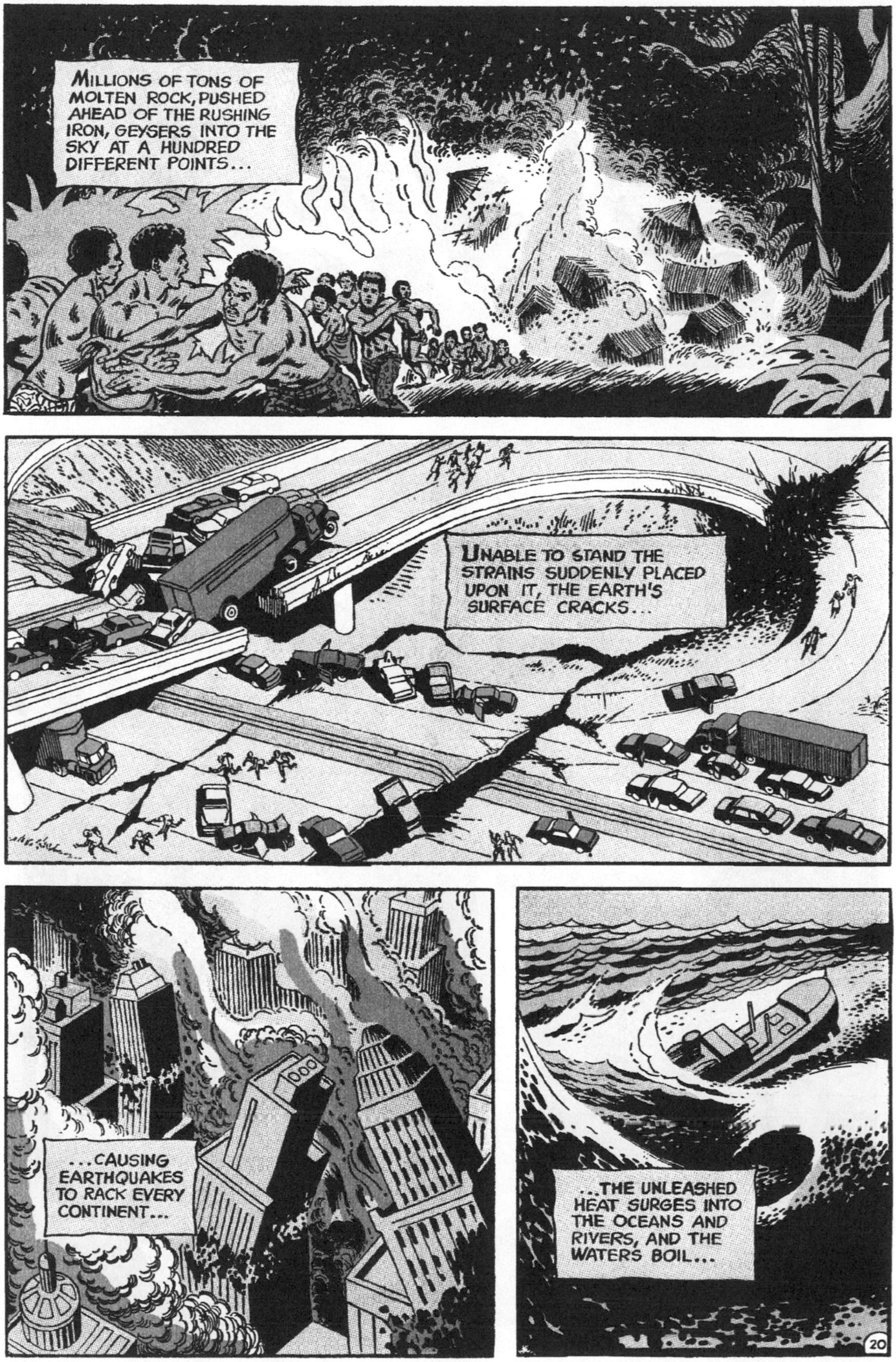
MILLIONS OF TONS OF MOLTEN ROCK, PUSHED AHEAD OF THE RUSHING IRON, GEYSERS INTO THE SKY AT A HUNDRED DIFFERENT POINTS...
UNABLE TO STAND THE STRAINS SUDDENLY PLACED UPON IT, THE EARTH'S SURFACE CRACKS...
...CAUSING EARTHQUAKES TO RACK EVERY CONTINENT...
...THE UNLEASHED HEAT SURGES INTO THE OCEANS AND RIVERS, AND THE WATERS BOIL...
20

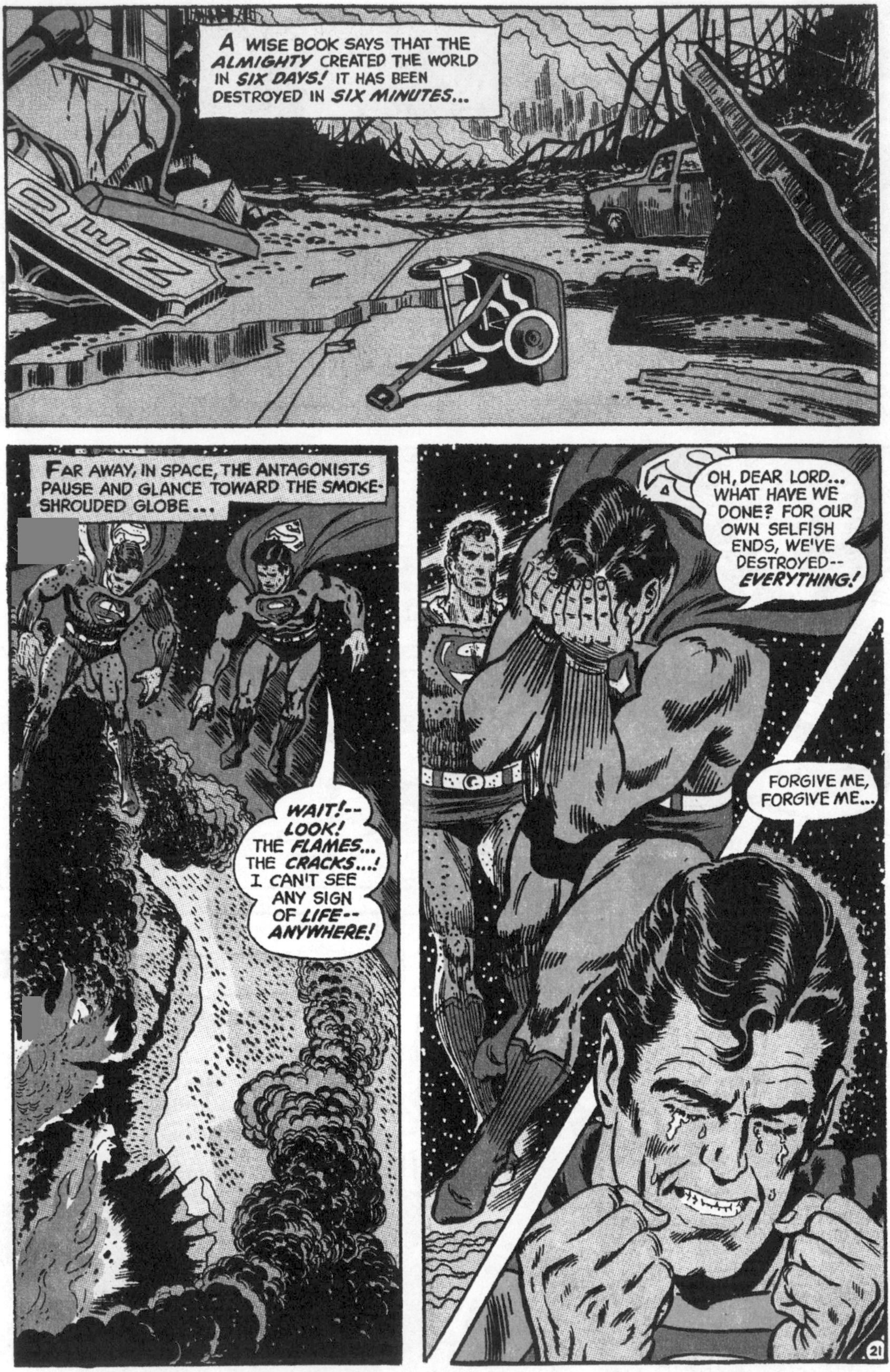
A WISE BOOK SAYS THAT THE ALMIGHTY CREATED THE WORLD IN SIX DAYS! IT HAS BEEN DESTROYED IN SIX MINUTES...
FAR AWAY, IN SPACE, THE ANTAGONISTS PAUSE AND GLANCE TOWARD THE SMOKE-SHROUDED GLOBE...
WAIT!--LOOK! THE FLAMES... THE CRACKS...! I CAN'T SEE ANY SIGN OF LIFE--ANYWHERE!
OH, DEAR LORD... WHAT HAVE WE DONE? FOR OUR OWN SELFISH ENDS, WE'VE DESTROYED--EVERYTHING!
FORGIVE ME, FORGIVE ME...
21

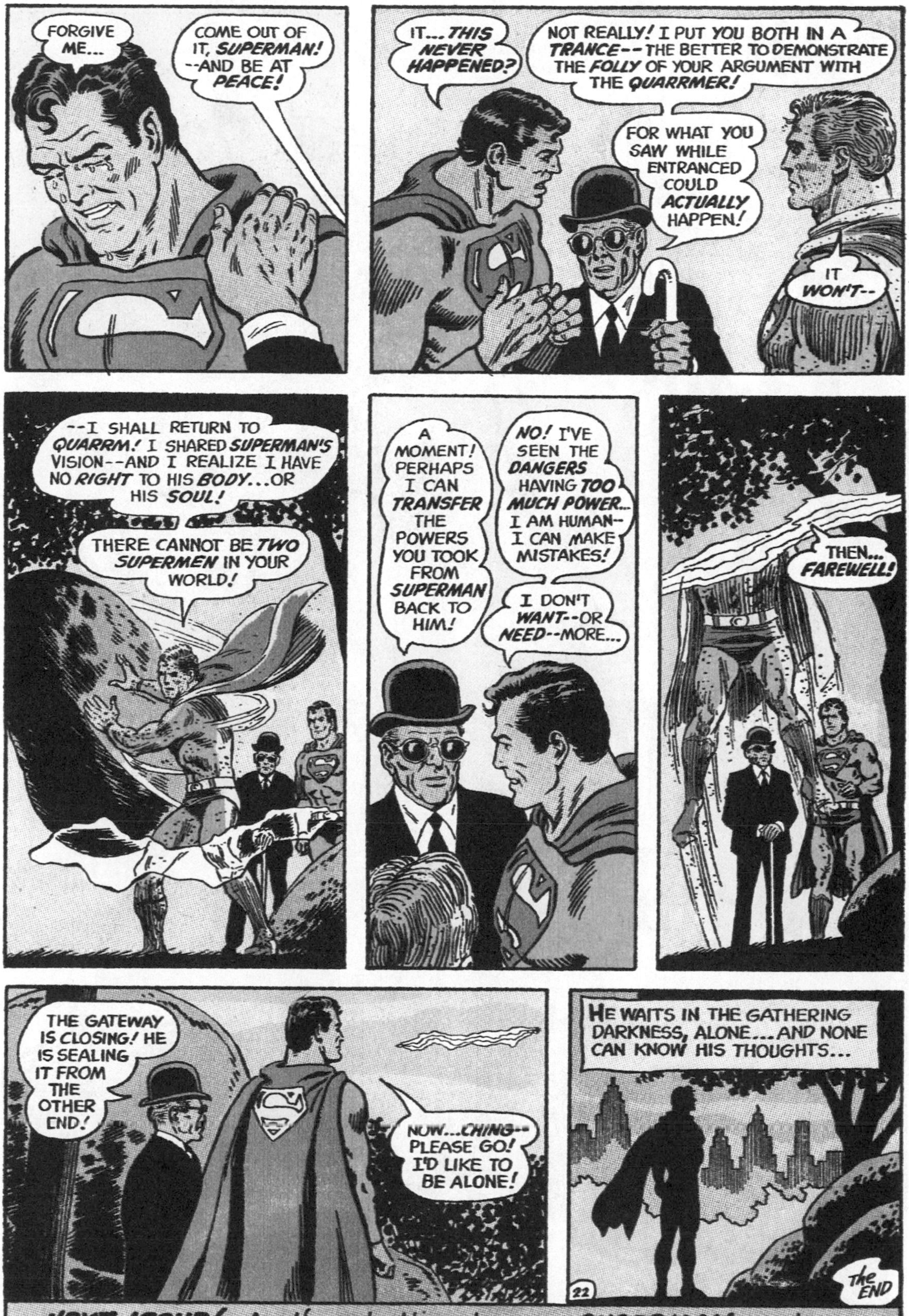
FORGIVE ME...
COME OUT OF IT, SUPERMAN! --AND BE AT PEACE!
IT... THIS NEVER HAPPENED?
NOT REALLY! I PUT YOU BOTH IN A TRANCE--THE BETTER TO DEMONSTRATE THE FOLLY OF YOUR ARGUMENT WITH THE QUARRMER!
FOR WHAT YOU SAW WHILE ENTRANCED COULD ACTUALLY HAPPEN!
IT WON'T--
--I SHALL RETURN TO QUARRM! I SHARED SUPERMAN'S VISION--AND I REALIZE I HAVE NO RIGHT TO HIS BODY...OR HIS SOUL!
THERE CANNOT BE TWO SUPERMEN IN YOUR WORLD!
A MOMENT! PERHAPS I CAN TRANSFER THE POWERS YOU TOOK FROM SUPERMAN BACK TO HIM!
NO! I'VE SEEN THE DANGERS HAVING TOO MUCH POWER... I AM HUMAN-- I CAN MAKE MISTAKES!
I DON'T WANT--OR NEED--MORE...
THEN... FAREWELL!
THE GATEWAY IS CLOSING! HE IS SEALING IT FROM THE OTHER END!
NOW...CHING-- PLEASE GO! I'D LIKE TO BE ALONE!
HE WAITS IN THE GATHERING DARKNESS, ALONE... AND NONE CAN KNOW HIS THOUGHTS...
22
THE END
NEXT ISSUE! Another startling story, as SUPERMAN meets... "THE STARRY-EYED SIREN OF SPACE!"

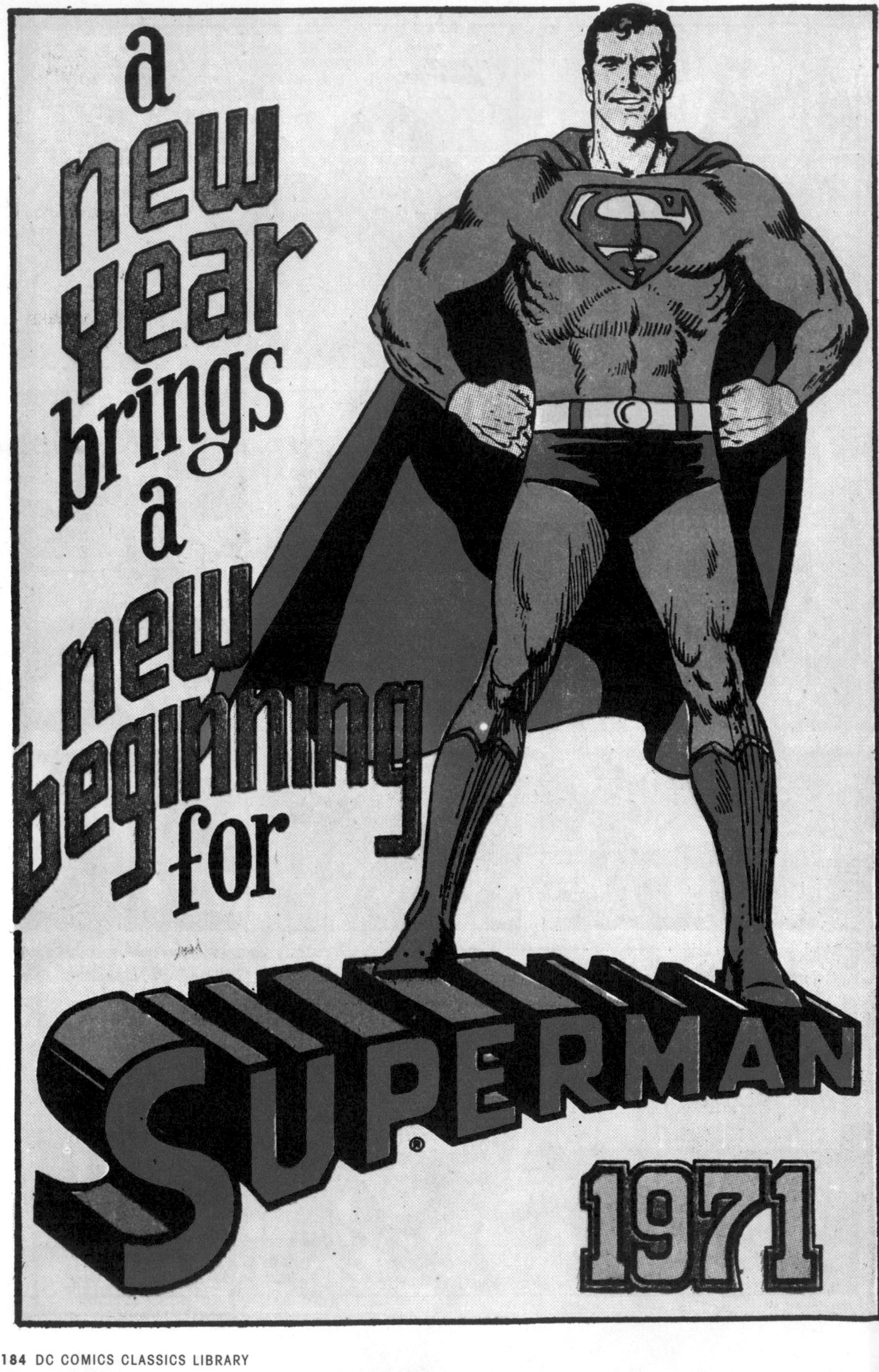
a new year brings a new beginning for
SUPERMAN®
1971

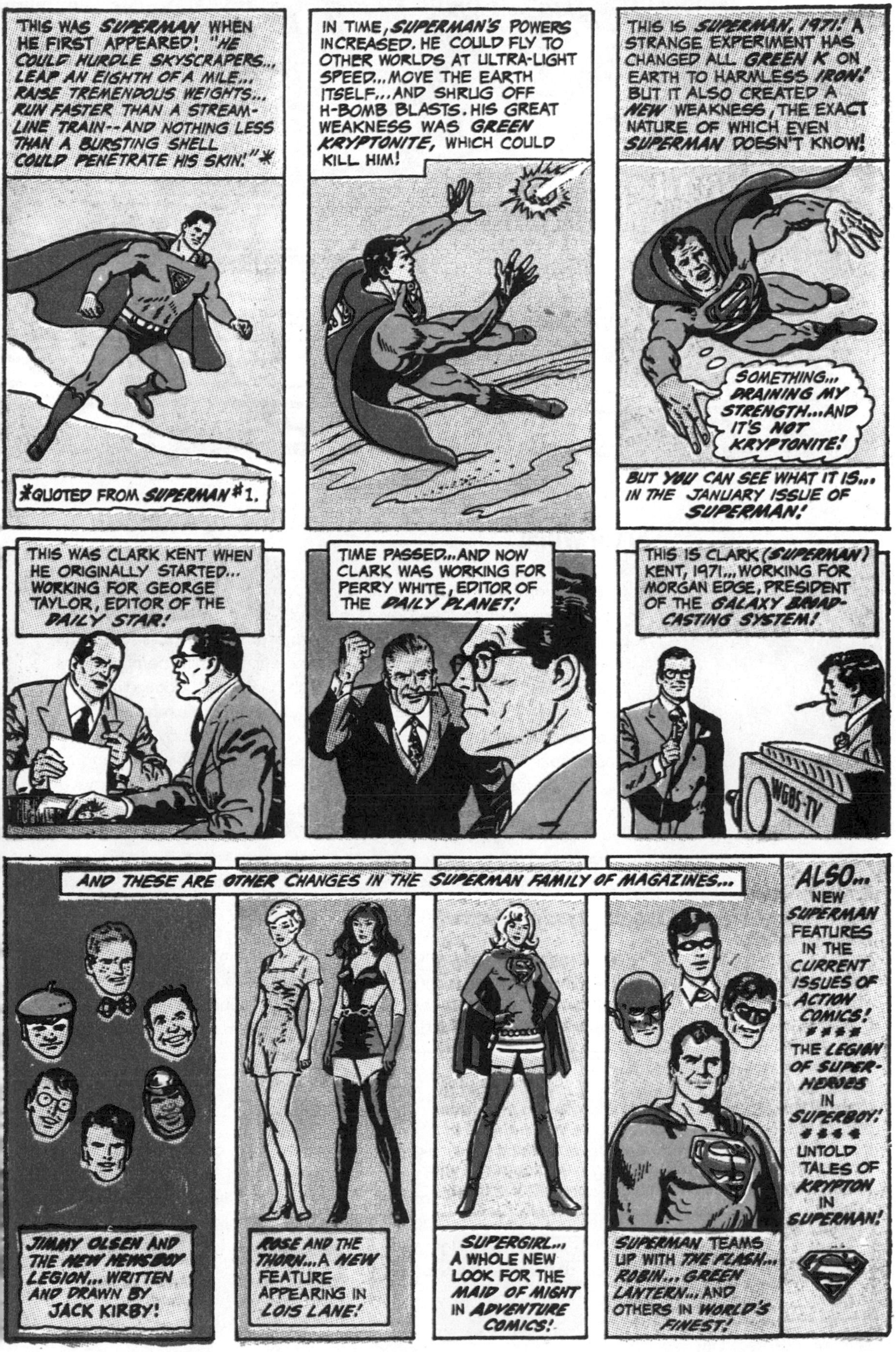
THIS WAS SUPERMAN WHEN HE FIRST APPEARED! "HE COULD HURDLE SKYSCRAPERS... LEAP AN EIGHTH OF A MILE... RAISE TREMENDOUS WEIGHTS... RUN FASTER THAN A STREAM-LINE TRAIN--AND NOTHING LESS THAN A BURSTING SHELL COULD PENETRATE HIS SKIN!"*
*QUOTED FROM SUPERMAN #1.
IN TIME, SUPERMAN'S POWERS INCREASED. HE COULD FLY TO OTHER WORLDS AT ULTRA-LIGHT SPEED...MOVE THE EARTH ITSELF...AND SHRUG OFF H-BOMB BLASTS. HIS GREAT WEAKNESS WAS GREEN KRYPTONITE, WHICH COULD KILL HIM!
THIS IS SUPERMAN, 1971! A STRANGE EXPERIMENT HAS CHANGED ALL GREEN K ON EARTH TO HARMLESS IRON! BUT IT ALSO CREATED A NEW WEAKNESS, THE EXACT NATURE OF WHICH EVEN SUPERMAN DOESN'T KNOW!
SOMETHING... DRAINING MY STRENGTH...AND IT'S NOT KRYPTONITE!
BUT YOU CAN SEE WHAT IT IS... IN THE JANUARY ISSUE OF SUPERMAN!
THIS WAS CLARK KENT WHEN HE ORIGINALLY STARTED... WORKING FOR GEORGE TAYLOR, EDITOR OF THE DAILY STAR!
TIME PASSED...AND NOW CLARK WAS WORKING FOR PERRY WHITE, EDITOR OF THE DAILY PLANET!
THIS IS CLARK (SUPERMAN) KENT, 1971...WORKING FOR MORGAN EDGE, PRESIDENT OF THE GALAXY BROAD-CASTING SYSTEM!
WGBS-TV
AND THESE ARE OTHER CHANGES IN THE SUPERMAN FAMILY OF MAGAZINES...
JIMMY OLSEN AND THE NEW NEWSBOY LEGION...WRITTEN AND DRAWN BY JACK KIRBY!
ROSE AND THE THORN...A NEW FEATURE APPEARING IN LOIS LANE!
SUPERGIRL... A WHOLE NEW LOOK FOR THE MAID OF MIGHT IN ADVENTURE COMICS!
SUPERMAN TEAMS UP WITH THE FLASH... ROBIN...GREEN LANTERN...AND OTHERS IN WORLD'S FINEST!
ALSO... NEW SUPERMAN FEATURES IN THE CURRENT ISSUES OF ACTION COMICS!
THE LEGION OF SUPER-HEROES IN SUPERBOY!
UNTOLD TALES OF KRYPTON IN SUPERMAN!

Afterword

Jerry Siegel and Joe Shuster can be forgiven for not realizing that they created a meme when they gave the world Superman because Richard Dawkins didn't coin the word until 1975, some 42 years after the first version of Superman appeared in an amateur magazine Jerry and Joe edited. The word is pronounced to rhyme with "seem" and, according to no less an august authority than the Oxford English Dictionary, it means "An element of a culture that may be considered to be passed on by non-genetic means, especially imitation." Dr. Dawkins was, and is, a geneticist and he writes, "Memes are tunes, ideas, catch-phrases, clothes fashions, ways of making pots or of building arches. Just as genes propagate themselves in the gene pool by leaping from body to body via sperm or eggs, so memes propagate themselves in the meme pool by leaping from brain to brain via a process which, in the broad sense, can be called imitation."

Jerry and Joe's meme was, in the words intoned at the beginning of Superman's first television show, a "strange visitor from another planet with powers and abilities far beyond those of" us lame Homo sapiens. One of the interesting aspects of memes is that, like biological genes, they change over time, in a process very like Darwinian evolution. Some of the mutations — the popular ones — last, and some don't.

Got all that?

What Jerry and Joe did was give us the meme of the costumed superhero. Not much of their brainchild was completely original; very little in popular culture is ever original. What they did do was take ingredients from here and there — Greek mythology, the Bible, science fiction — and assemble them into a neo-mythic hero who was appropriate for Twentieth Century America and, more important, for a brand-spanking-new medium called "comic books."

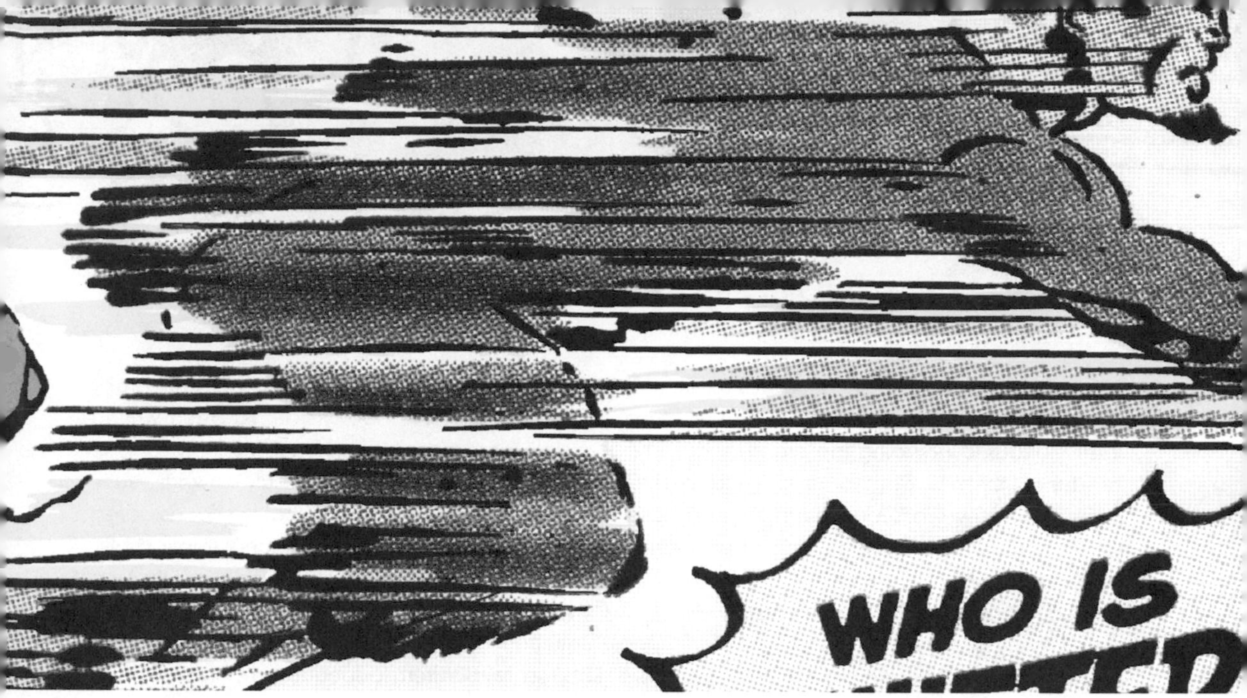
WHO IS

Superman began evolving almost immediately. In his first appearance, in a short story, he was a bad guy; in his second, unpublished, iteration, he was a good guy; and in his third, completing the meme, a costumed good guy. That third, crucial, appearance was in the debut issue of ACTION COMICS, one of the first comic books to use original material, instead of reprinting newspaper strips. There he was, on newsstands from Maine to California, clad in a blue costume with red cape and boots, lifting a car. Lifting a car! Well, a lot of fellows and gals had to see what that was all about!

They did, and Superman became the proverbial overnight sensation. Superman-the-character quickly migrated to other media, and Superman-the-meme generated a lot of imitations. Some of these barely resembled the original; some others were close enough to become lawsuit fodder. Some are long forgotten except, maybe, by historians and really old fellows and gals; others inspire megabucks movies attended by children.

And he evolved. He began as a relatively modest swashbuckler who was, in the words of the Superman radio show, merely "faster than a speeding bullet, more powerful than a locomotive, able to leap tall buildings in a single bound." An early adventure established that nothing short of an exploding shell could pierce his skin — but, presumably, something greater than an exploding shell could. He didn't remain so frail for long. As Joe and Jerry developed their creation and as other writers and artists did Superman stories, his powers grew. Leap tall buildings? No sir — fly over them.

Exploding shell? Try nuclear bomb. Speeding bullet? This guy could go faster than sound, and that was before he got his full growth. Pretty soon, he could see through anything except lead and travel in space and, well...do almost anything he, and his writers, found interesting or awesome or convenient for plot resolution purposes. If Superman had coexisted with the Greek gods, Zeus would have held his cape.

I don't think anyone ever planned to make Superman so mighty. Nor do I think consistency was on anyone's radar. There were no company guidelines that I've ever heard of, no equivalent of the "bibles" television producers provide to writers to ensure constancy of characterization and milieu and to establish parameters. The stories were largely plot-driven, like their pulp forebears, and characterization probably wasn't a priority. And — what the heck! — the stuff was just light entertainment. Although, if

sales estimates are to be believed, millions of Americans liked comics, but did anyone take them seriously, including the creative folk who produced them? Well, some kids did, a little, and some New York businessmen must have taken seriously the money comics were generating, but grown-up commentators and opinion-makers? Probably not. Comics were kid stuff.

Along the way, Superman's various biographers in comics, radio, movies and, later, television, and in at least one novel, expanded and modified his world. He had friends, coworkers, super heroic colleagues, an on-again off-again girl friend, foster parents and, courtesy of a radio scripter, a weakness: Kryptonite, which was matter from the planet of his birth. There must have been a lot of the stuff around the Earth because plenty of evildoers found enough to use against the hero.

Later writers added a second problem to Superman's list of woes in the form of a cosmic travel restriction: he was plain old human under a red sun, so he had to pretty much stay in the vicinity of our yellow sun.

Kryptonite, and, to a lesser extent those yellow suns, served Superman's writers well. They gave the guy weaknesses, and, for purposes of melodrama, weaknesses of some sort are necessary. The engine that drives these kinds of stories is conflict and unless the protagonist can be beaten, some way, somehow, he won't come into conflict because he's invulnerable. Later, very skillful writers were able to use psychological flaws as Superman's nemeses, but for the middle-period Man of Steel — from maybe 1950 through 1970 — Kryptonite and red suns were pretty much it.

Enter me.

In 1971, I was a young writer who was still pretty new at the comic book trade; I'd been writing scripts for five or six years, most notably for one of comics' greatest editors, Julius Schwartz. Julie and I had done some stuff that was considered successful, had a solid professional relationship, got along amazingly well considering that he was a fifty-something, white shirt-and-tie-wearing Jew from Queens, New York, and I was a frizzy-haired Midwestern peacenik who lived on the Lower East Side. In those days, the comic book business was, despite the prevalence of suits and shiny shoes behind editorial desks, a pretty informal, loosey-goosey sort of enterprise. I was kind of the flavor of the week for a while, so when Julie asked me if I'd like to try working on Superman, all I had to do was say "yes" and the deal was done.

I don't know why Julie picked me for the job. Maybe simply because we worked well together? Or maybe because I'd done a revamp on some other characters, under Julie's direction, he may have felt that the Man of Steel was due for a makeover?

And make him over, we did. Not drastically: I think we both sensed that we were dealing with an icon and some elements should be left intact. The costume, for starters, was familiar, serviceable, colorful, did the job. The costume stayed. And the story of Superman's origin, how his scientist father sent him in a spaceship away from an exploding world — we didn't fool with that, either. We might have updated the science a bit — it hadn't been established exactly where Krypton was, for example — but nobody was expecting a primer on cosmology, and the familiar story was good enough. We didn't change Superman's city, friends, enemies or workplaces.

But Kryptonite? That, we felt, should go.

Those green- (and sometimes red- and some-times gold-) glowing rocks had become a writer's crutch. When in doubt — when the story lacked drama or conflict or interest — have the nogoodnik flip a chunk of Green K at Supes and then figure out a way for it not to kill him. What had started as a valuable addition to the mythos had become at best routine, at worst clichéd. Away with it!

Actually, Kryptonite was merely a symptom. The disease might be called elephantiasis of the powers. Superman was just too mighty. If we were to be consistent in our plotting, there would be few problems he couldn't logically dispose of by page two. If we weren't consistent — if we had him not deal with a difficulty by doing something he did just last month, for instance — we were guilty of bad fiction and we risked alienating our readers who were, we finally realized, paying attention. Consistency wouldn't have been a concern in what's labeled comics' "golden age" — the '40s and '50s when conven-tional wisdom had it that a title's readership completely changed every three years and anyway...it's just kid stuff. We knew our audience to be bright, and we may have had an inkling that what we were producing was much more than tomorrow's birdcage lining, a narrative form that was both episodic and serialized.

The solution to our hero's elephantiasis? Obvious: Depower him.

But we shouldn't do it sneakily. We, by then, had enough of a sense of the kind of storytelling our work was becoming to realize that we might get plots from Superman's alterations. I don't know how much of this Julie and I discussed at the out set.

Maybe not much: loosey-goosey business, remember? But once I began work, we settled into what was already a familiar and pleasant process: I came in and talked plot with Julie. If I had it already parsed, the visit was short; if I came in with little or nothing, we'd talk until I could go home to my doughty portable type-writer and begin a script. Then I worked, time passed, I gave a script to Julie, more time passed and voila! I was holding a comic book.

After a year, I asked Julie for an exit from the world of Krypton. Forgive my aging memory; once again, I can't be certain of details. But I recall a vague sense of discomfort, of not fitting with the assignment somehow. Anyway, Julie agreed that Superman and I would part ways, and on the cover of the first Issue after the end of my run, here was the Man of Steel towing a planet. Obviously, his time of frailty was past.

Now decades have passed and Joe and Jerry's brave meme soldiers on, continuing to evolve, as must everything that does not perish. What you have in this book is one stage in his devel-opment, one that might be just a tiny bit more worthy than many people, including me, thought when it first appeared. For me, it's a bit like running into a classmate I didn't know I liked until he moved out of my neighborhood.

Good to see you, Superman. Hope it's all good.

Dennis O'Neil
Nyack, N.Y.
September, 2008

Biographies

DENNIS O'NEIL began his career as a comic book writer in 1965 at Charlton, where then-editor Dick Giordano assigned him to several features. When Giordano moved to DC, O'Neil soon followed. At DC, O'Neil scripted several series for Giordano and Julius Schwartz, quickly becoming one of the most respected writers in comics. O'Neil earned a reputation for being able to "revamp" such characters as Superman, Green Lantern, Captain Marvel — and the Batman, whom O'Neil (with the help of Neal Adams and Giordano) brought back to his roots as a dark, mysterious, gothic avenger. Besides being the most important Batman writer of the 1970s, O'Neil served as an editor at both Marvel and DC. After a long tenure as Group Editor of the Batman line of titles, Denny retired to write full-time.

CURT SWAN entered the art field intending to become not a cartoonist but a "slick" magazine illustrator like Norman Rockwell or Joseph Leyendecker. While serving during World War Two illustrating the Army newspaper *Stars and Stripes*, Swan worked with DC writer France E. ("Eddie") Herron. On Herron's suggestion, Swan found work at DC after the war. Swan's versatile pencils, which he remembered applying first to BOY COMMANDOS, soon appeared on various DC features, including Superman, Batman, Newsboy Legion, Big Town, Mr. District Attorney, Tommy Tomorrow, and Swan's longest assignment up to that time, Superboy. His familiarity with both Superman and Batman specially suited him to draw the original Superman-Batman team-up in 1952. Swan served various stints, regular and semi-regular, on almost all the Superman titles of the 1950s and 1960s, and remained the near-exclusive Superman penciller throughout the 1970s and much of the 1980s. Although he "retired" in 1986, Swan continued to work for DC until his death in 1996. To generations of professionals and fans, Curt Swan's Superman will always be the definitive version.

MURPHY ANDERSON entered comics in 1944 drawing features for Fiction House and, after a tour with the Navy, worked for a variety of publishers. In 1947, he took over drawing the Buck Rogers syndicated news-paper strip. Anderson began his long association with DC in 1950, drawing countless super hero and science-fiction stories, including Captain Comet, The Atomic Knights, Hawkman, and The Spectre. In addition to pencilling, Anderson was one of comics' best and most versatile inkers, with numerous credits on such strips as Adam Strange, The Atom, Superman, and, of course, Batman. His most famous collaborations were with pencillers Carmine Infantino and Gil Kane. Anderson has also produced instructional comic books for the U.S. Army and headed a publishers support service company that provided color separations and typesetting for the comics industry.